Barbara Will

I Was Glad

Christopher Campling

St Mary's Bursham

2 June 2013

I Was Glad
The Memoirs of Christopher Campling
(Dean Emeritus of Ripon Cathedral)

Christopher R. Campling

JANUS PUBLISHING COMPANY
London, England

First Published in Great Britain 2005
by Janus Publishing Company Ltd,
105-107 Gloucester Place,
London W1U 6BY

www.januspublishing.co.uk

Reprinted 2009

British Library Cataloguing-in-Publication Data
A catalogue record for this book
is available from the British Library

ISBN 978-1-85756-616-1

Cover Design Janus Publishing

Printed and bound in Great Britain

"I was glad when they said unto me: We will go into the house of the Lord."

Psalm 122

Juliet helped me to write this book.
We dedicate it to our children and grandchildren:
Penelope, Angela and Peter;
Rosalys, Bethan, Patrick and Natasha; David and Alice;
Josephine and Laurence Christopher.

Contents

Preface

When my father died in February 1972 1 shared with my family a disappointment that he had left us so little information about his life. There were his war diaries, which I had found and deciphered and typed during my sabbatical in 1994, but nothing else except a few old photographs and family snaps and the very few anecdotes that he had told us about himself.

Yet he had lived an interesting life. His father had worked on the Great Western Railway. Father himself won a senior scholarship to Trinity College Cambridge, where he was financially supported by "Uncle Willy", who owned a jewellers in the Strand. He was awarded First Class Honours in the Examination for the Natural Science Tripos in 1911. Then, to Uncle Willy's disgust, he was converted to Christianity by the Chaplain, and decided to read Theology. To his own disgust he only got a "second", which is hardly surprising as he did it in a year and had to start Greek and Hebrew from scratch. The rich Uncle Willy withdrew all communication and financial support, but Father continued to pray for him all his life! After Cambridge, Father went to Cheshunt Theological College and was ordained to a curacy at Wimbledon Parish Church, where he met my mother, Phyllis Russell Webb.

Mother had been born in Leatherhead, but at this time was living in a house on Wimbledon Common. She used to tell us with glee how she and her friends pinched the golf balls on the Common from the red-coated golfers, whom they regarded as the Enemy. Her father was a coach-builder; but as he did not believe in the new-fangled motor-car, he kept losing money and moving the family house "down the hill". Her family was descended, on her father's side, from the eighteenth-century pastel artist, John Russell, RA. Their house was full of his pictures, of which I inherited (from Mother's elder sister, Sylvia) the one I like best, *The Young Artists*. Mother and her brothers and sisters were brought up to love books.

One of Mother's brothers, Harold, was killed in the Great War and another, Basil, my godfather, served as a midshipman at Gallipoli, where he was made to stand for hours in the water, passing ammunition ashore. They kept him going on lashings of rum. He became an alcoholic, left the Navy under a cloud and later committed suicide.

Father joined the Army as a chaplain; he had adventures in the trenches which he described with dull nonchalance punctuated by blazes of anger in his diary. He was recommended for the Military Cross by his colonel, but this was disallowed by an order from above denying medals to chaplains. He became a tutor at Knutsford pre-ordination college; married Mother; and was appointed to be Principal of St. Francis Theological College, Brisbane, Australia, where John and I were born.

Father spent seven years in Queensland running the College and going on pastoral visits into the Bush, riding on horse-back from cattle station to cattle station, with a companion – for weeks at a time. He was made a Canon of Brisbane Cathedral, and then returned to the UK to spend the rest of his ministry in the Southwark Diocese. For several years he was in the Church Assembly; and he was made an Honorary Canon of Southwark Cathedral. He was a man of huge stature (6 feet 6 inches) and ability, under used by the Church but greatly valued by many people who encountered him on retreats and missions and were able to respond to his deep spirituality and his intellectual, sacramental, Bible-centred faith.

Most of what he did is now lost, so I have decided to write memoirs. I have lived through a war and seen many changes. I am not six-foot-six as my father was, but I have a story to tell: of school in war-time, evacuation and bombs; of service in the Navy, on a Greek destroyer and two battleships; of post-war Oxford; of ministry in schools, parishes, archdeaconry and as dean of a cathedral; of twenty-two years of controversy in the General Synod; of change, numerical decline and much that is faithful and hopeful in the Church of England.

Nearly ten years ago Juliet and I retired to Worthing where we live in our delightful "Pebble Ridge", close to the sea. On Sundays I help (when asked) in the Worthing churches, and I have written *The Food of Love: Reflections on Music and Faith* and some book reviews for the *Church Times*. Mary, my sister, lives with our cousin Francis just around the corner: it is a joy to have them so close. My brother Michael (also a priest) lives with his wife Anne in Bexhill. We meet at Seaford for needly golf and to discuss the world and how to put the country and the Church of England right. Lancing is nearby for old friends' and old times' sake. The friends include Brian Wallas who has helped me most generously with the publication of these memoirs.

Our three children gave us a truly amazing Golden Wedding party last year, and our greatest joy is to visit them and our eight grandchildren. Or they come to us and enjoy our house, garden and beach-hut.

Juliet and I feel ourselves to be singularly blessed.

Chapter 1
Beginnings

I was born in Brisbane in Queensland, Australia, on 4 July 1925. Father was away at the time on one of his "Bush Brother" trips. Mother was in the care of the Sisters of an orphanage across the road.

Mother was quite unsuited to the life in Australia, where she found herself "mothering" a college of twenty male students as well as her own growing family. She had never as much as boiled an egg. All their wedding presents were destroyed in the voyage out to Australia; and Father was often away in the Bush. But they survived and Father left a strong mark on the College, insisting upon a disciplined pattern of worship and learning, but frustrated by the poor academic quality of the students.

Father decided to leave Australia and return to the UK. The reason was to have us boys educated in England. Career-wise (the last thing Father would have thought of), this was a mistake. In Australia he might have ended up an archbishop, like my godfather, the Archbishop of Perth; but back in England no one knew him or was interested in his great gifts. Anyway, we all came home. He went ahead of us with John. Mother and I followed with Anne Jones, her school friend, who had come out to be with her: the best "sham aunt" there ever was.

I am told that on the voyage home I was a favourite with the ship's officers, who used to queue up to hold me and walk me up and down the deck. It seems unlikely. I was only six months old, just a brawling brat. But the voyage may account for my love of the sea and the excitement I always feel at the sight of ships.

1

Father was appointed Vicar of Forest Hill, of which I have very few memories. For instance, I cannot remember my brother Michael being born, but the story is that, aged two, I went out of the vicarage and made my way up the steep hill, Tyson Road. Mother rushed after me and that brought Michael a trifle early into the world.

I can remember going to the station in a hansom cab drawn by a horse and driven by a cabby with a long, curly whip which he cracked sadistically over the horse's rump, as we trotted off with a jolt. I can also remember sitting in the garden watching the R 101 airship pass by; a giant whale moving slowly across the line of the trees. This was the beginning of the flight to the South of France where it crashed. That was in November 1930. I was five.

We then moved to Coulsdon, the first syllable of which, according to Father, should be pronounced to rhyme with "coals" – as to Newcastle. I have golden memories of Coulsdon, nearly all of them happy. It is true that Michael and I were spanked once because in our excitement we made a lot of noise in bed early in the morning of "boat-race day". Father said that he would not take us but, prompted by our nanny, we asked to be spanked instead: we were, very gently, with Father's bendy bedroom slipper. The boat-race was always strangely exciting – with Father determined that Cambridge should win; and they always did, despite Mother's feelings for Oxford. We had the advantage of being able to perch one each on Father's tall shoulders at the critical moment, which was in fact very short, such is the nature of boat races.

There was a curious mystical moment when I was given a new bicycle. The sight of its huge, endlessly round wheels gave me a strange feeling, as if of eternity. I can still feel this if I go back in memory to that awesome moment. More down to earth, Michael and I used to cycle round and round the house, sometimes just idling, sometimes racing. We also cycled quite long distances, for instance to see Aunt S. at Horsham. On this occasion Mother insisted on tying labels to the bicycles, to our intense annoyance. Had we not "Passed the Test" on a strictly supervised and criticised ride with Father? Our bikes were an important part of our lives.

In the garden there was a lawn on which we played cricket or, in later years, tennis, and a side-lawn on which we could hit a tennis ball against the house, only once breaking Father's study window. We were given a tent for the upper part of this lawn in which we had a jelly tea on the afternoon of 16 September 1931, when Mary was born. Michael said that she was the same size as our marrow. We had our meals in the nursery with a nanny, and there was the quaint custom of dressing up nicely to go downstairs at about half past five to see Father and Mother in the drawing-room. Once we all had whooping-cough together in the nursery; and I can remember the fire flickering all night. In the nursery we sometimes played "sea battles" using upturned chairs for ships.

We also played "church". Chairs were put out for pews: Michael and various toy animals were placed in them to be a devout congregation and I stood on a chair (the pulpit) and preached the sermon, which, according to my mother, who was a silent witness and liked to tell the tale, consisted of the very proper exhortation, 'Bretheren, what I say unto you is, "Be good".'

My first school was Sherborne Kindergarten, down the hill. I was once sent to the headmistress for talking when I shouldn't. Miss Horsey was tiny but severe, and I decided that going all the way to this cane-armed lady was too risky; so I stayed outside the classroom and then went back when I thought a suitable time had elapsed. Of course I was found out – and had to repent bitterly; but with no physically harmful result, I noticed. I could read almost as soon as I got to the school; and I remember nothing else about the school except getting ticked off on a "nature walk" and, more creditably, giving a talk to the whole school (without a note!) on the subject of worms – which Father helped me to look up in the *Children's Encyclopedia*. Also I sometimes conducted the form band.

After Sherborne I was sent to Downside, a famous day prep-school which is still flourishing. At this school I played my first game of football without any idea of what the object was; but enjoying it all the same. I remember nothing about the class room except doing tables and spelling "round the form". David Hill (now – literally – my oldest friend) was there at the same time, and his mother sometimes took me home in her car for a treat. Usually I walked the mile and a half to and from school, and when I was flush with pocket money (six-pence a week) I could stop at a shop and buy aniseed-balls for five, or gobstoppers for two a penny. Another friend was John Tanner, who later came to Lancing and left for India where he died in an accident with gun-powder. He was always in trouble and was regarded somewhat distastefully by my parents, who thought he was a bad influence. Certainly his Christmas party, to which I went in an Eton collar, was a riotous affair with dancing, a crude game of murder and cider.

At Couldson we used to have Family Prayers every day, sometimes followed by a "quiet time", a period of silence and silence and silence and endless silence. Altogether it could last half an hour or more. We bore it; but John bitterly resented it and was put off religion for life. Father could be so insensitively solemn. Prayers would end with a long list of intercessions, mostly family. "And Grandma," Father would intone. Long silence. "And Aunt Sylvia," piped in Mother, her family not to be forgotten. Long pause. "And Aunty Win," said Father, not in the least deterred. "And all the rest of the so-and-sos," said John, furious, getting up to leave. Father looked sad, and we tried not to giggle. In the end Father gave up, as he gave up ordering us to have a cold bath every morning. His self-discipline (for he always had them himself in our Coulsdon days) and his devotion were signs of his great strength; but such discipline does not necessarily make other people strong.

One day Father took me for a special walk over the Farthing Downs because he wanted to talk to me. The secret, when it came out, was that I was to leave Downside and join my brother John at Belmont School as a boarder. I was excited by the prospect and could hardly wait. But Mother was distressed, and that spoilt it as it made me feel guilty for being so pleased.

Chapter 2
Belmont

So, at the age of eight I went to Belmont School, Hassocks, Sussex, to join my brother John. Michael came two years later. I remember being introduced on the first day to my fellow inmates: an awkward boy called Fontanaz; a tiny boy called Webb; another called Lumby; and a little tough Jewish boy called Harris. Max Burr (the headmaster and owner of the establishment) hated Harris and would often beat him; he somehow managed to impart an anti-Semitic prejudice in all of us, because far from pitying him in his persecution we tended to turn against him. I look back on this in shame but also in observation of the fact that this is how human beings tend to react, turning against the weak rather than turning to their support. In our company there was also Paul Attlee, nephew of Mr C.R. Attlee who was to become the country's prime minister. His son, Martin, also came to Belmont a year or two after me.

My best friend in those days was John Fife. He was the main strength of our "centre-half/right-half" partnership for three years running in the First Eleven at football. He was a very good player; I was quite good, although the school magazine *Characters of the First Eleven* described me as "inclined to be clumsy with my feet"! John's parents lived in the neighbouring village of Hurstpierpoint, which was a major advantage in our friendship because we could sometimes go to tea there on Sunday afternoons.

On one occasion the school went for a Sunday afternoon walk over the beautiful Woolstenbury Down. I was exhausted and Fife and another boy almost had to carry me back to school as I walked along between them. When I got back I reported sick – with scarlet fever; I was in hospital for the rest of the term but nobody else caught it from me.

In hospital I lay in bed for ages feeling awful, but not at all sorry for myself. My parents came and looked at me from a distance through a window. When I got better I was allowed to go for a walk on my own in the hospital grounds and some fields beyond. I remember hearing the eerie sound of a fox in distress, and bolting back to the hospital ward, terrified.

I had a special friend, Keith Ritherdon. He was a very "good" boy, never in trouble, though he got himself beaten once with the rest of us for some dormitory rag, as he did not want to be left out. I sometimes stayed with Keith at Newtimber and had a wonderful time roaming the countryside with an air-gun and exploring everything within reach. On one occasion his father took us to see what must have been one of the first ever television sets, and I can still remember the black and white figures dancing a spotty, snowy ballet.

Mr Burr built a chapel in the grounds of Belmont, in which I was confirmed on my twelfth birthday. I was prepared for confirmation by Keith's father. The only thing that I can remember about the classes is the sound of Mr Ritherdon's voice droning on and on, the rival sound of bat on ball outside, and a longing to join the cricketers.

On the day itself my parents were late because the train had broken down. Max Burr made an awful fuss and told the whole school that lunch was being delayed "while we wait for the Camplings". For a short time I thought that I would not even be allowed to have lunch with the other confirmandi and their parents at the High Table, and I banished myself (choking back tears) to the lowly rough and tumble of a boys' table. But they did arrive and I was found and reinstated. At the service, conducted by the Bishop of Lewes, I kept wondering what on earth – or in heaven? – my mother found to pray about for so long.

Belmont Chapel had a stained-glass window and other objects that we had made as part of our "handicrafts". I once sang a solo at a service and Roy Henderson was there in the congregation. He was perhaps the best singer in England at that time and he gave me good advice. 'You were obviously nervous," he said, and then added comfortingly and surprisingly, 'as I always am. The best way of dealing with nervousness is to concentrate on the meaning of the words.'

Words? Meaning? I had never noticed that Purcell's *Evening Hymn* had any words or meaning. In my later "Dean" days, I often found Ripon choristers singing beautifully without any idea at all of what they were singing about; and I used to remonstrate – as much as I dared without offending Ronald Perrin, the Master of the Choristers – and make them say the words to me. Particularly I remember this of Alexander Field singing *Love Bade Me Welcome*. But what could one say about, *O for the Wings, for the Wings of a Dove?*

Max's "bates" were frightening affairs. He would take someone off and beat him; or inflict an unreasonable punishment on all of us, and go around shouting at anybody and everybody – even, once, his wife Nilla, whom we all loved. She was a sweet and beautiful "mother" to us and she used to read to us smaller ones by the fire in her sitting-room on Sunday evenings – high spot of the week. We learnt to make ourselves scarce when it was known that Max was "in a bate", and lie as low as possible. It did give us practice in dealing with awkward people.

But he could also be utterly charming and winning, for instance when prospective parents came around the school, but also sometimes to ourselves. He would come to the dormitory to put our lights out, sit on a bed and, calling us "Gentlemen", tell us fascinating things about the world and his own past and his ambitions for the school and even the particular hopes he had for some of us. 'Christopher,' he once said (making me inwardly hop at the use of my Christian name), "flat out, please, this term. We want you to get a scholarship to Lancing; and Mr Houghton tells me that you have a good chance of getting an award for your singing. Well done. And, Michael (Gregory-Jones), you are to try for Haileybury. With your brain you should manage it …' He would leave us, sleepy, but ten feet taller in our cold beds.

The routine beatings were not all that bad. I was beaten four times, always for the same offence, ragging in the dormitory. The first time was in my second term when I was bouncing about on John Taylor's bed pummelling him in a friendly way. Mr J. came in and rebuked us; and then, quarter of an hour later, came back. 'You two,' he said, 'downstairs.' So down we went, in our dressing-gowns, into Max's study and after a short ticking-off I was banished from the room while they dealt with Taylor. Three whacks with the rope, and he blubbed like anything. 'I'm for it,' I said to myself as J.T. was ushered out of the study and I was ushered in. 'Kneel on the stool,' said Max de W.B., which I obediently did. He lifted up my dressing-gown, told me to bend over, and gave me two whacks with the knotted rope, the knots stinging like anything. Then Mr J. gave me two more. (One more stroke than Taylor; fair enough because it was undoubtedly me out of bed.) Then, Max said, 'I must ask you never to do that again, Christopher.' I fled, feeling, really, that I had hardly been hurt and if that was a whacking I could take it and many more.

Looking back I am amazed at the high moral tone that Max assumed on this occasion over nothing at all. Also, how extraordinary that they gave me two strokes each, as if it were part of a ritual; or were they just sharing the pleasure? My feeling at the time was that I had "paid the price" for my (tiny) misdemeanour, so the slate was clean and I could perpetrate the crime again if I wanted to, at the risk, at quite long odds, of being beaten again. This was a good bargain because by the next morning all the school had heard about it and Taylor and I were heroes.

The last of the four beatings was more serious because I had responded to a "dare", to go down the dormitory fire-escape, on to the bottom of the garden, there to collect a fir-cone which I brought back in triumph. I was not caught; but some other silly ass was; and on due enquiry several of us were beaten with a cane, quite hard and painfully, making me dread the possibility of the sort of cruel beatings that were said to be meted out in public schools.

It is a fact that of all the peccadilloes I must have been guilty of, the only ones I can remember are those for which I was beaten. This cannot be good psychology.

There was lots that was happy and good at Belmont, for instance the games nearly every afternoon. I was in all the first teams, but never a star, except perhaps at tennis. There were also exciting adventure games in the huge grounds, organised by Max, and sometimes ending with someone "lost" by-mistake-on-purpose, probably hiding up a tree.

We had very advanced handicrafts, including printing, which we did and ran as a "company"; silver-work, stained-glass windows and weaving. We did much singing, during which my particular gift was discovered.

There were long school walks over the downs in which we walked crocodile-style till we got to a certain point, at which we were allowed to go our own way at our own speed. There was archery, for which we once went to Cowdray Park and competed against an adult club (Mrs Burr became the world champion lady archer). In the summer we swam in the school pool. I did my "two lengths" in my first term (aged eight). I had been taught by Mr J., who had me dangling on the end of a pole with a band round my chest, he holding the pole and walking up and down. Eventually I found the pressure of the band gone, and myself swimming, but very, very slowly, and the two lengths took me ages. I was highly praised and awarded four "plus marks".

There were plays, in which I excelled. I was Alice in *Alice in Wonderland* and am told I was very good, though, according to an extant photograph, my feet were too big! Apart from *Alice in Wonderland*, why did Max write his own silly plays instead of giving us the experience of good drama?

Every year we had an "interview" examination for which we had to fill in "application forms" and then appear before a "Board", sometimes with some distinguished guest present to be chairman and judge. Of course the "charming" boys, like John Ommanney (later Captain, RN), always won. I never did, but I am grateful for the experience and the lessons learnt.

One enterprising episode in my Belmont career was when Gregory-Jones and I started a "sweet insurance" scheme. Sweets used to be given out twice a week from our private supplies, which were kept by the matron, locked in a cupboard. But for punishment you could have your sweets "stopped". So Grex and I offered, for a twice weekly premium of one sweet, to pay boys their sweets when stopped. The premium would go up after every stoppage that a miscreant incurred. It worked well for a few weeks and it meant that we always had a huge supply of sweets to hand. Max got to hear about this and called us in for an explanation. As he liked to encourage enterprise, he was rather nice about it; but enquired into the precise arrangements to make sure that they were businesslike and that there was no corruption, apart from our endless supply and enjoyment of other people's sweets! He then found some pretext to stop the whole school's sweets. We shared out all we had; and that was that.

I was once summoned to the study for a reason I could never explain. Max sent for me and David Jenkins, not the great and wonderful Bishop of Durham to be, but someone who became a splendid priest, Chaplain of Hurstpierpoint and, later, Eastbourne College. Max began to lecture us on the "seventh commandment" in mysterious, moral and slightly indignant terms. But what could he be on about? Eventually we made our escape, bottoms unscathed, and looked up the "seventh commandment" in the Bible, then rushed to a dictionary to look up the word "adultery". We then dissolved into laughter and decided that Max really was nuts.

One rather endearing custom at Belmont was that every night after school prayers the masters lined up and we boys went to each one of them, shook hands, and said, 'Goodnight, Sir.' Sometimes you would be feeling furious with a particular master (and possibly he with you), and this ritual could assuage your bad feelings. He might even call you by your Christian name and a sense of mutual humanity would be created.

I still possess two *Charles Letts's Schoolboy's* diaries from Belmont days and will quote some typical extracts. I was hardly a budding Pepys, and the information these diaries contain in their appendices about career structures, melting points, physical and chemical constants, trigonometry, books to read, facts about football and cricket, Oxford and Cambridge boat-races, public school athletic records, French and Latin irregular verbs, is probably their most interesting feature.

21st January: "Went back to school, King died." (This entry is ringed in black: but for which of the reasons?)

"Listened to proclamation of King Edward VIII."

"No church because of colds. Couldn't say collect. Bad argument with Harris, I won." (We had to learn the day's collect by heart before we could have our Sunday sweets.)

"Had to go to Miss Rose in the night for Jenkins, bother the boy."

"Mr Burr in quiet bate" (when he was most to be feared). "Hard maths but jolly good, beat Archdale." (Did I or Mr Burr beat Archdale? Could have been both.)

"Had chat with Max about character."

"Had fight with Gilbert in morn, I won. Mummy and Daddy came; they watched match v Springfield Park. Got my colours."

"Went back to school. Had chicken for last dinner."

"Bad latin with Mr J."

Mr Jeffries was the junior partner headmaster. He had a crusty temper, but was a good man, being even and dependable. When he put out our dormitory lights he would tell us stories about the trenches, and gas warfare. He also taught us history and his "history stories" were the only history I ever knew till I pieced them together and filled in some of the gaps later in my life.

The diary goes on about cricket:

"Scored 22 my record this term."

"Good nets with Mr Vidal, learnt a lot."

"Rotten nets with Mr Hatch, learnt nothing."

"Good match, took three wickets and two catches."

"Mr Roger Williams acted *Mid Summer Night's Dream*. It was very funny indeed."

"Bad whacking for ragging in dorm."

And so to the summer holidays and the camp in Cornwall at Pol Green Farm, near to St Mawgan. We used to go to the beach every day in a trap pulled along by the horse, Nimble, on whom also we learnt to ride. What a life, with the trap fully laden bounding along the road and Michael and I running behind holding on and being pulled along in huge strides.

Beacon Cove was our favourite beach, though there was always the danger of being cut off by the tide. We were once, and only the most strenuous efforts saved us. On one occasion a woman was cut off and screamed to us that she was getting out of her depth. Father went and rescued her, we thought very bravely, but he didn't seem to notice. The lady was more cross with her situation than pleased with him.

We used to play cricket on that beach. Having it to ourselves we could change the pitch whenever we needed to. Once we played a rival family, the father a clergyman friend of Father. It was a needle match and Father let them win by helping Mary to catch and spill the vital catch; so we lost, and were all cross with him and Mary.

On one occasion at camp John and I went off in the evening by ourselves and had a memorable walk along the cliffs in the moonlight. He told me all his plans for life which were centred on farming. We had a smoke and returned, I feeling rather conspiratorial and immensely flattered by his attention.

It was a wonderful series of holidays with each year offering more fun and adventure, with days on the farm, harvesting, catching rabbits and riding back astride the huge cart-horses, Prince and Princess; days of mackerel fishing from Padstow; the rocks and the huge seas at Bedruthan Steps; bathing amongst the breakers at Mawgan Porth, Father nonchalantly catching us if we should happen to be swept out to sea; days of solid rain, spent in leaky tents; the daily walk to the "latrine tent", situated in another field, which became annually spotted with more and more patches of luxuriant growth; an arduous cycle ride with Father to Truro and back; meals round the camp fire and singing and dancing to an old wind-up gramophone. There was the time when the pigs got into the field and ate the soap and were chased out by Father with a stick; and evidence, once, of rats in the store tent.

I had a life-and-death adventure on the water-wheel in the farmyard. This was part of a water-mill that was still in use. The farm boys could climb over the wheel, so I tried to copy them; but I went too fast and the wheel began to turn, so I went faster and the wheel turned faster still. Eventually I was defeated and found myself being carried down into the water underneath the wheel. John was there to haul me out, very wet and frightened. The farm boys made off. The farmer (Mr Hockin) would have beaten them raw had he known; we once saw awful evidence of how he treated his daughters when they erred. But Mrs Hockin had us into her kitchen for Sunday lunches and gave us turnip and cream pasties, and I never dared say that I did not like them! But the end-of-holiday's turkey was utterly delicious.

Back to the diary and the Christmas term, 1936: lots of football; and rotten latin preps and a good maths one in which I got 74 per cent in a common entrance paper.

One entry says "Had a jolly good feast after lights"; and there was the school play. I was Slughop, a dirty boy, in Mr Burr's play. See what I mean about the "drama"?

One day early in the summer term of 1938, Max took John Fife and me to see Lancing College. We were met by the Headmaster, F.C. Doherty, who took us into the Chapel and told us that it would never be finished in our life-times. How high it was and how green – due to the bottle-glass windows, most of which we changed years lated when I became Chaplain. Mr Doherty showed us what he called the "Brere Rabbit tower", and gave us a short conducted tour. I think Max hoped that we would win our scholarships there and then by our charming behaviour; but we returned to Belmont with the feeling that we had not impressed enough.

However, Father was keen for me to try for the scholarships, music and academic. For the music I sang Handel's *Where E're You Walk*. I was up against more experienced musicians, especially David Gould who had been a chorister at Salisbury. He could sight-read, play the piano and compose with easy competence. But they gave me a choral scholarship, just for my voice; while David and Julian Dale got the music awards. I went home for the weekend and during lunch my future housemaster rang up to tell my parents the good news. I went to London for the academic tests and did better than was expected, but did not win a further award.

As a reward for our crop of exhibitions and scholarships Max took some of us to *Snow White and the Seven Dwarfs* in Brighton. The tunes of this still take me back to those golden days in the summer of 1938, when I finished my career at Belmont. I had achieved some degree of credit – but I was glad to be leaving and I looked forward with relish to going to Lancing in the Michaelmas term, 1938.

Chapter 3
Lancing College

One beautiful day in September 1938 my father drove me from Coulsdon to Lancing College, up the drive, under the lee of the Chapel, round the College into Fields House, where we were met by Patrick Halsey, the Housemaster. Along with other nervous "new men" and their anxious parents we were given tea: doughnuts and lapsang. Father had wanted to talk to me about "the facts of life" on the way down, but I was in no mood for them, having already had a clinical account from Max Burr, and thinking them somewhat bizarre and not at all what I wanted to talk about at that fraught moment. Father wisely decided to leave me to make my own way; and very soon Philip Haynes came up and suggested that we "pal up" together as there was no one else he much liked the look of.

So we did. There were four of us; he and I, Meredith and Durlacher, with both of whom I used to fight, Meredith in playful friendliness, Durlacher in some hostility. Philip was very strong and intelligent, but slow in speech. He became known as Boosey. There was a mild attempt to call me "Hawkes" after the music publishers, Boosey and Hawkes: but it never stuck.

All my fears of new-boy rituals and bullying were quickly dispelled. There was none of it; and Fields House from top to bottom was a friendly and happy community, with the seniors a bluff and kindly lot. There was discipline, of course; "lines", which consisted of writing out dates on special paper which one had to draw from the Housemaster. Knock at the door. 'Come in; yes?' 'O – can I have a hundred lines, please Sir?' 'Hoh' (a curious Tiger noise made through the nose. 'Tiger' was P.J. Halsey's nick-name) 'and what have you been up to?' 'I am afraid I was late for call-over.' 'And so begins your career of crime.' It took me about an hour to do a hundred lines; but I got quicker at it with plenty of practice! Once I was nearly beaten for forgetting "call-over" altogether; and on an another occasion I had been told to wipe up a mess of water I had made in the bathroom (squeezing a sponge over Meredith); and I did it with the House-captain's towel. I deserved a whack or two for that but talked my way out of it, saying that I thought the towel had been put there for that purpose.

Sometimes a boy got punished quite severely; David Hollis, for instance, lost his study because he let off a stink-bomb in the House-room. Once a boy was mysteriously sacked and the Headmaster came to the House and lectured us most solemnly; but I had no idea what it was all about. I suspect, looking back on it, that it was some sexual misdemeanour, but in my innocence I never heard of such things going on in all my time at Lancing. There were some close and perhaps unsuitable friendships, but homosexual practice, never, as far as I knew. Being "one of the lads" in all sorts of other ways, there was no reason why I should not have known.

Men in other Houses (at Lancing all the "boys" were "men" – until they left, when they became Old Boys) thought that Fields House was "wet" because we did not have their harsh discipline with lots of beatings. We just laughed and thought ourselves sensible and civilised. After one term, Ben Forster became Head of House, and he was much liked and admired for the cheerful, well-ordered society he maintained and his kindness to everyone. I "under-schooled" for him, which meant that I had to clean his study once a week (they were known as "pits"). I also had to be prepared to cook tea for him and his friends on Saturday afternoons; baking the beans, making the tea and toasting the crumpets. I always got one, well buttered, as a reward, except for the time I forgot to put the tea into the teapot: a beating offence in many of the other Houses at that time.

However "wet", Fields House was keen on games, and I played in all the Under 16 teams. My sadness was that I did not excel in football as I had done at Belmont. I used to be beaten to the ball and pushed off it by other boys who were faster and stronger than I was and gave me no time to exercise what skills I had at positioning myself, dribbling and passing. However, I was in the House teams and eventually got my soccer colours, with a beautiful tie that I still wear occasionally. I did well at boxing, fighting for the school at seven stone, and thus making friends with a different set of boys outside my House. I once volunteered to represent the House at Fives, never having played before, earning good "Brownie Points" for being brave enough to try and save the House from the ignomony of not being represented, but not actually winning any games!

When I first went to Lancing in 1938, my head was full of stories about public schools and the terrible things they do to "new men". But I need not have worried. We became liable for under-schooling after three weeks at school, by which time we were supposed to know all the rules and the names of everybody important. On the twentysecond day, a wet and stormy Saturday, my name was on a list for "dyke under-schooling" with the instruction "Take order at Cow Top". This was to do with the cross-country race, five gruelling miles over the downs. "Dyke under-schools" were posted at various points of the race to open gates, write down the order of runners, and to stand by the twelve dykes over which the runners had to jump at the end of the race. Cow Top was at the furthest point of the course and to get to it you had to go down into a deep valley and then up the other side of the downs where there was a farm and a yard through which the runners made their muddy way before the long descent back to the Coombs Road, the Dyke Field and the school. So off I set, paper and pencil in hand. Of course I got lost, and returned to school, very wet and miserable, having missed the race altogether and dreading the consequences.

At supper a large boy (could he be a prefect?) came and asked me if I were Campling. Miserably I said that I was. 'Were you supposed to be at Cow Top taking an order this afternoon?' (Alas.) 'Yes, but I couldn't find it.' 'Never mind,' he said. 'I was at Cow Bottom and Johnny here was on the Coombs Road. We'll get together after supper and concoct an order between us.' So we did, knowing the final order and inventing our own with likely variations. I handed in my well-cooked list. That was that; and I decided that human nature in public schools was not as bad as I had feared.

We were expected to "work", and I shall now write something about this aspect of school life, beginning at Belmont. I went there at the age of eight and was soon double-promoted, well above my age group. This had the serious disadvantage that I was never taught to write properly, and my hand-writing has always been poor. In other ways the promotion was an advantage, and John Fife and I worked our way into the scholarship set of about eight boys who were expected to pass Common Entrance (the gateway to public schools) with ease, and were being trained for the much harder scholarship papers.

Maths teaching at Belmont could be terrifying because it was given by Max Burr, who would sometimes fly into tirades. But – in a way – I loved it. The joy of the logic of an equation, or the beauty of a "rider" in geometry, duly proved, with a flourishing "QED" at the end, was utterly satisfying. And Pythagoras! I learnt where to draw the squares and what points to join up, and out came the "many cheerful facts about the square on the hypotenuse" duly demonstrated.

I enjoyed English grammar, taught by Mr J., with the intellectual exercise of parsing words and learning to analyse what each word does in a sentence. But Max Burr also taught us, and he insisted upon enterprise and discovering the taste for words. He read to us "Q" (Quiller Couch)'s book on the *Art of Writing*, and every Sunday morning when we wrote our letters home we had to show him at least one unusual word or expression. However, there was little emphasis on poetry and literature. We "read through" Shakespeare plays in a way that made them utterly boring, an opinion I revised when I did *Julius Caesar* at Lancing for School Certificate, along with Chaucer's *Prologue*, and got my "credit".

History was nothing: just Mr J. telling us an endless story which has remained, patchy, in my head ever since. Divinity was equally nothing, except when Mr Burr's brother Alan joined the partnership and dictated notes on the Synoptic Problem and Q! Geography was less than nothing. French was terrible because we ragged the French master. Latin was good, and I can remember the satisfaction of being able to translate a Latin story about Horatius and the Bridge, revelling in the neat logic of the language. But I never learnt it properly. The rules were easy to me; but I never mastered the vocabulary and the tricks of irregular verbs and the case-demands of prepositions.

I failed to win an academic scholarship to Lancing, though I came tenth out of fifteen. But I did get a choral scholarship, and they upped it a bit because of my academic efforts. I was still a year younger than the others. I gave good value for my choral scholarship as I was still singing treble when I was in the "Forty" (Lower Sixth) and then continued as an alto, good enough to sing solos in the St Matthew Passion.

So at Lancing I found myself straight away in the Upper School along with the successful "scholars". I found it hard to keep up. I was best at English. Christopher Chamberlin (known as Monkey) taught me to "construct" my essays, but there was always a tense atmosphere in his classroom. He was the master whom all boys (and staff) could imitate, and the "monkey voice" was a universal Lancing shibboleth. "Gordo" (E.B. Gordon) taught me "additional maths" with the utmost patience, and helped me through the "panics" which would sometimes get hold of me when I could not see my way through a problem. But I passed in School Cetrificate, all because at the moment of despair I remembered (as I still do) the magical fact that the coefficient of friction is tan mu!

I was driven out of science. 'Get out,' shouted Johnny Walker (we later became good friends over music: he was an excellent clarinet player and offered to teach me; but we could not get hold of an instrument). 'Get out,' all because I picked up the weights with my fingers, 'and report yourself to your housemaster.' Many a housemaster would have beaten me without any question or explanation; but Tiger just said, 'Perhaps science isn't for you' and allowed me to drop the subject altogether. Thus ended my scientific education, a fact of which I am much ashamed; yet the truth is that I have studied the philosophy of science, including the mysteries of Einstein *et al.*, more than most people I know, especially those who assume that science is "against" religion.

In my first year, we studied "ancient history" with Mr. Handford. He was Head of Classics, the best brain on the staff – all-knowing, it seemed to us. I enjoyed his lessons, especially as he could be so easily diverted into talking about the day's tense affairs, with Munich settled but settling nothing, and war looming up. School Certificate History was done with the Chaplain. I did not take it seriously and failed. I took it again the next term under Mr Chamberlin and passed with distinction. He pressed me to do history in the Sixth Form instead of classics. I should have done this, but Father insisted on Classics, having premonitions that the Greek would be useful if I were ever to think of being ordained, which I was not at that time. Curiously the best use of my Greek was when I was posted to serve on a Greek destoyer, HHMS *Kanaris*, through the influence of John Terry who was on the staff of the Commander in Chief, Mediterranean Fleet, in Alexandria. That was to come about in 1944.

Meanwhile, I started Greek with this same, brilliant, double-first, but hopeless disciplinarian, John Terry. He insisted on calling us all by the names of the characters in *Winnie the Pooh*. I was Tigger. But we spent that year ragging about, and the Head Man was very shocked to find how little I knew when I tried the scholarship papers the next year. The same was true of Latin, with the result that when I started on the Classics after School Certificate (which I just passed in sufficient subjects) I found the reading of advanced books extremely difficult. Even at Oxford where I had to be able to read Latin and Greek, I found it difficult, especially when (for the ethics paper) I had to read a letter of St Augustine in Latin, for which there was no English translation.

In my second year at Lancing I experienced the reign of terror exercised by Stephen Bell. He was a short, squat, red-faced individual, a kind friend outside the classroom, a devout Christian, as long as you kept firmly to the old forms, but a notorious "terror". I think that he must have known that we had wasted a year with John Terry, and to make up for it and exact revenge on behalf of his colleague, he drove us as hard as he could, harder than I could stand. He gave us huge amounts to learn in "Evening School", always more than I could manage, and that meant being punished with hours of extra work, writing out irregular verbs many times over, as well as copying out sentences correctly that had been done incorrectly. Worse, he would put us on "report cards" which we had to have signed up at the end of every lesson and show to our housemasters at the end of each week, indeed, the Head Man, if they were bad. This happened to better and cleverer pupils than I was and caused a furore (so I heard later) amongst the staff.

On one shameful occasion when I had done my best to master some Greek verbs, I cheated in the test and answered the questions with my book on my knee. S.B. came and stood behind me for a terrifying minute but failed to spot the book. I think he was looking for it but did not like to challenge me. I made a few deliberate mistakes, but got away with it on this occasion with two huge disadvantages. One was my conscience, which gave me awful stick. The other was that S.B. got it into his head that I was really quite clever and raised his sights of what he expected of me thereafter. Looking back, I think that he was in the wrong almost as much as I was. If a pupil's only resort is to cheat, the master must be to blame.

Classics in the Forty (first year Sixth) was mostly taught by John Handford, plus Virgil with the Head Man. As he (the Head) did all the translating himself, he made life very easy for us, but this was fatal when it came to exams. John Handford was an inspiring teacher, who appreciated my appreciation but was sad (and sometimes very angry) about my "carelessness" which was really ignorance of the words and rules.

But I did love the books. The atheist Lucretius inspired me to think sensibly about religion and to begin to take a philosophical approach towards it. I can still quote lines of it (e.g. *"Tantum religio potuit suadere malorum"*, "Such is the degree of wickedness that religion can induce", a text which, alas, still stands). I loved the orgies in Euripedes' *Bacchae*, the schatalogical humour of Aristophanes' *Birds*, the power of Aeschylus' *Agamemnon* (bits of which remain in my memory), the relentless logic of Plato, the eloquence of Cicero and Demosthenes (but why did we have to read *De Senectute – Concerning Old Age –* when we would have enjoyed *De Amicitia – Concerning Love –* so much more?), the adventures of Aeneas, the easy (as far as the Latin was concerned) campaigns of Caesar, and the biting irony of Tacitus – and much more.

But the books set for Higher Certificate were too long for mastery. I worked very hard at them in class and at all sorts of unsuitable moments, such as a day hiding under a bush in soldier's uniform during an OTC field day in which the Fields House Platoon managed to get itself lost. I still think that the intellectual exercise of putting difficult bits of English (from Burke, or Carlisle or Gibbon) into Latin or Greek, reducing language to its essential meaning, and then building it up again, abstracts turned into concretes with as many verbs as possible, was an excellent training for someone who would spend a lot of his professional life writing or teaching.

But I failed Higher Certificate in Classics, twice, on each occasion passing the books but failing the Greek "unseen translation"; and in those days you had to pass all or nothing. I did well in ancient history; and really well in music, which I did as a subsidiary instead of French. In both years I got a distinction and nearly full marks in the paper on history, analysis and appreciation. The music was a joy to me, though I found the harmony difficult. I could apply the rules correctly, but never "heard" the difference between what was supposed to be right and what was ruled as wrong. However, I was good at writing tunes, and have kept that going ever since. But the ancient history and the music did not count, all because I had failed the Greek unseen translation.

Jasper Rooper taught me music, but it was the Gramophone Society in Fields that turned me into a classical music buff, along with some of my friends. The "Gram. Soc." met every Friday in the Housemaster's study after Evening School, and was always the high point of my week. We would lie around on the floor and listen to a programme chosen by the society's "Dictator", and drink the Housemaster's lapsang in the interval. None of us would have thought of reading during the music (in contrast to what I found in later days) and a programme would consist of something like the *Water Music, Eine Kleine Nacht Musik* and Beethoven's Seventh Symphony.

Besides the weekly Gram. Soc., some senior boys in pits had gramophones and stacks of records. These were the old 78s which lasted less than five minutes a side and were played with wooden needles that had to be sharpened between sides. To this day there are mistakes on records or blurry bits of recording when the music was too heavy for the needle, which remain in my memory as part of the music. But at Lancing I could sing to you any tune you asked for out of any of the Beethoven symphonies and concertos, all the Brahms orchestral works, lots of Mozart (especially piano concertos), Tchaikovsky (which for one term I affected to despise) and much else. No opera and very little chamber music, though Beethoven and Mozart quartets and the G Minor Quintet came to me at the end of my time at Lancing. My difficulty was that I could not afford "discs", so I had to rely on other people's. We once had a concert in Great School with Mozart's G Minor Symphony, and I can still feel the thrill of hearing this supreme work for the first time. Also we went to a concert at the Dome in Brighton and heard Brahms' Third, Beethoven's Eighth and *En Saga* by Sibelius. These still take me back to those early days of loving music, which was a very important part of my life at Lancing.

Incident. Christmas 1939. Received a telegram saying, "College frozen up. Delay return for a week." A joyful week.

My first term (September 1938) was the time of the Munich crisis, a crisis that sharply divided the staff. There was a debate in which Patrick Halsey took the pacifist line, saying that a country's "honour" was not a matter of going to war. Parnell-Smith, who later commanded the corps and disliked Mr Halsey, said that as a country we had betrayed another country and hence had indeed betrayed our honour. I wanted to be on Tiger's side (was he not my Housemaster?) but I found Parnell's arguments much stronger, especially if you translated the country's affairs into personal affairs and thought in terms of personal ethics. You could not, surely, make a promise to a friend and then leave him to his fate.

Meanwhile, Westminster School had been evacuated on to us and we had Westminster boys everywhere, in our dormitories, dining-room and classrooms. We took instant dislike to their prefects, who swanked about the place with swagger-canes bedecked with pink ribbons. Ted Longford (later the Precentor at Ely Cathedral) was there at that time; also Tony Benn; also Donald Swann, famous for *Salad Days* and some hilarious animal songs. He won the two schools' composing competition – in which I came second! But after three weeks, "Peace in our Time" was declared and the Westminster boys returned to London.

We spent Easter 1939 at school, a fact I remember for trouble I got into, which was serious at the time. A hymn chosen for evensong on Easter Sunday, the last service of the term, was *The Day of Resurrection*, which, because of its dreary tune, I hated. I told Wilfred Derry, the

Chaplain, who said, 'Why not change it, then?' So I did. I got hold of the keys of the organ loft from the Porter's Lodge and changed the number on all the hymn-sheets in all the stalls and the organ loft. Whoever was respsonsible for the hymn-boards naturally followed the change. Unfortunately Mr Howitt (the senior priest) noticed the alteration and tried to change it back by giving out in his high, thin voice, the hymn that he had originally chosen. But the organist didn't hear his announcement, so there was delightful chaos, such as the school loved.

But who had changed the hymn? The porter described me as the boy who had borrowed the key of the organ loft. Jasper Rooper – that sleuth – asked me direct, was it me? 'Yes', I had to admit. Trouble. He would have to report me to the Head Man. Perhaps W.R.D. (the Rev.) would help, I thought. But no. He did not take any responsibility for what he had said to me (thus forfeiting some of the respect I otherwise had for him).

At the final school assembly the Head Man gave out notices and exhortations before dismissing us for the holidays. He finished by saying that he wished to speak to the boy who had changed the chapel hymn-sheets. So – terrified – I waited behind whilst everybody else left and made for home. The Head kept me waiting around as he chatted to people, and then turned to me and walked me up and down Great School. How dare I take it into my own head to change a hymn? I was there to be taught, not to choose. It was the College's responsibility – and therefore his particular responsibility – to teach me good manners and the appreciation of what is best in music and poetry and – er – hymns. Did he appreciate the painful irony of what he was saying when I was already such a "classical music maniac" – as we were known, in contrast to the "jazz maniacs"? Anyway, on and on he went. I soaked up the reproof and the criticism of my tastes and longed to answer that the hymn I had chosen was a far better hymn – in every respect, literary as well as musical – than *The Day of Resurrection*. I was also in some fear of what physical pain he might be about to inflict on my behind; but it did not seem likely because he had a name for not being a "beater".

At last the harangue came to an end: but it wasn't the end. He told me that I must, of course, go and apologise to Mr Howitt. So, feeling like a wet rag, I dragged myself off to his room, and there made my apology, only to receive another long lecture on my irresponsible behaviour, and then be sent to my Housemaster. Tiger just looked solemn and said, 'I expect by now you have heard enough.'

The Chapel loomed large in our life at Lancing – but not all that large. It is a huge building, French gothic in style, all height and length, after the manner of Beauvais Cathedral. From the bottom of College Hill it stands like a huge hand pointing the way to Heaven and witnessing (as Woodard, the founder, meant it to) to the preeminence of the Christian faith. Inside it is utterly beautiful. As you step through the West Door your gaze is taken straight up to the High Altar and the huge tapestries at the East End. All is light and height and uplifting glory. Indeed the feet of the Celebrant at the altar are above the heads of the congregation; but so good are the proportions that you do not feel it to be so. The involuntary raising of the eyes is part of the inspiration.

We had sung evensong in Chapel every day and a full noncommunicating Sung Eucharist every Sunday. I was in the choir as the leading treble, and so always found the services interesting. But they did not make much impact upon me at the time. They were part of my growth, the spiritual growth, matching the intellectual and physical – with ups and downs.

There was one curious school custom to do with Chapel that got lost when the school evacuated. Before a service, boys would get into friendly lines abreast, sometimes linking arms, and walk down the wide steps that lead from the Lower Quad, past the Headmaster's house and the Common Room (now Teme House) to the parapet which looks down the hill. We would scan the view: over the River Adur, to Shoreham Airport, Shoreham-by-Sea with its two ancient churches, and the power station and the cement works away to the left: a gorgeous view on a sunny day. Then, About Turn – and back into Chapel for evensong.

A bizarre but important feature of Lancing life was the OTC (Officers' Training Corps), or just, "the corps". It happened on Monday mornings after break, and on Wednesday afternoons in full, ghastly uniform. Ghastly, because of its discomfort. It included puttees wound round the leg in a prescribed pattern so that the top end arrived exactly level with the outside of the knee. The trick was first to make that happen, second, to tie them in such a way that they stayed up, withstanding all the stamping and marching and countermarching that one's legs had to perform. Besides that, various brassy bits of the uniform had to be brightly polished in a way that did not mark the hideous khaki material of the uniform itself. The present Megarry Room was the armoury, with rifles padlocked round the pillars. Here, as "recruits", through the kindly barking of the BM (band master), we learnt our rifle drill ("At the Command One, throw the rifle up, catching it at the Outer Band ... So"); and from here we poured out into the Chapel Quad, lined up in House platoons and marched down College Hill, with bugles sounding and drums beating, led – would you believe it? – by the BM and the Corps goat! Tedious marching manoeuvres then took place around the Upper Field; followed sometimes by a bit of fun, attacking someone or other, and learning how to give firing instructions on a target described by the face of an imaginary clock. There was a great deal of "sweaty" (a Lancing word meaning "braced"), stiff, quasi-disciplined behaviour, especially by those who enjoyed this caper and liked hearing themselves shout: but most of us just endured it stoically, hoping to avoid trouble in the form of extra parades. Once a term there was a Field Day when, in full uniform and carrying our accursedly heavy rifles, we would career over the downs, "attacking" one another (i.e. another House's platoon), being sure to let off our allotted blanks before it was all over. I can remember once, very tired, marching back to College, and Ben Forster, the Platoon Commander, offering to carry my rifle and making another House-captain carry Meredith's. The corps will reappear in the course of these memoirs, no doubt, because in war and evacuation it became more important and, as one grew in seniority, slightly less unbearable.

Some snatches of Lancing vocabulary. "Don't look here", said to a junior, implying that though cats may look at kings, junior men have no right to look at their seniors. Rather more edifying, "Good on you for ...", meaning, "Please pass ...", whatever is required, the mustard or the butter. Or any sort of "please": "Good on you to tell me how to translate this unintelligible piece of latin verse", but also "Thank you", "Good on you for that bit of help" – even a nicely passed football.

And an absurd custom, indeed, rule. "New men", for their first year, had to keep all the buttons of their jackets done up: after a year, one button could be undone; after two, two. But only House-captains and prefects could swan around with all their buttons undone, their jackets flying behind them in lordly disarray.

One day in the summer term of 1939 my Housemaster summoned me to his study and invited me to join a party of three who would go with him on his annual tour of Europe; Ben Forster and Tony Dodgeson being the other two. I was much the youngest, but who cared? It was an opportunity not to be missed and my parents (who had to find the money – £20!) did all they could to encourage me.

So I left the family holiday in Devon to go by train to Chatham to stay the night with Ben's parents, his father being the Officer in Command of the Royal Marines. We had a grandly served dinner with me much in awe but enjoying every moment. The next day we set off in Tiger's Wolseley sports car, crossed the Channel and made our way to Amiens for the first night in a hotel which was spread around a courtyard and which fed us with delicious fish.

We drove through France, over the Alps, into Switzerland, where at Basle we bathed in the Rhine and I was nearly swept away. We were convinced (Halsey was convinced) that there would not be a war, so I said as much to my parents on a postcard home, telling them also that we were about to go into Germany. It was the last they heard from me before I turned up on the doorstep at Coulsdon on 30 August. In Germany we drove to Freiburg where Patrick nearly killed a pedestrian boy by his outrageous (as I later thought of it) driving. Strangely our German visas, applied for in Berne, only gave us permission to stay four or five days, up to the day, we later realised, that Hitler invaded Poland. So we hardly stayed at all in Germany; returned to Basle and then – in panic – made a dramatic dash (everything Tiger did was dramatic – or, rather, dramatised) for France and Calais. We went through Belgium and nearly got detained at the frontier. On our last night in France mobilisation notices were being issued and Patrick (was he mad?) tore two of these down from a station window and displayed them proudly in his study when he got back to Lancing. *"Avis Aux Reservists"*, it said; then a list of things the unfortunate reservists were to bring with them.

We crossed the Channel from Calais in one of the last car ferry boats to leave before the war began. So back to Coulsdon, having dropped off Ben and Tony to make their ways by train. I think my parents were more relieved to see me than angry with Mr Halsey for the risks he had taken. He stayed the night with us, looking very ill, and the next thing we heard was that he had got a duodenal ulcer and was unfit to return to school till half term, by which time war had been declared.

When the Michaelmas term began, Westminster School were with us again. We were fitted with gas-masks, which we were supposed to have with us at all times. Everything had to be blacked out at night, so we stopped using the Chapel after dark. Miss Carr, the House matron, urged us to knit scarves for the Finns, who were being invaded by Russia – but I doubt if my effort would have kept much of the Russian cold off the chest of a freezing Finn. Otherwise life went on as before.

In the summer term things hotted up. The news became dramatically bad and exciting. We used to rush back to our House-room in the break, listen to the news and move the swastika pins on the map in the direction of France and the Channel ports, according to the latest bulletin. The blitzkreig seemed unbearably masterful; indeed, "winning"; it was not until it was getting close and we could hear the guns across the Channel that we realised the enormity of what was happening. Rumours filled the air: we were going to be evacuated to Canada in HMS *Howe* (a ship just launched, which I later served in); the Reverend William Howitt had been arrested as a spy whilst returning from his daily dip in the sea at Lancing. All he had with him was a bicycle, a sandwich and a German dictionary, so it was said. One evening a gun appeared and was carefully sited on the Fields House tennis court, manned by two soldiers. It was there for the defence of England – but the next on day it disappeared, and we were told later that it was being moved around the coast to raise morale. We heard the infamous Lord Haw-Haw bleating his persuasive nonsense, and David Gould could imitate him perfectly.

Patrick Halsey went very quiet at this time. He was such a lover of Germany and such a strong pacifist that his position was very awkward. I expect (looking back) that the Head Man had a talk with him, because never in our hearing did he say an unpatriotic word. When later I talked to him about my own prospects and whether I should wait to be called up or volunteer or even be a conscientious objector, he was sympathetic and sensible.

One day we were summoned to Great School by the Head Man, who told us that we were to evacuate the College within a week. But wouldn't the Germans be here by then? Fields, Olds and Heads were to go to Ellesmere College for the rest of the summer term, the rest of the school to Denstone. Meanwhile we were to pack the College furniture into the crypt. Mr Handford would be in charge of the stacking.

So for that week no school work was done at all. We worked in shifts, carrying chairs, desks, everything that could be moved, except our beds, down to the crypt. In off-duty moments I used to sit out on the Fields House lawn (the weather was perfect) revising my set books for School Certificate. John Bishop would be playing Mozart piano concertos loudly in his pit, and I still associate the "Little B Flat", K 450, with those evacuation days. So College furniture was duly stacked; and one fine morning in June coaches appeared and drove us to Paddington where we went by train to Ellesmere or Denstone – sister schools in the Woodard Foundation.

Mr Winston Churchill and General Montgomery met one day at the College to discuss strategy. When Monty visited the school in the 1960s he unveiled a plaque to that effect. The college was taken over by the Royal Navy and thousands of RNVR officers received their training there – doing fleet manoeuvres (according to John Terry who was one of them) on ice-cream tricycles on the Lower Field.

Chapter 4
Summer 1940

One hot summer day in June 1940 Lancing College – boys and staff – set off in a procession of coaches to Paddington Station; Fields, Heads and Olds on their way to Ellesmere College, the rest to Denstone. Fields House got into the train in a sensible and civilised manner; but Johnny Walker, the Housemaster of Heads, made his House "get out and get in again in House Order", much to our amusement. Perhaps it was his way of checking that all were present, but he was known as a fuss-pot. When we arrived at Ellesmere, we walked to the College, where we were met and ushered through the school-smelling buildings (mixture of chalk and polish) to the playing fields. There, lines of bell-tents were awaiting us. Fields had its line. Philip Haynes, Eric Wood, John Shepherd and I were in one tent, with John Bishop, a House-captain, put there, no doubt, to keep us in order.

We did very little school work while we were at Ellesmere, but spent a lot of time lying around on the grass outside the tent, revising School Certificate set books. We only spent a few weeks there and during the last of these I sat the School Certificate examination, held in the Ellesmere gym. Considering the circumstances I did surprisingly well, though to get the necessary exemption from matric., I had to take some subjects again the following term. I remember the despair over the French "dictation and reproduction". Arthur Cooper had taught us at Lancing, and with his comfortable English rendering of French I co   score good marks. But Arthur had joined the army, and the Elle   re French master who took us on that occasion seemed dete   ined to make us fail. I hardly understood a word of his rapid end   gs. I had already taken the oral exam at Lancing itself, and,   mil   se note, passed – rather well.

31

Apart from the little work and some cricket played in the mornings when the Ellesmere boys (of whom we saw practically nothing) were at lessons, we were left to amuse ourselves, and when we were not just lazing, we went for expeditions on foot or by bus over the countryside.

We were late back for Chapel one evening, due to a lazy fatalism about bus times; no harm came of this, only dire warnings. But a few days later we went to Chester, this time with our Housemaster. We walked the streets with the shops aloft (but no money to buy anything) and went round the city wall, a walk I did again a few years later when on leave from HMS *Cabbala*. But again we missed the bus, and this time it certainly mattered to Mr Halsey, who had himself uttered the dire warnings. We tried to get a taxi, but the only one big enough was a hearse. So we tore across the Cheshire countryside crammed into this gleaming black vehicle which, I guess, had never gone so fast, or been filled with such lively bodies, before. We got back to the College just in time to sing the praises of Almighty God in Ellesmere Chapel.

The person I remember best from those days was John Bishop, the House-captain who was detailed to keep us in order. He had a cynical sense of humour which made merry on all subjects, sacred and profane. Being a brilliant "classic" (later an Oxford scholar), he would do our translation for us when asked. He was also a classical music buff and, not having a gramophone or the necessary discs, we used to walk around singing through classical symphonies and concertos, though "singing" is hardly the right word for the mixture of wild noises and conductor-like gesticulations we made. We invented words for the *Ode to Joy* tune in the Choral Symphony: "Rum Funk Gildensenshafter Gottlebach Elisium. Gor Bech Gibow Orchesta ..." Fortunately I forget the rest. J.H.B. was in those days a cheerful agnostic who used to sing at the top of his voice in the appropriate hymn in Chapel, 'Firmly I believe and truly, One is three and three is one; And I next acknowledge duly, The earth is bigger than the sun.' But never mind, God. You got the last laugh, because, as You know, he eventually became a priest in Your service in the Episcopalian Church in Australia.

We were always hungry at Ellesmere and nearly went on strike because of the bad quality and thin quantity of the food we were given.

Wilfred Derry, the Chaplain, organised a "buns for boys" scheme whereby after the evening meal we went round to the sanatorium where he had trays of buns ready for our consumption. A popular act, but was it sensible?

In this same sanatorium our Housemaster had his study, where he kept the House-bank and the lines-paper in the oven. One day both of these disappeared. The money reappeared but not the lines-paper; so the first miscreant who went along for his lines was let off, and no more were given or needed. Rawdon Crozier, the Head of House, kept us in good order. He left at the end of term and joined the Navy, coming back to see us, resplendent in officer's uniform.

When term ended, David Hollis and I decided we would cycle home to London. He had a bicycle at Ellesmere, and I, with my father's approval and an unexpected birthday cheque for £5, went and bought one – a Raleigh with a magical three-speed gear. On this journey we rode through Pershore and I can remember thinking how endlessly long the cobbled Georgian high street was. I was to walk it often enough (without its cobbles) in the 1970s, when I became its vicar. We went on to Evesham, where we asked the way to Broadway and were deliberately misled, this being the time of spy-fever in England. All sign-posts had been removed, and all strangers (even fifteen-year-old boys on bicycles) were assumed to be German spies. When someone more sensible redirected us back to Evesham to start again, we decided to stop and find a bed-and-breakfast. All I can remember of the next day's ride is catching on to the back of a lorry going up Fish Hill at Broadway. That lift was very welcome, however madly dangerous the practice may seem today. We did it as a matter of course up steep hills. The much more dangerous feat was that of racing along in the slipstream of a lorry, but we all did this whenever we could.

We spent one of the nights at a monastery at Prinknash, where David had a monkish uncle. He was delighted to see us and the Anglican Benedictines in that community did us proud, giving us an honoured and well-equipped guest-room full of comforts, which the monks, presumably, lacked. At supper that night a monk chanted on one note to the assembled company: first a piece of scripture, then a homily from some devout book, then – would you believe it? – in the same voice, without a break of any kind, he sang the day's news from *The Times.* Some monks, I noticed, were eating their meal standing up, presumably because they were under punishment. David and I were much awed by the place and its inhabitants and were delighted by the sense of holy happiness that seemed to prevail.

The next day, we went on to Devizes, where David had an aunt who gushed over us in admiration for our arduous journey. On the final day we rode to London and made for Wembley, where my grandmother and Aunt Win lived. They too were proud, though slightly disapproving. They gave us bony fish for supper, because Grandma believed in the necessity of eating slowly. The next day we rested in the morning and parted company after lunch. I made my way back to Charlton and David to his father's parish at Widdenham, near Ware.

I made for the centre of London and reached Victoria Station in the dusk on a bike with no lights. I nearly wept when I found that it was the wrong station for Charlton. I had to half ride and half push my bike back to Charing Cross and the train to Charlton, on which I travelled in the guard's van with my bike. This was the time of the black-out. Stations were not lit; even their names were obscured. But at last the guard told me that this was Charlton. I did not know the way home, but I set off walking, pushing the bike in the dark, whistling the tune of Handel's *Water Music,* which I knew my parents would recognise. I had rung them, so they were out looking for me. Tune recognised in the darkness. Great joy. Home at last with a serious hole in my trousers, so there was no way I could go to church on the following morning.

Father had just moved to be Rector of Charlton, where he had two churches, St Luke's, a delightful Jacobean church, and St Paul's, much bigger and higher (in both senses of the word) next door to the Rectory. It was said to be a living with a good income; but unfortunately by the rules of the day Father had to pay one third of his income to his predecessor who had retired.

In those bad days there was no "Parsonage Board" responsible for the maintenance and upkeep of parsonage houses (a matter that I later gave so much attention to when I became Archdeacon of Dudley), so Father was left to pay when the Rectory was damaged again and again by bombs near or far. At the end of the war Father was the only incumbent left in the district, all the adjacent parishes having lost their vicars by death or resignation.

Mother's nerves never recovered from the stress of the bombs and war-time conditions. Although she lived to be ninety-two, she was always frail and would jump to the ceiling if you said "Bang" behind her back. Not surprising. Father used to sally forth whenever there was an air-raid and visit the underground shelters, leading prayers and giving comfort. At least one of these shelters was destroyed by a direct hit with awful loss of life. Father would return in the early hours exhausted but unperturbed by the danger – to a distraught wife.

I was at Reigate staying with my Belmont friend David Hill when the Battle of Britain was at its height. We were playing golf and, becoming aware of extraordinary activities in the sky, we lay down in a bunker, which seemed as safe a place to be as any, and watched the planes swooping and diving and weaving in and out of one another. But for the fact that this was a battle, it could have been an exciting game of chase or beautiful acrobatics in the sky. But there was also smoke. Twice we witnessed the appalling death plunge: a trail of smoke as a plane curved gracefully and silently down to earth, and the dull thud of an explosion some seconds later. Horrified yet fascinated we returned to David's grim-faced parents. I was sent home on my bike, another tricky ride.

The news bulletins in those days were immensely exciting and we rushed to hear every broadcast and to read every paper about the number of "enemy forces" shot down, and our own much smaller losses. On 16 September there was an evening raid on London. Hitler had turned from fighting the RAF to attempting to subdue Londoners and Britain by bombing the capital city, as he had bombed Warsaw and other cities to destruction and surrender. We at home were used to the sirens and were not particularly perturbed that evening. The family was gathered in the drawing-room, reading, talking, me on the large settee (which is now in the outer hall of Minster House, Ripon). Suddenly there was a burst of ack-ack guns; the drone of a German plane overhead (we could always tell them by the throb of their engines); the scream of a bomb; a vivid flash; a deep but not loud explosion; an acrid smell; and there was the drawing-room ceiling falling slowly down; Father looking worried over his glasses. My sofa tipped gently forwards and covered me up. I then crawled out to a shattered room with smokey dust everywhere; Father kneeling down most incongruously because his chair had also fallen forward and tipped him out; John around, calling us; and – panic – where was Mother?

The house was not badly damaged, apart from the room we were in, which had lost its ceiling and its windows and most of its outer wall; so we went on a Mother-hunt, calling and calling, until at last she emerged from the bathroom, naked with a towel round her waist. A family roll-call found us all present and correct; Father, Mother, John and me. Air-raid wardens were banging at the door to see if we were safe and telling us to black-out the lights. Having huge Edwardian windows we had always found it difficult to black them out properly and had had many a row with the wardens; but on this occasion they were sympathetic. The all-clear siren soon sounded and, most illogically, we decided to go round to the Bank in Charlton village where the churchwarden, Mr Butcher, was the manager. He led us to his safe-room where Mrs Butcher gave us cocoa and we sat on tins marked with money denominations. When at last we returned home we saw what had happened. St Paul's, the church next door, had been demolished.

It was the first London church to be hit, and next day it was in the news and hundreds of people came swarming past to gape at the no-longer church and the damaged Rectory. I made Father angry because I allowed a photographer to come into the house to take a photograph of the ruin from my bedroom. The picture was published the next day. Challenged, I admitted my deed. But I never thought it was a fault! I still have pictures of the ruined church and my father sadly surveying it.

A few days later a spray of incendiary bombs fell over the garden. One hit the house and fell into the coal bunker in the backyard. I flung a pail of water over it – without any effect. Father came and looked at it sadly and warily, rather as if it were a snowball thrown by a naughty child. He then filled a bucket with sand which he placed carefully over the spluttering bomb, thus successfully extinguishing it. We then went into the air-raid shelter, which we had constructed under the stairs. We had furnished this space and made it fit for sitting in; but we hated it and only went there with the utmost reluctance. The next morning I collected two or three incendiary bomb remains from the garden, good-looking things with fins, about nine inches long.

Very severe damage was inflicted on the part of the parish that was down the hill, nearer the river, a land-mine, for instance, destroying a whole street. Up the hill we did not have it so badly, but there were enough incidents to shake us up.

One morning I got on my bike and went exploring, across Blackheath and on to New Cross and the Elephant and Castle. At one point I came across a crowd of people gathered on a bomb-site, and there I saw the King and Queen, wearing helmets, looking very serious and talking to people with obvious sympathy. They too had been bombed at Buckingham Palace, which suffered bad damage, and much was made of this. But there was no commotion or fuss at this moment, and I rode back home, where my mother was not at all pleased with me, though she softened when I told her about the King and Queen.

I recounted this incident when the Queen, who was by then Queen Mother, came to Ripon for the city's festivities in 1986. She asked me afterwards where it was that I saw her; but I could only remember that it was somewhere near the Elephant and Castle. She seemed satisfied, and obviously pleased that I had seen her when she was Queen and I was a "boy on a bike".

I have no chronological memory of bombing incidents in the war. I was quite often at home in the holidays, but I cannot remember what happened when. I can remember Father's infuriatingly devout curate Gilbert Mansbridge saying to my mother, hoping to calm her nerves, 'It's only a gun, Mother,' when a bloody great bomb fell somewhere nearby. We had a maid called Nelly who was elderly and known to be dishonest, one of Father's lost souls. She was with us for her sake rather than ours or Mother's. She had hysterics whenever there was a raid, especially if Father was out in it, and this did nothing to assuage my mother's nerves.

One of my most vivid memories is of the great Fire of London raid in 1941 when the whole of the River Thames seemed to be alight. John and I watched from an upstairs bedroom window. It was a memorable sight: the snaking curve of the river glowing in deepest red with the reflections of the fires that raged alongside it; searchlights criss-crossing; an occasional plane caught in them; anti-aircraft shells bursting like fireworks; all to a hideous cacophany of guns thundering, bombs screaming down, percussive explosions and the drone bass of enemy aircraft. John and I (this may have been on another occasion) heard a stick of bombs coming at us, each scream louder and nearer. We ducked into each other's arms, but the last one went over and beyond.

Apart from the blitz, which dominated everything, I cannot remember much about life at the Rectory, Old Charlton. To Father it seemed the most unrewarding part of his ministry, though there were some who obviously loved him. He came there with the bombing, which began almost as soon as he arrived, and some people behaved as if they blamed him for it. I shall never forget his massive calm when raids were at their noisiest and he decided to go out into them and visit the people in the shelters. He would come back very late and very tired; but was up for the hardly attended early service the next morning. Mother used to put on a show of good humoured "not caring"; and it was only after it was all over that she showed how frayed her nerves had become. I used to play the piano, go for walks, try to compose, do some reluctant gardening, and bike around the place; but after the Royal Elephant and Castle escapade, I had to keep to strict topographical limits.

When I joined the Navy I became a keen supporter of Charlton Athletic; indeed I still am, and they are doing well in the Premier League. But this was so that I could play my part in mess-deck conversation, and I was bound to maintain that London clubs were better than Northern ones! But I never actually attended a match, though every Saturday afternoon the air was full of the noise of the football crowd. I loved football. Why didn't I go? It was just that no one else in the family was interested.

I grew to be fond of Margaret Butcher, the bank manager's daughter, and to imagine that I was in love with her. Like me she enjoyed listening to music, so we would do this together in her house or mine. Once I saved up every penny I had in order to be able to take her by bus to Trafalgar Square, there to attend a National Gallery Lunch Time Concert, organised by Dame Myra Hess, then to the Strand Corner House where we could get a meal for one shilling and six-pence, and so home by bus.

These concerts were a feature of war-time London and I went to several of them. I remember Pears and Britten performing Schubert and the *Michael Angelo Sonnets;* and Myra Hess herself playing Schuman's *Carnival,* which I was studying (not playing!) for Higher Certificate Music. And once (here's history) I went with Father to a Promenade Concert conducted by Sir Henry Wood himself at the old Queen's Hall, before it was bombed. There was an air-raid and we were not allowed to leave till the "all clear" had sounded. Members of the audience went up to the platform and performed, and to our great pride Peter Gould, then at Lancing and hoping to be a professional pianist, played some Beethoven followed, for an encore, by Mozart's *Kl.* Has *Kl* ever been performed again at a Prom? Home that night by a nearly empty, noisy, bone-shaking tram which jolted its way through bomb-scarred London to Greenwich, from where we walked up the hill to Charlton.

To conclude the subject of Charlton: John was in the RAF in those days, so my memories of him come from the times when he was waiting to join up or when he was on leave. Michael or Mary were sometimes with us but they spent most of their holidays in Shropshire. I had a room high up in the house, folded into the roof, where I used to shiver in bed, cold and listening to the air-raids, which were generally distant but sometimes horribly close. We had an extraordinary "butler" called Usmah, another of Father's "pick-ups". He helped a bit around the house but then mysteriously disappeared.

My last memory of Charlton was when I turned up in matelot's uniform, fresh from the Mediterranean on Christmas Eve 1944 – to the astonisment of myself and all the family – a story that must wait for a later instalment.

Chapter 5
Lancing at Ludlow

The Michaelmas term 1940 started with Lancing at Ludlow, Fields and Heads houses staying in the luxurious, Victorian/Edwardian mansion, Stokesay Court. This stood huge and pompous half a mile from Onibury, six miles north-west of Ludlow. One made one's way up a long, rhododendron drive to the bleak, barrack-like rear, through the ornate porch and front door, into a large hall with a gallery all round in dark, polished mahogany, behung with oil paintings of Scottish mountains, highland cattle and classical scenes. The hall was big enough to be the dining room for both houses, as we sat on benches along the oak tables. Off this magnificent hall were stately rooms with elaborate ceilings and imposing pictures, all so valuable that we were forbidden to write in ink; but this did not stop a particularly stupid "under-school" from scrubbing one of them with a yard brush when he was on House-room cleaning duty. This room had an ornate ceiling, elaborate chandeliers, and more lugubrious pictures and carved tables, around which we were allowed to sit on benches or out-of-character school chairs.

There was also a House-captain's room and the Housemaster's study which he opened at nearly all times to boys for a (not very) "Quiet Room". How he managed to have boys around in his room so much astonishes me, but we took it for granted.

Dormitories were up the stairs off the gallery round the hall. They were beautiful rooms with balconies overlooking the garden. This stretched across lawns and shrubberies and a fish-pond, to a lake and the Shropshire countryside and the Three Sisters beyond, and

Titteston Clee hill, nobly shaped, away to the east. From the garden side, Stokesay Court had a magnificent, three-bowed front which spoke of its opulence and comfortable grandeur.

Here we lived. Every morning we went by two coaches through Ludlow to Moor Park where we met the rest of the school and had our lessons. For me this consisted of "the Classics" plus English plus Music (history, analysis and composition).

After school we would return by coach to Stokesay for lunch; and then real life would begin as we roamed the countryside on foot or bicycle, sometimes going far afield, returning to work (inkless) in the late afternoon and evenings.

Games were difficult because of the shortage of pitches, though most of the Houses managed to make their own in the grounds of their mansions. This gave us good excuse to visit one another's Houses and survey but not envy them. Ours was exceptional, and we valued the incovenient distance we were from the others. We used our bikes a lot and sometimes preferred (with permission) to cycle the twelve miles to Moor Park, and cycle back, enjoying the freedom of doing so. On Sundays there were no coaches and we had to cycle the twelve miles to church at Richard's Castle, the other side of Moor Park. If, happily, the weather was bad enough, we went to Matins at Onibury church instead, thus swelling a small congregation and reducing its average age.

The grounds at Stokesay were extensive and included a stream which ran into the lake at the bottom of the garden. One weekend we dammed the stream and made our own lake; then let the water through with a rush. Once it snowed so much that we were marooned for a blessed week in Stokesay Court, in the course of which we had a fierce snow fight against Heads around the stables at the bottom of the garden. I did a heroic deed, separating myself from the Fields House troops to cause a diversion. This led some of the Heads men away and enabled ours to capture the spot. I was much be-snowed as a result, but we won the day.

You would think that Stokesay Court would have no room in it by the time Fields and Heads plus some staff were settled there. Wrong. The owner, Mrs Rotten, and her daughter Jewel continued to live with us. They were both very large: grandmotherly and aunt-like. But they were kind to us and tolerated our presence with generosity. I do not remember any rows. They treated us to seats at the Ludlow cinema to see *The Great Dictator* with Charlie Chaplin doing his Hitler act, saying that it was a film that we "ought" to see – though I remember Mr Handford being scathing about it during a Greek lesson. They also gave us a farewell party at Stokesay Castle, with its ramparts and dungeon, which they owned.

We in turn invited them to all our home-made entertainments – including the Christmas concert with Haydn's *Toy Symphony*, which I conducted with the greatest pleasure, though I found the Housemaster an unmusical cuckoo. David Gould played a complicated composition of his own, Mr Walker played Mozart's clarinet concerto and Mr Halsey and two House-captains rounded off the evening with a rousing performance of *The Stately Homes of England*.

School life went on at Stokesay, with discipline still intact; but this was very different from what it had been at Lancing. Traditional rules which separated the generations (such as the number of buttons you were allowed to have undone and who could do what where and who could mix with whom, when and where) were forgotten and we became more like a large family, benevolently presided over by the Housemasters; with the Heads House regime being considerably more fierce than the Fields.

By extraordinary coincidence, my Aunt Sylvia evacuated Parkfield, her girls' prep-school in Horsham, to Witty Tree House at the bottom of the Stokesay Court garden, just beyond the lake. Michael had left Belmont with a scholarship to Lancing and had gone to stay at Parkfield for the last half of the summer term. Mary was also a pupil at Parkfield, so for the Christmas term, our first at Stokesay and Michael's first at Lancing, the three of us were all together, within half a mile. Sometimes Michael and I stayed at Witty Tree for the holidays rather than go back to London. We explored the countryside on our bikes and discovered the Long Mynd Hills and Ashes Valley.

These became part of our life, especially at weekends and on saints' days. The ride there; the walk up the valley and the attempt to find the source of the stream; the ride back, some of it behind a lorry; the stop for an illegal glass of cider in a pub; Mr Halsey's dramatic pronouncement (because he sometimes came with us) that this was the best thing he knew outside the Bavarian Alps; me with a Virgil in my pocket in the wishful pretence that I would include some "revising" in the course of the expedition: all of this was all part of the agreeable way of life that we led in those golden days.

For one week of holiday, Charlton being considered unsafe, Michael and I stayed on a farm at the foot of Ashes Valley and spent the time exploring the hills and valleys around; fortified by huge breakfasts and coming back to huge farm suppers, with a "wireless" to listen to in the evenings. It was a very pleasant week and M. and I became close, as brothers.

On another occasion Philip Haynes and I climbed Caradoc and had a rare experience. We were on the top of the hill with the sun behind us. A mist floated up the valley and, suddenly, we each saw our own (but not one another's) huge shadow on the mist, bestriding the valley. It seemed at the time a strange, quasi-mystical phenomenon. Years later I preached about it in Ripon Cathedral and after the service a member of the congregation told me that this is known as the "Brocken Spectre".

Towards the end of the summer term 1941 the Head Man came to see us at Stokesay and addressed each House separately. He told Fields that we would not be returning to Stokesay next term; but that we would occupy The Lodge, which was about three quarters of a mile from Moor Park. The Heads House? Boys in the Heads House would be divided out amongst the other houses, as far as possible according to their choice. It was to the great credit of all that had happened in our year at Stokesay Court that almost all the Heads House men wanted to come to Fields. Amongst those that did so were Douglas Bean and Brian Wallas. Douglas was later to marry my sister, Mary. Brian became Head of Fields and Head of the School, and later still Assistant to the Fleet Appointments Officer of the East Indies Fleet in which post he appointed me to HMS *Nelson*.

Life at The Lodge was extraordinary, unique. It was the nearest thing I have experienced to Christian, community living: "Christian" because we had daily chapel, understood the point of forgiveness (which was often necessary), were told by Wilfred Derry, the Chaplain, that the most important element in Christianity is giving thanks to God, and did this with unselfconscious awareness of the God-dimension of a very happy life.

The house itself was an elegant Georgian mansion of the size, I suppose, of the one Jane Austen's Bennet family would have lived in. There was a long drive leading to stretches of lawn and cedar trees; a spacious hall with a grand-piano and a large open fireplace; elegant sitting-rooms; a sweeping round-the-hall staircase; pleasant bedrooms with balconies and views over the woods or the valley or the receding Shropshire countryside.

There was room for the Housemaster and Mr and Mrs Neville-Smith. Neville was on the staff and Mrs Neville became Housekeeper, Matron and Mother-in-general. Wilfred Derry, the Chaplain, also lived with us. We "pits" had one room to ourselves, and the House-captains were next door. The Housemaster's study was downstairs, off the hall, where he knew everything that was going on; and the biggest room in the house, presumably the "withdrawing-room", was the House-room. There was also a cellar where people kept tuck-boxes, and smoked.

There was a stable block behind the house, built over a central archway. We kept our bikes downstairs on one side and had extra elsan loos on the other. Upstairs on one side was the dormitory for us seniors, and on the other side we made a chapel. This had beams at head height going across it, benches enough to accommodate us all, the altar one end and the harmonium, played noisily by David Gould and sometimes rather more tentatively by me, at the back.

We enjoyed our daily evensongs more than we had in the chapel at Lancing, breaking away from the plain-song, and singing our favourite hymns, led by the Housemaster, with some fervour. It always seemed to me to be twenty minutes of peace and spirit-filled solitude, generally to be enjoyed. We also had daily Eucharists there for the Chaplain and Housemaster and server and one or two boys in the congregation.

Once when I was serving I put clean water in the cruets before the service, and the water was frozen by the time of the Offertory! So it could be cold; and so could that dormitory. But we would not have exchanged the "pits' dormitory" in the stable block for any of the more comfortable ones in the house itself, for it gave us a lovely freedom to go off exploring if we wanted to.

The house was situated on the top of a hill at the end of a wooded valley, with a lake in the valley below. The valley itself stretched two or three miles to the High Vinnals hills. We explored it to its limits; did forestry work in the afternoons; went for runs and walks; looked for badgers; did our Home Guard exercises; and John Fife and Keith Ritherdon and I went shooting rabbits with bows and arrows, and John once hit one though it was generally unsuccessful and too wasteful in arrows!

Archery had been a Belmont thing. We never managed to establish it at Lancing because of the impossibility of getting bows and arrows; but on one occasion I went round the Ludlow golf course with Brian and Bill Wallis, they hitting golf balls and I shooting arrows. It made a good contest. They could hit balls further than I could shoot arrows, but they often went astray. I was more accurate until it came to the equivalent of the "putt" when the target they insisted on was always difficult to hit.

At the top of the valley was Mary Knoll, a beautiful, timbered, but not grand house. It looked down to the hills of Herefordshire in the far distance. I think it was the nicest dwelling, with its comfort, its views, its garden and its friendly atmosphere, that I have ever known. Keith Ritherdon discovered it when out walking. His story was that he saw Mrs Fletcher chopping wood, and he offered to do it for her. He was then invited to tea, and so began a friendship that spread from Keith to about six of us. We would go up there to work – and for tea! But it was more than that. Mrs Fletcher and her daughter Barbara made a home from home for us. My parents and others stayed there when they came to visit us on rare but happy occasions; and I went back twice in later years, once when on leave from the Navy and once with Juliet.

School work definitely suffered. We "classics" in the Pits' room used to prepare our books by sitting round the fire in co-operative effort. John Shepherd would do most of the translating, aided by the scholarly Philip Haynes; I would look up the unknown words in the lexicon; and Eric Wood guarded the "notes". He would take no part in the proceedings for several lines at a stretch, and then suddenly blurt out a useful bit of translation that the notes provided. Good fun; but not a good way of mastering the language or the text with a view to impressing the examiners. But I did enjoy those texts: the *Agamemnon; Oedipus Rex;* the *Birds;* Plato; some Homer; Theucydides; Lucretius, Virgil, Tacitus; and the delightfully salacious Roman poets. Proses, of course, and unseens had to be done by ourselves alone. My proses were supposed to be rather good, though riddled with mistakes. I was also good at the ancient history, which can nowadays be done on its own without the trouble of learning the languages!

In the pits' and House-captain's rooms we continued to listen to a lot of music, including the *Leningrad* symphony by Shostakovitch at its first broadcast. We thought it tediously long but not so ugly as "The Bloody" Vaughan Williams Fourth. I started an anti-Tchaikovsky phase, much derided by Brian, who said that he was a hedonist at heart, and Wilfred Derry who accused me of being "highbrow" just for the sake of it – a charge I indignantly refuted.

The Gram. Soc. continued to hold sway on Friday evenings, and on one occasion Benjamin Britten and Peter Pears (O.L.) were our guests. They stayed in The Lodge for a week, guests of the Neville-Smiths. Ben played us tennis and beat us hollow, though we thought of ourselves as respectable players. Peter sang Schubert and the Britten folk songs, some of them still in manuscript; and the *Michael Angelo Sonnets* which I also heard them perform at one of the National Gallery Lunch Time Concerts. We also had the argument (mentioned in *The Food of Love*) about Beethoven's late quartets, which at the time I did not know – but this did not prevent me from defending them!

(Years later I went to a performance of *Death in Venice* at Covent Garden. I went back-stage after the performance to see James Bowman, an ex-pupil from Ely days. He had left the theatre, but there was Peter Pears who had just come off the stage after taking many bows, looking drained and exhausted. But he took one look at me and said, 'O Christopher! How nice to see you again after all these years.' I could hardly believe that he would have remembered me, but he wrote to me later, a very sad letter, after Britten's death.)

One summer term the College Choral Society performed Bach's *St Matthew Passion* in Ludlow Parish Church, along with the Ludlow Choral Society. The soloists were all home-made from Lancing: Wilfred Derry the Evangelist; Brian Wallas and David Gould basses; a lady soprano from Ludlow; and I did the alto aria *Thy Mercy Show*, with some Ludlow ladies standing a few paces behind me. The Roman Catholic priest who wrote about the performance in the local paper said they were good, but I was "beautiful"! I also sang in the duet with the Chorus singing *Bind Him*; and the alto piece in the penultimate chorus. It was a searing musical and spiritual experience, made more so by the fact that I had lost my voice about a week before the performance with a chesty cold; and prayed like billio to have it back. The voice returned – and I sang, nerveless, as well as I could possibly sing. After this Jasper Rooper wanted me to take the choral scholarship to King's, Cambridge. They said yes, but not till after the war, by which time I had lost my alto voice, which had really been a deepening of my treble voice.

Games continued to be played. There was the Five-Mile race which Fields were hoping to win, Brian being an excellent long-distance runner, and he was well supported. But illness struck and we needed one more runner for a full team without which we could not win. So I was persuaded to run – much against my inclination because I was no good at it. I can remember now the sight of the other runners disappearing into the distance as I heaved myself along, with a few other stragglers, far behind them. I thought I would never make it. However, I finished the course, and that was all that mattered. Fields won – and people were quite pleased (if somewhat amused) with my effort.

At football we had a series of thrilling matches with Seconds before they eventually beat us and went on into the finals. I played right-back and got my colours! I played a lot of tennis, especially with Eric Wood, Douglas Bean and Brian. Our tennis rivalry was resumed in Colombo in 1945. Douglas was the most stylish; I the most inspirational and erratic; Brian, who generally won, the steadiest.

Playing games involved much cycling as the ground used by the school was the Grammar School's on the far side of Ludlow. Often we would stop at De Grey's café or the Castle Lodge Annex and feed ourselves on beans-on-toast after the match. Sometimes the

Housemaster would join us and would even pay! One wicked practice in Ludlow was to cycle, full tilt, down the steep hill and under the narrow arch without knowing if a car was coming up from the other direction: a wild and foolish "dare", which met with severe punishment the first and last time someone was caught at it.

Home Guard for us seniors was serious fun. There was a Fields House Patrol which had to fight its way through the woods. 'Campling,' said Sam Jagger in his sing-song voice, 'you can be Arse-end Charlie.'.Sometimes we had to do night duty guarding a bridge or part of the Birmingham waterpipe. Eric Wood and I played chess in the hut, whilst John Shepherd and Philip kept watch. When it was our turn to keep watch, we stalked a loving couple on the river bank. The next morning, the Head Man decreed that no lying-in concessions should be allowed for Home Guarders, so I staged a "fall-to-sleep" during his (the Head's) Virgil class. He threw a book at me but then relented and agreed with our reasonable request.

One Sunday the Lancing College platoon, which was the only mobile one in Shropshire – because we had bicycles – took part in a major exercise involving the defence of Ludlow. We took up a defensive position overlooking the Ludford Bridge over the River Teme. The local Ludlow HG unit had to charge out of the town, cross the bridge and attack us on the hill-side under cover of a smoke screen. Unfortunately they were too liberal with the smoke and we watched with fascination as men raced into the smoke and emerged minutes later coughing and spluttering and then collapsing. The exercise had to be abandoned and the ambulance service had a busy afternoon.

I learnt to fire a curious gun which could lob hand-grenades with doubtful accuracy. You had to be careful to get yourself clear of the muzzle. I was also asked by the Commanding Officer to study the army codes, which I was able to do very happily indoors whilst the others re sweating around in uniform on their tummys; a foretaste (the   g) of things to come.

Officers' Training Corps was less entertaining. There was much   g and clever parade-ground manoeuvres to place a squad on a ri   hand marker, something some boys could not do. I passed Cer icate A well because when I was set a tactical exercise and asked what I would do if my platoon were fired upon from a bush at the top of the hill, I said, 'Put covering-fire over there, and attack!' unlike some of my friends, who thought of long and ingenious ways to get behind the desired point without danger: but they were given no credit for this.

Mr Halsey had a row with the Corps Commander, Major Parnell-Smith, who complained of the Fields House platoon's behaviour during a field day (we had taken an order literally and managed to get ourselves lost) and demanded that Williamson be beaten for having dirty shoes on parade, which Brian steadfastly refused to do. Patrick wrote a blistering letter to Parnell and showed it and the subsequent correspondence to us House-captains at a Sunday evening "Hot Air" – always our favourite occasion in the week. He gave us a dramatic account of his interview with Parnell, whose voice he could mimic to perfection. This was an amusing episode at the time, almost a crisis, because the Head was brought in: but I felt very differently about such behaviour when I was Chaplain in the 1960s and Patrick was disloyal to me.

Fields House at the Lodge may have been a "Christian" community, but this in no way implies that we were pious or particularly well behaved. Far from it. When we were sleeping in the pits' dormitory we were late for bed for the umteenth time and Tiger made us do "digging for victory" on the potato patch for a tedious week. Once Rusby and Williamson made a bomb in an out-house which blew up unexpectedly and hurt them a bit. Johnson min. similarly let off a stink-bomb during dinner one day, challenging me (then Head of the House) to beat him; but I refused to break my record and instead gave him one hour's digging to do on the morning of our departure for the holidays. As he had intended to get up early and catch a special train to Birmingham and then make a series of connections which would get him home in record time (he being a railway time-table buff) this punishment really bit him deep and made him regret his wickedness. And when three boys told the athletic officials that they were with Jasper Rooper doing music and told Jasper that they were doing athletics, whereas in fact they were having a binge in Ludlow, Brian beat them all – much to their pained surprise.

There was nearly always some interesting crisis, affair, escapade, row, in the offing. On one occasion the cook upped and left. He was a jolly

German refugee called Kurt, and we used to tease him in a good-natured way, though we liked his cooking. So some of us were sent for from Moor Park to return to The Lodge at once and help cook the dinner. I made dumplings on that occasion; and repeated the trick when I was cooking for the mess-deck on HHMS *Kanaris*.

Often in the summer we slept out on the lawns and could see air-raids going on over Birmingham, as at Stokesay we had watched with horror the sky lit up with the dreadful raid on Coventry.

A sad thing happened one Sunday in 1942. John Fife fell on his head when cycling to church and was unconscious for a long time. Some of us kept watch over him at night, dozing in a chair in his sick room (I with a Tacitus on my knees) because he was not allowed to be unattended. When he began to get better (his mother having come to stay) we used to sit and chat with him. However, he recovered. He has recently been reading my memoirs, saying that he would have written the Belmont bit very differently!

But a nice thing also happened at the beginning of the summer term 1943.

Brian Wallas was called up into the Navy, into which I was to follow in September. Patrick summoned me and told me that he was making me Head of House; and I deserved to be, he added, because I had been so loyal to Brian. The truth was that I had never thought of being otherwise. Brian was one term my senior, and has been a friend for life. True, if he had gone from Heads to another House, I would have been Head of House for the whole year. But one term was quite enough; and I did manage not to beat anyone! I was also made a School Prefect with all sorts of flattering privileges in the school, which I rather enjoyed.

I had a serious talk with my Housemaster about what I should do after leaving school. For a short time I discussed with my friends the possibility of being a conscientious objector but came to the conclusion that it was essential to resist the evil of Germany and that this was not something that one could leave to other people. This view was reinforced by reading an appalling paperback about the Nazi concentration camps. I did not think that conscientious objectors had a good case, and I get cross when post-war generations take a lofty view against war as if to suggest that we were war-mongers. Conscientious objectors were certainly brave, but they had to assume that other people would make things better. Dodgeson was one. He became an ambulance man in the Red Cross, was badly wounded and died very young.

So I tried for a Naval Short Course at Oxford University, but was turned down because I wore glasses. So I tried for the same again but in the Air Engineering branch only to be told that my education was insufficiently scientific. So I voluteered for the Navy, intending to become a coder, which seemed suitable in view of my classical education. Naval codes could hardly be more difficult than Greek, and Brian was managing them, even though he had only been a "historian". To volunteer meant that, if accepted by the Navy, I would not be liable to be called up as a "Bevin Boy" to work in the mines, which I would have hated. The process of being called up was generally slow and P.J.H. had the idea that I should have another term at Lancing by trying for the difficult "Special Entry" into the Navy. This was agreed in principle. The Head Man summoned me, and I was duly appointed Captain of the School for the coming school year. But as the call-up papers came in the summer holidays, this was a post that I never took up; so I left Lancing to join the Royal Navy.

Chapter 6
Into the Navy

Gloom came over the breakfast table one morning in August 1943 when a letter arrived "calling me up" and ordering me to report to HMS *Royal Arthur* at Skegness. Father asked me what the matter was and I told the family the news, which was not unexpected. There was a general tut-tutting of excitement and sorrow, but I think Father thought that this was a "good thing". He had a less rosy idea than I had of the advantages of another term at Lancing, especially as he would have to pay for it! He also felt that the extra term at school just for the fun of being head boy was bogus. I would miss my friends, and would have no work to do. He was right. From everything that followed I am pleased that I joined up when I did.

I decided to go to Skegness via Ludlow in order to clear up my possessions and say goodbye to friends, including the Fletchers at Mary Knoll. Then I made the tedious journey eastwards across England from Ludlow to Skegness, changing trains many times. I remember the sight of Lincoln Cathedral, looking enormous, gracious, time-defying. At Skegness I was met by an elderly chief petty-officer who ushered me to the "ship", HMS *Royal Arthur*, formerly a Butlin's holiday camp.

Everyone was kind. I was fed well and put into a dormitory to sleep. I then made the brave decision to wear pyjamas, in defiance of what anybody else did or thought, only to discover that no one took any notice. "Live and let live" was the common attitude. There was enough to do fighting the system without having to worry about other people's odd habits, such as swearing or wearing or not wearing pyjamas.

In the morning I was paid what seemed a handsome wage and made the decision to allot a weekly sum to my mother. Then there were two or three days of kitting-out and lectures. We were instructed in naval morale and discipline, venereal disease, which I had never heard of, naval ranks, whom to salute and whom not to, whom to call "sir" or "chief"', naval traditions, the mystery of the daily tot of rum (not for me because I was under age) and much else – all laced with humour, making the Navy out to be a pleasant service, superior in every way to the Army and RAF, an opinion we were happy to share.

But I was beginning to feel unwell, drained of energy, my mouth perpetually dry and my head aching. I put it down to tiredness, the food, the boredom of queueing and the uncongenial – so far – companionship. It was in this condition that I took the all-important intelligence tests. I felt I did badly, but this did not bar me from my first choice, which was the coding branch.

I was at Skegness for a week. The weather was cold. I remember freezing walks up and down the camp; stuffy nights in huts, which slept three; early morning bugle-calls and a rasping voice on the tannoy shouting "Wakey, wakey, show a leg, show a leg, rise and shine, the morning's fine"; some desultory parades and rudimentary marching; noisy crowds of sailors; trying to get used to my uniform and tying and helping others to tie the "silks" which pass round the neck under the sailor's collar and are tied in a bow at the front; the ridiculous lanyards which had something to do with olden-days gunnery; long queues for dreadful meals; all this and more whilst feeling increasingly limp and listless. I endured it because I knew that I would soon be moving to HMS *Cabbala,* which I did not want to miss, knowing that Brian Wallas was still there. On Brian's advice I had brought good books to read at Skegness, which helped to overcome the tedium of the place. In fact I read *The Cloister and the Hearth* and later, at *Cabbala, Les Miserables.*

So I was posted to the camp at Laughton St Mary's near Warrington called HMS *Cabbala.* I felt dreadful on the journey, but cheered up when I saw Brian standing there waiting for me, trying to look like a salty, hard-swearing Jack. We were soon standing together before the Commander at "Commander's Requests" asking for one of us to change his duty watch so that we could go ashore together; and could we have some extra leave on Saturday so as to be able to play golf? 'Request one, granted. Request two, certainly not. Dismissed!' So, no golf!

Soon after I arrived the petty-officer in charge called me out and demanded to know if I was always that colour. I did not know what he meant, but he ordered me to report at once to the sick-bay. There I was told I had jaundice, and was ordered to bed. I was there for eight days, but cannot remember much about it, except that every morning there was "Doctor's Rounds", to prepare for which we were ordered to "lie to attention". I have quoted this when instructing people how to pray: be relaxed, yet concentrated; lying, sitting, kneeling, as it were, "to attention". I also remember having to endure awful music played loudly on the radio, especially a stupid song called *Johnny's got a Zero* about an American hero who always got "zeros" for his work at school, but then shot down a Japanese "Zero" plane in combat. I can sing the tune now, and it takes me back to that ward.

I emerged to find myself in Keith Class, in which I soon made good friends. There was Johnny Wilson, who was older than the rest of us and went straight for the commissioned cypher course after leaving *Cabbala*. He paid me one of the most pleasing compliments I have ever had, saying that I was "the best example of my religion he had ever met". We met again in Colombo. My best friend was Ronnie Wylie. He and I came top together in every test we had. We met again when he was a coder in the *Nelson*, as I shall recount. Then there was Bill, who too easily got drunk. We sometimes had to get him back to camp after evenings out, known as "runs ashore", and into his bunk without being noticed. There was the dour Donald McClintock, who criticised everything and everyone, but specially the officers; and two rascally butcher boys whose names I have forgotten. We helped them through their tests, and the fact that they passed at the end of the course was a triumph, we thought, for all of us. There was a devout person called Jones who wanted to read the Bible with me in Chapel in the evenings; but I found it too cloying and tried to get out of it without offending him.

We were taught by a petty-officer, considered the best teacher in the place, called Smith; a man of great ability who was against all officers, probably because he ought to have been one, and whose mind was dominated by sex. This made his teaching prattle hilariously funny. An instructor once had his leave stopped for a fortnight because the dreaded Mr Deighton, the warrant officer in charge of instruction, came into the classroom and found someone asleep. That would never have happened in Smithy's class.

I mastered the morse code immediately using musical phrases to help: for example, "B", *Walze Brilliante*. I was too slow for a telegraphist but fast enough for a coder. Coders had to know enough morse to be able to detect the likelihood of "corrupt" letters or numbers. Ronnie and I both got 97 per cent in our final coding examination. As I had supposed, naval coding was much easier than Greek.

My two cabin companions were not so easy to get on with, though we managed, and our cabin became popular, attracting three different sets of people to it. We had a good scheme for keeping the cabin clean. We took it in turns to be responsible, and the one responsible would do the sweeping and tidying until he could be bothered to scrub the floor. The turn then passed to the next.

Although Brian and I never had our golf, we sometimes went to concerts on Saturday afternoons. Indeed, one memorable day I went to Manchester to hear the Hallé in the afternoon, and on by lorry to Liverpool to hear Sargent and the Liverpool Philharmonic in the evening, and made it back to camp, just in time. That was later and by myself, Brian having left *Cabbala*. My diary speaks of many expeditions to Oldham, Manchester, Liverpool, Chester, with or without companions, for concerts, plays, churches and Liverpool Cathedral, using buses and trains and lorries. These expeditions were not always successful and sometimes I missed the concert altogether. There was one much despised concert at Warrington at which the orchestra omitted the "Trio" of Beethoven's Eighth Symphony, presumably lacking a horn-player of sufficient competence; and there was a memorable visit with Ronnie and Johnny to *The Marriage of Figaro* at which, being sailors buying the cheapest seats, we were nevertheless ushered into the front row of the dress circle. To prove our pedigree we ate sausage rolls out of my soap-bag in the interval.

There were dreary daily duties to do and every morning we would be paraded and sent off to parts of the "ship" to scrub floors, wash bathroom basins – or worse. There was one occasion when I was "in the rattle", that is, up for a disciplinary charge. My friends assumed that I was being summoned to go for a commission, such was the belief in the class system for choosing officers. But no: I had hung my cap on the light bracket in my cabin. Asked why, I said I thought it was a sensible place to hang it; but this was against some regulation and I was sentenced to "One Day Number Sixteens", which meant loss of leave and extra work in the evening. I survived. When the course was over we had a week of "working ship", which could mean anything from peeling spuds to weeding the ward-room garden. I had a good "number", namely to be Officer of the Day's messenger in the orderly office by the main gate. I did this by "watches", which meant that I had a lot of time off as well as some hectic hours "on". I went all over the camp looking for officers and others to give messages to, and once had to be very insistent with an officer who did not want to come out of the ward-room. I also used to take food and illegally chat to a man who had been sentenced to five days' "cells" for taking more than his allowance of tobacco out of the camp – an offence that most of us were guilty of occasionally. I used to take cigarettes to my mother and pipe tobacco to my father, and pray rather untheologically for good luck.

We ended with a grand and drunken party (vividly described in my diary) along with Smithy, our chief, and went our various ways on a week's end-of-course leave. This was just before Christmas, and with one or two others who were good at working the system, I sent a telegram to the Commanding Officer, RNB Chatham, requesting extension of leave over Christmas and Boxing Day. To my surprise I received a telegram at home granting the extension. This made a huge difference to my future, because those who reported to barracks before Christmas were all drafted away at once, Ronnie, for instance, to the *Nelson*. Whereas I had some weeks at Chatham before being sent to Alexandria, for further drafting in the Mediterranean Fleet.

So, a few days after Christmas 1943 Ordinary Coder C.R. Campling, C/JX 614876, reported to the Royal Naval Barracks at Chatham, to see what the Navy had in store for him. A "battle wagon" somewhere out there on the oceans of the world? Or a speedy destroyer cutting its way across the Atlantic? Or some safe but boring naval base in Lowestoft or the Outer Hebrides? Whatever it was to be, there was the business first of mastering the system of the ghastly life in Chatham barracks.

At Charlton I had joined a train stuffed with sailors of all degrees of saltiness with badges and stripes and hooks on their arms, tattoos on their hands, their breath smokey, their language foul, their resentment loud as I tried to push my way from the platform at Charlton on to a train that had been filled to overflowing at Waterloo. Half asleep they woke and snarled at me; but at least there was the certainty that this train was bound for Chatham, where we poured off the train and made our way like a human river down the road to the barracks. At the gate of the barracks I reported myself to an angry petty-officer in charge. This sort of man always seemed to be angry, like the family aunt in *Angela's Ashes*, as if your mere existence were an affront to his. I was told where to go, so off I went across the parade ground, urged to hurry as a piercing voice screamed at me to "pick up the double", i.e. run, which I did till out of sight.

Nobody could possibly forget the horrors of the underground tunnel at RNBC in which we slept at night. There was a steep slope down to what looked like the London Underground; then the tunnel went straight forward with branch tunnels going off each side at right-angles. From enormous hooks across the ceiling of the tunnel hung hammocks, with sailors sprawling in them in various stages of sleep. But there were no spare hooks to be seen, so where was one supposed to sling? I went in search, down byways and tributaries, turning sharp corners, looking for space, and at last found a patch which seemed to be less densely populated than the rest. There was a hook, two: so for the first time I slung my hammock and clambered into it – an operation requiring considerable gymnastic effort. No pyjamas on this occasion. Life was difficult enough without the complication of undressing more than a minimum. I hid what I took off in the recesses of the hammock because I had been warned that anything left exposed, especially boots, would be stolen. So I and all my possessions were enshrouded in what looked like a stuffed, bulgy, banana. Therein, fitfully, I slept my first night in barracks, to be rudely woken at five the next morning and ordered to get up and go on parade. Why? Because this space was reserved for "men under punishment". I managed to persuade the idiot who had woken me that I was not "under punishment", only to be told that I ought to be for slinging my hammock in that place; but I made off quickly and reaped the advantage of finding the wash-house fairly free. So I gave myself the wash that I badly needed, not having bothered the evening before.

I spent my first two days at Chatham going round the barracks with a group of ex-*Cabbala* friends doing the "joining routine" by which we had to report to a number of authorities and offices for an inspection or injection or the issuing of kit, getting our cards stamped at each one. Most of my friends were ahead of me but decided to go round again escorting me to the various stamping-points. This procedure took at least two days, for we kept it going for as long as possible.

There was no serious attempt at "routine" in Chatham barracks. We were supposed to parade at certain times and if we did so were liable to be peeled off for "working ship" duties, cleaning, peeling spuds, washing up; but the odds were against this because there were too many of us and generally we would be dismissed and expected to find our own occupation. This was awkward because if you were found doing nothing you were in trouble. The trick was always to have a broom in your hand and to use it industriously if an officer or petty-officer hove in sight. It was also possible to lie up amongst the mountains of hammocks which had been stowed ready for night use in the tunnel. I always had a book at hand and did a lot of reading at that time.

The important thing was to keep an eye on the "draft board" on which your name would eventually appear showing that you were to be drafted to a ship or foreign station. Dreadful days went by without this happening, so much so that a friend and I dared to go to the drafting office to find out what was going on and what the prospects were. I believe that they had lost my file, perhaps because of that extended leave, or perhaps they thought I was with my *Cabbala* contemporaries who had already received their drafts. Anyway, our action was immediately effective and I found myself drafted to the signal-training camp at Cookham, just a few miles out of Chatham.

One odd thing about the RNB Chatham was that on pay-day, which occurred once a month, the population of the barracks swelled enormously. I was told that there were literally hundreds of sailors who were on the pay-roll but had somehow been forgotten and were living comfortably ashore going about their own business, turning up only to be paid. If they failed to turn up they would be noticed, chased and arrested as deserters!

Cookham camp was a boys' borstal, and we shared some of the site and its amenities with the inmates. We also played football against them. But the camp was mostly Nissen huts in a wood and was preferable by far to the barracks. I was given a bed in a hut and most of the time was occupied with signals exercises, which I enjoyed. We were taught the rudiments of decoding "corrupt" messages when the text seems to be indecipherable. It was all a matter of intelligent guesses, and I found I was rather good at it, after my practice with Greek and Latin "unseens".

I also had my first experience of guard patrol by night, which I enjoyed. I was given a rifle, and I walked up and down a beat on the perimeter of the camp for a watch of two hours: a nice opportunity for thoughts, prayers and music in the head, and not much fear of interruption unless a stray officer came round to see if I was there and awake. Once one did, and we had a conversation about public schools and the relative merits of soccer and rugger.

An important feature of those days, both at Chatham and Cookham, was that every other evening and night I got leave. I did not always want to bother with it, but a wise old hand, when he heard me say this, took me aside and told me how much I would regret it once I was abroad or at sea. So I decided to go home to Charlton two or three times a week. I did not enjoy this as much as I felt I should. It always ended with me getting up at 5 a.m., having tea with Mother in her room and then catching the train to Chatham, thinking each time that I might never see my home again.

One day when the camp Chaplain found that I was a possible ordination candidate he sent me to see the Bishop of Rochester. The Bishop was very pleasant but there was nothing he could suggest except that I should keep faithful till the war was over and I was demobilised. But it made a nice day off; and having been given the whole day for this encounter I made the most of it and enjoyed mooching around on my own. I ended up in the Cathedral, where I said my prayers and was very nearly locked in by the duty verger.

At last, I was summoned and told to pack my bag and hammock and be ready to proceed to HMS *Sphinx*, the appropriately named naval base at Alexandria. First we made our way by troop train to Liverpool. There was an air raid going on in London, just over Charlton, it seemed to me, and we spent hours being shunted around and waiting in sidings. Eventually we got to Liverpool and went aboard a trooper, a large P&O liner. We were "messed" in stuffy decks, and were warned always to sleep at the ready with life-belts on. We made our way to Scotland, cruised around in a loch waiting for the convoy to assemble and then zig-zagged far out into the Atlantic. It was rough, but the motion of the ship was slow and I was not as sick as others were. We were told by old hands in a comforting way that rough weather lessened the chances of U-boats. After several days we reached the calm and warmth of the Mediterranean and found ourselves cruising pleasantly along the coast of North Africa.

There were a few of my old *Cabbala* friends with us, including the two cockney butcher boys who always made life lively, but none of my close friends. There was nothing to do on board this ship except boring bingo, which I could not be bothered with, so as usual I took to my books, and after finishing *Barchester Towers* began on *The Ring and The Book* by Browning. I am still the only person I know who has read it all through. It is worth the effort, except the section in which half of every line is in Latin. The book is a story of murder and rape told from the different points of view of those involved, including the criminal and the victim and the Pope. It would make an excellent television series, if it could be translated into intelligible English. Anyway, I used to bury myself away in a shady corner on the boat-deck and read for hours on end.

Occasionally we had intimate medical inspections to see that we were clean and disease-free, though keeping oneself clean was not easy. It meant queueing for ages behind people who lathered themselves for twenty minutes at a time, presumably in the hope of washing themselves clean from the contamination of the system, the imposition of other people and the stains of conscience – in addition to any physical dirt that might still be around on their necks.

Eventually we reached Port Said, and "entrained" to Alexandria and the sandy camp at Sidi Bishr in the desert outside the city, otherwise known as HMS *Sphinx*. The accommodation in this camp consisted of canvas tents pitched in the sand. One spent ages trudging across the sand to one's tent, to the loo (called "heads": they afforded no privacy whatever), to the dining-hall, and to places of duty or entertainment. There was a theatre and a sick-bay, where I spent a pleasant week having a mild form of dengue fever. In the middle of the camp was a compound with barbed-wire all round and sentries at the gate, in which men under punishment of "cells" spent their time. The Chaplain was often to be seen there chatting to them and I remember seeing him arguing furiously with a huge toughy who kept spitting at him.

The Chaplain in this camp was Canon Bill Burroughs, who later became Principal of Salisbury Theological College. He once gave me and a friend, Stephen Watson, a furious ticking-off because we "fasted" for our Easter Day Communion, having been on guard in Alexandria harbour all the previous night. Our business, he thundered, was not to be scrupulous and pious, but to be fit to do our duty at any time and at any place as ordered. He then took us to the canteen for a huge Easter lunch. He was a C. of E. chaplain to be proud of, and most people in the camp regarded him as a saint or, better, as "their friend".

Sometimes we were lined up in platoons and marched smartly off into the countryside, until we were out of sight of the populace, when we were allowed to break ranks and saunter along at our own pace. It was a way of keeping us occupied and exercised. On other days we would line up for duty and be sent to the galley to peel "spuds". With a huge pile beside us we sat round an enormous "fanny", peeling them, carving some into lewd shapes, tossing them in and telling bawdy stories.

One evening I was detailed to go on harbour-watch in Alexandria. This was because an Italian midget submarine had once penetrated the harbour defences and torpedoed a ship. So every night a patrol was set to watch for more hostile interlopers. Some of us had to spend the night in an open boat outside the harbour; but I was more fortunate. I was armed with a rifle, given a whistle and told to patrol the jetty, hour on and hour off, all night; with very little idea of what to do in the unlikely event of spying an enemy entering the harbour. This was Easter Eve, and I was delighted to have the time to myself and literally see the dawn breaking on Easter Sunday. It was also the occasion of my

Chaplain's "bottle", as we used to call rebukes in the Navy; but the lunch made up for that.

Sometimes I had afternoon leave and went and bathed in the sea and ate oranges. Other times I took a tram into Alexandria, with or without a friend and explored the city with its sweeping "Corniche", the name for the sea-front, and its well-filled, brightly lit shops – a welcome change after the black-out in the UK. Once, as I travelled in a tram, a little Arab boy leapt up beside me and snatched my glasses from my face. This was annoying as I was wearing ones with a decent frame. I had to report the incident and get issued with a new "pusser" pair from naval stores. Sometimes my friends and I would go to the Fleet Club and drink beer and enjoy an ENSA variety show. Generally the Fleet Club had nothing except tombola (otherwise known as bingo, or housey-housey); boring, unless, of course, you won, in which case you had to be escorted back to your ship lest you be robbed. There was also the YMCA at which one could have a meal and relax in a happy atmosphere. It was here that I met someone whose father kept the paper shop opposite St Luke's Church in Charlton. This seemed to both of us a suitable bond for an evening's drinking, and I really thought I had found a friend. I have sometimes spoken of that evening's feeling of "community" with a stranger, when preaching about the "Communion of Saints". How surprised that particular person, whom I never saw again, would be. I am still a strong supporter of the YMCA.

Three pleasing things happened when I was stationed at HMS *Sphinx*. One was that I bumped into John Terry, who used to teach me Latin and Greek at Lancing, now a naval lieutenant on the staff of C.-in-C. Eastern Mediterranean. He made me go to his mess, a flat which he shared with some other naval officers, and take off the uniform bits of my clothing so that I could visit him and his friends on natural terms. When John found out that I had been in Alexandria awaiting a draft to a ship for four weeks, he spoke to someone on the staff, and I was promptly dispatched first to *Canopus*, then to the Greek ship, *Kanaris*.

John introduced me (the second pleasant thing) to a high-brow Egyptian Gramophone Society which met in someone's luxurious flat. They could hardly believe that an English matelot knew so much music and knew Peter Pears and Benjamin Britten personally. They introduced me to Britten's *Les Illuminations,* which I heard Heather Harper sing many years later, when she came to stay with us in Ripon. I went to this Gramophone Society about three times. It was a musical home-from-home in a strange, foreign setting.

The third thing was that I came to know Lady Goldsmith, the wife of a commodore who was commanding a convoy at sea. She lived in a yacht, *Madelena,* in Alexandria harbour, and she kept open house for people like me. Amongst other things we sailed her dinghy in the harbour, had lovely meals, and gave talks to one another. I gave one on Classical Greek naval tactics – remembered from my Higher Certificate days. I also visited *Madelena* when I was aboard the *Kanaris.* Lady Goldsmsith's kindness shines like a jewel in my memory of those days.

Almost immediately after meeting John Terry I got a draft to *Canopus* to await passage to Massawa where I was to join His Hellenic Majesty's Ship *Kanaris.* But before going to Massawa I had to endure two weeks at the ghastly naval base in Alexandria harbour, HMS *Canopus.* This was reputed to have been barracks abandoned by the Egyptian army as unfit for habitation. Certainly I swear that I awoke one night to see a rat making its way along the hammock-bars, and stopping to look at me with great green eyes wondering whether or not to turn left along my hammock lines to join me in my hammock. It decided not to, I am glad to say.

In *Canopus* I was put on dining-hall duty. I had to scrub the floor every morning, from one end to the other, watched by a sadistic petty-officer who bawled at me whenever he thought I had left a dirty or a damp patch. I set myself to do it as well as I could and derived some savage, masochistic delight in this two hours of wearisome chore. At meal times I stood at the exit of the dining room with a fanny of hot, soapy water. As the matelots finished their meal and left the hall, they threw their knives and forks into my fanny. When it was sufficiently full I gave it a vigorous shake, picked out the knives and forks and wiped them on a wet cloth. I then put them into another fanny which was taken to the entrance of the hall so that they could be used again. This went on till dinner time was over, and with luck I could wash, change and go ashore.

On D-Day, while thousands were sailing and landing and fighting and dying in France, I was doing just that: washing up. Perhaps I should have thought myself lucky because I was at least safe. But I pined for something more – and throughout one dreary lunch composed a poem, the product of despairing boredom.

More knives! O dear!
Soon I shall hear them rattering, clattering
into the tin I dry them in.
I dry, I drop: I dry, I drop.
I dry I drop two:
I dry I drop two.
They've been eating stew.
Are there many left or few?

Twelve o'clock.
Let the rhythm rock
My thoughts away
across the bay,
in ceaseless motion
over the ocean
to the home I adore.
At half past four
They'll be having tea.
Will they think of me?
Will they see me tossing
in a cruiser crossing
the broad Atlantic?
Are they frantic
with fear and dread
lest I their second son be dead?
Am I saving people's lives?
No! I am only drying knives.

Mercifully I have forgotten the rest. But I know I felt wasted as the days went by and I awaited passage to Massawa. At last it came. I was ordered to get my bag and hammock and make my way to a jetty where I boarded a cargo ship on its way south through the Red Sea. I was the only lower-deck passenger on board, and I was given a comfortable mess and the run of the ship. I spent a lot of time reading, mostly *The Ring and The Book*. One beautiful, starry night one of the crew pointed out to me a rarity. Looking south over the ship's bow I could see the Southern Cross; whilst looking north over the ship's stern I could see the Northern Star. One is more aware of the sky at sea. Stars are very close. I never ceased to be amazed at the sight of the star-spangled heavens.

Chapter 7
HHMS *Kanaris*

My first sight of His Hellenic Majesty's Ship *Kanaris* was in the drydock in Massawa. Her whole bulk was on display – huge, bulging, ugly – nothing like the sleek vessel she would be when relaunched and sailing in the sea. She was propped up by heavy stakes which held her hull erect, and she towered over other ships in the dockyard. Perhaps she seemed big because of her dominating importance upon my life; but she was not large at all. She was a British Hunt Class destroyer, made over to the Greek navy, with five British communication ratings and a liaison officer aboard, so that she could sail and communicate with the British fleet.

The signals office, I was to discover, was under the bridge on the port side; our mess aft and below decks on the starboard side. The ship had two guns for'ard, and oerlikons in gun-turrets each side of the bridge. I used to sit and watch the sea go by (and up and down) on one of these when I was off duty. But that would be later. Meanwhile, I had to find my compatriots' mess ashore and was given an Arab "boy" messenger to take my bag and hammock and conduct me there. The mess consisted of a house between the barrack square and the sea-shore, about half a mile from the dock.

Massawa is situated at the bottom of the Red Sea, in the south corner, opposite, but north of Aden. It is one of the hottest in the world, and it certainly seemed so as Ali and I made our wa the *Kanaris'* communication ratings' mess. There I found that I had a bedroom to myself. There was a kitchen presided over by an Arab cook ("Ali") and some Arab boys (all "Ali", as far as I remember): quite a pleasant dining-room (mess) and a very pleasant verandah overlooking the sea.

There were five of us: a leading telegraphist ("sparks"); two signalmen ("bunting tossers") and two coders. The Liaison Officer lived in a house nearby, in some style, but rather lonely. I dumped my kit and made myself known to my new messmates, as anxious in meeting them as they were anxious in meeting me. It was important that we should get on well together, we Britons in a Greek ship in a foreign land. And we did. We were a mixed bunch in background and personality, but we liked each other and were able to have arguments, discussions and the usual exchange of banter and gossip, without dissent.

The Liaison Officer was Lieutenant Claud Richardson, RNVR, bearded, cultured, soft-speaking, but decisive. He kept us at a distance, but was invariably friendly and sympathetic when he needed to be. He was certainly nice to me, and at our first meeting suggested that he would start "CW" papers for an eventual commission. This was in ignorance of how I would perform, though presumably he had my papers. He insisted on high performance once we were operational and at sea. 'Only one mistake allowed,' he said to me; and when one day at Ancona a signal he had sent was returned as "not understood", my head was on the block and he insisted on examining the coded signal himself. But the mistake turned out to be a mistake in the drafting for which he took responsibility and laughed – and I, much relieved, was allowed to enjoy the joke.

The "leading hand" in the mess was Ben Clapham. He was a leading telegraphist, about as old as you can be in the Navy – nearing forty, perhaps even more. He had been in the "Andrew" (as sailors called the Navy) all his life, starting as a boy telegraphist. In the course of his training, he once told me, he was caned for some misdemeanour: 'made to bend over a horse [as in a gym] wearing PT shorts, and have my arse cut to bits by a bloody great petty-officer with a stick.' He never forgave the Navy for this painful indignity, and despised all officers and authority. But he was an able man who knew his signals procedures better than anyone I ever met. He could chat to his friends in the fleet when we were in harbour and seemed to be known by everyone. Telegraphists have their own personal morse "hand-writing" and much scatological jargon. Ben knew everyone and everything about the Navy: all the gossip; what ships were where; who would be promoted, courtmartialled, dismissed; how much liquor they could consume; and anything else you did or didn't want to know.

To me he was kindness itself. He showed me the ropes with regard to life at sea, the messing, the duties and chores, the meanings of the boatswain's whistles, how to cope with sea-sickness (ignore it and get on with your work) and much else that I have forgotten. He also insisted on "double-banking" me when I was on watch until he thought I knew enough about the procedures to keep watch by myself. He "took me under his wing" (hence the lower-deck term "winger"). He also confided a lot to me. Perhaps in his drinks he did the same to everyone. When he went ashore, as we all did together most nights, he used to drink thirteen pints of beer, when I could only manage three at the outside most. He was never to my knowledge drunk, yet always beery. To me he seemed a kind, wasted, unfulfilled person of great, untapped ability.

Then there was Les Arundel, the leading signalman: a Geordie, strong character, excellent leader, kind enough but impatient of weakness. Like all signalmen he had very good eyes and could read a flashing light amidst a confusion of other lights with ease. Like Ben on the radio, Les used to chat with his friends in harbour and seemed to know all the signalmen in all the ships around. At Massawa he was impatient of the shore life with nothing important to do, and he used to start furious arguments at meals about boxing (these were the days of Tommy Farr), football, the relative merits of North and South (of England: the South being given no credit whatever), politics, religion.

The lower-deck lawyer and politician in the mess was Jack Kirby, voluble in his left-wing views, utterly opposed to all officers, the Conservative Party and Winston Churchill. I was known to be a CW candidate and therefore "officer class", but despite this we got on well together and had a few heart-to-heart talks about the war, society, the Navy and life in general; even religion with which he (like all of them except for Jock, a Roman Catholic) had no acquaintance whatever, thus opening my eyes to the fact that not all people one met were "lapsed Christians".

There was a sentimental signalman who used to croon Bing Crosby songs; popular with us all till things got difficult and the sea rough when he would stay all his off-duty hours in his hammock. Another signalman was a Cornishman, Arthur. He loved animals and was shocked when we caught and cut up a baby shark. He was slow in everything he did and was completely unmoved by hardship or disaster or rough weather or disagreement or unpleasantness. He was as strong as an ox. Arthur Berry was another young signalman who joined us later. He was my age (I had my nineteenth birthday at sea on the *Kanaris*) and we became good friends and used to go ashore together in Ancona and other Italian ports.

When I first joined at Massawa there was a tall, elderly (by our standards), lugubrious coder, Jock, a Scot, who was waiting for me to relieve him. He used to lie on his bed all day when not working, reading Dante's *Inferno* and giving us harrowing descriptions of Hell at meal times. He was very religious in just the way I wasn't: a stern Calvinist, anti-drinking, anti-games, anti-(it seemed) all pleasure and enjoyment.

My fellow coder, and though so young, my senior, was Jock Kerr, another Scot; intelligent, well educated, a delightful friend. We could not go ashore together very often as one of us had to be on duty. He was everyone's favourite in the mess and I suspect, judging from the agonised shouts I heard from him late one evening and the soothing noises from Ben Clapham, Ben had a crush on him. Ben was by no means "gay" (a word with no sexual implications in those days) judging by the stories he used to tell us of his exploits in the various ports we visited: but you never know. Jock was a devout Roman Catholic and we gave each other mutual support in many a mess argument. We found to our surprise that there was very little we disagreed about – even the value, religious and therepeutic, of confession.

In later days Ben was replaced by a leading telegraphist who was another "real Navy" type. According to himself, he had a wife in every port and he used to talk about them disgustingly whenever, at sea, we knew our destination. He was unscrupulous in all respects, truth and kindness as well as sexual morality.

*   *   *

Life at Massawa carried on at a slow pace because of the extreme heat and the fact that there was nothing much to do. We spent our forenoons correcting books by the "correcting signals" that had been mounting up for weeks when the ship was at sea. Corrections are a necessary but boring business, and the Liaison Officer (LO) kept us at it remorselessly because he would have been in trouble if a failed correction had led to a mistake.

In the afternoons we slept through the stifling heat. In the evenings we went off to the open-air cinema in the dock-yard and cheered whenever there were pictures of London or somewhere we knew in the UK. Sometimes there was a question and answer session before a film began. I asked a question about the tides in the Red Sea being so considerable when tides in the Med. are almost nonexistent. The answer was unsatisfactory. The officer should have said that he did not know.

Sometimes we gave the cinema a miss and went into Massawa itself to explore the eating and drinking possibilities. That was when I discovered what enormous quantities of beer sailors could consume. Jock had the same difficulty as I had, but he whispered to me that when it was my turn to stand a round I could miss myself and him out. That helped; and it was also possible to spill quite a lot of beer on to the floor without being noticed. The others went on drinking their twelve or thirteen pints. We then lurched back to the mess, singing boozily. No nonsense about cards or gates or patrols; but the LO used to count us carefully the next morning.

Two odd incidents I remember. One was when a baby shark got into our swimming-pool. We put out a line and baite and with great difficulty got it ashore and cut it up. But what to do with the bits? I think we threw them back and watched, hoping that other sharks would smell them and come along. But they didn't. This incident put us off from using the pool and we asked in vain for the net to be mended before we ventured in again. In fact the water was so milkily m that it was never much pleasure to bathe in, especially as it was rous to sunbathe afterwards. I got some painful boils on my leg ll have the scars. Jock got ear-ache, which was worse.

he other incident was witnessing, through glasses because it was a long way off, an Eritrean soldier being flogged. He was made to lie, stripped, on the floor whilst two men beat him with sticks, impassively watched by the company of soldiers. He made no sound that we could hear, and when it was over, he got up and was marched away. Ben said that it would be a good idea to mete out the same punishment to Jock and me whenever we offended in thought, word or deed.

It was so hot in Massawa that an order was given that everyone should go on leave at least once a month to Asmara in the cool of the hills. I was also given leave. We were only allowed to go one at a time, so I went with a man from another ship, a "writer", with whom I got on well. We had to hitch-hike out of Massawa and wait literally hours through the exposed heat of the day. At last a lorry stopped and allowed us on board in its empty, open back. There we hung on perilously while it tore up the mountain road, zig-zagging wildly and almost throwing us out at every double bend. This was the most scary drive of my life. It seemed that while the front end of the lorry might get round the corner, the back end was unlikely to do so. But it always did. The scenery, when we had time to notice, was dramatic as the pass cut its way through the mountains: precipitous, craggy rocks; cascading waterfalls; prickly pears everywhere on scrubby, dry rock; steep climbs ahead; huge views behind. Once we passed a monastery perched on the side of the mountain, without, it seemed, any access. I still have a picture of it, the Nefassit monastery.

After two or three hours of this we were dropped at the naval rest camp, some miles short of Asmara. Here we were logged in and registered. Then, as advised, we asked for permission to leave the camp and go on to Asmara itself. We were told to report back at the end of our leave, so as to be officially logged out. In this way the camp was able to collect our victualling allowance for the time of our leave. A year later I was in Brian Wallas' office in Colombo and he asked me if I knew anything about this camp and why it was that the officer in charge was so keen to stay on. I was able to hazard a guess.

The camp was no good to us because, although it was cool compared with Massawa, there was nothing to do there except play billiards and drink. So we went on to Asmara which we found abuzz with colour and sounds and people and every shape and smell of life. We stayed in the YWCA (W for women; but it was unisex) and were made very comfortable. In the days that followed we explored the town and enjoyed ice-cream, beer and coffee in the cool, bead-hung cafés. We went to *Gone With the Wind*, which, with intervals, seemed to last the whole day. One day we walked to the Abyssinian border, crossed it and walked a few hundred yards so that I could add Abyssinia to the list of countries I had visited. But we had been warned about hostile patrols, so we returned and made our way back to the YWCA. We returned to Massawa by the same terrifying lorry lift, to the news that the refit was completed and the ship was ready to sail for Alexandria.

So there was my sleek ship, slim, swift, warlike, with a hostile-looking gun on the fo'csle, anti-aircraft oerlikons each side of the bridge, and a clutter of mine-sweeping gear across the quarter deck.

The first thing to do was to find the communication ratings' mess. You had to descend the after-hatch and there it was, on the starboard side. It consisted of a table with a bench each side; room at one end to stow kit-bags; the bulkhead with portholes (always closed at sea) one side; a penned-in area for stowing hammocks on the other side. That was all. It was immediately apparent that there was only room for three hammocks to be slung, so Jock and I slept, when we were allowed to sleep, he on the mess table, and I on one of the benches. Would you believe it? On a never-still ship, always rolling or lurching or both, I had to sleep on a twelve-inch-wide bench, with no support on either side, except the top of the mess table.

My gear stayed in my cylindrical kit-bag, which stood about three feet high. I learnt to know my way round this by feel. I stowed "rabbits" (presents bought to be taken home and distributed to family and friends) at the bottom. My "tiddly suit", which I had tailor-made in Alexandria and only wore on the grandest occasions, was neatly folded on top of them. Everything else (including the never-worn-at-sea pyjamas) was jumbled in on top. The bag could be locked – but it never was on board ship. "No need", my friends told me; for the Greeks, I discovered, had fiery tempers, but never stole. I can remember the feel of a small cylindrical object that I kept coming across. Months later when the kit-bag was unpacked, this turned out to be a tube of asprins which my mother had given me in case I was ill.

We soon settled into the routine of life at sea. There were three of us coders, Jock, myself and Ben, who was in general charge of the w/t (wireless-telegraphy) office but who also kept a coding watch; and we worked in three watches, as follows. There were seven watches: "first", 2000 to midnight; "middle", midnight to 0400; "morning", 0400 to 0830; "forenoon", 0830 to midday; "afternoon", midday to 1600; and the "first" and "last" "dog-watches", 1600 to 1800, and 1800 to 2000 respectively. But the schedule was more complicated than having one watch on and two off. We kept them as follows: first, morning and afternoon; last dog, forenoon (thus having a whole night's rest); first dog, first and round again. It sounds easy, but it wasn't: (a) because we often had to be on duty at dawn for "dawn action-stations" when we were most likely to be attacked; (b) forenoons "off" had to be spent on mess chores, such as scrubbing out or preparing dinner. One generally slept in the afternoon if off watch, and I used to do personal things such as writing letters, reading, mending or washing whatever needed it (including myself), saying my prayers and contemplating life (over the side of the ship) when off duty in one of the dog-watches.

Mess chores were hard to cope with, but I did my share of scrubbing the table and benches and floor as well as I could. As I wrote in *The Food of Love*, "Have you ever scrubbed a heaving deck?" It was quite tricky, even sick-making! Once a week on a dog-watch I did my "dobhiing" and dried clothes surruptitiously wherever I could find a place to hang them. Once I tried to dobhi my hammock blanket, into which I had been sick, in a bucket, which really was difficult. This was on deck, and the Greek sailors stood around laughing and teasing me in Greek.

My "Greek", despite my hard work at Massawa on a modern Greek primer, was a ship's joke, though, alone of all the British sailors, I did at least try. I found that what I had learnt at school helped me with the writing and reading but not at all with the speaking; and to add to my difficulty all the sailors seemed to speak with different accents, depending on whether they came from Alexandria or Greece itself or one of the islands. Indeed it was their atrocious accents that were to blame!

After the first few hours at sea I was feeling horribly sick. The ship was making about fifteen knots northwards through the boisterous, choppy Red Sea. It was the unevenness, uncertainty, unpredictability that made it so hard to bear. One moment you were heaving upwards;

then suddenly everything twisted and fell in a dreadful cork-screw motion and crashed downwards; pause; then up again, leaning over to one side or the other; up; an awful moment of hovering; then down again, and down and down and suddenly with a jerk, upwards and down, screwy down: never still. When the ship was going at speed, there was less "pause", more bone-shaking violence.

'Just forget it, Chris,' said the comforting Ben. 'What about those spuds? Have you peeled them yet? Well, chop chop; and then come and keep watch with me in the w/t office and we will file those situation reports.' Ben Clapham. Firm, kind, no nonsense, no gainsaying.

Peeling spuds was all I was allowed to do cooking-wise as my shipmates had no confidence in my culinary skills. But they were prepared to teach me, especially Arthur who was a good cook. We could have gone to the galley and taken our share of the Greek food: but certainly not. Never. We had to have real English stews with dumplings and spuds, jam tart, and fry-ups when we could get anything to fry.

Arthur taught me to make dumplings, and one day in the forenoon watch I made my way up to the bridge, where Arthur was on watch, to show him a handful of embryo dumpling, a curious tacky mixture, before submitting it to the oven which the Greek cook let us use when he was in a good temper. On this occasion the Captain saw me and demanded to know what I was doing. I showed him the dumpling mixture, and he laughed, fortunately, for the LO was ready to be "not amused" if the Captain had taken exception to my cookery class on his bridge. My cooking that day was a distinct success, pronounced "just edible" by my critics. Sometimes, before the end of a morning watch, I used to sneak out of the w/t office and visit my friend the cook in his galley. If I could pronounce it correctly in Greek, he would give me one of his superb waffles (doughnuts I would have called them) dipped in treacle. Opposite the galley was the officers' "heads", which I always used in preference to the awful ship's arrangements – at some disciplinary peril, but it was fairly safe at that time in the morning.

So up the Red Sea, through the Suez Canal to Port Said, where I went to Evensong at the Missions to Seamen church; and then on to Alexandria where for a few days I was able to resume my friendship with Lady Goldsmith and company in the *Madelena*. But now

I was two feet taller, and my cap was worn at a jaunty, Jack-like angle, because I had been at sea, watch-keeping.

An odd episode. Jock and I were drinking in a bar in Alexandria (leaving Ben on watch) when in came some Americans, who, seeing us "limeys", came over and began to pick a quarrel, fists raised. Fortunately, a party of Greek seamen from the *Kanaris* saw us in trouble and strode over to break it up. A couple of punches, and the Yanks fled. If it had been military police instead of our Greek friends, Jock and I would have been in trouble from them, if not from the fight.

Alexandria was our base and, once, returning to it and about ten miles away, we tried to send an urgent signal to the Commander-in-Chief, only to find that despite Ben's efforts, skill and colourful vocabulary, we could not make contact. However, a w/t station in Canada picked up our signal and transmitted it to Alexandria. So much for the marvels and limitations of wireless-telegraphy.

Ben kept a coding watch, but he was also responsible for the Greek w/t operators whom he used to chivvy and curse with an amazing string of totally uncomprehended expletives. No one seemed to mind, and when he wasn't there, one of them, "O Kurios Burgos", a friend of mine because he tried to speak English and I Greek, used to have long and rather confused discussions with me about life in general and Greek politics in particular. But usually there was nothing but concentrated work on watch.

We shared the w/t office with the telegraphists, the coder working at a desk with all the books and a voice-pipe up to the bridge, the telegraphists rattling away on their keys and receiving the shrill staccato morse signals relentlessly. Most of the signals were of a general nature "to all shipping", and these included the long "situation reports" which gave position, course and speed of all the ships at sea in the Med. There was once a coder ashore who left out the mention of a hospital ship, which was consequently sunk. These were tedious signals, but important.

When the South of France and Greece itself were invaded (we were in touch on both occasions, and much engaged in the second) I knew all the forces involved. Sometimes there were signals particular to ourselves, and these would go straight to the LO; and sometimes, but rarely because we tried to keep radio silence, we sent coded signals ourselves. There were a lot of these when we were in harbour. When we were in convoy with other escorting destroyers, we used to talk to one another on the radio telephone, speaking our coded groups. Our codename on these occasions was "Hook Nose"; and we used to try to put on a nasal, "hook nose" sort of voice. Ben did it so well that we were rebuked by the Senior Officer of the flotilla!

Once we were sent by "urgent" signal to Malta to convoy a fast merchant vessel to Taranto. We put in at Sliema, the destroyer base, but sailed early the next morning without getting any shore leave – to Jones' fury, because he had a very special wife in Malta. We then made our way at full speed through a sharp Mediterranean storm. We bounced and pounded and got hurled about, followed by the much steadier merchantman, carrying troops. 'What's the weather like up there?' I shouted through the voice-pipe to the bridge as the w/t office began to reel about in an unacceptable way, books flying everywhere, and Burgos being sick. The answer was a bucket of sea water poured down the speaking tube by a fed-up Leslie Arundel, soaking me and everything I had, as those on the bridge were already soaked. It was a terrible day and night, though I know, old salts were always telling me, it could have been worse.

Taranto harbour was full of Italian warships that were badly damaged by a raid by the Fleet Air Arm which had put them out of action earlier in the war. Taranto was a quiet rest and assembly place for British troops who were fighting their way through Italy, so there was plenty of provision for us ashore. Once I went to a concert of light classical music at the YMCA, including a tune that takes me straight back there, Boccerini's *Minuet.* It was at Taranto, too, that I went to the naval HQ for mail for the *Kanaris.* There wasn't any. 'There must be. What's that sack there?' 'O yes, *Kanaris.* I thought you said –. Here you are then.' For this I was very popular when I returned aboard and exaggerated the story just a little. Mail mattered terribly.

From Taranto we used to take convoys up the Adriatic to Bari, B.....lisi and, disappointingly, to Ancona. "Disappointingly" because we we.. routed to Venice but had to return back after receiving a signal sayi.... "Venice still in enemy hands. Return to Ancona." However, ltho..gh there were no provisions for us ashore there, I did get to like ..cona and could walk out of it into nice countryside and cliffs by the s.. – which I used to do with the like-minded Arthur Berry. Once we were drinking in a bistro with Jones and couldn't get away from him. But we were grateful in the end because, however drunk, he could always find his way back to the ship.

There was a German submarine in the Adriatic operating from Venice. We played a cat and mouse game with this sub, but it always seemed to me that neither of us wanted an encounter and we managed to avoid one another with ease. Once there was a fishing vessel lost off the heel of Italy and we were sent to rescue the crew. The sea was rough and we tossed violently when the way was taken off the ship. The cutter was lowered and the Greek sailors showed impressive seamanship as they manouevred it and got the men aboard. Great excitement; and a congratulatory signal from ashore was written out with flourish by me.

We went up and down the Adriatic several times and I got to know the ports of Taranto, Bari, Brindisi and Ancona, as well as the look of the east coast of Italy, and the headland at Argostoli, where the sea was always extra choppy. (That's the name I remember, but I cannot find it on a map. Was it S Maria di Leuca, or – further north – Peschici or Vieste?) It was, in many ways, an enjoyable life. We were relaxed and friendly with one another. The air was often full of music, Lilly Marlene being popular with the British and the Greeks and, indeed, the Italians and Germans. It was a cross-battle-lines friendly war-song.

I was glad to be in the *Kanaris*. Once at Ancona we were moored alongside a British cruiser, HMS *Ajax*. There were some men with rifles on their shoulders doubling up and down the deck doing "No.11 punishment" – poor chaps. There were no punishments in our ship, at least amongst us British, though for a forenoon entertainment I would sometimes watch from a discreet distance while Greek seamen stood charged before the Commander, gesticulating and proclaiming their innocence in voluble Greek with more histrionics than would have been allowed on a British warship.

To the excitement of all aboard, Greece was invaded and we were dispatched to cover the troops going into Piraeus, the port of Athens. Sailing along the shore as part of the convoy escort I thought of the ancient triremes and the Battle of Salamis twenty-four centuries before, and pondered the possibility of a battle to come. But there was no battle to come. The troops went ashore; we made fast alongside the jetty in Piraeus harbour and were immediately invaded by undernourished Greek children. We fed them with all they could eat and take – too much so, because after that we were on short rations.

We were in Piraeus for a week – time for a trip (with Coder Paris) to the Acropolis to climb the hill and see the Parthenon and the Erechthaeum and other temples on the site. To me it was utterly moving and I was in a fever of excitement as I saw the famous friezes on the Parthenon, high up, but designed so as to look right from ground level, and much else which I had written essays about in my far-off Classics Higher Certificate days. There was hardly anyone about, the place being of no interest to other sailors on leave, and of course no tourists. But there was a photographer, so I have photographic evidence of the occasion showing me and Paris both looking very sailor-like. I was also delighted with the Areopagus, Mars Hill, where St Paul made his famous speech in Acts 17. It was a stiff climb up the hill and down again into Athens, and Paris and I, not at all used to walking, gave ourselves a good Greek meal, washed down with retsina wine, before returning to Piraeus (by train) and the *Kanaris*.

One distinguished visitor aboard the *Kanaris* was Archbishop Damaskenos. He was a dignified ecclesiastical figure, huge in stature with a long flowing beard. But he was more than that. He became an important political figure who was able to negotiate terms between the contending factions and the British government. He stood on the bridge, addressed the ship's company and blessed all aboard, sprinkling the crew with holy water, to the amazement of us British sailors.

On another day Jones went ashore in my overcoat (the weather was cold) and burnt cigarette holes in it, and tried to persuade me that he had got "shot up" by some Greeks ashore. This was not impossible because there were some wild Greeks about belonging to different political (we would say "terrorist") groups; our hat-badges with the letters HHMS on them made us share the unpopularity of the Greek king, who was being stoutly supported by Churchill. Indeed there were ELAS and EAM bands everywhere, and lest there be trouble with the Greek ships, we were quickly dispatched from the scene.

So we were ordered to sea to guard a slow convoy to Salonika (Thessalonika) in the north of Greece. This meant making our way up the heavily mined coast with mine-sweepers in company, sweeping a passage as we went. We passed Mount Olympus, and crawled up the beautiful coastline; a peaceful but tense trip, punctuated by the occasional explosion of a mine. Finally, we edged our way through the syrupy smooth water into the harbour, and heard that the convoy and the mine-sweeping operation were important enough to be reported on the BBC news.

We went ashore for a hilarious evening of drinking with Greek sailors from the ship and Greeks ashore, and I exceeded my limit of retsina. So we staggered back to the ship, led, as usual, by the nose of Leading-Telegraphist Jones, and managed to get a decent night's sleep: but I noticed the LO looking at me quizzically the next morning as I tried to soothe my thumping head.

We sailed swiftly back to Athens, unaccompanied. I managed to get ashore and bought a load of sponges to give as presents to my dear familiy – one day. But a strange thing happened, and that "one day" came sooner than I had expected. I passed an old lady in the street, with a lovely face and deep, still eyes. She wanted to tell my fortune. 'I don't believe in it,' I said. 'Why not? You believe in God.' 'That's different.' By this time she was reading my palm. 'You are about to go on a long journey,' she said. 'Of course,' said I, 'I am a sailor.' 'Ah! But you are going home.' 'Obviously – eventually.' 'No – you are going at once and will be home for Christmas.' Impossible. It was now December; and even in a perfect scenario, there was no way I could get back to UK by Christmas.

But – as soon as I stepped aboard the *Kanaris* there was a message that I was to report at once to the LO. Had I made some awful mistake? Or had he seen me lurching about at Thessalonika? What trouble was I in? 'Oh Christopher,' (he had never used my Christian name before) 'you are to return to UK immediately for an Officers' Commission Board. You will take the first passage available to Alexandria and then on to UK. But I can't let you go without a relief, so you will be with us for a bit longer.' That seemed to spoil it all; but I was delighted in a shaken sort of way, being very happy where I was, but ambitious all the same to get a commission. Meanwhile, there seemed to be no prospect whatever of a relief arriving miraculously while we were still in Athens.

However, the first signal I decoded when back on watch was a "most immediate" to *Kanaris* and other Greek ships to leave Piraeus at once and proceed to – Alexandria! I think the LO thought I had drafted the signal myself, but the reason was clearly the political trouble that was brewing up. Anyway, we weighed anchor and made for Alex by way of Haifa where we filled our lockers with oranges bought for almost nothing from a vendor on the jetty. A signal was sent requesting my relief to be ready for when we arrived.

I left the *Kanaris* sadly, but not all that sadly. My special friend, Jock Kerr, had already left, and the others were none too pleased about the purposes of my leaving them and my brilliant luck in getting the coveted "UK draft chit". However, I was taken, with bag and hammock, complete with sponges, pictures, and presents, to that delightful spot in the desert, HMS *Sphinx*. There I was told that there was a long queue for UK passages and I might have to wait for weeks. But almost immediately I was summoned from my tent and told to report on board a corvette, which was sailing the next day.

This was a "flower class" corvette. I was messed with the communication ratings and told that I did not have to work my passage. But I wanted to work and asked if I could do a seaman's watch, for the experience. This was courteously refused; but I was allowed to do a coder's watch, much to the delight of the other coders. There is all the difference between keeping one in three watches and keeping one in four. I was teased a lot and was always hailed to "lunch" when ship's hands were piped to "dinner". And it was specially funny that I found the passage through the Bay of Biscay so sick-making. The corvette has a different movement from the fierce violence of a destroyer; it rolled and dithered and rose and sank in a slower rhythm, more dignified, but just as deadly.

By now Christmas was approaching. The Battle of the Bulge was on and we heard bulletins continually about it on the radio. It was Germany's last desperate attempt to beat the Allies, and for a few days it looked very serious from our point of view as the Germans drove a wedge between the allied armies. But Monty took charge – even of the American army – and all was saved. For a few days Churchill was in trouble in Parliament, and we listened agog to the news.

We reached Portsmouth in a fog, with no hope, it seemed, of entering harbour. But again I was lucky because I was sent ashore in the ship's cutter. I was then taken to Pompey barracks and immediately sent on leave. 'Anything to declare, Lofty?' (Which I was often called by those who did not know me; though I was more thin than tall.) 'Cigarettes? Tobacco?' 'Only my ration of pipe tobacco' (destined for Father); 'O, and some sponges.' 'Sponges? Let's look.' There was my "duffy bag" bulging with sponges – illegal, I was sure. But the petty-officer just laughed and sent me on my way. Train to Victoria. Tube. Train from Charing Cross to Charlton. A walk up the hill. Knock at the Rectory door. (I can relive the excitement even as I type.) No one could believe it. That was Christmas Eve, 1944.

I have never been sceptical again about little old ladies with wise eyes who could speak English in Athens and seemed to know all about me, past and future.

Chapter 8
Sub-Lieutenant (Special Cypher)

Christmas 1944 was spent in idle happiness. Mother seized my kitbag and had everything out and washed. Despite the glamour of uniform I dressed in old, civvie clothes and stared down someone in church who whispered to her neighbour that "he ought to have joined up like everyone else". I distributed the sponges and other "rabbits", went to church, no doubt, and enjoyed Christmas dinner. Margie, John's wife, was staying at the Rectory at that time with her baby, Anthony. She was a WRNS officer stationed at Chatham. We had a long talk about the prospect of my getting a commission, both agreeing that it did not matter one way or the other, both knowing perfectly well that it mattered like hell.

After my leave I reported back to Portsmouth barracks and handed over the sealed envelope from Lieutenant Richardson containing my commission papers. He had told me that sometimes they get lost and the only guarantee was to hand them over in person to the right authority at the right time. This I now did and so found myself put in a mess with other ratings who were also waiting for the CW board.

This was an edgy time because any hint of trouble could end in ing sent back to sea. For instance, there was an unexpected kit and ock inspection, which happened, fortunately, almost at once. My in fine shape after Mother's laundering and sewing operation; b my hammock was black. I explained that I had just got back from leav after seven months at sea. 'All right – but get it cleaned today.' I scrubbed the outside till it looked respectable, then tied a bit of bunting to it so that I could recognise it in the heap of hammocks in which it wa wed.

There was another incident, amusing in retrospect, awkward at the time. We were lined up ready to go on weekend leave. We were expecting the order "Right turn. Quick march". But instead came the order, "Out gas-masks!" Horror. No one – but no one – carried his gasmask. All we carried was our gas-mask cases in which our Fridaywhile[1] possessions, pyjamas, tobacco allowance and toothbrush, were neatly folded. The Officer of the Day, who was expecting this, was amused and lenient. He told us to report back in an hour for the next muster of "liberty men" – complete with gas-masks. One friend of mine could not find his, but he risked it and this time got away without it. We missed the train, but there were plenty more.

I was then sent to Chatham barracks for the CW Board. But no tunnel! We were messed in the luxury of Nissen huts outside the barracks, being trusted to make our own way in and out as required. Our delicately poised situation was enough to ensure good behaviour.

When the time for the Board came I was relaxed and ready for it. The day was spent in a large hall, waiting to be summoned, one by one. I read *Villette*, while others tramped up and down in their anxiety. When I went into the Board Room I was ushered to a chair with a crescent of officers around me at their desks. What had I made of my sea-time? I told them about the Greeks and the convoys and the invasion of Greece and the hasty departure of the Greek ships from Athens. I told them that, yes, I had done my best to learn modern Greek but that my attempts, influenced by school Classics, were considered a joke by the Greek sailors. Why did I want to be commissioned? (I had thought about that.) 'Because I want more responsibility.' Was I fit for it? That was for the Board to decide, but I had a clear conscience about what I had done so far as a coder. What did I do in my spare time? Played golf, and Bach on the piano.

After a day of fevered waiting, a chief petty-officer came and called out a list of people to "line up". My name came third. The letter "C"? Or "order of merit"? It might have been merit because John Whitworth

---

[1] "Friday while" is short for "Friday while Monday" and means a "Friday to Monday weekend" as opposed to a "Saturday while", a "Saturday to Monday weekend."

came first. Surely he could not have beaten me! But remember, his uncle was an admiral! Anyway I found myself with the favoured few. I would have been terribly disappointed if I had failed. But most did; and I wasn't as sad on their behalf as I am sure I should have been.

The cypher course took place at a "stately home" at Privett in Hampshire. Cyphering is like coding, the difference being the importance and security of the signals being handled. But we were also introduced to the Cypher-X machine, which was new to me. I was slow on this at first, never having typed. Not that this was real typing: you had to use the weight of the wrist for each letter.

We had lurid lectures from the Commander about security, with plenty of horror stories, which ended in courts martial; and descriptions of traps, easy to fall into. The course was not so simple for those (the majority) who had not been coders, and one seaman candidate, Rogers, failed and was sent back to barracks, poor chap. The rest of us were hit by this as if we had been bereaved.

We were much pandered, as a way of being introduced to "officer class" living. We were waited on at meals and had our beds made for us. One of our number, who joined when I did, was Lady Patricia Mountbatten. She was tall, elegant, friendly, in every way delightful and very clever indeed. She was the only one of us to get an A; though Colin Mann and I got B plus. She came with us to the cinema at Petersfield one Saturday evening, there being no home leave during the course: six of us cuddled together in a jeep.

Colin Mann, older than most of us (all of twenty-five!), was openly a Christian, in a balanced, life-affirming way. He was expert in sophisticated matters such as good wine, the best restaurants, films that we "must see", and books that we should have read. John Whitworth was my special friend – but I never made him out. He was well educated, the nephew of Admiral Whitworth, C.-in-C. Western Approaches at Liverpool, a connoisseur on everything that mattered, such as politics (the people rather than the principles), the Navy and how to get the best out of "the system". He was vulnerable, affectionate, a good friend, much teased, but able to ride it. We had long walks and talks and I was pleased when I found that he was on the same draft as me to Colombo.

I decided that I was not fit, so I took to going on long, fast walks round the countryside, sometimes persuading John to come with me, once Colin, but not, alas, Patricia! Towards the end of the course we were visited by one Sammy Goode, a tailor from the waterside at Portsmouth. He measured us up for suits complete with one wavey, green-on-gold stripe, and tropical gear as well, in case we were tropics-bound.

During our last day at Privett we were each interviewed by the Commander who told us how we had done and recommended the sort of appointment we should have. I had done well, except in Cypher-X in which I needed more practice. The Commander recommended me for a sea appointment.

One beautiful day towards the end of February we dressed ourselves in officers' uniform, piled into taxis and made for Petersfield, Waterloo and home. There I wore my uniform and practised saluting to my bedroom mirror: very smart salutes; casual, off-hand ones; formal acknowledgement of a senior officer, friendly response to a friend, gentlemanly acknowledgement of a known rating. You can put a lot of human communication into a salute. I came down to supper that evening, slightly ashamed of myself; but fortunately no one had witnessed my histrionics.

I had a week's end-of-course leave plus any extension that might be expected for embarkation leave. I was intensely irritated by the fact that one of the weeks was Holy Week and I was expected to make all the religious observances, including the Three Hours on Good Friday. I was at my most rebellious; but managed it and duly rejoiced on Easter Day.

When leave was over I had to return to Pompey barracks for additional "officers' training", a foolish business in which we were lectured by Lieutenant-Commander House (whom we called "Housey-Housey") on "officer like qualities" (OLQ) which we were supposed to cultivate. We were messed in a hotel near the sea in Southsea, where we ran up over-regulation mess bills, finding the drink and cigarettes exceedingly cheap. This was the only time in my life that I took to smoking – and gin! Fortunately I didn't keep it up. We even had some square-marching on the parade ground of RNB, and I was called out to drill the squad, a practice I had learnt in the OTC at Lancing. The chief petty-officer was a bully and enjoyed making young officers look silly, so he picked me out as a likely victim. But I did rather well, and so confounded him. Everyone was pleased.

At the end of the course we were subjected to an examination on the Navy, its ranks and customs. Those of us who had been to sea found it very easy and scored top marks – but our fellow students, doctors, chaplains and other new entrants, were stumped by much of it. The course ended with a formal, compulsory "Saturday-night-at-sea" dinner in the officers' mess – even although we weren't at sea, only practising. The bow-tie of one of my friends fell into his soup. This seemed typical of the course.

On leave again, I received a telegram ordering me to report to Liverpool and take passage to HMS *Mayina*, which I knew was the transit camp at Colombo, where Brian Wallas was stationed. With the order came a first class rail-warrant. Father saw me off at Paddington, complete with tropical gear and two huge suitcases that I had bought in Birmingham staying with Philip Haynes. In Liverpool I reported aboard SS *Lancaster*, a P&O liner full of troops and old friends, bound for Colombo.

The voyage took us across the Atlantic, through the Mediterranean, the Suez Canal and the Indian Ocean to Bombay. I played a lot of chess; occasionally we were made to do PT on the deck, which we did with petulant lack of enthusiasm. There were bridge groups (but foolishly I did not play in those days), a very poor ship's concert, plenty of time to read and write and then – the beginning and end of all rags.

It was Victory in Europe Day. We were in the Indian Ocean, heading south east. The news came through on the radio, and we went collectively mad. Out of the general drinking, rejoicing and excitement there evolved a game of rugger with an officer's cap, played from one end of the upper deck to the other; no sides, no direction, everyone against everyone, with uninhibited shouting, wrestling, rushing, tackling, falling, scrummaging, till exhaustion overtook – and it was time for dinner.

The underlying cause was not so much the joy of victory in Europe, though there was plenty of that, especially as regards the cessation of the bombing at home which we all feared. No, the underlying feeling was that it may be all over for them in Europe and at home, but for us it was not at all over. We were still in it, indeed, going out to it; and, seriously, could we hope to defeat the all-conquering Japanese without many of us getting killed first? In Burma, true, things had taken a turn for the better, but there was still Malaya and Singapore to recapture, and the Japanese forces seemed to sprawl all over the Pacific. So – all right for you in Europe: but don't forget us in your frizzling excitement.

As for myself – I record this with no pride, just a fact – I felt an inward but not an outward excitement and I did not take part in the madness of the rugger which ended with dinner, but also with one broken ankle and many painful bruises. I found myself apart, very serious; saying words that I remembered from Robert Bridge's *The Testament of Beauty:*

> Amidst the flimsy joy of the uproarious city,
> My heart was quiet within me, and felt a profounder fear
> than ever it had known in all the war's darkest dismay.

After five weeks, we arrived at Bombay. John, Colin and I went ashore to explore the city, its seething population, and its many dreadful beggars; "dreadful" because that's the way they made themselves look; but they were still to be pitied and surreptitiously tipped. We visited the cathedral-like railway station, with its hordes of people, officers, men, Indians, British, nuns of every religion, holy men, dogs, parties of school children. They say that if you stay around Bombay railway station you will eventually meet everyone. Then we had an absurdly expensive dinner at the Taj Mahal Hotel at which John Whitworth embarrassed us by demonstrating his panache for ordering food and wine and being rude to waiters. After this we returned, replete, aboard the SS *Lancaster* for the rest of the voyage to Colombo.

I would like to say that there was Brian waiting for me on the jetty. Almost true. He knew I was coming and left me a note at *Mayina* telling me to get in touch, which I soon did.

HMS *Mayina* was a camp in the jungle outside Colombo, just as the *Sphinx* had been a camp in the desert outside Alexandria. We were put into tents while the rain cascaded down – such as I had never seen before. Our daily duty was to censor mail. The letters we had to read were mostly illiterate and made me feel, many years later, that Tony Blair was right to call for Education, Education, Education. I had a conscience about it, too, because I told my parents in a letter that I was in a "Sunny Isle where only man is vile" (a bit of code that you will be able to decipher if you know the hymn *From Greenland's Icy Mountains...*).

Brian had everything organised. He knew just the place for a light lunch, drink and banana-split; just the place for a slap-up dinner to celebrate and meet his friends; and how to become a member of the Flower Club where we could play squash and tennis. Besides the Flower Club we used to go to the Galle Face Hotel for wonderful surf-bathing.

Soon, opting to work rather than do nothing, I began to work day shifts in the cypher office. The officer in charge was a Wren, known as Grizzle: a blue-stocking, gracious, severe, very clever indeed. She had her own rules of "procedure" which were different from those I had learnt at Privett, and she expected us to keep them. On one occasion she and I wrestled together over a high-priority signal that was corrupt. It was like doing a difficult crossword puzzle, but we managed to make sense of it. It was she, so she told me, not Brian, who recommended me for appointment to the Staff of the Admiral Commanding the Third Battle Squadron on HMS *Nelson*. So I am eternally grateful to her.

Whilst waiting for the return of the *Nelson* from shelling the Andaman Islands, I was given a week's leave; so off I went with Michael Whitehorn, a staff-officer friend of Brian. Michael was older than me and was an ordination candidate in the Presbyterian Church. We spent most of the first day standing together in the rain in a jungle village somewhere between Colombo and Galle without any chance at all, it seemed, of getting a further lift. However, a lorry came along at last and took us all the way. We stayed in a hotel on a promontory and were very comfortable.

The trouble with that leave was that it rained for the whole week, hard, non-stop. So we decided to go out and get wet. We had deep theological discussions and found that we agreed on everything except the centrality (according to me), the "possible prop" (according to

Michael) of sacraments and the "Church". I was glad in the end that I was C. of E.; but he remained equally glad to be a Presbyterian!

I was once required to take sacks of confidential documents up to Mountbatten's HQ at Kandi. I had about three carriages full of these sacks and, as I could only sit in one carriage, I said that it would be impossible to guard them all: so I was made to sign a paper recording my objection. It was a lovely journey into the hills, and Kandi, with its lake, is a beautiful place. Having safely delivered the sacks I was taken to a hotel for a comfortable night, disturbed only by a distant boy who played the same drum rhythm loudly and without stopping.

Before I left Colombo, Douglas Bean and Christopher Hollis turned up – coming from the UK as coders. No commission for them, and Brian and I could have refused to have anything to do with them! As it was we shed our uniform tabs so that we could all go about together. There was difficulty in getting them membership of the Flower Club as they were not considered "gentlemen"; but Brian wangled it somehow. We all used to go to the Cathedral for Evensong on Sundays and we came to know the Bishop, Douglas Horsley, later to be Bishop of Gibraltar. Douglas used to play the Bishop's piano – and we would all listen gratefully.

At last I took a train to Trincomalee where HMS *Nelson* was at anchor. Two arrogant midshipmen[2] (who by nature despised RNVR sub-lieutenants) came for me in the cutter and wafted me to the *Nelson*, where I climbed the many steps of the gangway, saluted, was greeted by the Commander and handed over to a midshipman who took me down many decks into the Officers' Flat where I had been allotted a magnificent cabin. It was almost next door to the Admiral's sleeping quarters. There a Royal Marine stood guard, keeping a wary eye on the Admiral's hook which he wore in lieu of a right hand. He kept it at night on a shelf outside his cabin. I longed to steal it.

---

[2] One of them may have become the Vice-Admiral on whose ship Juliet and I dined in the evening before the Battle of the Atlantic service in Liverpool Cathedral at which I preached when I was Dean of Ripon. Certainly he had been in the *Nelson* at the same time as I was.

Chapter 9
HM Battleships *Nelson* and *Howe*

I soon settled into the hectic life aboard HMS *Nelson*. There she lay in the harbour of Trincomalee, said to be the finest natural harbour in the world, huge, dominant, with the East Indies Fleet anchored around her: aircraft-carriers, cruisers, destroyers, a supply ship and many satellite ships of various shapes and sizes, like a large family. But that is too soft a metaphor. Here was a fighting force, a fleet with enormous fire-power, bent on an operation of decisive importance, the invasion of Malaya: Singapore the immediate prize, victory over the Japanese the ultimate goal. Orders, instructions, congratulations and reproof went streaming forth from the *Nelson* to all the ships in the fleet, by flag when they were open and general, by hand when they were personal and particular, by code or cypher when they were confidential. More than that, Lord Louis Mountbatten in Kandi, and the Admiralty in London were in constant communication with Vice-Admiral Walker in the *Nelson*; and the cypher office was abuzz with it all.

I was introduced to Captain Biggs, the Chief-of-Staff, by Lieutenant Jacques, the Senior Cypher officer, and then, over a quick sherry, to Vice-Admiral Walker himself. He was known as "Hooky" because of the hook he wore in place of a hand. He was a devout Christian and showed interest in the fact that I was an ordination candidate.

The Commander had told me that in view of my age (nineteen turning twenty) I would be messed in the gun-room with the midshipmen and other junior sub-lieutenants; but the Chief-of-Staff insisted that being on the Admiral's staff, I should be messed in the ward-room – where, frankly, I found myself rather friendless. I rarely saw the other two cypher officers, because they were on watch or resting when I was free, though one of them, Bill Tozer, later went to HMS *Howe* with me and I got to know him well. There was none of the rough, kind comaraderie that I had found on the lower deck, where, whatever the differences in rank and culture, we all messed together and made the most of a bad job, the common enemy being "officers". In the ward-room they tended to ignore my presence as if I did not exist. The other officers had no idea how hard we worked or the responsibility we carried; and of course we did not tell them. Their overwhelming concern was to keep their professional sheets clean, and hope one day for promotion. RNVR officers, who were in a minority in that ship, were more inclined to worry about home and family, and were looking forward to being demobilised. I had no strong feelings about that. I just had my work to do and my end to keep up.

There was a young sub-lieutenant (supply) in the gun-room with whom I played chess. He was always in trouble, poor chap, but I could give him little comfort. It was just part of being a junior officer in a big ship. There was a Lieutenant Prince who was also an ordinand, but he was ten years older than me and we never had any time together. So for my first few weeks in the *Nelson* I was lonely, but too busy on watch, and too tired off watch, to mind. I discovered a piano in the store-room near my cabin, and against the grinding noise of the ship's engines I used to play this to myself as loudly as I could.

I once made a mark on the life of the ward-room. Through going to the Cathedral I had got to know the American Vice-Consul in Colombo. He wanted to be taken aboard the *Nelson* and shown round. He persisted. What was I to do? I tried to chat up the Commander (the Executive Officer: the most feared man aboard) but could get nowhere near him in the ward-room. So I joined the line of ratings who were up before him for "requests" or (more likely) punishment. He was very surprised to see me at the end of a long queue of defaulters and he tried to shout me down when I began to ask him if I could have a guest aboard for guest-night. 'Of course you can, you –'.'But this is a special guest ...' 'I don't care a damn who it is. You're wasting my time.' 'He is the American Vice-Consul.' 'What? Why didn't you say so in the first place?'

Panic and much preparation and a rocket-like rise in my evaluation. Lieutenant Prince was summoned to take the American V-C and me and an escort round the *Nelson*. This gave me a fascinating insight into the enormous size and complexity of this vast man-of-war and a glimpse too of how men lived and worked in her. We were shown the bridge with all its technology; the complicated gun-control centre; the crowded mess-decks; radar, azdics, sick-bay, and the huge, huge engines. The American Vice-Consul was treated as an important guest of honour at dinner; and there was I sitting amongst the Most Mighty at the High Table.

After that little episode life became happy enough. When I was on watch I worked as hard as it was possible for me to work, four hours at a stretch with maximum speed and concentration. I became competent on the cypher machine and the typewriter and I soon learnt to make the right judgements about whom to distribute signals to within the ship. At the cypher books I was very quick indeed, knowing lots of groups by heart, and being able to subtract numbers as quickly as I could read them. Things were very tense. The war was not over; there was a Japanese cruiser in the vicinity when we were at sea, the subject of a furious exchange of signals between us and Mountbatten. Once we were dive-bombed by suicide planes, one of which, aiming at us, brushed the cruiser astern (HMS *London*?). But down in my office in the bowels of the ship, or in my cabin, only rarely on deck, and never so in time of action, I knew nothing of this.

One day, while we were still in Trincomalee, a signal came from the Chaplain of the Fleet, asking that I be allowed to go to Colombo for four nights to attend a selection course for ordination. 'Certainly not,' said Captain Biggs backed by Commander Colville, the Communications Officer; 'We are much too busy with plans for Operation Zipper.' 'But, yes,' said Hooky Walker, 'of course he can go. You can get a temporary relief for him. I am going to Colombo myself. He can fly with me in my aeroplane.' So I did. We hopped across Ceylon on a bumpy flight at low altitude, because the Admiral said that his ears ached if we went higher. He preferred the bumps. I then made my way by rickshaw to Bishop's College, where the Bishop of Colombo lived, and took part in a semi-retreat, semi-conference, semi-(but mainly) selection course. There were about thirty candidates of all ranks in all services, presided over by the Bishop, assisted by other members of his staff, including a Father Hunt who had spent the whole of his ministry in Korea. He was now a naval chaplain ('and a high security risk,' grumbled Brian who knew him as a member of his mess and was critical of his indiscreet conversation). In my interview with him, he asked me what book I was reading. '*Pride and Prejudice*,' said I. 'But does that help you to pray?' he responded tersely. I do not know what my answer was, but thinking it over now the answer is, 'Yes: all books that open you to new experience and new insights into the world, help you to pray.' I do not think he would have agreed. The secretary of the Board (Commodore de Pass, RN) wrote to me years later, when I was appointed Dean of Ripon, saying that he had kept in touch with all our careers – and was very proud of them. Vice-Admiral Walker also wrote to me in 1951 when I was ordained.

When I emerged from this pleasant and unworrying interlude (because I was not worried about the outcome), the first atom bomb had been dropped, and our world, the world of fighting forces in the East Indies, was utterly changed. Panic! What was going to happen now? Relief! Astonishment! How could splitting a tiny atom make such a commotion? Cynicism: 'I bet it's been exaggerated.' Scientific wonder by those who had some inkling of what it was all about. Horror by those who understood what had been inflicted on Hiroshima. A marine Lieutenant Williams, whom I had known as a senior and very clever boy at Belmont, tried to explain what these bombs meant in scientific and humanitarian terms. He expatiated about it to a tense audience of officers at dinner. It was mysterious, awful, terrifying good news.

My immediate concern was to get back to Trincomalee and rejoin the *Nelson*. But when I went to the airport I found that the Admiral had made his own way back and an army colonel had pinched the plane that he had left for me. There was no prospect of a flight and there were no trains, so I would have to hitch-hike. There was someone else in the same situation and together we started to walk across Ceylon. We got a lift at last, but it only took us halfway and then dropped us in the midst of a jungly nowhere. Darkness was falling, so we lit a fire (a) to keep ourselves warm and (b) to keep wild animals away. After a long wait an army truck came along and I had to pull what slender rank I had to persuade the driver to take us to Trincomalee. So, after most of a day and a black night, I reported to the Naval Officer in Charge at Trinco. He immediately sent a signal to the *Nelson*, which was about to leave harbour. The cutter was sent with the same two surly midshipmen, and I scrambled aboard. The cypher staff were pleased to see me, especially as my relief was still on board and there was no time now for him to return to duties ashore.

It seemed that Operation Zipper (the invasion of Malaya) was still to take place, but unopposed. By this time the second bomb had been dropped (unnecessarily in my judgement) and peace was soon declared. So the Third Battle Squadron under the command of Vice-Admiral H.T.C. Walker flying his flag in HMS *Nelson* sailed from Trincomalee. This was a moment of history. The *Nelson* was the centre of a huge armada of ships spread out over the ocean as far as the eye could see. There were no clouds in the sky, hardly a ripple on the sea. It was a scene of great beauty and great menace as the fleet steamed purposefully eastwards for the Andaman Islands, Penang, and Singapore.

"Heading east" reminds me of the worst row I had in the *Nelson*. Standing orders were that routine signals deciphered in the night should be sent up to the bridge at dawn. But with the ship heading east, dawn came earlier and the "zone time" changed. I got it into my head that dawn would therefore be later, not earlier; a silly mistake but understandable seeing that where I was in the bowels of the ship dawn made little impression. Suddenly the buzzer buzzed. It was the Officer of the Watch (OOW) demanding the dawn signals. 'But it isn't dawn yet,' I began. 'I'll tell you if it's dawn or not,' shouted the furious OOW. 'Report to me on the Bridge with the signals – at the double.' So I scrambled some signals together and asked the messenger to guide me to the bridge, I not having the least idea how to get there. Sure enough, to my shame and embarrassment, there was the sun well up in the sky; and I was ordered to report myself to the Communications Officer.

On the only other occasion that I was in trouble with the Communications Officer, my boss, he was much more angry, he being in the wrong. A very high-priority signal was received from Mountbatten's headquarters in the middle of the night wrongly cyphered, that is to say, in this instance, it was cyphered from a book that was out of date. So I initiated a signal of equal priority asking that the signal be recyphered correctly, and repeated. This was in accordance with procedures that were laid down; but the next morning the Signals Officer was furious with me for sending a signal without his permission. I said that there was no point, when I had a signal of such importance, in wasting time waking him up in the middle of the night and asking his permission to do something that I knew I would have to do anyway. As it turned out the urgency of the signal justified my action – but Commander Colville was no less annoyed. Meanwhile some cypher officer on Lord Louis' staff in Kandi was no doubt in trouble.

More trouble for me, of a different kind altogether. I had an old school friend who was three years older than me and inclined to be intimidating. He was very clever indeed, but unsuited to be a marine officer. He came to me and said that he wanted to see a secret signal which had been sent about himself. The reply to this had been "unclassified", so the coding office had sent a copy to him. Naturally he wanted to see the original. Of course I flatly refused to show it to him. So he went for me with fury, bribery, flattery and "old boy" pressure; and it took all my determination to fend him off. After he had gone, I went round to the coding office to have it out with the coding petty-officer who should not have allowed this signal with its "secret" reference to have been sent to the officer concerned. The petty-officer was upset at being rebuked by a green cypher sub-lieutenant; but he knew that I was right and he hoped that I would not take the matter any higher – which I didn't.

My reward was that there in the coding office, enormously pleased at what he could hear going on, was Ronnie Wylie, my best friend at the coders' training establishment, HMS *Cabbala*. This was a joyful encounter because I liked him better than anyone I knew in the *Nelson*. No outward sign of recognition at the time, except the hint of a wink. But later I sent him a note: he smuggled himself into my cabin and most illegally we spent hours talking together. I was so sorry that he was not commissioned. He was just as good a coder as I was; but he had been in the *Nelson* ever since he left *Cabbala*, notably when the *Nelson* covered the D-Day landings in France, with no opportunity of being noticed or promoted.

The fleet sailed to Malaya and anchored off Penang. Rumour had it that the assault troops that went ashore got stuck in the sands and could make no immediate progress. This did not matter because there was no military opposition. A Japanese admiral came aboard the *Nelson* and I have a photograph of him doing so, saluting the quarter deck. He came to give us the disposition of the Japanese forces and to make preparations for their surrender. Needless to say the pressure of work in the cypher office became intense as we coped with all the dispositions and informed and received instructions from London.

While the world waited I was sent ashore with a Signals Petty Officer and some ratings, who were armed with sacks of confidential books and other necessary equipment, to set up a temporary signal station. We went in a motor-launch taking an hour to reach the shore as the *Nelson* was anchored well out to sea. We landed, turned right along the harbour front and, led by me, came to the Pacific and Oriental Hotel. It looked good, so we walked in and I said, 'Right – we will have this one.' So the books were stacked, the signal and wireless apparatus set up and a party of signalmen and telegraphists was left to man this new signal station.

Other things must have been happening too because I had an hour or so in which to explore this hot, silent, deserted, utterly peaceful and beautiful place with its mountain backdrop. I bought an oil-painting of a fisherman sculling his boat, paying for it with the only currency available, a packet of cigarettes. I still have the picture, and I love it. We cruised back to the *Nelson*. I reported what I had done; and the fleet went on its way up the Malacca Straits to Singapore.

(When Juliet and I returned to Penang in 1993, having a week's holiday after our tour of Australia, I went back to that hotel and tried to tell the story of that far-off day in August 1945; but I do not think that the man at the reception had any idea of what I was talking about. He was too young to know.)

Soon after we reached Singapore Lord Louis Mountbatten, the Supreme Commander of the South East Asian Command, came aboard the *Nelson* on his way to take the surrender. He made the ship's company gather round in his usual informal, theatrical way and managed to pick out by name some of the ratings who had served with him before. Very impressive. He then came into the ward-room and I found myself near to him at the bar. He asked me what I was, and when I said, 'Cypher officer, Sir', he snorted and said that cypher officers should be Wrens, who were better at it than men. 'Your daughter Patricia was,' I dared to say, 'and she was top of our class. But in general the men are better.' He was pleased and said that Patricia was now on his staff at Kandi. This left me wondering if it were she who had made that mistake. But I doubt it, knowing her.

I was not, of course, one of those detailed to take part in the surrender ceremony, but I was well aware of it; and I was pleased to see it represented in wax in the War Museum in Singapore, which we visited in 1993. It shows a naval rating standing by with "HMS *Nelson*" on his cap-badge – quite right; and I have some snaps of the ceremony itself.

I also possess a Japanese sword. This is because General Slim gave orders that all Japanese officers were to surrender their swords to British officers. Three of these swords were allotted to the officers of the *Nelson,* and I – quite the most junior and insignificant – drew the lot for one of them. I still have it and am very proud of it.

Singapore was a dull, listless place in those days of surrender, the population quite unmoved by the turn of affairs. Everything was jaded and needed a coat of paint. But when I ventured into the market to shop I found the Chinese Malays lively and vociferous and pleased to see us, especially if they could sell us things. I bargained my best and bought a china tea-set (teapot, tray and cups but no saucers), some silk pictures and other items most of which I gave away as presents when I got home. Meanwhile, they adorned my cabin and gave it a new look.

News of the prisoners who were being released from Changhi gaol sent a ripple of consternation through the Fleet, people of all ranks talking about it together in hushed indignation. Some of them, we heard, were not fit to travel back to the UK. They were in hospital trying to recuperate. I was an ordinand, destined for the priesthood. Should I not visit them? I would not forgive myself if I did not at least try, so when I next went ashore, I found out where the hospital was, walked backwards and forwards past it in indecision, decided that the worst (living with myself) would happen if I funked it, so in I went. I was allowed into the ward and went from bed to bed, but got no response at all, except for one stretched face which turned to me and said, 'Got a fag, mate?' When I said I hadn't, he turned away in disinterest. I crept out of the ward and out of the hospital, dejected and useless.

About this time the Bishop of Singapore, Bishop Leonard Wilson, came to stay with us aboard the *Nelson*. He had been a prisoner of war and had been flogged by the Japanese; but he did not seem to bear any hatred against them. He told me cheerfully that the way to survive such ordeals is to pray for the perpetrator. In saying this he was saying more than he knew, because at a later date he baptised and confirmed the very officer who had beaten him.

Bishop Wilson had with him his chaplain, the Reverend John Hayter who had been at Lancing and Teddy Hall and Cuddesdon. I was proud at the prospect of following in his footsteps (having already endured Lancing) as I liked him immensely.[1] I was sent for by the Captain (Captain Caslon, RN), who told me that Vice-Admiral Walker (whom I used to meet regularly at the eight o'clock Holy Communion service on Sunday mornings) wanted Prince and me to look after Bishop Wilson whilst he was aboard. Prince could not be spared from his upper-deck duties, but there was little cyphering to do now the war was over, so this duty, which I regarded as a huge privilege, fell to me. So I spent a day or two with the Bishop and his chaplain, not hearing their stories because they were reluctant to speak of them, but telling them about England, Mr Churchill, the black-out, rationing, bombing, the Church of England (what little I knew about it), Lancing in evacuation, the Navy, the *Nelson* – and anything else that they could pick from my brain.

---

[1] I am sorry to say that I lost touch with John (later "Canon") Hayter; but when he died, as Vicar of Boldre in the New Forest, he left a sum of money to the Friends of Lancing Chapel, of which I am the Chairman. We spent the money on a door in the South Aisle of the Chapel, which I dedicated at our Festival in 1999, with many of his parishioners present. I told them about our meeting in 1945. They were pleased. He was obviously much loved for his long and faithful ministry at Boldre.

I have already written and published some words about Bishop Wilson, who had such a strong influence upon me, in *The Food of Love*. I quote them now:

> Never have I known such a man as Bishop Wilson. He was very prayerful and devout; kind and interested in everyone and everything, but not himself; physically as frail as could be; but spiritually, calm: with no complaining, no aggression, just the strength of serenity. God was most certainly with him, I thought.

I had a letter from him years later when I became Vicar of Pershore and he had just retired as Bishop of Birmingham. He said that he remembered me well and would certainly come and preach in Pershore Abbey as soon as he was able to. Unfortunately he died very soon after writing to me.

A few days later I was summoned by the Communications Officer along with Bill Tozer, to be told that as there was now so little work to do in the cypher office we were to "trans-ship" to HMS *Howe* and change from cyphering to the Supply and Secretariat branches of the Navy. Bill was given first choice and chose to do "supply" (which would have bored me stiff), leaving me, to my great satisfaction, to go for secretariat. The *Nelson* was known to be going home soon, and was being filled with officers and men who were going to take passage to the UK. HMS *Howe* had only recently come out and the rumour was that she was going to cruise around showing the flag. Unlike everyone else, I had no desire to go home, having only been away for six months, and I was delighted with the idea of a new ship and new reponsibilities and cruising around the world waving the British flag. So with little regret and with the help of a marine I moved my gear from the *Nelson* to the *Howe*.

HMS *Howe*

Once aboard the *Howe* I reported to the Captain's Office and was introduced to the Captain, Captain Hugh McCall. I then started work under Lieutenant-Commander (S) Tony Palairet, the Captain's

Secretary. He was pleased to have me because the Captain's Office was at that time burdened with the responsibility of going through the papers of everyone on board to decide which medals each man was entitled to as a result of his war service. For example there was the Defence Medal, requiring service in the UK such as air-raid warden or the Home Guard; the 1939–45 Medal, requiring six months' sea-time in a theatre of war; the Atlantic or Burma or Mediterranean stars, requiring sea-time in these areas over and above the 1939–45 qualification; and the Victory Medal for everyone on active service during the war.

So, for instance, I was entitled to the 1939–45 Medal for my time in the *Kanaris*, the Burma Star for my time in the *Nelson*, and the Victory Medal. Sorting this out for everyone aboard the *Howe* was a big task, especially as there was the complication that time spent under serious punishment did not count towards medals. Tony Palairet gave me a huge pile to do and told me to get on with it as quickly as possible because many of the men were about to go home to be demobilised. I also had to calculate their demob numbers; and if they did not agree with me they came and told me so! Sometimes I beguiled myself by reading juicy things about some of the men, their courageous doings and their crimes. This was responsible work because there was no time for independent checking. I denied myself leave day after day in order to get it finished, and I believe that Palairet was pleased with me because he began to trust me with more duties and to train me in the work of a captain's secretary.

By the time the *Nelson* had gone home, her complement hugely swollen by men returning to UK for demobilisation, the *Howe* had sailed round to the naval dock-yards in the channel between Singapore island and the mainland. I had one run ashore when I walked across the causeway to the Sultan's Palace, its throne-room sited so that from the throne itself there was a huge view of the Malayan jungle.

By this time I had a new friend, Lieutenant (RN) Jimmy Woodward, Navigating Officer of the *Howe*. He was an ordinand, and I met him years later with his wife when he was vicar of a south London and an Honorary Canon of Southwark Cathedral. When I knew him in the *Howe* he was a "Dart.", that is an RN officer trained from the age of thirteen at Dartmouth. He was, therefore, strongly versed in naval affairs, but he wanted to leave it in order to be ordained. We struck up a friendship, being different from one another in matters of education, training and standing in the Navy, and yet so much alike in faith and purpose. He was quite unsolemn, a hundred miles from being pious. We used to take taxis together across the island to Singapore town where we rode around shamelessly in bicycle-rickshaws (such as Julie and I took – ruinously – during our stay in Singapore in 1993), bartered in the market and ate huge Chinese meals.

Once we went dutifully but dubiously to a Quiet Day for ordinands organised by the Chaplain of the Fleet at St Andrew's Cathedral, urged to do so by the Chaplain of the *Howe*, the Reverend Bill Sandys. I had disliked the Chaplain in the *Nelson* who, it seemed to my judgemental self, never left the bar of the ward-room but we hardly ever saw Bill Sandys in the ward-room except at meals. He was more likely to be found in the seamen's messes or the sick-bay or with those keeping a middle watch on deck in a storm. He was a friend to all on board from the Captain downwards. He had a strong influence on me at this time.

At the Quiet Day in Singapore Cathedral I met up with some of those who had been on my selection conference at Colombo. I remember nothing else about it except that I enjoyed the peace and the absence of any responsibility. When Juliet and I visited Australia via Singapaore in 1993 we went to the Cathedral and once more found it an oasis of peace amidst the roaring city, also a successful centre of Christian mission. The Dean told us that literally thousands attend services there every week.

HMS *Howe* did not stay long in Singapore. First we sailed to Colombo, and I shared the agonising panic that Jimmy, as navigating officer, felt when Colombo failed to appear over the horizon at the moment he expected it to. However, after a nervous minute it crept up out of the haze and all was well. We stayed long enough for me to go and see Brian Wallas who was impressed with my adventures and surprised to find me now in the Secretariat Branch of the Navy, though I never actually changed the colour of my stripe from green to white.

We then sailed for Mombasa, "crossing the line" in the process. There was suitable ceremonial on board, and those who had not crossed it before lined up to get themselves covered with foam by "Neptune", shaved and ducked. I found myself separated from the officers and jostling with the men. I rather enjoyed this: the anonymity, joining in the banter, with no end to keep up; and at the end of it finding myself the proud owner of a certificate.

That evening there were boxing bouts on deck, and I watched with dismay, as I had once thought of volunteering to box. These bouts were brutal and skill-less, the contestants fanatically cheered or booed, depending on their status in the ship. There was also a deckhockey competition between messes. I was the ward-room's goalie and we played the Royal Marines. I managed to keep the puck out of the goal by a series of swoops and dives which amazed myself and my brother officers and left me heroically bruised; but in the end there was a scrummage in front of our goal and the massive weight of the marines propelled everybody, everything, me, puck and all into the goal.

At Mombasa I went ashore, bought a watch, and walked along the beach where fishermen were working their nets from the shore. Bill and I had a meal together. We saw little of each other in the *Howe* even though for a couple of weeks we shared a cabin. He was an ultra-polite person whose smooth reserve was difficult to break. He was also scrupulously tidy, so it was just as well that we did not have to share the cabin for very long, though this might have broken down his reserve! Mombasa is a curious port with ships lying alongside the jetty almost in the town itself. Strangely, it is a place that recurs (along with the *Howe* and its scrubbed deck and its white awning) in my dreams.

We sailed on to show the flag to the Seychelles Islands, where beautiful girls came aboard for a typical naval party with lots to eat and drink and all the officers in their best white uniforms. I went ashore one afternoon and walked over the hill and down to a beach which smelt exotically of the rich herbage. But no girls about, alas! There was another party ashore at which our Marine Band played old-fashioned tunes. I bought some tortoise-shell things which I added to my collection of presents to be distributed when I got home. I kept and still have napkin-ring.

the Seychelles we sailed to Adu Atoll in the Maldive Islands. The was a military and naval establishment there, no doubt highly secret; a canteen for drinking beer; sand, coconut trees and the ocean all around: nothing else at all. I remember thinking, 'I am on a real desert island'. I believe that the place is now a holiday resort. But resort for what? I wonder.

Back to Colombo; then home via the Red Sea, Suez, the Med, "Last-Port-of-Call" Gibraltar (or, indeed, the first if you are going the wrong way) offering the last chance for buying presents, and so home to Portsmouth. I was disappointed at Suez because half the crew was given leave to go to Jerusalem and rejoin the ship at Port Said. Tony Palairet tossed me for it, and won. But I was rather pleased at his confidence in leaving me in charge of the Captain's Office.

One memorable incident on this voyage was the notorious "Saturday Night at Sea". As the youngest officer I had to propose the toast to "Sweethearts and Wives". Bill Tozer wrote a poem in terrible rhyming couplets which he gave me to recite; but I had my own ideas and wrote my own speech – which I then left in my cabin on purpose, deciding that I would dare to deliver it without notes, as Father preached his sermons. This was a decisive moment because it taught me that, however nervous, I was able to speak in a way that sounds "off the cuff" but in fact is the result of careful preparation. I have not used a note since, except when delivering lectures and broadcasting on the World Service. I did not tell jokes, but tried to lace the speech with humour and sly references to people and events. They seemed pleased with me and plied me with drinks when the ordeal was over.

We spent Christmas Eve 1945 in Aden. I joined the Chaplain and the carol-singers who went round the ships in harbour, in the ship's launch, before going to the midnight Eucharist in the Chapel. (I hope that ships still have chapels.) I also went ashore with Bill Tozer to see the ancient and impressive Queen of Sheba wells. New Year's Eve and Day were spent at Suez and, as the youngest officer, I had to ring in the New Year on the ship's bell.

By this time I was well established on board. I was the Assistant Captain's Secretary – and was duly called "Scratch" as captain's secretaries always are. I used to attend the Captain to take orders, issue instructions and type confidential letters and reports. I also did the coding and cyphering for the ship when it was needed. My Captain later became Rear Admiral of the Dock-yard in Malta, when I was Scratch in the *Ranpura* in 1946, with Tony Palairet (now promoted) still his secretary. He was pleased to see me again and Tony gave me particular help over a tricky disciplinary case that my Captain had to deal with. There was a determined attempt to take me off the *Howe* when she left Colombo to return to UK, but the *Howe* wanted to keep me; so I was on board when she proudly sailed into Portsmouth harbour in January, 1946. We were welcomed home by a huge crowd of cheering people, a Marine Band, Princess Elizabeth and Lieutenant Philip Mountbatten, her fiancé. Also my mother and Mary, my sister.

I could not believe it, having no idea that the *Howe's* return to the UK was national news. But a Royal Marine knocked at my cabin door and told me that there were two ladies to see me. There was Mother with Mary on her arm, very excited. So was I. We had a long talk and exchange of news; then I showed them round the *Howe* with polite sailors obligingly handing them up and down companion-ways and ladders, and we had a joyful tea together in the ward-room.

I remember nothing about my home leave after returning to the UK except that I went round all my family and relations distributing gifts – with a feeling that they did not appreciate them enough!

One evening was memorable. I went to Sadlers Wells to see *Peter Grimes*, still in its first run. I had read about it but was not prepared for the searing impact it made on me: the poetic, strong, pathetically weak fisherman (Peter Pears); a criminal action (albeit an accident) on his conscience; pursued by a heartless crowd of prigs, harlots, a clergyman and self-righteous gossips; succoured, mothered, wooed by the one sympathetic character (played by Joan Cross); his hot-headed determination to succeed; another criminal accident and the spoken advice by his one friend, a sea-captain, to put out to sea and sink the boat. All these were there against a background of village life, the mending of fishing-nets, a church service, boisterous behaviour in a pub and a storm that kept blowing in, the wild, salty sea, the fog-horn and the interval of the ninth which scorched my mind all the way back to my ship and for weeks afterwards. I have never been the same person since, and I go to every performance I can get to.

Soon after that a signal came appointing me to be Captain's Secretary of HMS *Ranpura*, a heavy repair ship which was moored nearby and was rumoured to be about to sail – to Singapore!

Chapter 10
HMS *Ranpura*

I was pleased to be appointed to the *Ranpura* as Captain's Secretary. It meant that Tony Palairet in the *Howe* thought that I was up to the job; and it was much more fun to be going to sea again – even back to Singapore – than to be spending my remaining nine months in the Navy at some boring shore establishment. So I lugged my gear over to the *Ranpura*, established myself in a magnificent office under the bridge, facing for'ard, and found myself a decent cabin in the officers' cabin-flat.

The *Ranpura* was an ex-P&O liner, a sister ship to the heroically lost *Rawalpindi*, sunk by the *Scharnhorst* in the early days of the war. *Ranpura*'s middle deck had been removed and a giant foundry put in its place. With a medical contingent and a strong team of ship-building technicians of all grades of skill and experience put into uniform (we called them "dock-yard mateys"), we could do anything for anybody – and indeed were to do so later at Malta and Greece and the islands of the Aegean Sea.

The ship was just commissioning so at this time there were very few officers and men aboard. This gave me the satisfaction of being able to establish myself before they arrived. Then they came. Sub-lieutenant (S) George Anderson, who became my special friend: we helped each other out in all sorts of difficulties. Then there were sub-Lieutenants Peter Trumper and Brian Cleaves; and Arthur Fosh, who joined us in Malta. We were to have hilarious runs ashore together in Plymouth, Malta, Greece, the Greek islands and Corfu. Then there was "Uncle" (because he was all of thirty years old) Philip Vaughan. He took a fatherly interest in our behaviour and well-being, and on one occasion gave me stern but sound advice. There were many engineering, electrical and shipwright officers aboard for the repair work which was our *raison d'être*. There was a dentist, and a doctor, Surgeon-Lieutenant David Bett, who became a friend for life, godfather to our daughter Angela, and I to his second son, Andrew. This was his first appointment in the Navy, and he was the life and soul of every daily happening.

And there were the three commanders. There was Commander (S for Supply) Baird, Commander (E for Engineering) Jeans and the Commander of the ship, Commander Norrington, RNR. They were excellent professional sailors, stern but kind to the likes of me who were only there out of necessity and for the fun. I learnt to get the best out of the commanders in their varying moods. I would go to one just before, and the others just after their midday drinks: the one being gentler when he was free of alcohol but looking forward to it; the others when they had been made a little happy by it.

There was also Lieutenant-Commander Pond, the "Number One", fiercely efficient as Number Ones are supposed to be; and Mr Ward, the Gunner (T), who was very able, and anxious to get a full commission. He had been in the Navy all his life and had worked himself up through efficiency and hard work. How ridiculous that in the naval hierarchy I should be senior to him. There was also the Chaplain, the Reverend John Castledine, known by all as "The Bishop", who was very important to me, though I do not think that I appreciated him at the time.

The Captain himself, Captain T.W. Marsh, DSO, RN, was one of the few naval officers who achieved the rank of Captain from the lower deck, having joined as a "boy seaman". He ran the ship fairly but firmly and was much in demand in Malta as President for courts martial, which I used to attend with him. He saw issues clearly and had the knack of cutting through the haze of rhetoric and dissemblance and getting squarely to the point.

Captain Marsh had a delightful wife and a fourteen-year-old son, Geoffrey, who came to stay on board the *Ranpura* during the summer holidays. I had to take the Captain's launch to an aircraft-carrier (HMS *Ocean*) when he arrived in Malta from UK, go aboard and ask permission to take Captain Marsh's son to the *Ranpura*. After lots of saluting, permission was given. 'Carry on, Sub,' said the Commander of the ship; so away we went, down the steep gangway of the carrier, into the *Ranpura*'s launch, which the quarter-master had hailed; across the harbour and up the gangway into the *Ranpura* – all to Geoffrey's boyish delight and my relief that nothing had gone wrong.

Captain Marsh was kind to me and made allowance for my inexperience. He used to ring me to report to his sea-cabin on the bridge. I would go up with loads of papers under my arm for signing and instruction, and would go away again with loads more to deal with. On one nasty occasion, the commanders got together to complain to the Captain that I was overbearing in my manner towards them. Captain Marsh realised that they were suffering from "shoot the messenger" syndrome, and was understanding both of their position and mine. No row developed, only gentle reproof; and I resolved to be perfectly tactful for the rest of my life.

I had three writers in the Captain's Office "under" but really "with" me. We were the same age and equally inexperienced. We all worked hard, but I worked hardest, sometimes far into the night. There was Trevor Dawson, known as TD: he could imitate perfectly the particular way I used to say "Nonsense". Then there was Derek Bromfield (DB) whom I recommended for commission just before we returned to UK, and Ian Hay who was the Commander-in-Chief's nephew.

A day or two after I had established myself aboard, HMS *Ranpura* filled up with her complement of officers and men, seamen and dock-yard workers, temporarily in uniform. She then did her commissioning trials, of engines, compass, signals and administration. A fault was found in the engine-room, so we were sent to Plymouth to have it repaired. This delayed us for a week, and I went ashore to explore the much bombed city of Plymouth and the cliffs and the beaches nearby. We sub-lieutenants had an outing in honour of the madness of going off again to the other side of the world. What were we doing in a ship bound for Singapore, when the war was over and all sensible people were returning to civilian life? We ate and drank as we pondered the question, then tripped back aboard with no answer but very jolly indeed, a little after midnight.

109

We set sail across the heaving Bay of Biscay to Gibraltar, then through the Mediterranean to Alexandria. On the way out I edited a *Ranpura* magazine, which was typed and distributed from my office. We also started Radio *Ranpura*. George Anderson was responsible for this and became a popular announcer. The magazine was rather high-brow, but popular all the same.

There was no shore-leave at Alex, owing to the stormy political situation that was gathering. A crisis was looming between England and President Nasser of Egypt; we were sent back to Malta to reinforce the British Fleet. There we stayed, moored in the middle of Grand Harbour, for many weeks as Heavy Repair Ship for the Eastern Mediterranean Fleet.

Most of my work up to that point had been helping the Captain to establish the ship's routine and distributing his many and various orders; also in bringing up to date the records of the men in the ship – some twelve hundred of them – and keeping them properly filed. But from now on, besides everything to do with the ship itself, we had to deal with the requests that came for repair from ships in the fleet. These had to be received, logged and passed to the departments concerned. There was also welfare work to be done, now that we were abroad. The Divisional Officers were responsible for this, but most of the paperwork fell to me. I was surprised at the amount of trouble the Navy took to help someone whose wife was ill or (sometimes unexpectedly) pregnant.

Despite the work there was time to explore Malta and enjoy some of its amenities, especially the tennis club where I had some fierce battles. Malta is a steep and dazzling island with many steps and the blaze of brilliant sunshine on white stone. Once George and I went to St. Paul's Bay in a rattling old bus, and didn't think much of it; and there was the memorable occasion of my twenty-first birthday party, when my friends took me ashore to Valetta and dined and over-wined me. I enjoyed this immensely but hated the after-effect of being overwined, with my cabin going up and down and round and round unasked. I decided not to let it happen again.

One curiosity about going ashore in Malta was that Captain Marsh decided that officers should wear caps or hats ashore (even in civies) so that they could salute the quarter Deck when they left and returned to the ship. We should have worn caps anyway because of the glare of the sun; but we did not want to, especially for such a bizarre reason. Now it happened that the porthole (called the "scuttle") of my cabin was by the steps of the gangway up and down which people went on leaving and returning to the ship. I kept this open so that my friends could leave their caps, having duly saluted the quarter deck, on their way ashore and then retrieve them, ready for saluting again, when they returned aboard. Captain Marsh once met us ashore and was puzzled and not too pleased to see us without our caps; but he saw us again from his cabin when we crossed the quarter deck; and there we were, be-hatted and saluting as large as life. If we hadn't been, there would have been trouble. When he next saw me, my arms stuffed with papers for him to sign, I could see that he was itching to ask me how we managed it; but he didn't and I didn't tell him.

I had the job of typing the confidential reports on all the officers, so I was much in the Captain's trust. The most important part of these reports was the section devoted to an officer's professional ability, indicated by a number ranging from one to nine. "Five" had to be the average, but as we had so many highly qualified technical officers aboard, the average was more like seven or eight. This meant that the Admiral's Office would reduce all the assessments by two or three, which was bad for the genuine RN officers who needed a high mark for their prospects for promotion. I wrote a covering letter to the Admiral's Office to explain this matter and persuaded the Captain to sign it. Whether it made any difference or not, I do not know. On one occasion he wrote a scathing report on an officer and this was returned by the Admiral's Secretary saying that it should have been underlined in red and signed by the officer to show that he had seen it. So I had to get hold of the poor chap, show him what the Captain thought of him, and get him to sign. After which we went and had a drink together.

Captain Marsh deplored the general ignorance of seamanship throughout the Navy. When "ordinary seamen" came before him to be rated "able seaman" – an automatic procedure worth quite a lot of money – Captain would bark questions at them, such as, 'Box the compass.' If the candidate did not know what this meant or how to do it, the Captain would refuse him promotion. I then had to go to him afterwards and point out that by the new King's Regulations and Admiralty Instructions he was bound to promote the man however little he understood about boxing the compass. Captain Marsh gave in with a sigh and told me to see to it; so I summoned the man and told him that the Captain had changed his mind and that he was now in the lucrative position of being an "able seaman".

There was a concert party which was held ashore in aid of the hospital, produced by a senior surgeon. HMS *Ranpura* was asked to help with technical matters to do with staging and lighting. This was something that we were well able to do, and we were duly given the "credits" so much desired by the Captain. But as we became involved, an additional request came aboard for two men who could sing, to take part in a "Schubertiad". The Captain, anxious to oblige, pressed me hard to volunteer and to find someone else who could sing. It happened that Writer Webb (from George Anderson's office) was known to have a good tenor voice, so he was "volunteered" to me by my own writers and was accordingly press-ganged into joining me in this sacrificial act. We found ourselves playing the parts of "merry peasants" in a performance of the sickly (to my mind) *Rosamunde*. My colleagues were much amused and I never lived it down.

There was a row in the ward-room caused by some senior officers refusing to sign their mess-chits at the time of drinking in the evenings, and then editing them the next morning at breakfast. I objected to this in the complaints book in the mess; not very tactfully, I suspect. Uncle Vaughan took me aside and gave me a lecture on the subject and made me retract before serious trouble boiled up. So I apologised for any aspersions that I may have cast.

Once an officer's steward was caught stealing and was sent to detention. I suspect it was the same discontented steward who had thrown our caps overboard into the Solent when we were at Portsmouth at the beginning of the commission. The amazing sequel on that occasion was that the next afternoon I went sailing with Sub-Lieutenant Cleaves, and there on the "port quarter" (or whatever) was a floating object, which turned out to be an officer's cap: indeed, my cap! The result of this coincidence was that I always wore a scruffy, sea-salt's cap which made it look as if I had been to sea for years. My friends were quite jealous.

One day we set sail with the Eastern Mediterranean Fleet, Vice Admiral Sir Algernon Willis flying his flag in the cruiser HMS *Ajax*. We were soon detached from the fleet with orders to sail to the Aegean Islands and give whatever help they needed with repairs, supplies and medical attention. This we did, visiting Andros, Skiathos and Skiros, Limassol in Cyprus, and harbours on the mainland of Greece; but unfortunately not Piraeus.

To these we offered our services, medical, supply and repair. I remember David Bett looking after a boy with a broken arm; Smithy the dentist being made to earn his passage; watches coming for repair to the Ordnance department; trouble cured with regard to an island's electricity supply; and a fisherman bringing his boat with a fault in the diesel engine. We also put on lavish parties for the local inhabitants and then went ashore for the return match. No wonder we were popular.

I had nothing to do with the repair side of our activities, except to receive the letters (which sometimes required a little knowledge of Greek) and pass them to the appropriate department; and as no one was leaving or joining the ship, I had less to do than usual and plenty of opportunity to enjoy the islands in all their beauty. They are jewels floating on the deep blue sea (Homer's "wine-coloured" does not seem the right word for the sea). Ashore they are mostly olive groves and steep, stepped terraces. There was little opportunity for walking, such as I had enjoyed on the Sussex Downs or the Long Mynd. It was better just to sit and sniff the air and gaze at the sea and talk and drink retsina. But I did manage a walk with Uncle Vaughan, over the hills of Corfu with oysters for supper, which he taught me how to eat.

We went to Limassol, on the southern shore of Cyprus. This was like our other visits, except that the Mayor came aboard and begged audience with the Captain. In the Captain's eyes I was supposed to be able to speak Greek which surely I should have learnt when serving in the *Kanaris*; so I was told to stand by and listen to the interpreter to make sure he was doing his job properly – something that was far beyond my linguistic capacity, but Captain Marsh thought that I could at least look as if I understood. The gist of the Mayor's plea was that we should extend from him an invitation to the British government to make Limassol the naval headquarters of the Eastern Mediterranean. Captain Marsh ummed and ahed in a friendly and diplomatic spirit and promised without commitment to pass the message on to his superiors. The Mayor went ashore satisfied; and the Captain reported the conversation to C.-in C.-Med. by a long signal cyphered by me; but we did not hear any more. This story shows how popular we were in Cyprus in those days.

One day some of us took a long, steep walk up a valley at Argostoli in Cephalonia. When we got back news had come of the mining of two destroyers, HMS *Saumarez* and HMS *Volage*, off the Albanian coast. The Captain decided to get up steam immediately as we might be needed; and sure enough we soon had an "urgent" signal from the Commander-in-Chief to proceed "with utmost dispatch" to Corfu, where Captain Marsh was to act as Naval Officer in Command.

I had two embarrassing episodes as "Greek interpreter". One was at a party ashore at Samos. Captain Marsh turned to me and said, 'Tell this person that I have eaten rose-petal jam on Mount Athos.' I could manage it all but the "rose-petal jam" – and Captain Marsh, seeing my hesitation, lost all faith in my ability as an interpreter. To him one either knew a language or one didn't: not knowing the Greek for "rose-petal jam" clearly meant that I didn't.

The other occasion was when we were at Corfu looking after the *Saumarez/Volage* affair, with strict orders from the C.-in-C. to do all we could to please the Greeks. A message came aboard from the Greek authorities inviting "the Captain and Officers to a – something"; I did not quite know what, but the Greek word was a compound of "ecclesia", and I guessed that it would be some sort of church service, in honour, perhaps, of a local saint. The Captain decided that they ought to attend, so off they went in the ship's launch, the Captain, the Commanders (S) and (E) and a sub-lieutenant or two, all in their "Number One" uniform, swords at the ready, to the expected religious event. But two hours later they returned, pawed and grubby, having found themselves at a scout rally; for "ecclesia", as I should have known, means "assembly". They were unreasonably angry and it took a long time for me to live this down. So much for a classical education.

HMS *Saumarez* had been mined in what were supposed to be clear waters off the Albanian coast, after a cruiser had gone at full speed through the same area unharmed. This was a miracle because a mine hitting the cruiser would have caused much greater loss of life. The *Saumarez* was down by the bows, so HMS *Volage* towed her backwards into safety but got herself mined in the process, with serious loss of life. At Corfu our people went aboard to repair the ships enough to make them sea-worthy and fit to be towed to Malta.

Meanwhile the wires of communication buzzed, and for a few days we were at the centre of the globe with news bulletins every day bringing the world up to date with our affairs. I picked up some gossip ashore which was reported, but this was clearly an Albanian not a Greek action. Albania was eventually fined a large sum of money by the World Court, which, as far as I know, has never been paid. It was an act of aggression by the most communist of all countries to show the world that although the war was over, there was still bitter tension between communism and the capitalist West. The grey pall of the "Cold War" would darken the world for the next forty years.

While some of our crew worked hard on the two stricken destroyers, social life went on, with a deliberate attempt to fraternise with the Greek population. A football match was held and there was a "compulsory" dance following a notice from the Commander that "the following officers will go ashore at such a time to such a place". But despite my crude shuffling which went for dancing, and with the aid of a noisy "hokey-kokey", we enjoyed ourselves.

There was a strange incident with two submarines that came into Corfu harbour. Captain Marsh was critical of the way they had entered harbour and sent a signal requiring the senior commanding officer to come aboard the *Ranpura*. The signal was not the friendly RPC ("Request the Pleasure of your Company"), but the official "You-are-in-for-trouble" signal, ICU. But the reply came back, WMP ("With Much Pleasure") – which Captain Marsh took to be impertinent. So a row was looming – which Captain Marsh did not want, for he was a good man and there were plenty of more important matters occupying his mind.

So he asked me to go aboard the submarines and talk the submarines' CO into some sort of apology. I did this and was very well received. The Commanding Officer had misconstrued both the Captain's signal and (he said) his own hasty reply and promised that no offence was meant. Both captains looked tired and bedraggled after a gruelling time on and under the sea; and they didn't want any trouble either. So they came aboard peaceably and Captain Marsh, without losing his dignity as NOIC, spoke to them kindly but firmly about the correct way of entering harbour. Meanwhile I had greatly enjoyed my drinks aboard one of the submarines, the only one I have ever visited.

And there was the panatomime. It had started long before on our cruise of the islands, and there were those who wanted to drop it now, especially as the Naval Architect, Lieutenant-Commander Dale, was at the heart of the crisis; and he was our pianist. But the cause of entertainment prevailed and the panatomime, *Babes in the Gut*, went riotously ahead. In the pantomime (music by Dr. Bett – much of it after Sullivan) George and I were the "babes" dressed as matelots: we got into trouble in the Gut (the disreputable part of Malta) with drink ("Pussers' Limers") and some wickedly alluring girls. We were arrested by the Shore Patrol of Malta (after Noel Coward's *The Stately Homes of England*) and duly rescued by the Good Fairy, Electrical Commander Vaughan, a man of enormous girth. It went down well on the ship and the Captain watched it every night from the deck outside his cabin. On the last night he made an appropriate speech; and he mentioned my performance in the "flimsy" (personal assessment) he gave me when I left the Navy.

We sailed next day for Malta, with the destroyers being towed in company. It was a slow voyage.

When we reached Malta Captain Marsh thought that I looked tired and needed some leave, so I was sent off in a destroyer to Sicily with a travel warrant for the train to Taormina. There the grandest hotel in the place had been taken over by the Navy for officers on leave. It was a wonderful week of total idleness. I climbed the hill above the town and signed my name in a visitors' book underneath such names as field marshals Kesselring, Rommel and Montgomery; and I went to the market and bought a picture and a dog's head walking stick which the carver carved as I watched. I still possess it.

Two officers and I had a day in a Jeep with a driver – at no charge. We drove to Mount Etna, and most of the way up. We went to the beach at the bottom of the hill below Taormina and bathed – late at night. And on the last night there was a party with lots of Wrens and nurses from the Haslar hospital in Malta. I came over shy and decided that I did not want to go to it, mostly because I was terrified of dancing and making a fool of myself. I had never danced, and in those days one danced with a partner and was expected to know how to do at least the rudimentary steps. At Corfu I had been ordered to go to a dance, and had resented it. So why should I spoil my leave by joining in something I thought I couldn't do? But my friends (temporary because I did not see them again after the leave) came to my cabin, made me get up and dragged me to the party. There I met a nurse whom I liked very much and she told me that dancing was easy if you had any sense of music and rhythm; so I tried and enjoyed it, and have enjoyed dancing ever since.

I loved that nurse – more than any girl I had ever met, and in a different way, not to be repeated till I met Juliet. We talked together all the way back to Malta in our destroyer; talked and talked, side by side, oblivious of everything and everyone else. But at Malta the relationship ceased. The *Ranpura* was under orders to sail: there was a week's work to catch up; men were leaving the ship and others were joining, homeward bound for demobilisation; and for a few days I was frantically busy with no hope of getting ashore. We duly sailed for Gibraltar and the Gare Loch, through the steepest and wildest seas in the Bay of Biscay and the Irish Channel that I had ever encountered. But I was much too busy to be sick.

In the Gare Loch we prepared to pay off, with most of the ship's company going on long-term demob leave. Officers too; and I was on the list with only about ten days to serve before I left. There was an "end-of-term" feeling, but no festivities. Many were worried about what sort of future they were going to. The regular naval officers were desperate for promotion before it was too late. Gunner ("Mr") George Ward was one of these, and I took a lot of trouble writing the right sort of request for promotion to commissioned rank. The Captain was supportive – but I never heard the result. David Bett was another. He decided that he would like to stay in the Navy on a shortterm commission. This needed lots of paperwork and the right recommendation from the Captain, duly, indeed, enthusiastically given.

As regards the ship itself and its daily routine, nothing seemed worth doing; and the prevailing attitude amongst us about-to-be-demobbed lot was "Couldn't care less", an attitude that I found was typical of the whole country at that time, and it took me, to whom such an attitude does not come naturally, some time to shake it off. There was a row in the wardroom because one of the senior officers struck a rating, an appalling steward who almost literally asked for it. It seemed to me to be a likely end to this officer's promising career. He was RN and, like Captain Marsh, had come up from the Lower Deck. But I have since learnt that he went on to become a captain RN himself.

At last the day came for me to leave the ship. I left the Captain's Office to the one writer still there (Trevor Dawson); Captain Marsh gave me a family Bible which he possessed and had duly inscribed. He also gave me a very generous "flimsy"; except that by my own suggestion, for reasons already explained, he assessed my "professional ability" as five, the average. This enabled George Ward's and David Bett's eights to mean more.

My steward, Briers, who painted my initials on my green pusser suitcase in letters that only he could have done, packed all my things and was almost tearful at my departure. I was in a state of suspended excitement. I could not believe, let alone feel it. I was leaving the Navy. I would go to Portsmouth to collect my demob suit and, literally, a bowler hat, though I cannot remember ever wearing it. I threw away my officer's uniform and the very "tiddly" rating's "fore-and-aft" uniform that I had had made in Alexandria in 1944 and had only worn at my interview for commission and in the *Ranpura's* pantomime. So with these symbolic, sartorial actions, I turned my back on the Navy. I can honestly say that in terms of responsibility and good work, I had done well. Now I looked forward to a vague, cloudy future with thoughts of university. I had a place booked at St. Edmund Hall, Oxford. But would I go for teaching? Ordination? I really didn't know.

However, my leaving the *Ranpura* and the Navy was delayed for two days by fog! Would you believe it? Fog descended on the Gare Loch. One of the ship's boats had failed to return, and others were forbidden to leave the ship. So – back to the deserted wardroom and my empty cabin. Eventually the fog lifted and there was the Gare Loch in its bare, wintry beauty, saddened by the line of naval ships that were paid off and deserted and waiting to be scrapped. *Ranpura* herself was not scrapped and she became a depot ship for deep-sea fishing.

Meanwhile, I took the train to Glasgow and then a first class (for the last time in my life) sleeper to London, King's Cross. *Ranpura* had the last word because I was rudely awoken at midnight by three ratings, who were making the same journey. They burst into my cabin singing George Anderson's and my pantomime song, *Two Little Green ODs Are We* (tune as in *The Mikado*), from *Babes in the Gut*. I was rather moved.

Chapter 11
St Andrew's, Eastbourne

After my first return from the Far East at the end of 1945 my father had moved from Charlton, SE7, to Roehampton, SW15. At Charlton he had been the only vicar left in the neighbourhood, all the adjacent parishes being vicarless through bombing or natural retirement. He was exhausted, my mother more so. The war years, with the bombing and the V1 and V2 rockets, which I had learnt about with horror from letters from home, and the rationing and deprivations, had made an indelible mark on her. Now they were at Roehampton, a village on the edge of the greenest part of London and Father was happy in his ministry there with many parishioners who had a hunger for "the things of God". He became Rural Dean of Richmond and Barnes with a ministry that was creative and fulfilling.

But I was not enamoured at the prospect of living at home, back in vicarage life; and this period was the most unsettled of my life. There was little of the bubbling fun of school days, nor was there the responsibility and the challenge of life at sea, with the world to visit and history in the making. Nor was there the sense of purpose and demands and fulfilment of my later days in ministry.

Vicarage life at Roehampton was difficult to settle down to. The war was over, Father busy in his new parish, Mother still shattered by the bombing and seemingly in bad health, though she lived to be ninety-two. I spent hours playing the piano, strumming through music that was too hard for me to play properly – for instance Beethoven's *Storm Sonata* which I could play by heart, except that I could not play it! My arms used to seize up at the difficult bits, even though I played the last movement slowly, loving its rippling flow, as it runs out into nothing in the last bar. Mother was once asked what she thought Heaven would be like and she answered, 'No music, I hope,' with reference, I feel sure, to my practising. If only I had spent some of my demob money on having piano lessons!

I had nine months to fill in before going up to Oxford, so I applied to the teachers' agent, Messrs Trueman and Knightly, who quickly fixed me up with a job to teach for two terms at St Andrew's Preparatory School at Eastbourne.

This was a top-class prep-school snuggling under the downs at Eastbourne, with splendid playing fields, fine buildings and a separate house for the assistant masters. There were four Heads, all partners. The senior was Philip Liddell. He was tall, gentle, shrewd, understated. I never knew him angry, but he had firm control of everyone, partners included. Mr Harrison had little to say, but was an excellent teacher of scholarship maths. J.L. Bryan was the third. He had played cricket for England, touring Australia. He ran the cricket and the rugger so well that to watch the first teams playing was like watching a professional team in miniature; the cricket especially with its fast bowlers, cordon of slip fielders, who practised every evening on the "slips machine", and some solid and some exciting batsmen.

The fourth partner was my particular friend, John Beales. He had been a major in the Army and much of his talk consisted of improbable tales about what he had done in Palestine. He also ran the boxing and persuaded me to help him. On his duty days I used to accompany him as he patrolled the school, keeping a wary eye on all that was going on.

There were two features of "break" at that school. One was the incessant roller-skating which the boys did, up and down, spinning and turning, rarely coming to harm, and strengthening their muscles and their balance. The other was a wired-in courtyard where they could do anything with balls without hurting property or losing the balls. Yard cricket and yard football went on all the time, and the boys acquired their ball-skills.

There was a pianist on the staff who played in the evenings in the masters' house but was bored with the school with its limited scope for music in which none of the headmasters showed any interest. He was nice to me because I used to listen to him and could "talk music"; but he thought nothing of my piano-playing and said that I was doing it "all wrong".

Why parents should pay huge fees to have people like me and David Stafford (a colleague, ex RAF) teach their sons is a mystery. Neither of us knew anything about any subject, let alone how to teach it. He and I were told to take the bottom form for mathematics, together. I did not want to push myself, but I realised that one of us must take charge, so at the first lesson I decided to count slowly up to ten and then take charge if he had not already done so. He didn't, so I did.

We started by making a plan of where the boys sat and tested ourselves on their names. After that I gave them sums to do and made them learn their tables. They were aged seven or eight, and one of the brightest (I can see him now sitting in the front row) was Peter Snow of present television fame. I found him many years later taking his family round Ripon Cathedral. The glazed "I am used to this but it annoys me all the same" look quickly vanished from his face when I reminded him that I used to teach him mathematics at St Andrew's, Eastbourne.

I also taught the scholarship set history. Dreadful, because I did not know any except the ancient Latin and Greek history I had studied with the Classics at Lancing, and a few unjoined-up patches I could remember from Belmont days. However, having been in the Navy, I felt that I should learn something about Nelson. So, on the principle that the best way to learn is to teach (and quite a good way to teach is to be learning), I read what I could, studied his battles and then explained them on a blackboard in chronological order. I found myself delighting in the ingenuity of the tactics, the amount of trouble that Nelson was prepared to take (for instance, spending a night in an open boat taking soundings outside Copenhagen) and his moral courage when he took his fleet from Toulon in the Mediterranean to the West Indies to chase the French with nothing but his intuitive calculations to guide him. He had to agonise over his guess with all its consequences for the year and a half that he was at sea. This thrilled me, and I hope that something of it rubbed off on to the boys; for isn't teaching a matter of sharing enthusiasm as well as imparting knowledge?

I Was Glad

Once I was given a ten-year-old boy (Michael Fletcher) to coach. He had missed the first half of his first term at Latin. Would I help him to catch up? By the end of the term he and I were miles ahead of the others and I can still feel something of the excitement he had in grasping one firm rule after another and building up a system of constructing sentences, which means constructing thought. He was clever and had an excellent memory. We both enjoyed the lessons. I met his mother, once, watching him in a cricket match. She was pleased and slightly amused by my estimation of Michael's character and ability. I wonder what has happened to him. I also taught an able English set and grounded them in grammar which I did myself at Belmont. The sweet logic of it appealed. I also enjoyed their chirpy essays. I taught them to punctuate a sentence (by listening to it), but had to be careful to hide from them my own weakness in spelling.

I also taught "Scripture". This appalled me. I could not remember learning any at all at Lancing, except a book called *Christian Verities*, full of rude illustrations perpetrated by its former owner. What was I to do? It was generally known that I was "destined for the Church". I was therefore expected to be infallible on religious subjects and was allowed no pleas of ignorance. So I chose what was obviously the shortest gospel, St Mark's, which I read through with the class, I keeping a chapter ahead and finding it very difficult to comprehend. Why no birth stories? Why such short stories, barely linked together? How sharply pointed they were! What did some of the sayings of Jesus mean? Was he deliberatly putting people off with his parables? What a lot of the book is about the death of Jesus; and what a skimpy account of his resurrection, hardly more than a "happy ending". Was I really going to Oxford to study all this? Yes, indeed; in Greek with Professor Lightfoot; and many of these questions would be raised and discussed in the detail of the text and in close comparison with the other gospels and the wider context of Christian theology. Meanwhile these lessons at St Andrew's were not easy, and I was as pleased as the boys were when they lured me away from the text into moral and religious discussions which we all found more interesting. (And even, occasionally, alas, I confess, into stories of "what I did in the Navy" and what life was like at sea.)

Do I have rosy spectacles about those two terms at St Andrew's? I did enjoy them. I liked the boys and had no disciplinary difficulties. It was a happy school with hardly any use of the stick. John Beales and I would go round the classrooms and day rooms and dormitories when he was on duty, he shouting with harsh, kind humour at everyone for all the misdemeanours being perpetrated or planned. Occasionally it would be, 'Firbank, stop that at once. Bend over.' Whack (with a slipper); but the Firbanks never seemed to mind and no one thought his methods reprehensible. Boys did well. Some got scholarships to public schools. I found myself sucked into the life of the place.

On one occasion all the Heads went off in the evening to celebrate Mrs Liddell's birthday, leaving me in charge of the school. Philip Liddell paid me the nice compliment of saying that I had a calming effect on the boys and didn't make them excited and silly. He summoned me to his study one day to beg me to stay in the school and to take up prep-school teaching as a career. This was tempting (and, of course, flattering); but as so often with temptations, when they are explicitly stated and faced they are already halfway to being defeated. Boys pall after a few weeks of term. Prep-school teaching would close me in. I wanted to open out. And I would never be able to buy a school of my own even if I thought that this would be a good thing to do.

There was very solemn religion every day in the school chapel, with a morning assembly consisting of a psalm (Anglican chant), a lesson from the Bible, a hymn and prayers. J.L. Bryan used to read the lesson, which was nearly always an Old Testament story – good for the Common Entrance scripture examination. No one seemed to question or rebel against chapel. This was 1947 – I had to wait till the 1960s to find the rebellion I expected, at Lancing. St Andrew's chapel would not have put people off, but it might have inured them against the excitement and challenge of Christianity.

Games were more important. I was once playing with the boys in the nets on a summer evening, and Mr Bryan came rushing out to tell me to stop batting at once lest the boys should copy me! I was cross and went off in a sulk to play tennis with my colleagues, one of whom had had the same treatment. There was a tennis court, but the boys (for some good cricketing reason?) were forbidden to play on it. However,

I was allowed to play cricket in the staff match and (a) I shared a stand with J.L. Bryan of England and (b) I caught a heroic catch at point which was sheer self-defence, the ball sticking to my hand just in front of my face.

All this for £50 a term plus full board; and teaching at St Andrew's led to teaching and tutoring jobs during the Oxford vacations. I spent the greater part of one Christmas holiday with David Roscoe, staying in a hotel in Grand Avenue, Hove, and coaching him in the daytime for Common Entrance. He was bright and did not need extra tuition. In fact, I was more child-minder than teacher because his parents were too busy to have him around in the daytime. I also tutored Christopher Halliday who lived in Wales. He was from another school. His parents (Professor and Mrs Halliday) were intimate friends of Matthew Smith, the English painter. Their house in mid-Wales was full of his pictures which I came to love in a way that I had never loved pictures before: warm, exuberant colours, golds, browns and reds, voluptuous nudes, the sun-baked hills of France, satisfying groups of fruit and flowers; all in blazing oil which leapt from the canvas and drew me into their glowing, vibrant worlds.

Matthew Smith used to stay with the family. At first he was kept apart from me, like a treasure that couldn't be handled. But he came into the drawing-room once when I was playing the E Flat minor Prelude of Bach. He sat and listened and told me that he was sure it had been written in one blaze of inspiration. Some of his pictures, he said, were like that and if he did not finish them in one sitting they would become lifeless and dull. We had some long talks and I felt immensely privileged to have got to know such a great Englishman. I always feel angry when people say that they have not heard of him. Art education in this country is appalling. Mine at Belmont and Lancing was nil. Juliet shares my feeling about Matthew Smith and we go to his exhibitions if ever we hear of one, as we did recently in Bath.

The Hallidays were kind to me, seeing that I was living on top of them for the whole of the summer. Christopher changed from being resentful at first to quite a friend later. He was mad on cricket and I used to bowl to him in the garden nets. Professor (of German) Halliday and I had long talks. He was amazed that someone who could talk about art and music and politics and the world was nevertheless bent on being a priest. Mrs Halliday was more sympathetic about my religious propensities; and we even went to church together, she, Christopher and I, on Sundays.

My other tutoring job was preparing Christopher Gault for entrance to Uppingham, living with the family at Harting in Sussex. I slept in a pub in the village but worked at their house all the day, with lots of teaching but plenty of time to do my own work as well. There were some enjoyable social occasions with this family – tennis parties and dances – and I fell for a doctor's daughter who (it seemed to me) was promptly whisked away and sent to see her cousin in New Zealand! Once I stayed with Christopher and his own father at a large estate in Surrey. I was met by the butler but declined to give him the keys of my ill-packed suitcase. We dressed for dinner in that establishment; and I felt like a character in *Villette*!

I had two enjoyable touring holidays: one in the Summer of 1947 with Brian Wallas, Douglas Bean and Patrick Halsey, our erstwhwile housemaster, my future colleague at Lancing; the other to Spain with Brian and Douglas in Brian's car. We drove through France into Spain as far as Burgos and back via Pau and Calais. It was enjoyable in a frothy sort of way. Brian and I shared the driving. The distances were enormous – too much so.

The other earlier tour was of the "three northern capitals", Copenhagen, Stockholm and Oslo. We travelled by air and it took all my hard-earned demob gratuity. After it was over I wished that I had bought a motor-bike instead. It was essentially a "looking back to school-days" holiday. But we three had grown up since Lancing days and Lancing humour and mimicry had worn thin. However, just to see these cities struggling back from the drab war years was interesting, though Stockholm was irritatingly prosperous and expensive.

By the end of the summer holidays 1947 I had shaken off my demob blues and was ready to go to Oxford University, study Theology and enjoy self, before buckling down again to that task-master, "responsibility".

Chapter 12
Oxford

One day, on leave from the Navy, I went with my father to look for an Oxford College. First we visited St Edmund Hall (known as Teddy Hall), where some OLs had gone before me. The reports were good, and I fell for the place at once: its intimate quadrangle with wisteria growing up the walls and the acacia tree leaning gently across; the pleasing well in the middle, around which much beer would be drunk; the chapel, small, dark, intimate, with its own smell of polish and hymn-books; the library in which you could sit and read and watch what was going on in the quadrangle below; the dining hall with its portraits and raised High Table and the pleasant gallery which, in later days, I loved to eat in because my friends and I could sit there, all-seeing but unseen by our superiors below.

I was invited to meet the Senior Tutor, who said that although my academic record was poor, it was good enough for me to be admitted. Perhaps they were short of potential students, or was he impressed with my naval officer's uniform? Anyway he gave me an immediate "Yes", and asked me to sign my name on the roll. Father said, 'Shouldn't we look at some more colleges?' No: I liked this one.

So, in September 1947 I matriculated at St Edmund Hall in the University of Oxford to read Honours Theology. My tutor was the Vice-Principal, later to become Principal and one of the greatest patristic theologians of his day, the Reverend Canon Prebendary Dr J.N.D. Kelly.

My room was one of the most desirable rooms in the College, in the far right-hand corner of the quadrangle as you enter it. In the next room was Robin Day. We were to inhabit different spheres of university life, he and I; he amongst the talkative and opinionated greats in the Oxford Union, of which he became President; I more Teddy Hall orientated. Robin and I were on friendly terms, but not close friends. His was a noisy room with people constantly in and out causing gales of excited laughter. He often burst in on me (whether I was there or not) to "borrow" my sherry.

Amongst my many friends was Nicholas Stacey, who had been in the RN. He had been educated at Dartmouth Naval College and had all the personal characteristics of a naval officer. He was also an Olympic runner. Indeed to see him running was like having a close-up view of a steam engine in full throttle. Nick followed me to Cuddesdon where he picked my brains on theological subjects. Later he came to Basingstoke at my request to address the youth guild in the parish church. He went for them! "The Holy Spirit doesn't expect you to sit around playing ping-pong": hot stuff.

I threw myself into Hall affairs with enthusiasm and enjoyment. I spent too many hours, no doubt, in the bar – known as the buttery – drinking beer and playing shove-halfpenny with a fellow reprobate, Teddy Morgan, and others. Teddy and I were the best, and I once did the whole board in one go. I used to play the common-room (JCR) piano when I thought there was no one around. I sang with the Chapel Choir and worshipped in Chapel regularly, as, indeed, John Kelly expected us ordinands to do; and I wouldn't have missed his sermons for anything. They were the best sermons I have ever heard.

I played tennis and achieved the distinction of being the first reserve for the Teddy Hall Second Six and played in several matches. Once I played in the Parks with J.N.D. Kelly himself and two others, and we hit the ball as hard as we could trying for winners all the time. It was a rare, almost mystical experience to find perfect co-ordination between all the parts of my body and my brain and my partner's intentions. (Would that I could do it today at golf!) Sometimes I played squash with plenty of puff and lather – but found it difficult to win points.

I tried soccer but was not good enough, so I resorted to being the Hall's tame referee, which I enjoyed, except when the team were cross with me. Once I played rugger, persuaded to do so because there was no one else to fill the last place – but never again. It nearly killed me.

Also in the scrum that day was Elvet Lewis, who became Vicar of St Stephen's, Worcester. In our vicar days (I was at Pershore) he was strongly opposed to all liturgical change. I debated this with him on a Worcester Deanery occasion and used the Teddy Hall rugger scrum as an analogy of two people who were really on the same side but got in each other's way as they scrambled for the ball: it was to explain how at heart we were one, but disagreed about almost everything!

I once played hockey for Magdalen, persuaded by Brian Wallas, who explained the rules as we cycled to the pitch.

I also rowed – or rather, coxed, being tall (an advantage) and light. After a few outings in which I learnt the jargon and the peculiar feel of steering the long, low craft, propelled by large men, I was asked to cox the Hall Second Togger for the lower-class races in the Lent term and then the Second Eight in the summer. I also coxed a scratch crew at a regatta at Marlow. In my heart of hearts I thought that I should have coxed the First Eight, but the place was taken by an abrasive American called Pat Murphy. I learnt to steer a cunning course through the notorious "Gut" where the river narrows and winds, and I could come up to the Green Bank very close to the trees, where the current was slowest. Paul Foote once complained that his oar brushed some leaves, but he did not seem to mind as on that occasion we bumped the boat in front, Queen's Two. In the previous day's race I had "washed off" Trinity Two, who were overlapping and trying to bump us, so my coxwainship was adjudged a success. We were a happy crew and I did my best to encourage the rowers with my loud voice and cheerful vocabulary. At the end of Eights Week I was thrown into the river.

And I boxed! Training every week at the University Boxing Club gymnasium in Alfred Street. I had boxed at Belmont and Lancing with some success; but now I found myself out-classed, not so much in boxing skill as in strength. I was a tall light-weight with a long reach which my opponents had to avoid if they were to hit me. The captain was also a light-weight, so there was no question of a blue; but I ran and trained and sparred and made myself useful at home matches, held in the Town Hall.

Mike Carr was my favourite sparring partner, a Teddy Hall geologist who got a First, but died young in Canada. We were good friends and I particularly enjoyed his company as he was not a "theologian", indeed not in our chapel circle. He was a searching agnostic but a positive atheist. I had to work hard to persuade him that I did not believe that the world was made in six days in the year 4002 BC. We had many talks together, and I always thought that he was a much better person than I was. After our last sparring session in the gym he said, 'Chris,' (very few people call me that) 'I think you are beginning to get the better of me. I'd better be careful or you'll have me converted as well.'

My most painful sparring was for one minute with the Welsh heavy-weight champion, Johnny Williams. He punched me on the nose, which was mildly broken and has remained so ever since. I remember drinking Teddy Hall soup with painfully cut lips at many a Hall dinner. Why? I do not know. I have a picture of me in the Boxing Club trying to look tough amidst some really strong – but very gentle – boxing friends.

Besides these athletic activities I went to as many plays and concerts as I could afford – which was not enough to satisfy. They included *Julius Caesar*, predictably in modern dress; *Macbeth*, badly produced by Ralph Richardson, who came onto the apron-stage to give the audience a lecture in decorum because we laughed when the witches' cauldron kept flicking on and off; and *A Midsummer Night's Dream* in the gardens of Worcester College, with the fairy world dancing over the lake in the dusk.

For music I remember a performance of the Vaughan Williams Sixth Symphony at the Sheldonian with the hushed fugue at the end disappearing into a thunderstorm. And I sang in the Bach Choir, with rehearsals every Monday evening. We sang the *St Matthew Passion*, Parry's *Job* (which we later broadcast in London under Sir Adrian Boult), the *Sea Symphony* (Vaughan Williams) and the *Hymn of Jesus* by Holst. Our conductor was the affable Tommy Armstrong, though occasionally in his absence Dr Andrews of New College would take over. Andrews used to put us through it, insisting that we sang the right notes at the right moment. We also did a performance of *The Dream of Gerontius*, made memorable by a young contralto called Kathleen Ferrier. In the summer vacation I scraped up enough money from tutoring to go to Glyndbourne to see *The Marriage of Figaro, The Rape of Lucretia* and *Albert Hering*.

I joined the Oxford Union and once made a speech on "Religion and Politics". It was well received but was important for one reason only. The President kept ruling that speeches had to be shorter and shorter, and by the time I was called I had to cut my speech to only a few minutes. Doing this I learnt that I am capable of "thinking on my feet", which is by no means the same thing as delivering a well-prepared speech without notes. I was to need this trick in later years when I was in the General Synod. But my attempts to do well in the Union were half-hearted. I once prepared a speech against the motion "This House Would Rather be a Dustman than a Don". I planned to give a murky description of a dustman's work, and end by saying with a snort, 'I'd rather be a Don.' But I wasn't called, so this funny oration was never heard, and that was the end of my interest in the Union.

But life was not all games and theatres, the Union, beer and shove-halfpenny. There was also the study of Theology, which I enjoyed far more than I had expected to. John Kelly was my tutor and I shared tutorials with Philip Haynes, who was ahead of me and was able to guide me in such tricky matters as "What was The Penteteuch and What was its Literary Problem", this being the subject of my first essay. I had been reading through the Old Testament before going up to Oxford and found it incomprehensible. But not so with J.N.D. Kelly. He helped me to learn about the formation of the Bible and the developing understanding of God that it contains. He also taught me that intellectual integrity is a vital part of spirituality.

This realisation transformed my religious outlook. It gave me my life-long conviction that sound teaching is an essential part of sharing the gospel with other people; and that this is all the more necessary today because (quoting Hosea) "My people are destroyed through lack of knowledge". This is what I find to be the case with 99 per cent of the non-believers that I know.

John Kelly taught me to understand as deeply as I could the complex literary, historical, philosophical and religious elements of the Bible: revealed through the Word of God Incarnate in Christ and developed by the Church, despite its mistakes and patchy understanding of the God of Love. Unfortunately, neither my memory nor my grasp of the minutiae of scholarship (linguistic variations in the text, for example) were good enough for academic distinction, especially where Greek and Latin were involved; but my conceptual understanding seemed to be good and I could grasp the twists and turns of doctrinal development.

The system of learning was that we were given a number of lectures to attend on the subject of the term's work; and had to write an essay each week, to be read aloud to our Tutor. We worked in pairs, Philip Haynes being my tutorial colleague. My essays were considered lively but not well researched: I found it difficult to read and digest all the books to which we were directed each week, though I was able to grasp the gist of a subject. I started one essay on the Eutychean heresy with the sentence, "Once upon a time there was an Archimandrite and his name was Eutyches and he lived in a convent near Constantinople." At the end of each term I had to appear before the Principal and the Fellows and hear a report on my progress. The understanding I showed was commended; but I was berated for not reading widely enough or in sufficient depth. But this was not for lack of trying.

I used to enjoy my tutorials with J.N.D.K. immensely, even when my essay had been finished at 3 a.m., or, once, not finished at all but bravely ad libbed! John would listen, quote you back to yourself, point out all the deficiencies in your argument, list the things you had omitted or misunderstood, and even know what you had read as well as what you hadn't. Once he said, 'I can see that you will become an eloquent preacher,' and even, 'You will have to write a book; but I do not know what on.' Once he strode over to me in the Quad, be-gowned and be-capped, when I was drinking beer with my friends by the well just after a tutorial, and said (in his most imitable voice and in the hearing of my friends, agog), 'Ah, Mr Campling, I believe I omitted to point out to you a mistake in that essay I had the pleasure of hearing you read this morning. The word "ilk" means "likeness" so it is tautologous to say, "Of similar ilk". You may say, "Similarly" or, "Of an ilk".' With which he strode away leaving me to finish my beer with my much tickled friends, all of them and me having for ever improved our English vocabulary.

John Kelly gave me no help at all with regard to the examinations themselves. I did a "collection" for him at the beginning of each term (a paper on last term's subject matter), but he rarely commented. I once pressed him a",' which I found disappointing, especially as he had told David Thawley that he might manage a "first". But he didn't, nor did the scholarly Philip Haynes. We all got "seconds", even Ivor Church who had come all the way from Australia to get a "first".

Parallel to my study of the Bible and the History of Doctrine and Ethics with J.N.D.K. was my study of the gospels in Greek with Professor R.H. Lightfoot. Philip Haynes introduced me, and I found myself one of a privileged group of six who studied with R.H.L. every week. We worked our way through the Synoptic Gospels – and woe betide anyone who had not prepared the Greek carefully. It was not enough to have read through an English version just before the session. Ivor Church was nearly turned out one day by a ratty Lightfoot who suspected him of memorising the Authorised Version. To me these sessions plus the lectures he gave on the gospels were immensely valuable, and much of my teaching and preaching has sprung from Lightfootian insights. For instance I taught the Fourth Gospel for A-Level at Lancing to Bruce Hawkins, who went out to the West Indies on VSO to teach in a secondary school. Bruce wrote and told me that he was now teaching the Fourth Gospel to West Indian girls. They little knew the learned source of what they were studying. I hope it reached them in its pristine form, but I doubt it.

Because of my time in the Navy I was excused the preliminary examination, Responsions, and I took my final examination, "Schools", at the end of the Michaelmas term 1949. My heavily annotated Greek New Testament shows how hard I worked at the text. I was badly caught out in the paper on the Apostolic Age (Acts and Epistles). I read through a book on the Pastoral Epistles the night before the exam and got a question on which I wrote reams on the theory I remembered from this book. 'Dreadful,' said John Kelly later when (as one of the examiners) he told me how I had done. 'You had clearly read one book and had been taken in by it.' However, I did satisfactorily on the Old Testament papers, well on the gospels, very well on the History of Doctrine (although I had revised for the wrong paper the night before: this shows that having actually to think is more important than churning out what one has just revised). In my best paper (ethics) I only answered three questions – going to town with my own conclusions about the ethics of punishment, a subject which I later used to discuss with Sixth Formers at Lancing working for scholarship General papers and with Angela on a walk in the rain in Wales before her Oxford entrance exam. I thought I had muffed it, but it turned out to be my best paper.

For my second year at Oxford I had to move out of Hall into digs. Nigel Grindrod, Peter White and I decided we would set up digs together, and we explored the city trying to find something comfortable, within easy biking distance, and affordable. Eventually we found just the place in a side-road off the Cowley road, with a delightful couple as our "landlords", Mr and Mrs Simpkinson. Mr would wake Peter every morning and say, 'Give Mr Campling's toe a pull."' We would then go down to a nicely cooked breakfast. We each had a desk in our bedroom, and the house had a piano on which I learnt to play Bach's E Flat Minor Fugue and Sibelius' *Romance* – to the delight, no doubt about it, of the others!

Nigel Grindrod remained one of my best friends until he died quite recently. He was one of the most Christianly and sensibly devout people I have known. He became a probation officer and then Head of Social Services for Croydon. Nigel and Ruth had a caravan near Pately Bridge, and Julie and I, Penelope, baby Angela and Wanda, our au pair, went to stay with them in extreme discomfort and hilarity. On one occasion we went and looked at Ripon Cathedral, and I thought, 'Just the place for me!'

Peter White was an ordinand, different from me in churchmanship, having a strong evangelical father who was Vicar, then Bishop, of Tonbridge. I stayed at his home one vacation and heard my first "evangelical" sermon, all about personal conversion. Peter rowed Seven in our boat. He was strong and always good-tempered and he took his part in throwing me into the river with particular relish.

I duly got my "second" and J.N.D.K. was pleased with me. If I were doing it all again I would try to learn less and think more; but I am not sure that that is a sensible judgement when I recall the extreme ignorance from which I began. You can only think from the basis of some knowledge, tempered by experience. Certainly the theological knowledge, thinking and attitude that I acquired at Oxford have affected me ever since. When I was asked by the Bishop of Winchester, prior to going to Basingstoke, what living person other than my parents had had the greatest influence upon me, I answered without hesitation, 'John Kelly'.

Towards the end of my time at Oxford I was uncertain about my vocation. I was tempted to go for teaching. Spiritually I had kept up with the basic disciplines, but although I enjoyed theology I found no priest at Oxford who inspired me or helped me at all. The Cowley Fathers once had a go, but I was appalled at their shrill opposition to the scheme of uniting the Church of South India with the Church of England, which I thought wholly good, and I detected a prying voyeurism in one of them who, when I made my confession, wanted to make me admit to sins I had never committed. J.N.D.K. was a devout and disciplined priest, but was not someone I could emulate, and when I consulted him he rightly made it clear that on the matter of vocation I would have to make up my own mind.

But teaching? Teaching what? Surely not Latin and Greek! A degree in Theology was not an obvious advantage for a career in secondary schools, and I did not fancy the delightful but unreal prep-school world. One day I had a letter from Canon Burrowes, my old chaplain on HMS *Sphinx*. He was now Principal of Salisbury Theological College and he invited me to see him at Salisbury with a view to going there for my two years' training. I did so – but could not bear the place, though I was delighted to see him again. The "pious young men" atmosphere put me off and I returned to Oxford determined to enrol for a Diploma of Education course and so become a schoolmaster. But – to my chagrin – there were no vacancies. I had left it too late. I would have to wait at least a year; and the fact was that with my degree the Diploma of Education people were not particularly interested in me.

Then – out of the blue – or perhaps straight from On High – a letter came from the Principal of Cuddesdon Theological College reminding me that I had once (when I was in the Navy, persuaded to do so by the Director of Service Ordinands over lunch at the Naval Club) put my name down to go there. Was I still interested? Would I care to go and see him and the college? John Kelly said that I should, so reluctantly I did – and loved the place at once. I fell for it and the people I met there. For instance, there was Ben Foster who had been head of Fields House when I first went to Lancing. Since then he had achieved high rank in the Royal Marines, had read History and was now preparing for ordination. What a person. He was manly, virile, good. I also liked the Principal, Kenneth Riches, later Bishop of Lincoln. So it was agreed that to Cuddesdon I should go, back on the main track of Christian ministry.

And you can see how God works through "non-theological" circumstances!

Chapter 13
Juliet (and Cuddesdon)

By now Juliet Marian Hughes had come into my life. We met on 18 December 1948 at a dance. Juliet was just eighteen. I can see her now: unique, standing as if she were apart, with an aura about her: a golden person. She made me tingle. She was very, very beautiful, and she spoke shyly in a husky voice. Michael offered to take her home after the party. But no way! She was mine, mine to escort and deliver to her home; and then to race back to my own home unable to think of anyone or anything else. This was different from mere "attraction" or even "admiration". I refused to discuss her when we discussed (as people always do) those we had met at the party. But more meetings occurred: on a bus (she was carrying chrysanthamums); at a dance; a dinner, along with Douglas and Mary and Michael, at Wimbledon. Then, more intimately, there were walks in Richmond Park when we talked about everything under the sun and I told her about the Navy and the seventeen countries I had been to and she told me about Devon and St Paul's Girls' School and her friends, the Shirleys Summerskill and Williams; and orthoptics. Then she came to the Worcester College Eights Week Ball at which we drank Pims without being aware of its lethal power and danced South American rumbas and sambas and tangos, she with grace, me with bounce.

In the summer of 1948 I stayed with Julie's Uncle George and Aunt at Stoodleigh in Devon. No one was good enough for their Julie, but I won Aunt Kitty's heart a little through the piano and singing, she being a good pianist; and I introduced her to the Britten folk-songs, which she liked as soon as she mastered the rhythms. Uncle George would have preferred me to have been in the Army, but was intrigued to find that I had served with Greeks on a Greek destroyer. He had had charge of Greeks in a prisoner of war camp in Eritrea, guarding the sailors who had been in the mutiny that my ship had avoided. So we had plenty to talk about and stories to swap.

One starry night Julie and I crept away from The Old Forge after supper. We leant over a gate looking at sheep; and I proposed and she accepted. Julie had cousins at Stoodleigh with whom she had spent her school holidays when evacuated from London. But we did not share our secret with them on that occasion. First we went to see Julie's alarming Uncle Roddy Williams, who had been in charge of Wakefield gaol, with his wife, Aunt Kitty. They lived at Iwerne Minster, deep in the heart of Dorset. I helped do things in the greenhouse, and I think I passed the test. Tony, Julie's brother, was a sapper in the Army, and, given that I had been in the Navy, he seemed to approve of me, especially for my much travelling. I liked him very much.

I really loved Kay, Julie's mother. She was a little dismayed when a future never-will-be-rich clergyman asked if he could marry her ultrabeautiful daughter; but she was very gracious about it, wondering, I think, whether Juliet had any idea of what she was letting herself in for. But she was assured by Curteis, her friend and golfing partner, that one day I would be a bishop (wrong! I became a dean – which suited us both much better). She was a mother-in-law to be proud of. Chute (my future vicar) once asked me about her, and I was pleased when he said, 'Like mother like daughter,' especially as he clearly fell for her, as he did for Julie herself. Anyway, after a tiny hesitation, Kay agreed, and she was always completely supportive. It's also true that Julie was much loved by my parents; and this was mutual, though she held my father in great awe – as everyone did.

We had a difficult time of "engagement", which was too long because the Church authorities insisted that I be ordained for at least a year before being married. This was wrong in theory and nearly disastrous in practice. They seemed to think that a person like me had two vocations, one to marriage and one to the ministry; and that it was too much to embrace both together. Nonsense! I had one vocation which was to be a married-to-Juliet priest. She was not going to be there "to support" me. She was part of it. Anyway, this meant waiting till 1953. I became head over heels bound up with my parish (Basingstoke) and she was miles away, first in London, then in Swindon practising orthoptics. Also I was busy at weekends when she was free. We survived – but it was difficult at the time.

When I was at Cuddesdon people behaved childishly about our engagement, with silly excitement, like school boys; but I had to put up with it. Julie came to Cuddesdon a few times, staying with Peter and Jane Mumford or David and Molly Thawley. They were generous and understanding. My other friends kidnapped Julie the first time she came, meeting her at the bus stop before the one I was waiting at. Ha Ha. On another occasion they wrote me a dreadful letter, purporting to come from Bishop Carpenter-Garnier, a retired bishop living in the village, father confessor to many of us. In this letter he strongly advised me to reconsider the matter of my engagement, which he had read about in *The Times*, and asked me to see him before making any further arrangements. The whole College watched me go pale as I read this letter at breakfast. But they quickly confessed, and I still have Colin James' letter of humble apology. He was to become the distinguished Bishop of Winchester! Julie put up with this well, but found my first year at Basingstoke as a curate more difficult to cope with.

Cuddesdon is a village on high ground about twelve miles out of Oxford. There is a church, a pub, a shop and clusters of houses on the hillside, and a friendly farm where Norman Taylor and I used to go for tea and television – for instance to see Hungary beating England at football – and friendliness. And it contains the best theological college in England. The Principal was also Vicar of the parish, so College and village life were in many respects integrated. There is some rivalry between them, friendly, as in the annual cricket match, but not always The pub was out of bounds to us, which was sensible because we d have dominated it and it would have been a distraction. The e was on top of the hill and there were lovely walks around, in ng the three-mile "Garsington Grind", which we sometimes did alo with our thoughts or with one another in deep and serious talk. I used to stride round it learning my songs and sermons by heart.

The Principal was Kenneth Riches, later to be Bishop of Lincoln. He had a staff of clergy of varying degrees of ability and experience. Only the Principal had any influence on me. The others suffered in comparison with John Kelly; but Riches ("Princeps") was stimulating on the subject of Christian doctrine, which he never allowed us to separate from spirituality and pastoral concerns. Doctrine was not "in a box", he would say: it was to be lived and experienced and shared. Also he introduced me to the idea of "balance in creative tension", which I have developed and spoken about all through my ministry. Indeed, it was the subject of my Ivor Church Memorial Lecture at St Francis College, Brisbane, in 1993.

The students at Cuddesdon were mature and able, none of them coming straight from school and university. For instance, there was Basil Heatherington, who had been a Bevin Boy working in the mines, and proud of the experience; David Jenkins – not the future bishop but an old Belmont friend. We had shared many troubles in those far-off days. He became a school chaplain and we used to meet and drink beer together at chaplains' conferences.

Peter Hammond, ex-RNVR, was expert on the Greek Orthodox Church. He used to hold bridge parties in the sacred "silent" time after compline, at which people bid silently and drank retsina and mead. When he was a curate I asked him how things were going and he answered, 'Terrible, I sacked the organist while the Vicar was on holiday.' He was full of fun and wickedness and profound goodness.

Peter Haynes became Dean of Hereford. He tried to sell the Mappa Mundi and I defended him on a Radio Three programme, *The Third Ear,* against a very rude MP (Patrick Cormack) who tried to stop me getting a word in edgeways. David Scott became an archdeacon and we used to meet and growl together at sessions of the General Synod.

They were a splendid set of men, varied, devoted, humorous, scholarly, leftish, rightish, outspoken, wise: Birts the Spike; Jim Challis, the smiling evangelical; Ian McNaughton, an older statesman – rather naughty – he took a liking to Julie when she stayed with his fiancée in Oxford. Christopher Cooke became my father's curate at Roehampton, although Father was not "high" enough for him. Christopher Lee-Smith, his friend, became a Franciscan monk

(Brother Roger) and got to know my son-in-law, Robert Magor, and Angela when Robert was priest-in-charge of a church in Plaistow. There was the prickly but saintly John Norton and the rich John Huggins, who married a Russian princess.

Philip Haynes, my Lancing and Teddy Hall friend, suffered from bad health and had to delay his ordination for two or three years. He became a distinguished Vicar of Purley, and was responsible for the publication of Professor Lightfoot's books.

Peter Mumford was an ex-Army colonel and county tennis player, who became Bishop of Truro. I last saw him when I took the retreat and preached at the ordination service in Truro Cathedral. He was critical of the spikey young men he inherited from his predecessor, the princely Bishop Leonard, who was a tough opponent of the ordination of women and other forward movements in the Church of England and later joined the church of Rome with much blowing of trumpets. Peter asked me to "sort them out" but I could not quench the excitement they showed when they practised "dressing up" the night before. (And I remembered myself when I first put on my naval officer's uniform!)

Colin James had also been in the Navy. I once stayed with him in Lincoln, where his father was archdeacon; he stayed with me at Roehampton, and we had a week's walking together on Dartmoor. He was a brilliant conversationalist, ready to see the humorous absurdity in situations and people; clever, devout, an affectionate friend.

I used to admire Ronald Gordon from amongst the basses when he accompanied the Bach Choir at its rehearsals. He was then the Balliol Organ Scholar. Now at Cuddesdon he took me and my singing into care. (I also went to Arthur Cramner for professional lessons.) Ronald taught me to sing *The Mystical Songs* by Vaughan Williams and *Let us Garlands Bring* by Gerald Finzi. I sang both groups of songs at Sunday ning "Bright Hours" – and managed to do them from memory. On ccasion the clock in the common-room struck nine as I was in g. Afterwards someone commiserated with me, but I was able t y truthfully that I had not heard it.

*　　*　　*

Ronald and I became friends and he invited me to accompany him to Rome on his motor-bike (an Aerial 250cc). First I had to learn to ride the bike and pass my test, which I did without difficulty. One of my solo rides was to see Juliet when she was living at Highworth to give her her engagement ring. I kept stopping and feeling for it to make sure it was still there. Then in October 1950 (the "Holy Year") Ronald and I set off. Rome is a very long way away, especially on a motor-bike. But we made it, going through France, over the Juras to Monte Carlo, then down through Italy. In Rome we stayed in the British Embassy, where Ronald's father was vice-consul. But he was away, so we stayed in his flat and were looked after and much spoilt by his housekeeper.

We had a week of luxury and sight-seeing, concentrating on "old Christian" rather than "Classical" Rome; and, of course, "new Christian" Rome because we received personal invitations to one of the Pope's public appearances at Castel Gandolpho. We were not impressed with this. The Pope himself was a distant figure who hurried on to the balcony, said a few words in all languages and then hurried away. People behaved well throughout the long wait before his appearance, but fought like cats to get out afterwards and catch one of the few trams that were waiting to take us, squabbling and pushing, the air heavy with garlic and Italian swear-words, back to the Eternal City.

Unfortunately, our bike had gone wrong on our last lap to Rome. We took it to a garage for repair, but when we collected it, paying a lot of money, it was no better. So we limped all the way home with the pump that circulates the oil giving trouble, necessitating more and more oil to be bought and poured in. We went via Assisi, staying for two nights in St Mark's Convent, sweetly attended by nuns and enjoying the holy peace of the place; thence to Florence, where we stayed in a vile youth hostel full of drunken Germans. There was no time or money for sight-seeing. We stayed for two nights with Ronald's friends in France and were taken for some magnificent and comfortable (after the saddle of the motor-bike) drives. Then we toiled back through France with all our money going on oil and with very little to eat. And oh it was cold! Whoever was riding pillion did so for half an hour feeling that it was impossible to get colder; but then he would take over in front and find that this was much worse –

and so on for hundreds of miles. We finished knowing that if we spent the night at a B&B we would have to push the bike the last ten miles; but if we oiled the machine we would have no money for supper or bed. So we decided to ask at a farm if we could sleep the night in their barn. When Madame learnt that we were English and had been in the forces in the war, she would not hear of "le barn" (or whatever) and insisted on giving us hot onion soup and a bed for the night. Next morning we drove on to Calais and the ferry. At Dover we must have looked suspiciously disreputable and were made to strip the motorbike and prove that we had no illicit drugs or contraband on board. We hadn't; so on we went to Rye to stay with Aunt Sylvia; and the next day to Roehampton, which also seemed a long way off on the twisty English roads.

It was a wonderful trip. Our friendship remained intact. But I have never wanted to go on a motor-bike again.

Humphrey Green, now Father Benedict in the Community of the Resurrection at Mirfield, was my personal theologian whom I have consulted on theological matters to do with my books, sermons and controversies, all my life. When I was Dean of Ripon I used to visit him at Mirfield and take him away for a day's walking in the Dales, which we both enjoyed, I for the intellectual and spiritual elevation (as well as the fun) of his company, he for the wicked worldliness of mine.

An other friend at Cuddesdon was Norman Taylor. He was ex-sub-lieutenant RNVR and scholar at Corpus Christi College, Cambridge. We saw eye to eye in almost everything, except that he knew more about poetry and literature than I did, and tried to teach me; and I knew more theology than he did, and tried to teach him. He introduced me to the essays of Baron Von Hugel and, personally, because he was his mentor at Cambridge, to Canon Charles Smythe, and I him to John Kelly. He was a neophyte Christian, having been converted by Smythe. We had two holidays together: one in Devon, where we sailed and capsized a sailing dinghy at Salcombe – shameful business for ex-naval officers; and one after the College Mission to Sunderland (which I will describe later) walking from Hadrian's Wall South down the Penines in golden autumnal weather.

The professional training we received at Cuddesdon was not impressive. Most people spent their time cramming for the General Ordination Examination, which they all passed. I was excused it but had to take two general papers, which required no preparation, as far as I can remember. There was a good framework for spiritual discipline: meditation every morning at seven, followed by Matins (compulsory) followed by the Eucharist, which most of us stayed for; evensong in the church at five, with the "College Sermon", given by a student and torn to pieces at a discussion afterwards, once a week; compline every evening at nine and silence after it, with a devotional address (known as "The Emotional") given by the Principal on Fridays. There was rudimentary instruction in speaking and singing; a few courses of lectures in the week given by the staff on such subjects as ethics (which in my proud Oxford way I despised), doctrine by the Principal, excellent in my opinion, but not "high" or "low" enough for the extreme tastes; and a smattering of "pastoralia" about what not to do in a parish.

In the evenings we sometimes had visiting lecturers, distinguished churchmen with bees in their bonnets, such as the vicar of a parish in Leeds (Ernie Southgate, later Provost of Southwark), who talked to us about the House-Church movement; the Bishop of Middleton on the Industrial Mission, then in its infancy; a lecture on the Railway Mission in South Africa, necessary, we were told, so that the whites could have "their own" church brought to them. The only question we bothered to ask was, 'What was the gauge of the railway?'

We used to go in pairs to neighbouring churches to inflict evensong and a sermon upon them, one to take the service, the other to preach, and both to meet later and criticise one another. It all depended on whom you went with. Norman and I used to say the nicest things about one another's efforts. I learnt then that I can best preach without notes; and this was confirmed when, by rule, I had to "read" my College Sermon (on "Fruit of the Vine") and felt very unhappy about it, though it was well received.

Many years later, soon after being installed at Ripon Cathedral, I went back to Cuddesdon to preach at their compulsory Friday evening "Parish Communion". The weather was unbearably cold, so that even with their heavy overcoats on, the students sat there in the unheated church, shivering. Also an appalling College Steel Band dominated the service which, even without this, was silly in its contrived informality. Besides all this, the service started late because a Jesuit monk had been lecturing the students on the Existence of God. So no one was in the mood for worship; I cut my losses by reducing my address to about four minutes. People said afterwards that they were pleased with me for being so sensitive, but it meant that I was not able to say anything of consequence. However, I enjoyed the feel of the College as I stayed the night there and went on to see my mother – for the last time.

She was so sweet, now aged ninety-two, rather forgetful of recent matters (such as other members of the family's visits: 'Michael has not been to see me,' though he had been the day before!) but still full of poetry and family traditions and strong, life-affirming Christianity. I was able to tell her all about Ripon and the Cathedral and my Installment Service; and she gave me her lovely silver cross, which she had acquired in Italy and which I have now given to Robert for his ordination. She died in March 1985. I gave some hymn-books to Ripon Cathedr"Praise the Lord, O my soul, and all that is within me praise his holy name: praise the Lord, O my soul, and forget not all his benefits."(This, to me, is "Mother's psalm".)

It seemed that my friends and I were teaching each other at Cuddesdon, more than we were learning from the staff. We must have been a difficult lot to cope with as we had nearly all of us seen more of the world than they had; and seen it too in a non-Christian context. In some ways I look back at my two years there as two years of missed opportunity. I could at least have read something about the history of the Church of England, as the only history we did for the General Ordination Examination was the Early Church, and the Reformation. However, it was an enjoyable two years in which spirituality (which I think of as "friendship with God through the living Christ") became a way of life, enriched by human friendships.

Chapter 14
Basingstoke Days

When I was still at Cuddesdon I took part in the College Mission to Sunderland. We were there for a hard-working week. There were prayers, conferences and services each morning, visiting from door to door every afternoon, and meetings of one sort or another every evening. In those days there were no barriers to visiting such as there are today, and even if many of the visits were "blanks" there were some at which I was drawn deep into conversation. I met no hostility, but was often asked, 'Why wasn't I visited before?' Sometimes there was an invitation to "tea", a huge meal with the family.

At the end of the week two vicars asked me privately if I would be their curate. One was Tommy Bendelow, who worked alone in a dock-yard parish, getting almost no response from the people except the respect and devotion they had for him. His was truly a ministry of "casting bread upon the waters", for no one in his parish, it seemed, went to church. The other was Jack Richardson who was vicar of the central parish of Sunderland, where people did go to church. This parish was run by the vicar and his curates on conventional C. of E. lines.

But the Principal of Cuddesdon would have none of it. This romantic "going up North" was good for some, no doubt, but not necessary for me, he said. He had had a letter from Archdeacon Chute, Archdeacon, Rural Dean and Rector of Basingstoke, and he had encouraged him to write to me. He did. So I went to Basingstoke to see him and liked everything about it. I then went to see Bishop Mervyn Haigh, the Bishop of Winchester. He had been a colleague of Father's in his Knutsford days just after the first war, and he was pleased that I was going into his diocese.

But there was one snag – Juliet, whom I was going to marry. Chute already had his ration of one married curate (Robert Arnold) and liked the other two to be bachelors living with him in the Rectory, so it was by no means certain that he would have me if I were determined to marry, which I was. However, he decided that it could be done and he agreed to have me with a starting salary of £220 p.a. plus my keep in the Rectory until I should marry and move into our own home. This would be a council house on the South Ham estate on the edge of Basingstoke.

So on the Feast of St Thomas (22 December) 1951, I was made deacon by the Bishop of Winchester in Winchester Cathedral. A year later I was ordained priest by Bishop Alwyn Williams, the new Bishop of Winchester, in Romsey Abbey. At both services I felt supported, strengthened, elated, by the Company of Heaven. That is to say, I felt strong spiritual support; but also very close, human support. Juliet was there with Kay, her mother, and all my family. After being made deacon we had lunch together at the well-named Manor of God Begot. I was then delivered to Basingstoke where I was soon involved in preparing for the Chistmas services. I read lessons at all the services, having rehearsed them first in front of Chute. He seemed satisfied, and then gave me detailed instructions about how to administer the chalice at Holy Communion. He left nothing to chance.

Basingstoke Rectory was a bachelor establishment where Chute presided over his curates, two or three in number, with paternal state and authority. At meal-times we sat down together with "grace" before and after, except at breakfast which was eaten in silence to the punctuation of growly noises about the news – we each had our own paper. There was a housekeeper/cook, Miss Caste, of whom we were much in awe. No curate's behaviour, however good or bad, ever surprised her. She was kindness itself, but she never smiled if she could help it. We loved Evelyn, her assistant, who always took our side. She made life easy with her sweet temper and her precise knowledge of our individual needs and tastes.

Archdeacon A.W. Chute was a doyen of his generation of clergymen. Born and brought up at the Vines (now a national stately home), educated at Winchester and Oxford, he was wealthy enough not to need a salary – indeed, he gave his salary back to the parish, which was not good for it. He was not only Rector, he was also Rural Dean and Archdeacon of Basingstoke. He had no secretary, but he sat up late every night writing his letters by hand in triplicate. He was everything to everyone in the parish, and much loved. He made few demands on his parishioners, his one aim, so it seemed to critical me, being to keep everyone happy: and he did not want curates rocking the boat! He was always friendly but never close. He presided daily at lunch and dinner at which we curates were expected to be "properly dressed".

These were still the days of rationing and at meals each of us had our butter for the week in his place. Chute divided his neatly into seven: the rest of us had generally eaten our ration by Thursday. Mine was always a mess. We had a strict rota – Chute included – for helping Evelyn with the washing-up. Chute worked with his scythe in the meadow between church and rectory on many afternoons, and we were expected to keep the lawn mown between us. David Howe was good with the engine of the mower; I used to toil up and down thinking of sermons, and somewhat resenting this "waste" of my time. But when I mentioned this to Kenneth Riches (Cuddesdon Principal) he was totally unsympathetic and gave me a lecture on the importance of fulfilling life's ordinary reponsibilities.

Dear Chute. I was often irritated by his gentle, middle-of-the-road attitudes; but looking back I admire him greatly. He was a genuine "curate trainer" with exacting professional standards. He was selfless, totally devoid of pomp or self-importance. He insisted on the disciplines of ministry: visiting, good accounts (he used to audit my St Michael's Guild accounts every quarter), administration, proper preparation for worship, and a strong pattern of prayer, daily offices and Eucharists. We had to be in church soon after seven every morning: Matins at seven thirty. Eucharist at eight, except Mondays and Saturdays. All this was more important to him than fervour or enthusiasm or too much interest into individual souls, or new, bright, boat-rocking ideas.

Chute was a "curate trainer" of the old-fashioned sort. Everything I did in church had to be done first in front of him: reading lessons, preaching, taking services and prayers and (later) baptisms, marriages and funerals. Chute had an odd idea about funerals, one which I later abandoned. This was that one should never mention the person who had died – that was up to the mourners: our job was simply to conduct the service and offer the appropriate prayers to God. Nowadays it is quite different, and with members of the family reading tributes and poems and the officiant expected to speak about the deceased, funerals are more personal and to that extent better.

Sermons had to be written out and read aloud to the vicar in his study – an ordeal, but one I appreciated because Chute had an acute mind and could put his finger on moments of bad judgement or illogical thought. He was wary at first of my ability to preach without notes and warned me of the dangers of doing this: that if it is not well prepared it easily leads to vacuous waffle. But for all my life-long sins and failures this, not preparing sermons, has not been one of them. I prepare them meticulously and always know within certain bounds what I am going to say.

At first my sermons were virtually learnt by heart. But with more experience I was able to learn the thought by heart, but not the words, though some words are precisely planned and rehearsed. I learnt the trick that came from the study of St Mark's gospel under Dr Lightfoot: that of having "stitch" words or phrases or ideas that come at the end of one paragraph and lead easily to the next. This helps the memory and the flow of logic; and when in preparation I find something that I cannot remember, I tell myself that this is because it is not logical. So think again and get it right! People sometimes say in kindness that they like to hear a sermon which "comes straight from the heart" (or worse: "off the cuff'"); but my sermons come from the head as well as the heart.

Whatever the difficulties, the advantages of not using notes are considerable. Eyes on the text make a barrier between preacher and congregation, though Ronnie Macfadden, Ripon's best preacher in my time, could always appear not to be reading his beautifully prepared texts. The other advantage is that I still – deep in retirement – do not repeat myself. No sermon gets preached twice, even when I preach twice on the same Sunday: they always come out different, which is why I still lie awake on Saturday nights polishing and trying to perfect (and shorten!) the address I have been thinking about all the week. Sermons are not painless, however easily they may seem to trip off the tongue.

There was the sermon to the NFU in Pershore Abbey just after a General Synod debate at which it was resolved that harvest festival sermons that year should be about the imbalance of the world's economy. Lots of statistics were to be quoted. I was obedient to the will of Synod, but did not find any other member who was so at his own harvest festival! No one liked what I said and I got some angry letters afterwards.

There was the very difficult sermon (at Ripon) about the Gulf War with the Royal Engineers present and just about to go out there. The Colonel told me afterwards that however seriously I took it, they in the officer's mess took the moral-political problems just as seriously; but in the end they had to do what they were told. He later become a candidate for Confirmation and, in his retirement, a strong supporter of the Cathedral. And there were the two "Judges' Sermons" in York Minster, with the Minster packed with the legal profession in their colourful gowns and wigs. I was much in awe and expected to be sent to the Tower if I offended. But I gave it to them strong, all the same! There was the sermon to the Worshipful Company of Wool Gatherers. I was told that it must be to do with wool, but was determined not to preach about sheep; so I used the story of Jason's fleece. There was also the sermon in Lancing Chapel on the occasion of the centenary of Nathaniel Woodard, the Founder of the Woodard schools. I reminded the huge company of the particular Christian aspirations of their Founder.

Chute once said that one of the choir boys (Derek: he later became Verger) liked my sermons because, he said, rather oddly, "they went on and on". I wonder what he meant! Meanwhile, I continue to _____ every time I go into the pulpit, praying that my memory will _____ me down.

Archdeacon Chute laid it down that all afternoons and some evenings were to be spent visiting. Woe betide us if we were found wandering round the shops! Each week at the Monday Chapter Meeting we had to produce a list of those we had visited. The total was expected to be between twenty and thirty. Robert Arnold, the senior curate, used to cheat by listing everyone he had met in the streets. I used to push my own list up by counting the visits I had made for settling such things as lesson-readers, Sunday school teachers or the organist about hymns at my "own" church, the mission church at May Street.

May Street was a working-class district, conservative with a small c. I visited every house in the area and got to know some of the families, whether they attended church or not. There was Eileen, for instance, who married Alan, an ordination candidate, later a priest: both strong members of St Michael's Guild. There was Reg and Mrs Stevens, who had lived there and moved away, and was still the wise churchwarden. Once there was a problem which I told Chute about. He said, 'We will go together and consult Reg.' Reg gave us sensible advice and this taught me a lesson about the neccessity of consulting the laity. Reg and his wife lived selflessly for the good of their church and all connected with it, including the training of the current curate!

I made a bad mistake with the May Street carol service. This had hitherto been a "sing-song" occasion; but I had other ideas and decided that I would train a choir of children, around the strength of one of them who had a particularly good voice. I planned that she should sing the opening verse of *Once in Royal David's City*. I persuaded her, trained her, got her to the point, lined her up at the back of the church. But at the last moment she wouldn't – and broke down in tears. Shame and consternation: a weeping girl; an angry family; and much cluck-clucking in the congregation. I told Chute about it afterwards and he said, 'It's not their culture, you see: and you mustn't try to push yours on to them.' This culture gap has been one of the chief stumbling blocks in the business of getting people to come to church. I have never solved the problem; and as I look around at some of the clergy who think they are solving it, I find that they are simply recreating it from the other side. Lots of worshipping people have been mightily put off by what is called the "happy clappy" culture, including the banal music and the repeated choruses that people use nowadays in church. But there I go again! Somehow Christian worship must be polyglot, able to be expressed through all cultural traditions. This requires sensitivity and an inclusive policy.

People were moving away from the May Street area of Basingstoke and new housing estates were springing up on the outskirts of the town, one of them called South Ham. I persuaded Chute that it was there, not May Street, that we ought to establish a church to serve the people. He had been thinking about this and had already acquired a suitable piece of land on top of the hill. Now, he decided, the day had come. A wooden church was designed and built by a builder-churchwarden, Mr Apse. I was allowed to inspect the plans and make suggestions, and the church was built: a fair-sized hall with a sanctuary curtained off at one end and a vestry at the other. It was big enough for a constant flow of weektime activities for various groups in the neighbourhood, including "youth services" such as scouts and guides; and there were chairs for a congregation of over a hundred on Sundays. In fact Julie and I reckoned that we had about three hundred children at the Sunday afternoon children's service, which I preferred to "Sunday school".

The most important thing I did when I was at Basingstoke was to marry Juliet. The wedding took place at Roehampton Parish Church. Father married us; Chute led the prayers; Ronald Gordon played the organ; Michael was Best Man; Tony gave Julie away; Elizabeth Hall (Julie's best friend from St Paul's School: I married her to her husband in 1999 in Bath Abbey) was Chief Bridesmaid, with Caroline Frazer and Sally Gillett in attendance. About a hundred and fifty people were present including my distinguished cousin, Professor Clement Webb, who gave us a valuable Georgian silver salver, wrapped in newspaper.

The reception was in the Parish Hall because of the rain, but we moved into the Vicarage garden when the sun came out. Kay's friend Curteis Ryan proposed our health. Juliet was utterly beautiful, beyond my words to describe; and she got delightfully jolly under the influence of the champagne and all the love and the fact that everything had gone so well. She – we – did not want to leave, but eventually we changed our clothes and were cheered away in a friendly and much decorated taxi to the Naval Club where Julie and I had a quiet supper. Nan Taylor turned up, having been to the wedding but with no idea that we would be at the club. Undeterred we drove to Victoria and caught the train to Southampton for the midnight ferry to Guernsey. Julie soon began to feel queasy and I was sleepy as a result of a pill I had taken, so reluctantly we went to our separate bunks. Confetti fell out of my suitcase when I opened it, causing fellow passengers to laugh; and Juliet, I am afraid, had an uncomfortable night, feeling sea-sick, pill or no pill.

Once Julie had got over her sea-sickness, our honeymoon was bliss. We had a hotel at the south end of the island, near the lighthouse. We walked the cliffs, explored the island – and persuaded the hotel keeper blushingly to put the twin beds together into a lovely double-bed. We were there for a fortnight and my rosy memory recalls sunny weather all the time.

I decided not to submit Julie to the ordeal of another rough crossing, so we flew to Portsmouth and took the train on to Basingstoke on the promise that I would pay the fare when I got there, being, as usual, out of cash. There were no credit cards in those days, but people were trusting, and a taxi took us back to the Rectory – via the bank. Our house on the South Ham estate was not yet ready for us, so we had to spend the first six weeks of our married life in the Rectory. Julie, dreading the council house, was happy, and Chute, who loved Julie, was hospitable; but I hated this arrangement and longed to get away and have Julie to myself.

Chute had persuaded the council to let us have No. 36 Cobbett Green, which was at the bottom of the hill near the main road. If you were to open the front door you would see the stairs going straight up to the lavatory. At the top was our bedroom on one side, the bathroom and spare room, which was also my study, on the other. There was a small L-shaped sitting-room at the bottom on the left with just room for a sofa, armchair, book-case and piano (no television in those days). On the right was the kitchen. Behind the house there was a derelict patch waiting to be turned into a garden. We got some of the youth from St Michael's Guild to give us a hand trying to put it into order, but without much success.

There we lived for two years. Julie got a job as an orthoptist, first in London, then in Alton, Winchester, Andover and Basingstoke itself. She became the Hampshire County Orthoptist. They sent a car for her every day and paid her enough to make our ends meet, just: they would never have done so on my salary alone. I was upset by this and put the matter to Chute. I wanted him to raise the matter of my salary with the PCC and the Parish Treasurer. But Chute said no: it would be most ungentlemanly and improper for the PCC to be asked to discuss a clergyman's salary. However, a cheque for £10 mysteriously appeared every month from Chute himself, and this had to do. I was not allowed to thank him for it.

I was excited about our first home, "my" church and my new area of responsibility. The church was duly dedicated and the Bishop of Southampton came and blessed our house, though Julie was upset about this because she thought that the house was not ready for such a visitation. I toured the area in a borrowed car with a loudspeaker and posters all over it. 'Do you hear there? Do you hear there?' I shouted in true naval boatswain fashion, which would have been recognised by many an old salt recently demobbed as I was. 'Your own church, St Peter's, is about to be opened this Saturday. Come along and join us. Muster in the church at 1900 hours.' Every house got a leaflet and a map of the estate, showing that all roads led up the hill to St Peter's. The church was packed for the occasion and we were off to a good start.

We made friends on the South Ham estate through the church life as it began to flourish. Every Sunday we had a Eucharist in the morning and a packed children's service in the afternoon. Julie played the piano, having practised the chosen hymns all the week. If for some reason she couldn't, I would play myself, shunting to and fro between the altar at one end of the church and the piano at the other. These services were hard work, but I was getting a steady stream of Confirmation candidates from them. If only I could persuade the parents to come along with their children! But even on special occasions such as the harvest festival I could only get a few. Most people regarded the services on Sunday afternoons as a splendid way of employing the children while they, the parents, slept or read the newspaper. 'Why should we go to church ourselves,' one of them asked, 'if we lead good Christian lives and send our children to the children's service?' I answered, 'If you don't come, your children, seeing that, will give it up. Their children won't come at all. Their children will grow up knowing nothing about the Christian religion either in theory or in practice. The next generation of children will have no Christian ethical basis for their life whatever.' I have been proved right.

Julie and I were much occupied with St Michael's Guild, the parish church youth club. In those days the youth club was an important feature in the life of any parish, and an important influence on the lives of the young people who joined them. St Michael's Guild was a particularly good one. It met in Church Cottage (an ancient tithe-barn next door to St. Michael's, beautiful in its rustic way, but not well equipped) every Sunday evening after evensong for instruction, which I took very seriously. So did they – for their use of the club in the week depended on it.

After instruction they would come round to my room in the Rectory – and just "be": argue, quarrel, drink coffee, sit around on the floor, canoodle, even play shove-halfpenny (which I could always win – having honed my skills at Teddy Hall). There were two or three meetings in the week in Church Cottage at which they danced, played table-tennis, did useful crafts (a reluctant few of them) and joined in any entertainment I could devise. We had, for instance, a mock trial, which I had worked out as a thriller, each person knowing only his own part, and some unlikely person emerging as the true culprit: debates and games, both physical (such as their very rough form of musical chairs) and intellectual.

What about doing a play? First I tried a "Revue" for which I wrote the words and music (some of it borrowed from HMS *Ranpura's Babes in the Gut*) and it was quite successful. At least I discovered who could and who definitely could not act. When Julie joined me we produced a play about the formation of the Union Jack and we entered it for the County (Hants & Berks) Youth Club competition. It fell at the first showing at Basingstoke, and the examiner, pressed by our angry members, said that it was the play's fault: it had no dramatic content. True – but for us it was step forward.

Next year we tried again with *The Red Velvet Goat*, which reached the finals but didn't win. We tried again and I insisted again that Julie be the producer. There were many difficulties and tensions. We had to teach most of the members to project their voices, and we did this by holding conversations with them through the walls of a room. Some of the members worked very hard and their talent was encouraging.

The play was *The Mayor of Torontal* about a girl in an East European village who bewitched the whole village by her beauty – and eventually the Mayor himself. We had just the girl; but she had to be taught word by word, line by line, movement by movement. She had no natural talent and a difficult temperament; but she triumphed – to everyone's delight. The Mayor was John Oliver, a natural, who later became churchwarden first of St Michael's, then of the parish church of Old Basing; then died, tragically, very young. He was one of the most responsive Christian boys I have ever had the joy of teaching. There was also Stuart Bell, who also painted my portrait, now in Peter's possession. He did the scenery with verve and imagination. The result was, first, local triumph with the whole parish there to watch the performance in Church Cottage. For this they were judged worthy to go to the finals in Winchester: finals which we WON. Tremendous joy throughout the parish and the town of Basingstoke, because it was well reported in the *Hants & Berks Gazette*. It was a particular triumph for Juliet, who had never done anything like it but had now truly made her mark.

St Michael's Guild also took to square-dancing, which for a short time, prior to Rock and Roll, was all the rage. I went to Winchester for a "callers' course"; our club could put on an evening of square-dancing with a band or just a gramophone, and make several hundred pounds whenever we wanted to till the craze stopped as suddenly as it had begun.

In my second year at Basingstoke (still not married) I joined the local Gilbert and Sullivan society; and was given the part of Grosvenor in *Patience*. I enjoyed it immensely, especially as in doing this I was meeting a new, unchurchy section of Basingstoke society. I learnt a lot, too, as I submitted to the instructions of the producer, who forced me into the accepted, traditional, G&S mould. I particularly enjoyed the "encore" I was called to do after *Prithee Pretty Maiden,* and the last hilarious duet with Teddy Mendham (Bunthorne) who was an experienced G&S tenor. He was also an atheist, and we liked each other a lot. He asked me once to accompany him on a business trip to Manchester, which I did, greatly enjoying the drive (no motorways in those far-off days) and the day-long heart to heart talk we had about religion and life.

I also got myself the job of being the unofficial music and theatre critic for the *Hants & Berks Gazette.* I had a three-fold objective: (1) to encourage people to come to professional performances. Peter Katin, for instance, gave a brilliant piano recital in a sparsely populated Town Hall and I gave him and the music a rave review, which must have been one of his first; (2) to persuade amateurs, whose shows were always sold out to mothers, sisters, cousins and aunts, to raise their standards of performance (I remember writing about the all-important "dot" in the tune of the *Unfinished Symphony*) and to be more adventurous in what they performed. Was I outspoken, and arrogant? I expect I made some enemies; but also (objective No. 3) I earned one halfpenny a line; and disciplined myself to write in a way that sub-editors would find hard to cut. Every halfpenny helped me in those days of financial penury. Also I was given free tickets to the concerts and plays, which was a bonus in itself.

I tried to bring to Basingstoke some enthusiasm for inter-church friendliness and activity. We had a monthly "fraternal", a meeting of all the clergy of the town of all denominations. Chute made it a "must" for us curates – but I do not remember seeing him there! I once read a paper called "Campling Puts His Neck Out". I forget what the daring thing was that I said; but I learnt that the Church's divisions are so institutionalised that they are hard to repair. The Congregational Minister became a friend and used to invite me to preach on his special occasions.

I also made friends with the Roman Catholic curate. We were both put on the management committee of the Town Youth Club, and decided to do something in the club on Good Friday. So we devised a way of acting out the story of the death of Jesus, laced with suitable prayers and actions. It was rather good. But a few days later he came to see me – to apologise! 'What on earth for?' I asked. It seemed that he had been rebuked by his Superior for allowing me to think that it was right and proper for him, a Roman Catholic priest, and me, a mere Anglican "nothing", not a priest in their eyes, to work together – indeed, pray together, in the context of a religious act on Good Friday. I just looked at him. We laughed; I accepted his "apology" – a fact he could report to his Superior; and we went off and had a drink together. Could the Pope forbid that? How sad! But how good that both churches have progressed so much (but not enough) since then.

I also unearthed a Basingstoke magazine from the year 1910. In one of these the Vicar wrote an apologia for his rough treatment of what he called "Dissension" – by which he meant the new Congregational Church. The Mayor of Basingstoke, who was also one of St Michael's churchwardens, had, in his capacity as Mayor, attended the opening of the new church. The Vicar was furious with him for this gesture towards a "Dissenting Church", and refused to allow him back into St Michael's on the following Sunday. So the Mayor and his party fought the Vicar and his party as the Mayor-Churchwarden tried to get into his own church and the Vicar and his men tried to keep him out. In his article in the magazine the Vicar explained that he had been ordained "to root out heresy and division", so he was only doing his duty. I used this story when I preached on some ecumenical occasion. Chute was rather pleased.

There was another ecumenical, political occasion which I initiated and pushed poor Chute into. It was at the time of a General Election. I suggested that we Christians from all the churches in Basingstoke should get together and have our say. So I proposed a meeting at the Town Hall at which the candidates would be confronted by members from all the churches and answer questions. Chute could see no good reason against this as long as I managed to persuade all the churches to take part. I had no difficulty with any of the "nonconformists", even the RCs: but the Anglican "low church", which was stuck in the middle of the town and opposed us in everything we did, was very difficult and at first refused to take part. But I persuaded the Vicar by inviting him to chair the procedings. He agreed; but then rightly insisted on Chute being in the chair. The meeting went well and it was the only occasion at which the candidates confronted one another. In their introductory addresses, all three candidates claimed that they had once thought seriously of being ministers in the Church!

David Howe joined us in the summer of 1952 from St John's College, Cambridge, and Wells Theological College. He was a fine musician who could read music and improvise easily on the piano. He composed a wicked "Anglican Chant" tune, which changes key in the middle. This makes every verse get higher so that by the end of the psalm the choir and congregation find themselves screeching far above their range – and wondering why. He tried – but failed – to write one that went down.

David encouraged me to sing, and besides the Vaughan Williams and Finzi songs that I used to sing at Cuddesdon, and *Lord God of Israel* from Elijah which the organist at Basingstoke persuaded me to sing for him on one occasion, I added various pieces from the *St Matthew Passion* and *B Minor Mass* to my repertoire. Also I used to sing leading articles from *The Times* in the style of the recitatives from the *Matthew Passion;* assisted by David's "continuo" accompaniment with sudden key-changes and unexpected spread chords – which set me off again. Fortunately there was never an audience for this nonsense. David could also play the bassoon and did a bouncy rendering of *Lucy Long* at a parish party – which went down much better than my *Songs of Travel.* But alas! He caught polio on a holiday in Spain and almost lost the use of his vocal cords. He was as good a priest as I have ever known. He was simply "good" in himself. Some are called (me?) to be teachers of the faith; some, "doers". David just was in his strong, gentle goodness a Christ-filled person.

Nigel Harley overlapped with me and then followed me to South Ham, having married Kate, a doctor's daughter from a family who were particularly kind to Juliet and me. We introduced them to one another, so we claim, at a tennis party we organised when Nigel first arrived in the parish. He was a county-class player. Kate was not! (But she was a good pianist.) We made them partners and he was able to tear about the court getting the ball back from all situations and smashing it whenever possible, heroically giving Kate her first ever victory at tennis.

We had two years of married life at Basingstoke. Then came a cutting from the *Church Times* which Father had seen and sent to me. It was about a vacancy at Ely for a minor canon who would also be the Chaplain of the King's School. It happened that we were going to see my brother John at Dunmow. Why not look in at Ely? So I wrote and was invited to interview. We both fell for the place: the Cathedral, its Close, the School; the friendliness of everyone; powerful Mr Brown, the Headmaster; the holy, humorous Dean, Simon Hankey's father (and, we were later to discover, his wickedly amusing wife); a delightful little house in the Close, "The Choir House", which was to be ours; and a double job, both parts being after my own heart: singing services with the choir in that superb Cathedral; and being the Chaplain to a school of about four hundred boys. They appointed me almost on the spot, and I got appreciative letters in confirmation both from the Dean and from the Headmaster.

When we got back to Basingstoke, Chute did not want to know; and it took him two weeks to agree to see me, strongly suspecting that I would be leaving him.

Chapter 15
The King's School, Ely

Juliet and I travelled to Ely in the late summer of 1955, perched in the front of the furniture van. As we approached, the Isle of Ely rose above the wind-torn fens of Cambridgeshire looking like a sandcastle on a flat beach. On the top, where the flag would be put, stood the Cathedral. As the road from Cambridge wound its way towards it, the Cathedral became a ship, changing its bearing and its shape with each twist of the winding road. Then the town appeared, and the ship was a Cathedral again; still, massive, the West Tower soaring up to Heaven; the Octagon Tower more humble, more of the earth. This monument to God's glory dominates the town; and behind it, in peaceful seclusion, with gates locked at night against intruders, we found the Close (known as the "College"), the Canons' houses and the King's School.

We found The Choir House (now a draper's shop) in the north corner of the College, near the Lady Chapel, adjoining school classrooms. There was no garden, only a courtyard for the boys to play in. The walls and ceilings sloped unevenly at curious angles. Nothing was square or sensible. The window frames were set in gothic arches. There was neither a larder nor a linen-cupboard, and only an ancient boiler. It was a delightful, impossible house, a million miles different from 36 Cobbett Green.

Outside the courtyard was the Sacrist's Gate, over which the Verger lived. Then, in the same style but on a grander scale, stood the house where Sir Will and Lady Spens lived, Sir Will being designated Cathedral Steward. Then came the Precentor's house, then the Organist's. We all backed on to Ely High Street and often had to put up with the prying eyes of shoppers and tourists staring in on us.

165

After a day spent settling in I went to see the Headmaster, Ben Fawcett. He too was new, having replaced Bill Brown. Fawcett was tall, upright, grey, with military moustache and bearing. He was principled, punctilious, an ardent highchurchman. He insisted on high standards of performance both in education and liturgy, telling me straight away, bluntly, that he was my "ordinary" – an ecclesiastical term I had not previously come across: it means "boss". Thus it was he, not the Bishop or Dean, who would lay down what was what in religious matters. I learnt later that he was irritated to find that Bill Brown had appointed me Chaplain when as the new Head he should have had that reponsibility. But he was friendly and welcoming. Although conservative in many matters, he was also creative – indeed, a visionary as regards the school. He considered this to be a slack establishment which in scholarship, games, spirituality and discipline needed (in the Lancing phrase) "bracing up".

The King's School, Ely, in those days was a school for boys, aged eight to eighteen, mostly boarders living in boarding houses with a sizeable rump of day-boys attached. It was a public (i.e. private) school with the Dean and Chapter as the basis of its governing body. Academic standards were not high, but a few boys gained admission to Oxbridge every year. The music in the school was especially good because the choristers in the cathedral choir stayed on after their voices had broken, and the Assistant Cathedral Organist (Dr Arthur Wills) was in charge.

Fawcett wanted a full sacramental practice of Christianity, with the School Eucharist celebrated on Sundays and voluntarily on weekdays. I was expected to offer the possibility of "confession", though this practice met with hostility from the staff. It was a life-line to some boys and one particular master. In all this I was in full accord with Fawcett, but to my surprise he then appointed another priest, Arthur Taylor, to be Deputy Head. I need not have worried. Father Taylor had no status in the Cathedral, and anyway we did not disagree about anything that mattered concerning religion in the school.

My position was made difficult by the fact that most of the staff of the school were opposed to my "high church" tendencies, whereas the Cathedral staff (led by the Precentor) regarded me as being "dangerously low"! Fortunately the Dean, the Very Reverend Patrick

Hankey, a man of strong catholic spirituality, saw the whole situation with his twinkling eye, knew what was important and what wasn't, enjoyed the joke of "piggy me in the middle", and gave me total support whichever way I found myself facing.

Part of my appointment was to be "Minor Canon of the Cathedral". This meant that I was responsible for half of the daily Matins and evensongs. The other half was taken by Ted Longford, the Precentor. It was he that had put me through my first singing test, with Michael Howard the organist listening. He (Ted) quickly let me know that my voice was good but my style was wrong! I was expected to sing the words in a semi-staccato way with every syllable equally stressed. This was how to sing plain-song, he said; and the choral settings had to be sung with clear, syllable-by-syllable phrasing. I thought at the time (and still do) that Ted had the best "precentor voice" that I have ever heard: a light tenor/baritone, clear and resonant. But I also thought that he exaggerated what the choristers called the "typewriter" style, and I could not bring myself to imitate this to his satisfaction. We both avoided the sickly, wordless, precentor's sob, which you sometimes hear; like that of the Minor Canon who used to begin the Creed, "MmmmmmmwhI believe in God"!

It was important to sing well because the choir was brilliant. I have known cathedral choirs all my life, and, of course, Ripon has to be my favourite, Worcester, with Peter singing in it, second. But Ely was something different. Michael Howard purposely produced a tone for the boys which was halfway between the continental gutteral sound produced from the chest voice, and the pure hard tone of the traditional English cathedral treble, as found at King's College, Cambridge. The "Ely sound" was harsher than King's, more flexible, more vigorous, always excellent in enunciation.

Singing services with this choir was a nerve-wracking experience for a humble minor canon. The Head Chorister would come into the Vestry as we were robing, bow to me and say, 'Smith in G, Sir' – or whatever the setting and its key were to be. I would have a tuning-fork in my sweaty hand and would clasp it nervously as we processed through the Cathedral to the stalls in the Choir. Meanwhile the organist would be improvising with crunchy discords that were clearly being played to put me off my note. Miraculously he would shuffle through the intervening keys and finish (if I were lucky) on the chord of the key I was to sing in. But I needed to empty my mind of all that he had been playing, strike my tuning-fork firmly, calculate the right interval between the note it gave and the note I needed, and then embark resolutely on the opening, "O Lord, open thou our lips". After that it was easy, and the one-note chanting of the Collects (plus correct inflections when it was plain-song) was a positive relief, until the end when the organ would come in angrily if I had gone out of tune, and the boys would look knowing. At my first broadcast evensong I was convinced that I had made a mess of it; but no organ came in to correct the pitch. The Choir sang its elaborate Amen, and I knew that all was well.

Although other people (such as the Headmaster) thought it an unwarrantable burden on an already well-burdened School Chaplain, I loved the Cathedral side of my work and would not have given it up for anything. Ted Longford, his delightful wife, Joan, and their young family were good friends to Julie and me, though he could sometimes be very squashing. Michael Howard, the Cathedral Master of Music, whose book about his own life has recently been published, pays high tribute to Ted as a pastor and friend. When Michael needed help, Ted, by his friendship and priestly guidance, gave it to him.

As Chaplain I was responsible for the pastoral care of the school, and my chief opportunity for this was when I prepared boys for Confirmation. I took immense trouble over this, taking boys in small classes and then giving them individual teaching on their prayer life and anything else they asked for. I had a clear object, which was to share with them the friendship of God through Christ, which enhances life at every point and leads to God-centred, people-centred living.

I was given a heavy timetable, being called upon to teach every class in the school (where the age-range was eight to eighteen) twice a week. But what was I to teach? And at what stage in pupils' development? My predecessor wrote to me and said, "I always keep a Gospel going." This was unhelpful. So I thought the matter through and came to the conclusion that my object was to teach the Christian religion: not to force it on anybody, but to present the truth as I understood it in a way that left people free to make up their minds about it.

My first encounter with the Sixth Form was difficult. Some respected me at once and some of my best Confirmation candidates came from that group of boys. Others rejected everything I said, as was their right. But the significant thing was that they had no understanding of what it was that they were rejecting. They would like to have found that I believed that the world is flat ("Flat as my hat, flatter than that", in Rudyard Kipling's words) and was created in six days. But I didn't. Mine was a pilgrimage, a search, an attempt to open my eyes and see more, not a closed certainty that I knew it all. Nevertheless, in their determined opposition to Christianity, they floundered and found me a most unsatisfactory opponent.

Gradually I learnt by trial and error what part of the study of Christianity was most helpful to what ages: the story-telling; the attempt to discover the history; the conceptual grasp of doctrines; how these relate to the Bible; how they relate to life; the ethical consequences to the individual and society; the objections in philosophy and science; and the relationship with other faiths. So a syllabus evolved. The principle was that everything – from the savage stories in the Old Testament, to the gospels, through the triumphs and failures of the Church, to the practice of worship today and the problems of living: everything is related to the central truth, that religion is relationship with God, the Christian religion relationship with God through Jesus Christ.

And what fun we had with the delicious Old Testament stories and the astonishing life and teaching of Jesus and the bungling history of the Church and the juicy ethical problems of the day. What arguments. And what insights intelligent, engaged boys can show. What a lot they taught me. What rows we occasionally had before I learnt to keep them working, and therefore keep them in order. And what disappointment with my first small set of O-level candidates who did not do as well as I thought they would because the examiners were looking for the details of the stories, not Professor Lightfoot's exegesis as explained by me.

On the staff, only Fawcett gave me any credit – and he did not always help. When I sent a boy to him for an enterprising and thoughtful piece of work for "Headmaster's commendation", Fawcett's concern was about whether or not it was written neatly. Any crossings-out (which to my mind are essential for good writing) disqualified the piece. But when the inspectors examined me they gave me very high commendation indeed. Their only criticism was that I tended to ask boys to make lists, for instance of what they could discover from St Mark's gospel about the growing opposition to Jesus, rather than write essays.

All these ideas about "Divinity teaching" were teeming in my head when I started going to the Schools' Chaplains' Conferences, held for the inside of a week each year in the Easter holidays at one of the schools. My first was at Wellington College. I was soon asking awkward questions about the teaching of Scripture, Divinity, RK, RE (I went through all these designations in the course of my teaching career), to find very little interest from some and strong concern from others. I was asked to write a paper for the consideration of the next conference and I did so "On Teaching Christian Doctrine". This was well received and it was decided that we would produce a book to be called *A Guide to Divinity Teaching*. This was published by SPCK in 1962 and it contained three chapters by me, on Doctrine, New Testament and Worship. The book was politely reviewed, but I never heard it mentioned again!

In these days of multi-faith awareness chaplains would write a very different book. But my point was a good one, and still is. In schools that claim to have a Christian foundation – such as cathedral schools, the Woodard Schools and many of the public schools whose origins are Christian – Christianity should be taught. "Bible Stories", "Every Day Life in Ur of the Chaldees", "How St Paul made Tents", "Religious Festivals", "Comparative Ethics": these may have a place. But Christianity must be taught for what it is, or, if you prefer, "for what it claims to be". Those who are expected to live in an institution with a Christian ethos, especially if worship plays a part in the routine, deserve to be taught this so that they can make an intelligent choice about its claims. Against the charge that this is "indoctrination" one can make the counter-charge that the opposite is "intellectual and spiritual deprivation". But disparaging words do not help. A way of life can be shared: but if people are to be able to accept or reject it, only knowledge of it will make them free to do so. The eighth-century BC prophet Hosea said, against the priests of his day, 'My people are destroyed through lack of knowledge.' Much damage has been inflicted upon our society by the muddy ignorance of the Christian faith in which the majority of people live their lives; and often in the media people flaunt their ignorance in the lava of scorn that they pour upon the Church.

One day I received a letter from the head of the educational publishing firm, Edward Arnold. He had heard of my views. Would I consider writing a course for RE which his firm would publish? I consulted Ben Fawcett and Juliet and both firmly said, 'Yes.' The preliminaries took a long time to settle. The first plan was a series that would lead to O-level; but as I had little experience with O-level and regarded the course I had used as being too tightly tied to the biblical text, I persuaded Mr Maddox (head of the firm) to free me from its restrictions. By this time he had passed me over to one of his partners, an intelligent person, not a Christian believer, but interested and sympathetic. He had a considerable influence on me by his wise and exacting advice. Whatever I proposed to him was put to the firm's School Representatives who peddled my ideas around the schools that they went to. Many private schools and a considerable number of state schools played their part in helping me to form the overall scheme for the books.

The first year's book was to be about Jesus Christ and was to include subjects for the pupils to explore for themselves from the gospels. "What did Jesus think about ...? What did he do for lepers, sinners ...? What part did 'faith in him' play? Find out by looking up..." It was to be illustrated with pictures of Jesus from artists of different ages and nationalities, all making some point for pupils to discuss. This was to be called *The Love of God in Action*. The second was to be about the Church, starting with the Apostolic Age, up to the present, with some lives of particular Christians (such as Edward Wilson and Gladys Aylward), illustrated by photographs of the Church today. It would be called *The People of God in Action*. The third book would tackle Christian concepts, doctrines and practices. It was to be illustrated by "stills" from films, each posing a moral problem for discussion. It would be called *The Word of God in Action*. And the fourth book (my favourite) was to be about the Old Testament, seen as the story of the development of Jewish religion from Abraham to Christ. This story would give a series of pegs from which to hang moral and religious problems, such as the so-called "wrath of God"; the ethics of punishment; religion and politics; rules and laws and love. It would be illustrated by Old Testament scenes from artists down the ages, all related to "problems" for consideration. It was to be called *God's Plan in Action*. As there was so much for the pupils to do and look up, two Teachers' Books were also published with "all the answers" – and a good deal more discussion.

I tested much of the material both at Ely and Lancing; especially the pictures with their "legends". Boys sometimes wrote brilliant essays on these; and I wished later that I had the time and energy to produce a book consisting only of pictures. Pictures take you to "life", and from the life-situation it is possible to draw probing questions to do with personal and social behaviour as well as relationship with God.

The books (called collectively *The Way, The Truth and The Life*) were duly published in 1964 and 1965. They did well for about ten years. But when schools stopped providing books for individual students, no more editions were printed. Also the ethos of the books came in for questioning as RE teachers felt the need to teach about all religions rather than Christianity by itself. I had my own way of dealing with the problem of "other religions", indeed "other denominations of Christianity", which I will write about in the chapter on Lancing. But, certainly, if I were writing the series today I would write with a broader spectrum, and try to show how with One God and many human ways of relating to God, religions should be able to learn from one another in the affirmation of their common humanity.

Meanwhile the Cathedral soared above us with its miraculous Octagon Tower, the construction of which no one understands. I used to take classes "up the Cathedral", even "up the spout", which was the name given to one of the eight massive oak trees that formed the Octagon Tower, high up above the Central Crossing. Very few of the public were taken "up the spout", but my classes were – when they were good! The boys enjoyed the climb, and sensitive boys were amazed at the construction, the huge size and the beauty of the Cathedral. My reward was oohs and ahs and whoops of joy. Ely Cathedral was a good "visual aid".

Very special were the choristers, who were treated as professional musicians. After a year a boy could read music as easily as you can read this page. They were treated harshly if they made careless mistakes; and intricate and breath-demanding solos were considered normal. Julian Thompson and James Bowman were the stars when I first arrived, both of them brilliant singers. Many years later Julian was ordained and became Precentor of the Cathedral. James' voice turned to alto, then counter-tenor, and as such he won a choral scholarship to New College, Oxford.

I claim a degree of credit for this. I started a Gramophone Society on the Fields House Lancing College model that had meant so much to me in my school days. James attended and we became firm friends. 'You must go to Oxford,' I said. But how when he could not do maths? By careful research I discovered that it was possible to get to Oxford with a scientific subject instead of maths. This included botany. So I went to Miles Amhurst, a musical member of the science staff, and persuaded him to teach James biology to the standard demanded by Oxford University. James duly passed and went to New College to be interviewed. They said to him, 'Why should we have you here when your academic record is so poor?' He answered, 'Please, will you hear me sing?' They did; and that was that. James says that the New College experience played a crucial part in his professional career; and he became the best counter-tenor of his generation. James Bowman, OBE, is still going strong; and is a life-long friend.

Another chorister was Paul Ives whose "Pié Jesu" from Faure's *Requiem*, performed just as his voice was about to break, was one of the most beautiful pieces of singing I have ever heard. He later played the cello in the BBC Symphony Orchestra, and is now a County Music Director. His brother Bill is a well-known composer. Then there were the Jeremiah brothers, excellent professionals, Bill's voice (slightly husky) being prominent on the famous record that the Choir made under Michael Howard, *Music for the Feast of Christmas*. There were the Keene brothers and naughty Miles who damaged the railway signal-box on behalf of the travelling public when the railwaymen were on strike; and the rebellious Smith whom I later met when I preached at Lewes Grammar School. When I asked after him it was found that he had cut the service! I hope he didn't, but suspect that he did, get into trouble. And there was a boy called Swabey with a voice like a cherub.

Other boys. Woods the grumpy Head of School when I first arrived. He was much more important than any new chaplain! Peter Keir whose father was a doctor at the RAF hospital, and himself went to Cambridge. He and his friend David Bowyer were in the Sixth Form and became devout, intelligent Christians. The Tamplin brothers, who came to stay with Julie and me at St David's when their sister was ill, were both ordained, and Peter still comes whooshing down to see me, always a delightful surprise. He once turned up at Ripon with his daughter, on bicycles. Alan Haydock, John Hall and Timothy Girling also became priests.

And there was the tough-guy, John Russell, who went bathing in an out-of-bounds part of the river with his friend, who was drowned. I had to look after him, much shaken, whilst he stayed in disgrace in the Sanatorium. I sorrowed with the dead boy's parents, tried to assuage the Headmaster's wrath and took the funeral service with many of the school present. There was an awful moment when the coffin slid away and all present gasped at the finality of it. I insisted after that that some better arrangement be made at cremation services.

The present controller of BBC Television Drama, Alan Yentob, was a Muslim boy in the school, over whom, unbeknownst to himself, I had a disagreement with Fawcett. He said that he should be excused Divinity lessons. I said (wrongly, I now believe) that he should at least attend them and so be able to learn about Christianity. Fawcett asked the Bishop for his opinion; and to my surprise the Bishop supported him. So here was a boy that I never saw in the classroom; though for a short time he was in my House.

And so I could go on, as schoolmasters do whose old pupils bubble up in their memory like water from a rock, vividly alive now because they were so important at the time.

On the staff there was an ultra-pious, ultra-low-church housemaster. He was reputed to have walked round the examination room during a chemistry exam. saying, 'I can smell the swimming bath,' which was evidently a hint to candidates about one of the questions they had to answer. Roger Firkins joined the staff to teach French and music and also to sing tenor in the Cathedral Choir, a fact which brought us close together. He is a life-long friend and his wife Elizabeth became Angela's godmother. David Scott had worked as a prisoner of war on the notorious Burma Road. Like all POWs I have met, he was reserved and loth to tell his story. He was a Christian agnostic, whose devotion and way of life was miles ahead of his beliefs. He confided in me: and I learnt much from him.

Rodney Saunders was my chief adviser and critic. Fawcett made him the first Headmaster of the Junior School, at which job he was immensely conscientious, but always over worried about different boys (who were really just "boys") and difficult situations. He was married to a Norwegian wife who did not understand the ethos of a public school, and did not agree with much that she did understand. Once, in the middle of a cricket match, she and a friend came into the ground and wheeled their prams straight across the middle of the sacred pitch, without even waiting for "over".

I played some cricket, once for the staff against the Second Eleven. I ran someone out with a flukey throw from the deep, and was just getting my innings going nicely, scoring the odd run and keeping the balls at bay, when Fawcett, a very solemn cricketer and impatient with my face-saving effort, declared the innings closed. On another occasion I played with the Cantores choristers against the Decani in a needle match,[1] as much between me and the Precentor as between the boys. I definitely got the better of it, having no reputation to preserve whilst he was known to be a good cricketer. He came in to bat, so I was put on to bowl. He looked around the field with interest, and at me with disdain, but I cunningly bowled him a full toss on the leg and he swept it into the hands of the boy whom I had just placed on the boundary.

---

[1] "Cantores" and "Decani" denote the particular side of the choir on which the boys sit. At Ely the "Cantores" sit on the left, the "Decani" on the right; the opposite way round to most cathedrals.

When I came in to bat in the Cantores' innings, he increased the length of his bowler's run to about a hundred yards, tore up to the wicket and bowled a ball which missed me, the wicket-keeper, and the longstop and went for four runs. This happened three times, except that on the last time I got a nick to it and so was accredited with the runs. The Cantores won.

We had interesting neighbours in the College, for instance Sir Will Spens (of the Spens Report) and his wife. They used to invite us in to drinks on Sunday mornings after the services. Then there was the saintly Bishop Gordon Walsh whose episcopal ministry had been spent in Japan. We would go to tea with him and find him more interested in us than the stories he could tell of the courageous deeds of Japanese Christians.

Professor Ratcliffe (the Ely Professor at Cambridge) would occasionally ask us to elegant, gourmet lunches on Sundays. Once it was in Lent, but he promised us that being Sunday there would be no fasting: 'No lettuce sandwich.' He lived in style and fed his cat as sumptuously as he fed himself. He was a man of encyclopaedic knowledge and was engaged in writing a dictionary of the Church. Asked one year where he had got to, he replied 'The letter H.' But asked again the next year he said, 'I have just found a gap in the letter G.' When he left Ely he gave us some bottles of excellent wine which, he said, would be ruined if he were to move them.

Canon Bernard Pawley and his wife Margaret came to live in the College, Bernard being the Diocesan Secretary as well as a canon. He could speak Italian fluently (having learnt it as a POW) and became the English Representative of the Archbishop of Canterbury in Rome at the time of the Second Vatican Council. He knew the leading Roman Catholic figures of the day and used to tell juicy stories of that epoch-making event. I used to meet him later in the General Synod, when he was Archdeacon of Canterbury. He was one of the few speakers who emptied the coffee room when it was known that he was going to speak. He sometimes had the Synod in fits of laughter as he told joke after joke out of the side of his mouth, as if they were caustic asides.

Presiding over everything was Patrick Hankey, the Dean: tall, handsome, now ageing but as sprightly as ever in wit and acute observation. We loved him dearly. Once Juliet had a bad bout of chickenpox. I was in despair trying to look after her and do the cooking for us both and manage the Cathedral services and my work in the school. The stew I was making was bubbling furiously in the pressure cooker. I slid the lid to have a peep, and "woof!" it all went up to the ceiling. Mrs Hankey chose this moment to call. She took one look round, ordered a taxi and carted Julie and me away to live with the Dean and herself in the Deanery. So for three lovely weeks we lived with them, mostly in the kitchen where Frances Hankey held court. We drank whiskey and exchanged news about the world, Cambridge, the Church of England, Ely, the Cathedral, the School, the College, the Town. Gossip? Never! Patrick and Frances were the epitome of kindness, Christian love and devotion. He was my confessor: the wisest, the shrewdest, the most vibrant instrument of Christ's love and strength and forgiveness that I have ever known. Michael Howard, in his autobiography, pays him generous tribute, despite the fact that it was Hankey who insisted on his dismissal from Ely.

The Bishop (Noel Hudson) was a bachelor who had had a brilliant career as the youngest brigadier in the Army, much be-medalled. He had been a successful Bishop of Newcastle, but Ely did not suit him. He was not academic, so he did not impress the University, and he found the clergy and church folk of the Fens slow and stuck in their ways. He used to take me to Diocesan occasions as his Chaplain and once told me that he was trying to unite two villages either side of a river into a single benefice, but had been told that it was impossible. Why? 'Because one of the villages was Danish, and the other Saxon.' He was an affectionate, emotional man who needed human life to be buzzing around him. He hated the seclusion of the Cathedral Close, living there alone with his cantankerous housekeeper, who kept everyone at bay. But she did us a good service. She wanted to have television in her sitting-room and so needed to put up an aerial. But television was a new toy in those days and aerials were forbidden in the College, to the dismay of Juliet and me when Anne Jones (Mother's school friend and an honarary aunt) gave us one unexpectedly. But the Bishop's housekeeper insisted. The Bishop backed her up, and aerials were allowed – ours included.

*   *   *

An extra burden that I was given early in my career at Ely was that of being a "form master". It was part of Fawcett's plan to bring boys and masters into a more creative relationship and to give boys a greater motivation to work. Boys were now given marks in all subjects and these had to be added up every fortnight, so that a boy's progress "up" or "down" could be noted with approval or disapproval as appropriate. There was much that was fortuitous in this process with only a fortnight's marks being considered, and I thought the whole thing a nonsense. Also the chore of adding up the marks and putting them into order was more than I could bear in a busy life. Sometimes (alas) I would put down a suitable "order" first, and concoct the marks to correspond with it afterwards.

One day the school secretary gave me a hand-written letter from the Headmaster calling me to account. It was a hell of a blast. Mr Saunders had checked my marks and found them to be seriously inaccurate. Also it was noticed ... Besides which, it seemed that ... And I was apparently guilty of ... In a word (but there were two closely written pages), as a schoolmaster, I was being unprofessional. I went straight round to B.F. to apologise and talk it through. He heard me out, then simply said, 'Would you like to be Housemaster of the new junior day-boys' house, to be called Oppidans B?' Of course I would.

(This episode nicely illustrates one of Fawcett's principles of "command" that I was to employ later in my life. "Rebuke: then, if the offender accepts, offer more responsibility.")

So I became Housemaster of Oppidans B. The "House" was centred in the school-room adjoining our house by the Sacrist's Gate. The object, said Fawcett, was to give the day-boys a sense of corporate identity and a sense of individual importance, because I would be for each of them "their Housemaster". I was to give them the attention and discipline that B.F. thought they lacked. He even gave me a cane and told me to use it. I did, but deeply regret it. I can only say in defence that this was a universal unquestioned method of punishment. On one occasion I had a nasty incident of bullying which I "dealt with"; but when things did not seem to improve in that respect, I consulted Saunders who said that if you use a cane yourself you will always get a degree of bullying (though he himself was a vigorous caner). So I gave it up.

As for the boys of Oppidans B, I really did love them, and so did Juliet. We have a delightful picture of us both with the two girls and all the boys of Oppidans B. They were a cheerful lot, some of them very able, some excellent games players. I wrote and produced a play for them which was a success; and, much encouraged, Julie and I produced *Androcles and the Lion*, borrowing a few boarders to help out.

We also produced the school play one year, at the request of the senior boys. It was a nonsense farce (*Youth at the Helm*) and went down well with the school, especially when Reg Atkinson lit his pipe. There was also a House competition which I was asked to adjudicate. I gave the prize to a production of *Waiting for Godot*. Roger Firkins kindly said that my speech on that occasion was the best thing of its kind that he had ever heard, which was nice of him. To me it was good to be so involved in the life of the school.

One nice thing about housemastering was that I got to know many of the local people whose sons were in my House. This was good for the boys when they found that I was prepared to take the trouble to see them at home and to see their parents. One such was Ian McKittrick, now a barrister. Ian was doing badly at work and behaving as if he had very little intelligence, which I did not believe. When I went to his home I found him engaged in his consuming hobby, which was to follow the movements of merchant ships round the world. He told me – all excited – pointing to a globe, SS "*Something*" was leaving Singapore today and would pass SS "*Somethingelse*" on its way from Perth tomorrow night, and SS "*Yetanother*" would cross their courses on its way to China somewhere between X and Z. 'Ian,' I said, 'if you can keep all this in your head, you should be able to manage Latin and French verbs!' He saw the point.

As Chaplain I used to organise Quiet Days for the Confirmation candidates. Then, emboldened by their popularity and effectiveness, I organised a Retreat for the older boys at Hemmingford Gray, the Diocesan Retreat and Conference House. This had the Headmaster's and the Dean's enthusiastic support, and roused the deepest suspicion from everyone else. The first Retreat was certainly successful. Boys are religious beings when encouraged. The subject matter of the talks was made suitable for them, and the services were designed to give them lots of scope for participation and contribution. The silences were awkward at first (as in Retreats for adults) and there was the expected giggling over such important exercises in communication as "Please pass the salt", which had to be made in sign language. But I felt – and the member of staff with us (David Scott) agreed – that a good atmosphere was achieved. On the last morning before breakfast, at which the silence was officially to be broken, the boys, led by Peter Tamplin, had a silent rag on the lawn, playing Tig. Then – back into the house for a noisy breakfast.

Unfortunately, the second one was not so successful. Word had got around that the Retreat was a Good Thing, and some may have decided to go for wrong reasons. All seemed to be well at the time, but two days later Fawcett summoned me to tell me that a Housemaster had complained that some of his boys had used the occasion to smoke. So that (in my time) was that. This is an example of how both at Ely and Lancing the staff would go to infinite trouble to prevent, and the boys to even more trouble to perpetrate, the crime of smoking, whatever the consequences if caught.

By far the most important events at Ely in our five happy years there were the birth of Penelope and then, two years later, Angela. During a walk along the river bank, on a gorgeous day off, Juliet whispered to me that perhaps, she could not be sure, but the indications were, that very possibly, she was pregnant. Dr Bamford soon confirmed this, sharing our delight. He particularly wanted Julie's first baby to be born at the Evelyn Nursing Home in Cambridge. And so it happened. A fortnight before she was due, Julie and I went to Cambridge to watch the bump-races on the Cam, my previous career as a cox for the St Edmund Hall Eight giving me a professional interest. That very night, things began to happen. I drove Julie across the Fens from Ely to Cambridge in our old Ford Eight. It was a hazardous journey. Snow was falling. The headlights failed. We crept along the slippery, twisty road with only side-lights to see by. But we arrived safely; and so did Penelope Marian Campling, all five and a half pounds of her. I was allowed to see her almost at once, and it is libellously affirmed that I put my finger into her mouth, no doubt affecting her health and character for ever after.

All that people have said about the joy of the birth of one's firstborn has been understated. No words can express it. The fact that love and creativity, new life, a new person, a character in her own right, should all go together in a sequence of pleasure and hope and suffering and ultimate joy, seems too good to be true. To us this joy has its God-dimension evoking awe and thanksgiving. Also our joy was enhanced by being shared by so many people in Ely: in the Cathedral, College, Choir, congregation, city, School. I shall never forget it; and the School was granted a holiday in Penelope's honour.

Angela was conceived at Hope Cove on a holiday that was memorable for having the one-year old Penelope with us chortling with pleasure at the beach and the sea and all the nice people who came and admired her. Angela was not so punctual as Penelope. Julie's mother Kay came to stay with us to look after Julie and Penelope in the critical weeks before the baby was due; and went away again because the baby refused to appear. Also there was trouble with the baby being upside down and Julie having to go to hospital for her adjustment. But at last Angela decided that it was time to be born. Once again it was a stormy night. Julie refused to believe the signs. At last she did. The ambulance came at the doctor's insistence and we drove across the Fens expecting Angela to be born at any moment. Once at Addenbrooke's Hospital things happened quickly. I was there to give moral support, despite Dr Bamford's tut-tutting; and when it was all over I walked through the streets of Cambridge in the early hours of the morning to catch the first train back to Ely, my heart and my head proudly rejoicing at the birth of our second daughter, Angela Mary Campling.

Ben Fawcett said that he would (a) grant the school a holiday in honour of Angela's birth, but (b) cancel it for some collective misdemeanour which had been committed – something to do with tampering with Miss Arbor's rain-gauge. Julie objected most strongly – so he relented and the boys had their holiday.

At about this time our first au pair girl, Wanda Fora, came to live with us. She was from the Italian part of Switzerland and already spoke four languages fluently. She was delightful and she adored the children. She was also highly intelligent and I taught her English, getting her to write essays which I corrected. She was a Roman

Catholic, and unfortunately the local priest would not allow her to come to the Cathedral. She became a firm family friend. On a later occasion, when Julie and I went to America, she had Penelope to stay with her in Switzerland. (Penelope's adventures getting home again deserve a book to themselves.) Later still she came with her husband to stay with us at Pershore, where we took them to the County Ground at Worcester and introduced them to the mysteries of cricket.

One day in 1959 the Provost of Lancing (Canon Browne-Wilkinson) wrote to me to say that I might be the right person, as an Old Boy and in view of my recent experience, to be the new Chaplain of Lancing. My heart leapt at this suggestion, and despite a warning from Lady Spens that "it would not be good for my career" (about which I never thought at all) it seemed to me that nothing could be better. So Juliet and I went to Chichester to see the Provost, then drove on to see the Headmaster of Lancing, John Dancy. He cross-examined me fiercely, but was obviously interested in what I had to say about the centrality of the teaching. There was virtually none at Lancing (he said) except the O-levels in Divinity for everyone, and A-levels for the few. Cuthbert Shaw, the present Chaplain (also an OL) was a fine priest, but was determined not to be a schoolmaster. I felt strongly that the two should go together, and I told Mr Dancy that I would want to be identified with every side of school life, and that I would want to teach the Christian faith as I was trying to do at Ely. I also told him about the prospect of my books. He decided to appoint me and wrote a formal letter offering me the post of Chaplain of Lancing College.

In the summer holidays of 1960 Juliet and I took two coach-loads of boys to see the Passion Play at Oberammergau. Two Lancing boys joined the party. The adventures we had in the course of the long journeys, the time at Oberammergau itself and the five days' stay in the Alps are most memorable. There was the fuss over the tickets which did not arrive in time; the hotel where, although booked, there was no accommodation, forcing some of us to sleep in broomcupboards; the friendly fight with pine-cones that the two coaches had with one another in a forest near Lake Garda; the member of the public who was very excited to meet our famous choristers (this was just after *Music for the Feast of Christmas* had been issued); the profound impact which the play itself made upon everybody; the walk in the mountains with James Bowman; Simon Davey going off on his own for a botanical exploration, and us thinking he was lost. All this would take another book to describe.

There were generous farewell speeches, and the gifts of a fine oak table and a chandelier when we left. Christmas in the Cathedral that year was glorious. The choristers, now under Arthur Wills, Penelope's godfather, stayed in accommodation sparsely adapted for them in The Choir House, looked after by Julie. Despite the discomfort it was a happy Christmas for everyone; and we managed to keep them entertained in between packing things up ready to leave for Lancing.

Roger Firkins drove us to Sussex and we moved into St Nicholas Lodge in time for the new term at Lancing College. This was January

1961. A new life lay ahead, full of hope, fulfilment and disappointment.

Chapter 16
Chaplain of Lancing College

Lancing College had never had a married chaplain before, so a new house was built for us in Hoe Court, a pleasant group of houses situated across the Sixteen Acre Field. St Nicholas Lodge looked down to the coastal strip of Sussex, and then to the sea beyond. It was an attractive house, built in an open style with kitchen, dining-room and sitting-room running into each other, my study tucked round the corner. As a family we spent seven happy years there.

Our nearest neighbours were John and Heather Chaffer with their two children, Jason and Tamsin. On the other side, with a wild wood between us, was a large house with a spacious downstairs flat where George and Mary Shaw lived with their children. George Shaw was the successful Head of Biology. His hobby was academic gowns and he used to wear his own shimmering Oxford doctor's gown with great solemnity in Chapel, even though in those days he did not believe in God. He must have changed his mind, because in later years he became Churchwarden at Granchester. At Lancing he was a firm "behaviourist", who strongly opposed my views, though we and our families were good friends.

Above the Shaws lived the Bohemian Powers (as the Shaws described them), Michael, Jane, Dominic, Caroline, Adam and Alice. We loved the Powers. They were always pleasant, friendly and ready to help in day-to-day domestic matters, even if they did bang on the Shaw ceiling and overflow the family bath once or twice. Michael was not a worshipping Christian. He was one of those appointed by Dancy for his many gifts, not his religious convictions. But he once told me that he liked my "life-affirming" Christianity; and when it came to the crunch he was a "supporter".

Round the corner lived Alan and Cheril Evans-Jones and their son Gareth, who used to get up to mischief with Peter. Gareth is now a housemaster at Eton, and Peter is Deputy Head of a comprehensive school in London. They should meet again!

Hoe Court was a good place for the children. They could roam about the woods, go up the downs, and play wild prisoner games in the gardens which all ran into one another. I lurked one day at a bedroom window aiming my Super-8 camera for a long picture of the children creeping up on one another, with boistrous fights, captures, rescues and recaptures, all going on around our hut and Peter's tent. At times our house would be left in eerie silence, because the children had gone elsewhere; at other times all the Hoe Court children plus many from the College houses seemed to be squabbling and socialising in our garden.

When we first went to Lancing, Angela was a baby in a pram, and she spent most of her life under the apple tree. There were still workmen doing their final touches to the house, and Angela used to throw things out of her pram for their entertainment.

Peter was born in Worthing in a very old-fashioned hospital where fathers were not encouraged to be present at birth or even to see their offspring at close quarters. No Daddy's finger in the mouth for Peter! When I went to see Juliet, who was very shaken after the birth of her nine-and-a-half pound son, I was shown a room full of babies and told that Peter was "the third on the right", the largest and noisiest on view.

We had a succession of au pair girls to live with us, and we loved them all. Several Lancing masters had au pairs, so the girls had a social life of their own and they used to go to Brighton and Worthing together for evening classes and other activities. There was Ruth, who had been a friend of Wanda, and a jolly French girl, Chantal, who was a particular favourite. She came with us to St David's, where we had holidays in Father's cottage, Craig y Mor. She used to wheel Peter around the narrow Welsh roads in his pram, with Angela on her shoulders, singing naughty French songs at the top of her voice. She was always smiling and laughing. She told us that her parents were *tres libres*; but, alas, on one occasion she was out all night in Brighton. This was against the rules so we thought that her parents should be told. It turned out that they were not at all *libres*. Father was over the next day and took her home. Then there was Elspeth, the beautiful Swede whom I gently rebuked for overdoing her determination to slim. And there was Francette, a particularly pretty girl from Paris, who was around when Peter was born.

Beyond the little world of Hoe Court, up the hill, across the Sixteen Acre Field, was the College itself. Sometimes we went *en famille* and watched the activities on the games field which stretched in huge steps down the hill on the other side of the College under the lee of the Chapel. The nearer to the Chapel (and the pavilion and the "grubber"), the higher the class of players. In the spring term athletics in fascinating variety were performed all over the Lower Field. They made an entrancing spectacle as we wandered from discus-throwing to high-jumping and long-jumping, hurdles, putting the weight, hurling the javelin and various lengths of running and relays. The girls would eye the boys, the boys the girls; and Peter would sit up in his pram, watch everything that was going on, and be much admired. Sometimes, instead of the playing fields, we would walk along the rough track between Hoe Court and the College drive, and visit the College farm. There we could watch the pigs being fed, amidst a cacophany of piercing squeels.

Our family life at Lancing was varied and entertaining. It included the formal dinners to which we went and which we gave, and children's parties. Eventually the girls went to the local school; and so did Peter. Penelope learnt the violin from Jean Pounier, a top-class professional who had turned teacher. The children would walk back from school over the downs, and Julie or I would meet them at the chalk-pit at the top of our lane. Sometimes we had exceptionally cold weather, and I can remember a hazardous walk over the snowy, slithery, frozen downs with Peter and Gareth, both behaving with courage and stoicism.

In term time I was rather an absentee father. I would leave the house at seven every morning, walk up the Sixteen Acre, past Fields House, round through the College to the Chapel, where I would say my prayers before the seven thirty Eucharist. On "my days" I would celebrate the

Eucharist with a server and a congregation of about six, masters and boys. On Henry Thorold's day I would be in the congregation for his "Mass", but he would never attend mine, preferring to celebrate by himself with a server in a separate chapel. Then I would have a cooked and silent breakfast in the masters' dining-room (now the McGarry Room); "silent" because the masters were all reading newspapers.

Then I would go to my study, which was on the first floor of the Masters' Tower, where the common-room was situated and the bachelor masters lived. From my room I could see everything that was going on in the Upper Quad. There I would make last minute preparations for whatever classes I had to teach, and see any boys who wished to see me. There were prayers in Great School twice a week at which any religious feelings that I tried to impart were likely to be dispelled by the Head giving out notices, congratulations, public and collective rebukes, or whatever.

Then lessons. I taught a nearly full timetable, which, being in addition to everything else such as Confirmation classes and Chapel services, was extremely demanding. After a morning's teaching I would have lunch in Hall, sitting with the staff at the High Table. Then, after coffee and gossip in Biddy Shearwood's kitchen, I would sit in my room to be available to any who wanted to see me; perhaps one of my own personal "pupils" who would bring me his card for scrutiny; or perhaps someone in some kind of trouble or doubt, or just for a chat. In the summer there was afternoon school, after which I would go home to tea; or I would be asked to umpire a game of cricket; or, in winter a game of football. Chapel was at six every day; after which I would go home if I was lucky. But there were lots of evening meetings, clubs, pupils to see, Confirmation classes to take and candidates to see individually; not to mention services and sermons to prepare, teaching preparation and book correcting to do: all before I was free to drag myself home to wife and family.

At Ely I had taught each boy twice a week, which was demanding, but it kept me in touch with them all. At Lancing this was impossible, so I decided that I would teach all the new men and the Sixth Form and as much as I could of the rest. I later started an A-level group in the "Forty" (Lower Sixth). In its first year there were about eight candidates who did well in the two-year course; but later it grew to about eighteen, which was more difficult. This happened because the idea had got around that Divinity was an easy option. For that reason and because the set was not so interested or intelligent, the second group did not do so well. Sometimes my sets included boys who had already done Classics and were able to do Divinity in a year with a gospel or an epistle in Greek. This was stimulating for me, and I learnt a great deal by doing it. As the syllabus changed in its details every year, the whole exercise was taxing but rewarding. I have been preaching and lecturing on the strength of it ever since.

My aim at Ely had been to teach the rudiments of Christianity to all the boys so that they could at least know what it was they were accepting or rejecting. This proved impossible at Lancing where other masters (especially Henry Thorold) shared the teaching. They were too individual to take their share in someone else's syllabus; and H.C.T. told me firmly that he had his "own method", which he had been using for years. This did not include the teaching of Christianity. What he did was kept from me, but I suspect that it was more to do with Christian art and architecture, about which he was enthusiastic and knowledgeable; and only indirectly to do with the Gospel of God. He had an abundance of relaxed charm, emphasised by his idiosyncracies. He always kept the door of his classroom open, and there were invariable rituals for every lesson. Asked by a nonplussed inspector what he used for visual aids, he answered, 'I am my own visual aid'. Which was true. Patrick Halsey, on the other hand, when asked the same question, said that somewhere or other, he couldn't remember where, and he couldn't actually lay hands on it at the moment, he had a ram's horn. He then went round his colleagues accusing them of pinching his ram's horn; and Fields House boys were made to look for it in their lockers.

With my first years' class I followed the developing pattern of Book 3 (*The Word of God in Action*) in my series *The Way, The Truth and The Life*, which I was in the process of writing. It starts with the challenging question, "What is religion?" I took the answers seriously, pointing out that a "judgement" ("It's a lot of nonsense") is not the same as a definition. The boys helped me a lot in the writing of the book, especially the illustrations from films which I selected with Harry Guest's expert help. These would be set for "Evening School", and stimulated some lively and provocative essays. Book 4 on the Old Testament was also in its formative stage with lots of trial and error. David Thistlethwaite, an artistic boy in Fields, did the Old Testament time-chart which I still use when I am giving sermon courses on Old Testament subjects.

Donald Bancroft, in charge of English, invited me to teach English to a class in the First Year, and another class for O-level. This made a huge extra demand upon my time and intellectual resources because I had to do a lot of thinking and reading and preparation. But I decided to accept on the grounds that it would be good for me and for my standing in the school, even if it meant giving up some divinity classes.

The English teaching was deemed successful and I got a good crit. from the inspectors. I had devised a scheme (borrowed from Max Burr at Belmont) by which we invented a small-town community with every boy being a particular character within it. They then had to write letters to one another. Some fine correspondence was produced as the town's life grew and polite invitations and angry demands and threats of legal action were hurled across the classroom. I was also given an O-level set and we studied *The Diary of a Fox-Hunting Man*, and some science fiction. These classes contained such future literary giants as David Hare and Christopher Hampton. I also had Tim Rice in a divinity group, but cannot remember much about him except his uncommited charm.

The problem was the Sixth Form. These were not the mild-mannered 1950s; they were the contemptuous 1960s, with everyone in revolt against something – *towards* The Beatles and "King" Elvis Presley, and *against* all restrictions and authority, both as regards truth and behaviour. Chapel and Christianity made an excellent target, and I experienced this immediately on my arrival.

On the first day of my first term at St Nicholas Lodge, as I was engaged in the task of settling books into my study, there was a knock on the door and the tall, lanky, fifteen-year-old Julian Reindorp, eldest son of the Bishop of Guildford, presented himself. Could he please see me? 'Of course.' Well, he was a committed Christian and very anxious that the Christian religion, which meant the Chapel and divinity lessons, should do well and recover lost ground. People had liked Cuthbert Shaw my predecessor very much; but the Sixth Form made mincemeat of him in the classroom, and the compulsory services with their plain-song and ritual, though prized by the devotees, were disliked by everyone else. Much of this was due, said Julian, to the fact that Cuthbert Shaw could not hold his own in the classroom. I would have to be careful. The Sixth were waiting to take me to pieces. He did not advise gimmicks either in class or in the pulpit. Jokes were funny at the time but were often counter-effective. Sincerity by itself would not be enough (no one could be more sincere than C.S.). I would have to be … etc.: all rather discouraging but definitely helpful.

At my first Sixth Form lesson I had a list of those who should be there. But one was missing. Where was he? 'Oh, I expect he has forgotten, Sir.' 'Then will you kindly go and remind him, and we will start the lesson when he gets here.' That lesson started and ended ten minutes late, ten precious minutes into break.

It was about the concept of knowledge, which is a relationship through awareness. Contrast the direct knowledge *of* with the more tenuous indirect knowledge *about*. There are degrees of knowledge (both kinds) according to the closeness and strength of the relationship, which itself depends on the strength of the links between the known and the knower (with plenty of examples from science, history and types of love). Religions claim to be the *knowledge of* and *knowledge about* God. The "links", of course, have to be tested. There would be plenty of time for that. End of lesson.

One of them had just won a scholarship to Oxford. 'Did you get a scholarship to the University, Sir?' asked the arrogant Neil. 'University? We didn't even think about the University in my day. We went into the Army or Navy or Airforce to serve our country. Several were killed before they could get to the University.'

That was a small and clever set – and we got on rather well; but soon a new arrangement of the timetable was made by which Divinity for the whole of the Sixth Form was to be held in the Physics Laboratory during the last period of Saturday morning. Could anything be worse? There I had to stand at the focal point in the centre with tiers of boys at the desks rising up above me to the back of the room. Thus I was confronted, and whatever I planned there were always one or two who would question, argue and dominate the proceedings. Some of them were actually quite angry, not with me personally, but with a system which gave them too little liberty in all sorts of ways, especially in the obligation to worship God every day in Chapel, whether they wanted to or not. I had to support the system, and I argued hotly for God, but I could feel their anger, and I was aware of the discomfort of those who were on my side, but felt that I was being defeated by the situation.

So the next holidays I thought the matter through and came up with a scheme for Sixth Form divinity groups. Instead of meeting en masse at a set time every week, pupils would be divided into small groups of six to eight each and do their divinity with "Divinity tutors" at a time convenient to all concerned. In these groups they would study in ways that suited themselves, boys and tutors alike. Some would study (say) the Epistle to the Ephesians in Greek (with John Bell), or St John's gospel in much easier Greek (with me). Some, on the other hand, might prefer to read *Why I am not a Christian* by Bertand Russell.

This particular book was popular, but it played into my hands; because anyone could see that Russell's objections to Christianity sprang from his rebellion against his upbringing; in the same way that Clement Freud rejected God as he rejected his own father. Some were ready for the recently published *Honest to God* by Bishop John Robinson. This suited the sort of person who found the Christianity he had been taught to be too small and restricting, with its Sunday school God and stained-glass-window Christ, rather than the "Man for Others" that Robinson writes about. Also the book contains a useful chapter on prayer which was liberating for those who had been brought up to think of prayer as childish acts of petition. "Science and Religion" was a popular subject, and I recommended Archbishop John Habgood's book, because it tells the story – of the clashes that need not be clashes. And some were drawn to ethical problems, even to "Christianity and Politics".

Obviously I could not do this all by myself, so I appealed to my colleagues, not just the "Christians", to help. I said that I did not mind about a person's present state of belief or unbelief; what mattered was that he would be prepared to take the subject seriously and be a "seeker" along with the boys. Many agreed to help, and then I had the job of arranging the groups and fitting them to suitable "tutors". Sometimes a tutor would agree to help on condition that he could pick his group. Harry Guest was a liberal agnostic with a mind not as open as he thought it was. He was popular and he took two groups of the sort of boys who would have been difficult with me, though I insisted on taking one particularly difficult group myself.

One boy (the son of a vicar) asked me angrily why he should study divinity at all, especially if it were confined to Christianity. Why not Buddhism, for instance? 'All right. Study Buddhism.' I replied. 'You can be excused divinity classes and groups, and I will expect an essay on Buddhism, comparing it with Christianity, by the seventh week of term.' This plan was popular and was taken up by several boys, making me order lots of books for the library on world faiths; and I found myself reading essays from which I learnt a great deal. They were done seriously, and the requirement that they should "compare it (a faith) with Christianity" was invaluable as it opened people's eyes to see, for instance, that whereas Buddhism is dualist, Christianity isn't. And to study Islam and Christianity brings you to think about the One-ness of God in "simplicity" (Islam) or in "Trinity" (Christianity); and to compare "God is merciful", even "God loves" (Islam), with "God is love" brings you face to face with the Christian doctrine of the Trinity.

There were still some who did not fit at all and did not want to study anything with anyone. With one or two I entered into an "essay dialogue", telling them to write what they thought about Chapel and Christianity, the only provision being that there should be nothing insulting and no mention of personalities. I then wrote back as forthrightly as they wrote to me; and sometimes (but not always) the air was cleared.

The scheme went ahead with all the risks and no doubt a number of group and personal failures. Some of my Christian colleagues were doubtful. It seemed wrong to them that boys should actually be encouraged to read *Honest to God* and (even worse) *Why I am not a Christian* especially as they were doing so with doubting colleagues. But the Head (E.W. Gladstone by now) agreed with the scheme and took a group himself on the Reformation, he being a Historian. The general atmosphere improved immensely. It was like a boil being lanced. I do not think that any such scheme could continue indefinitely; but it was what was needed at that particular time in the life of Lancing.

John Dancy had hardly finished appointing me to Lancing when he announced that he was leaving to become the Master of Marlborough. This was a great disappointment to me. John had given me a tough, aggressive interview before he first appointed me; then, just before my first term, in a much gentler spirit, had told me of his dissatisfaction with religion at Lancing, how, in an intellectually "braced" school, the divinity teaching was third rate – indeed, how he longed for reform both in the Chapel and the classroom. But it would be up to me. He did not want to carry out major changes in his last two terms – he had made enough already; but he would help me to prepare the way for what he was sure his successor would want to see carried through.

I liked John Dancy immensely. He was unpopular with the staff at Lancing for the changes he had made, for instance, the easing out of some elderly, comfortable members; the appointment of new, able, "not our sort of Christianity" masters; the tightening of discipline and the insistance on excellence in all the interlocking circles of school life, particularly the academic, which he regarded as central. I also found John such fun to work with. He was inclined to question everything you said, not to down you but to draw out the best. He was a deeply and intelligently committed Christian; after my own heart, but more so. His was the highest combination of tough intelligence, Christian commitment and human sensitivity that I have ever met.

J.C.D. left a school thriving in all departments with a happy, steely, purposeful air. The boys seemed to me to be exceptionally bright. In my first "new men's" set, for instance, I had David Hare, Christopher Hampton and Richard Taylor, who changed his name to Carrington, and was the Vicar on *The Archers* programme for many years, and other sparky individuals who responded to everything with lively and irreverent enthusiasm. (You should have heard David Hare's imitation – both in subject matter and voice – of the Queen's Christmas Broadcast.)

E.W. Gladstone, called from being a housemaster at Eton to become the new Head of Lancing, was a very different kind of person from John Dancy. Perhaps he was what Lancing needed for it to settle into gentler, easier ways. He was one of the nicest men I have ever known, certainly the nicest headmaster, as a gentleman and a friend: perhaps too much so. He was very good on the estate, the College drive, the trees, the buildings and their surroundings, and he civilised the school in all sorts of ways, putting a stop, for instance, to the tradition of school-bathing being done in the nude. I can see the notice in his neat hand now. "All boys who bathe will wear bathing-costumes." But things began to get slack and there were too many departments proceeding on their own steam in their own direction.

I got on well with Willie Gladstone man to man. We were the same age, both ex-RNVR, and had served roughly the same length of time in the school. On one occasion he and Rosalind took Juliet and me and the parents of John Hadley to a ball at Hurlingham, and we had a lovely time together. I baptised their children, witnessed his will, and generally thought of myself as a friend.

It was a pleasing arrangement at Lancing that towards the end of his first term each boy would invite a master of his own choice to be his personal "tutor" whom he would meet regularly throughout his school career with his work-progress card in hand for probing, assessment, discussion, pats on the back or metaphorical kicks, according to desert. These sessions could be tense as well as happy and constructive occasions. I used to get my share of pupils up to the agreed limit and I established a good relationship with them – one that for some has lasted to the present day.

One pupil (now a clergyman) brought me his card with a "black", which I knew all about from the master concerned, not filled in. 'Oh, I have not got time for this today,' I said, 'bring it back tomorrow – complete.' (Did I know about the "black"? Surely not.) So he returned after lunch the next day. 'Sorry,' I said, 'that's no good. Try again tomorrow.' (So perhaps I did know.) I forget how many days this went on for, but he got the message and the "black" at last appeared. Clearly I had been waiting for it; and now that it was there and acknowledged it did not seem to matter all that much.

Another of my pupils was renowned for his smoking and the skill with which he evaded detection. After leaving school he became the

Head Perfume Taster (or Sniffer?) of a major London store. So presumably the smoking had not affected the sensitivity of his nose.

Another pupil was Jeremy Sindon, the son of Sir Donald, who became a top-class actor in his own right. He was an unusual boy. When he was acting, even in small parts, he had that mysterious quality of stage presence, a kind of relaxed concentration, an unselfconscious focus, that only the very best actors have. He hated games, and did his best to avoid them on all occasions. Patrick Halsey, his Housemaster, and I consulted together, and as a result Patrick allowed him to go into Brighton on Saturday afternoons to watch a play; on condition that he wrote a full review of it within the next few days. This arrangement suited everyone concerned; and was typical of the freedom that P.J.H. was ready to give to those whom he trusted.

Jeremy died in his early forties in the course of a brilliant run as the monstrous but loveable Mr Toad. I went to his memorial service and wept along with many famous people. Lady Sindon thanked me warmly for what I had done for Jeremy as his Tutor and for preparing him for Confirmation, to which he had been faithful all his life.

Boys came to me with problems, personal and religious. One wanted a precise definition (no fudging) of some of the sexual words and innuendos he had been encountering. Sometimes a boy had fallen out with his Housemaster, and I had to be very careful. One had quarrelled with his parents; and one came to tell me of his consuming interest in Romany, the history and culture of gipsies, and how he would like to live the gipsy life himself.

My personal pupils, Confirmation candidates and A-level pupils used to come down to our home in Hoe Court. Julie would feed them and the children beguile them. Angela made no secret of the fact that she hoped one day to marry Nigel Wheeler (who now teaches at Eastbourne College); sometimes a couple of boys would come together to "baby-sit" when we were going out. Most of the married masters used baby-sitters in a way that was sensible and civilised, until one master kept his sitters up far into the night. A housemaster complained, and the Head put a stop to it.

I had ordination candidates amongst the boys, but no more, I suppose, than in other generations. Some were clearly cut out for it, with clerical, even episcopal parents – though this did not qualify them for virtue! Some of the most determined rebels were parsons' sons. There were, for instance, in the former group, the Reindorp boys, sons of the Bishop of Guildford. He, the Bishop, gave me strong support when a housemaster complained that I had had a speaker to address the boys in Chapel about the problem of drugs. Bishop Reindorp heard about this and wrote a strong letter to Willie Gladstone squashing the objection and commending my action. There were also the Mortimer brothers, Lawrence, now a senior priest in the Coventry Diocese, and Christopher, who became a policeman. Their father was a priest and the owner/Head of a ballet school, Elmhurst, at which, most curiously, Julie had once been a pupil. He came down with his troupe, who performed in Great School and were extremely popular!

There were also some unexpected ordinands. One Sixth Form boy who was strongly opposed to me in my first term came down to see me on his last night at school and decided (later) to be ordained. He is a priest now in the West Country. Another, John Hadley, was one of the cleverest boys I ever taught. He won a Classical scholarship to Oxford when he was sixteen and then, at my suggestion, spent a year with an OL priest in Lesotho, where he had to ride long distances on horseback between the far-scattered Christian communities. This made us laugh because John was adept at not taking exercise at Lancing. He had a brilliant academic career at West Berlin, Oxford and Leeds universities, getting three "firsts". He invited me to preach at his ordination and I took a Quiet Weekend for his parish, at a lighthouse in Sussex. He became Chaplain of Bristol University and wrote a book on the Eucharist, *Bread of the World.*

David Hare was a star pupil. He became a Sacristan in Chapel and was my right-hand man when we organised the Chapel fête which raised the huge sum (for those days) of £1,500. David wrote the brochure for the fête and helped me with the publicity. When I was Vicar of Pershore I went to see one of his plays at Worcester College of Education, and later he wrote to me because he wanted a "guide" to the General Synod. We spent a day together in the gallery, I trying to explain the complicated procedures of the Synod and some of the personalities who were on view that day. He was beginning to write

Racing Demon. Later, he sent me a typescript and asked for my comments. I wrote fully about the theology and relevant details of church life which he portrays so brilliantly. He took my advice on some matters, not on others; and he gave me two tickets to the National Theatre when it was first produced. This play shows a deep understanding of the predicament of clerical life and work in the East End of London and, although it is now dated, I enjoyed it very much when I saw it again recently in Chichester. I find in his plays (especially *Acting Up,* the monologue about Palestine) a compassion underlying the spare and sparkling wit of the dialogue.

The Chapel fête included a star-studded film by Richard Taylor, who had hung around the Pinewood Studios in the holidays asking film-stars if he could film them for twenty seconds as they emerged. Each would light a cigarette, or something like it. Round these snaps he strung a story, and then showed his star-ridden film at our fête. His film also included a remarkable shot of the Chapel being "launched" (like a ship) and careering down College Hill into the River Adur.

Obviously the Chapel "touched" the boys who worshipped in it throughout their school days, and many were profoundly responsive at the time. But how they kept their faith later was up to them. I know that many of them still feel indebted to the Chapel and the Lancing Christian ethos; but of course there are also those who took against it. Christianity properly presented has to be divisive. A boy once said to me, 'Sir, I have lost my faith.' 'You mean you have stopped being faithful,' I replied.

But lots of my life at Lancing was outside the Chapel and outside the circle of "the faithful". I used, for instance, to referee football matches and was once seriously embroiled in a row when I was presiding over a needle match between Fields House and Gibbs. Of course, I was accused by the Gibbs House of monstrous bias; all in good fun, until the winning goal was scored. Or was it? If the goalposts do not have nets behind them to encage the ball, and if a speculative shot is kicked from twenty yards out, and the sun is in your eyes and the ball sails just over or just under the bar, how are you to tell if it's a goal or not? I couldn't, so I asked the advice of a spectator who was standing on the line by the corner-flag – only to find (when I had taken his advice) that he too was

Fields House and therefore equally biased. This row was allowed to burgeon because Henry Thorold (the Housemaster of Gibbs) said that of course I was biased, being ex-Fields; and Patrick Halsey, still the Housemaster of Fields, said that he agreed, but who could blame me? Both were enjoying the joke; but needle matches are no joking matter to those involved, and Gibbs House boys were not pleased.

Nigel Wheeler, however (of Olds House), had plenty of confidence in my refereemanship and he invited me to be the travelling referee for his Third Eleven. This was made up of boys who were not in "First Club" but were keen journeymen, as I had been in my school days. It was important to Nigel that they had a referee who understood the offside rules, because he proposed using the offside trap on enemy teams; so he took me aside and drilled me in the rule, which I knew anyway. I enjoyed Third Eleven occasions immensely, but I think that Nigel found that I was not such a compliant referee as he had hoped.

Meanwhile, Ken Shearwood – the Housemaster of Sanderson's, famous footballer; the most loyal and understanding person on the Lancing staff as far as I was concerned and, of course, the master in charge of football – invited me to help with the coaching of the younger boys. He gave me a method. I was to get them to practise first in threes, two against one; then in fives, three against two; then in sevens, four against three: so that they learnt to think collectively and to make space for the "one over". It was great fun and a lesson that I have often thought about; that individuality and collectiveness go together.

It was not by chance that I got engaged in this and similar activities. I wanted to get as much integrated into school life as possible, to "dirty my hands" in the kind of things that were important to the boys. Obviously this policy had its dangers. I hated making mistakes and making myself look ridiculous (or monstrously biased!) but on balance I think it was a good thing not a bad one that I was found to be human, sometimes bad-tempered, and altogether fallible.

For pastoral reasons I used to go "visiting", as in a parish. I would go to the boys' "pits" (their studies) and chat with them in as friendly a way as I could. There was difficult territory here between being too much "one of them", on the one hand, and being a "master in authority" on the other. I always tried to give warning of my approach, so that "lights could be put out"; and if I happened to smell a little smoke, so what? I consulted the housemasters about this policy, and they agreed that pastoral opportunity was more important than disciplinary precision. Sometimes I would "go round a House" in an evening and end up with the Matron and then the Housemaster himself; and then go home, rather tired.

Visiting extended to the domestic staff. My vision was that Lancing College should be a community in the fullest sense, and this had to include all who lived and served in the place. There were children around, so I organised a Children's Service on Sunday mornings. We even had a Sunday school outing to Chessington Zoo with all the children in the place, including our own. Some housemasters' wives came with us, including Biddy Shearwood, who was the sweetest person and the slowest driver I have ever met: she told me that she always slowed down when she saw a car coming towards her. When we got there, all the children wanted to do was to go on the swings and roundabouts.

There were also the College servants, the married ones living in the drive, the unmarrieds in a kind of hostel presided over by Mrs Kentall, the verger's wife. I saw them all once each holiday, and went to Lewes gaol to visit a young man of very low intelligence who had got himself into trouble on Brighton beach with some sex offence which I do not think he understood. "I don't know why they have put me in this place," he kept saying. What a terrible dank place that gaol was, and how hard the warders were – even to me.

There was also at Lancing a set of "in betweens", women who served the school faithfully and got little thanks for it. The house matrons were all right. They had the boys and the housemasters to tend and chivvy and grumble against and they could enjoy the "community" of the House. But the two caterers, for instance, lived lonely lives stuck away in some remote room high up in the College, and did not feel themselves to be part of anything. They too were on my termly "rounds", and one of them, Lavender, became a friend of Juliet.

When I left Lancing both Provost and Head told me that this particular work had been unnecessary and distracting: my responsibilities began and ended with the boys, not the staff, certainly not the domestic staff. My successor would be thus instructed. Blow them! Is it not one of the first duties of the Church to create community? I suspect that the source of this rebuke was the Bursar who was very possessive about "his" domestic staff; just as it was he who stopped me taking boys "up the Chapel", as the insurance would not cover them in case of an accident; and he refused to let Lancing host the Public School Chaplains' Conference (of which I was the Chairman) in the Easter holidays. But we (Bursar and I) became friends when his son Nicholas joined my A-level Divinity set and through a lot of hard work by both of us scored a "pass". Bill Tydd wrote me an exceedingly gracious letter after that.

Broadcasting became a feature of my life at Lancing. There was an Easter Day celebration on the radio; a televised sung Eucharist with me celebrating and preaching; a week of evening meditations on Southern Television, which was recorded in Southampton; and a *Songs of Praise*, which I wrote and compèred myself. The Choir sang *Jesu Joy* from memory, athwart the Chancel steps, John Shaw, who became a professional, playing the oboe obbligato. I had an uplifting sense of inspiration as I said the lines that I had learnt by heart, between the musical episodes; and I remember consciously treating the camera and the men behind it as if I were sharing all the Gospel that I had in me with them.

Southern Television liked Lancing, so with their approval I devised a programme about the College, its founder and its Christian purpose and the present conditions of life and submitted it. 'This would do nicely for John Betjeman,' said George Egan, the producer; so J.B. took over "my" programme, though he was no good at learning the words or the facts: he kept making mistakes which required the filming to be done again. Anyway, the programme was considered a success; but I was given no credit for it, not even a fee for writing it. I could have done with the money (we were very poor in those days), but the matter of acknowledgement did not even occur to me at the time. I was just pleased to be involved.

Meanwhile the Public School Chaplains' Conferences were growing in numbers and influence as we met together each year and thrashed out our shared difficulties: the teaching syllabus; anger against compulsory chapel; conservative staff; uncomprehending headmasters; the ethics of the 1960s, with rebellion in the air. Our book, *Guide to Divinity Teaching*, had been published; I read a paper on Sixth Form Groups (the general feeling was "Good: but it would never work in my school"). I was Chairman for two years and we had a particularly enjoyable meeting at Stowe where we played wild golf in the intervals between sessions. Also we had a talk from the BBC Religious Broadcasting chief, who asked me if I would consider a job with them if invited to do so.

I also joined a smaller, selected group of headmasters and chaplains who met at Lambeth Palace, arranged for us by Ted Fisher, who was a son of the former Archbishop and Headmaster of St Edward's, Oxford. I became friends, at that time, with Oliver Thistleton-Fiennes, who was then Chaplain of Clifton, having great troubles, and later became Dean of Lincoln, where he had even greater ones. Yet he was such an easy, gentle person, the last to be controversial for its own sake, but surprisingly awkward and tough when it came to matters of principle.

Meanwhile the Woodard schools became active. Heads and chaplains were summoned to Bloxham, and I was elected secretary to the first Bloxham Conference. Out of this grew the Bloxham Conference, which is now established on a permanent basis with a paid staff. It produces papers on everything that Woodard schools stand for. This happened after I had left the scene.

A special occasion was when Monsignor Gordon Wheeler came back to Lancing to address the school in Chapel. He had been Chaplain of Lancing before the war. One summer holiday he went to Rome with Patrick Halsey, and there, to Patrick's cynical amusement, he "poped". So when I became Chaplain in the 1960s I found that one of my predecessors was now the Episcopal Administrator of Westminster Cathedral. So why not confound my critics by inviting him to preach? No doubt he would be the first Roman Catholic ever to speak from the Lancing pulpit. I told the boys about him before it happened and begged them not to let the C. of E. down by negative behaviour or feeble singing. I need not have worried. They startled me by their bright response and robust singing at that service, and I felt that the Monsignor must have been impressed. He spoke well and made an excellent impression on everyone, without embarrassing us Anglicans. In the evening I asked him to my house to talk informally to the Sixth Form Theological Society. This was called the Eutychus Society, named after the boy who fell dead from the upper storey, because St Paul would go on talking (Acts 20, 9–12). Has any other Christian society been named after him? I regret to say that my terrible theologians (Henry Spier particularly) bullied the Bishop as they challenged him to defend his Church's attitude on birth-control and world population; I had to rescue him from the rapier lunges of their arguments. Monsignor Wheeler later became Bishop of Leeds and will reappear in these annals in the chapter on Ripon.

In the next chapter I will come to the crux of my ministry at Lancing.

Chapter 17
Leaving Lancing

My relationships with the staff at Lancing were mixed – and I now embark on the sad story which ends with Henry Thorold and me both being dismissed.

Some of the staff welcomed me back having known me as boy in the school. I do not think that Sam Jagger remembered me. But I remembered him, and I reminded him of how he had appointed me "Arse-end Charlie" in the Fields House Home Guard Section. Arthur Cooper remembered me because he had taught me French and had then left to join the Army. He was now Housemaster of Olds and with Pam his wife, was the first to invite Juliet and me to dinner. On that occasion he told me all his troubles, house-wise and (particularly) chapel-wise; and expected me to have answers at the ready. I fear that I proved a disappointment There were no easy answers. He was a good but simplistic man; always delightful company.

"Monkey" Chamberlin remembered me well, having taught me English and History. He was now Housemaster of Teme, and, to everyone's delight, had married his Matron, Audrey. Marriage had certainly softened him, but the boys, especially those in his House, were still much in awe. He was pleased when I told him that I had learnt the trick of composing essays (and so sermons) from his "fish" method. He supported me loyally, but unfortunately he retired from his House soon after I arrived, and so lost most of his influence. But he continued to give me good advice. 'Get to the point of your sermons more quickly,' he once said.

That was at the beginning of Holy Week at the end of my first term in the school. Easter was early that year so we had Holy Week and

205

Easter at school. The last time this had happened Father Trevor Huddleston had taken all the extra services in Chapel, and it took some persuasion for John Dancy to let me do it myself; but I did and this gave me an opportunity to make my mark upon the school. I gave one address a day to the whole school at evensong, then another to a voluntary congregation in the crypt, plus much time on personal interviews and confessions. I still have the Holy Week booklet which we produced. The school was responsive. No clouds on the horizon yet.

John Handford was still around, taking a few Sixth Formers for Classical scholarships. He also took a learned divinity group. He had been much hurt by Dancy's treatment of him and had taken himself off to Canada to teach in a girls' school. Back at Lancing, living as a widower with his two daughters, he rarely appeared at College. He was obviously pleased, in a schoolmasterly way, to have me back, and was astonished that I could still quote gobbetts of Lucretius and the Agamemnon and *The Testament of Beauty* (still can!) and could manage some modern as well as New Testament Greek. With me he was appointed a governor of St Michael's School, Camberwell, which in its special relationship with Lancing had taken the place of the school "mission" to the parish of St Michael's, Camberwell. John and I used to drive to Camberwell once a term and I would tell him all the developments and difficulties in the chapel situation. Once J.C.D. had left, John Handford was the only influential member of the older "Christian" set who understood the need for reform and could give me sensible advice.

But, O Patrick Halsey! I considered him to be the most influential man in my life (after John Kelly) for what he had done for me and the values he had given me when I was a boy in his House; especially faith in God and the love of music. As seniors we used to relish the way he mimicked his colleagues, his wicked accounts of common-room life with its gossip, above all his sharing with us the correspondence he had with Major Parnell-Smith about the corps: all this in our Lancing-at-Ludlow days. He had also taken me to Europe when I was fourteen; and then had visited Scandinavia with Brian Wallas, Douglas Bean and me just after the war. So by this time we were "friends", not just master–pupil; and he claimed to have engineered my appointment to Lancing. Perhaps he thought that he would be able to "run" me.

However, after two golden terms he became dissatisfied. One Friday evening I attended the Fields House Gramophone Society and, incidentally, was horrified to find that the boys read books instead of listening to the music. When it was over and lapsang had been drunk and spilled on the Housemaster's carpet as of yore, and the boys had gone, presumably to bed, we settled down and Patrick produced a long list of complaints. His favourite hymns had not been chosen lately; last Sunday's visiting preacher ...; he could not see why ...; where was the ...? What had happened to ... ? I forget the precise nature of his complaints, but I remember that he was anxious that the Carol Service (now looming) should have more congregational participation. I agreed with this and prepared to battle it out with John Alston, the excellent (and always loyal) Director of Music.

The most important thing was that he had heard that I was dissatisfied with the non-communicating sung Eucharist which the whole school attended every Sunday morning. Those who wanted to make their Communion could only do so by going to the earlier eight o'clock service as well. I was determined to change this state of affairs, and I had had the enthusiastic backing of Dancy and now the cautious agreement of Gladstone and the Provost. But Patrick said that he would go to the stake for the principle of "fasting Communion": that meant "no receiving of Communion after breakfast". So unless I was prepared to have the main service before breakfast, which would deny the staff and boys their treasured "lie in", and would be wrong in other ways too, there was no way by which the present arrangement could be changed. And, added Patrick darkly, many of his colleagues agreed with him.

That was a long evening. The gist of my reply (after the second whisky) was, 'Please trust me. I know what I am doing.' But he didn't. Perhaps I didn't.

The Church of Rome had given up insisting on fasting Communion during the war; and the practice of an after-breakfast whole-school Eucharist was one I had supervised and had no trouble with at Ely. I could not see what they were so frightened about; and I thought that if they would trust me they would find that everything would be all right. Also I knew that the majority, including people like Ken Shearwood and Arthur Cooper, as well as newly joined Christians such as Robin Reeve and Ted Maidment, would agree with me.

But I was reckoning without the Reverend Henry Thorold. He was ten years my senior; had been at Lancing a long time; was Housemaster of Gibbs and officially the "Assistant Chaplain". When I was first appointed, Wilfred Derry (my old chaplain) wrote to congratulate me and say how pleased he was that I was going to take Cuthbert Shaw's place. I would surely be a chaplain in the "proper Lancing mould". 'But what on earth will you do about Henry Thorold?' he added. It was the first time I had heard of Henry; but I went to Lancing determined to like him and work easily with him.

Henry Thorold had an estate of his own in Linconshire. He had been a Classical scholar at Eton; and he drove an amazing old Rolls. Indeed, it was his boast that he had driven all the way to Lancing from Lincolnshire without changing gear: he had also once been fined for parking where he shouldn't in Worthing and vowed from the dock never, ever, to enter the town of Worthing again. He was absolutely charming, a brilliant conversationalist with a fund of stories, quick repartee and a deep chuckling laugh. He was kind and generous with those he approved of. He had a profound faith in God, along with a love for all that is traditional in literature and art, architecture and Christian liturgy. He was an expert on architecture and he wrote some of the Shell Guides in his delicious, poised, enthusiastic yet slightly ironic style. He had two hates. One was what he called "public school religion", by which he meant hearty hymn-singing, moralistic sermons and services devoid of sacramental content. His other hate was "change".

Soon after we arrived Henry took Juliet and me out to lunch in Hove, driving us there in his Rolls. After we had talked about everything under the sun except Lancing (the Navy featured; he had been an RNVR Chaplain) he turned to me abruptly and asked me whether I liked public school religion. We discussed it, and on the whole I agreed with him. But then, did I want change? I could not say, 'No.' People have always grumbled (e.g. at Pershore and Ripon) about "change for change's sake"; and I have cheerfully countered that that is no worse (perhaps better) than "no change for no change's sake". What proud impenitence to be against all change! All of us, always, individuals and institutions, are in a state of change, development, growth, improvement – or deterioration. We can never "stay the same". Change will always happen, and it will be a shrivelling or growth, retreat or advance, retardment or development, deterioration or improvement. This is what I thought and still think. I forget what I said on that occasion; but I knew then that there would be formidable objection to any changes that I would come to propose. And, indeed, as P.J.H. had hinted, there was a strong body of opinion ready to back Henry in his "no change" stance.

Looking back I find that I have considerable sympathy for their point of view.

If you have a strong belief in anything of profound importance (such as God or, let us say, democracy), you find that this belief spreads itself into lots of little dependent beliefs which come from it and seem essential to it. If your "little beliefs" are challenged, it seems that the central belief itself is being threatened. And if this happens while your belief is being assaulted by "new thought" peddled by non-believers, you cling all the more stubbornly to the little beliefs that buttress your central belief. This is what was happening at Lancing. John Dancy had appointed some able young masters who had no religious beliefs at all and for whom the Chapel counted nothing. So, Christian Friends, unite! And when a new chaplain arrives on the scene and wants to change some of the traditional symbols of the True Faith (such as fasting Communion) you feel you must resist.

So here it was again: a belief in the absolute necessity of fasting before receiving Holy Communion. To me this was not the issue. The issue was the absurdity of having a service of Holy Communion at which the congregation was not able to receive Communion. I was strongly influenced by the "Liturgical Movement", which was sweeping through all denominations of the Church – not least the Roman Catholic. This was a move away from the obscurantist, priest-dominated service, "recited" by the priest, "heard" by the congregation. Henry used to use the expressions "saying Mass" (himself) and "hearing Mass" (the congregation). To me the Eucharist is something that the congregation *does*, not something it *listens to*. The priest *presides*. So my desire to restore Communion to the Communion service was not a personal whim: it was in accordance with the way the Church at large was reforming itself in those days. It was part of what was leading to the widely spread practice of Parish Communion; and it was what was being promulgated and enacted in the Roman Catholic Church through the Vatican Two Council.

But Lancing masters had not heard of this. To them I was guilty of abandoning Lancing Christian traditions. The less commited could not see what all the fuss was about, and William Gladstone (now the Headmaster) was 100 per cent on my side and encouraged me. The Provost also gave his consent to make the change, despite the opposition of H.C.T.

Of course, I did all I could to prepare the congregation, amongst other things persuading the Provost to authorise four of the staff to assist with the administration of Commuinion by taking the chalice. These were John Bell (Peter's godfather, Henry's House-tutor and later the Housemaster of Gibbs, a life-long friend), William Dovell, who followed Arthur Cooper as Housemaster of Olds, Dennis Day, Head of maths (and still a friend) and Paul Witherington, who succeeded Patrick Halsey in Fields. They trusted me and were prepared to go along with me. I owe a great deal to their loyalty, though I recognised the difficult position they were in. Another helpful person was Ken Shearwood, who fought my battles at housemasters' meetings and was prepared to stand up to Henry Thorold. Two others who helped were the new history teachers, Robin Reeve and Ted Maidment. Both became distinguished headmasters. They used to meet Ken every day in his kitchen after lunch for coffee and gossip in Biddy's gentle presence.

I found the new sung Eucharists, with very short sermons, moving and wonderful services. I had told the boys that the crux of their individual response to God was in the receiving or not receiving of Holy Communion. If in doubt they could talk to me or someone else about this; and it was perfectly possible, indeed, good, to have a "Lord, I believe: help thou my unbelief" attitude. To the Christian, practice generally precedes and reinforces intellectual conviction; as in life to give and to receive a kiss can start and strengthen a relationship. Loving actions create love. I added that if there was anything wrong about the "compulsory" situation that brought them involuntarily to this crucial choice of faith, then the responsibility for that was upon me and the school, not on them.

In the event many received Communion: many didn't. Some came to talk to me about it. Personally I was much moved at the sight of boys, staff, parents, visitors coming reverently to the Altar to receive the effective presence of God through the bread and wine; once when we broadcast this service a viewer wrote to tell me what spiritual inspiration this sight, caught on the camera, had given her. So in practice all seemed to be well, transforming, peace-bringing.

But no! Immediately after performing his particular duty at the service (perhaps having preached), the Assistant Chaplain marched out of Chapel. Another housemaster, complaining afterwards that he could not communicate "with all those boys about", also marched out. 'How did I know that the boys were properly prepared?' he demanded of me afterwards. 'Let us leave that to God,' I answered, wondering how much he was himself "prepared" if that was his attitude. Gradually the opposition grew. Some of the boys, so I was told, had not behaved well. There was talking and sniggering. So the Christian Eucharist, along with the Christian religion, was proving divisive, as I think it always has to be, even as it proclaims and promotes "the peace of God".

If that had been all, I would have won, my case for "Communion at Communion" being so strong. But now the wider problem of "compulsory Chapel" came to the fore. As things stood there was compulsory sung evensong every day except Saturdays when there was a congregational practice instead. In addition there was a voluntary Eucharist every morning; a voluntary eight o'clock every Sunday; the school Eucharist with sermon at ten; and full evensong with sermon on Sunday evenings; plus prayers in Great School twice a week.

I argued the case for compulsory worship, saying that if all worship is voluntary, then it becomes just one of the optional extras in school life, splendid for the few enthusiasts, ignored by the rest, along with the Chess Club or the Jazz Society. All pupils had the need and the right to be introduced to the central practice of the faith. Furthermore, in a Woodard or any Christian school, it was the institution, not just the individual that was concerned. Worship was an over-arching experience which brought the whole life of the school to God and God into the whole life of the school.

But the question I had to answer was this: "Is the experience we are giving the boys a true experience of Christian worship?" What we did was certainly not an action of the whole community, because in the absence of the great majority of staff, the "community" was not present. We had clergy and choir, Headmaster and a scattering of staff, and a largely silent, resistant congregation of boys going through the rigmarole of sung evensong, set to plain-song, which the boys, with the exception of the trebles who were kept hard at work singing every other verse, found extremely dull. Masters read the lessons, the clergy the prayers, and the rest had to be content with one hymn.

(At Lancing things were not that bad. When I went to preach for John Dancy at Marlborough the boys sang every other word of the hymns from side to side of the chapel, and there were acres of boys taking no part at all. The phenomenon I faced was nationwide in public schools.)

I wrestled hard with the problem and came to the conclusion that what was needed was a more obvious balance between the obligation imposed by the school, on the one hand, and the free choice of the individual, on the other. So I devised a scheme called (by me) "Choose your Service". For this I planned a variety of services in the week with, for example, evensong twice a week; an outside speaker, once; and less formal services on the other two days. The poor choir had no choice. They had to be at the sung evensongs; and Saturday "Congregaggers" remained compulsory for all. With this and the two Sunday services still compulsory, boys were allowed to choose three, and the seniors two, of the rest.

This scheme was popular for a time, but the staff hated it. The boys were no longer shut safely away in the Chapel play-pen for fortyfive minutes each evening; and there was no system containing choice which could not be evaded by those determined to do so. I felt that if some were determined to cheat the system, so be it. No harm was done, except to themselves, and the system. But housemasters were not as easy about it as I was. The difficulty for me was how to devise so many informal services week after week. Henry, of course, would have nothing to do with them. We had some of these in the crypt which, being an undercroft, was more intimate than the Upper Chapel with its huge, awesome spaces, and to that extent a more helpful setting for worship for those who found the Upper Chapel overpowering. I felt that for all its disadvantages this system had helped the situation by breaking the tyranny of compulsory, daily worship.

Some nice things before I get to the end of my story. Lancing was often accused of "living to itself" (as one local person put it, "with its nose in the air") but there were some of us trying to open the school to the world and the world to the school. My (and David Hare's!) Chapel fête brought people up to the College in their multitudes. It included a tour of the school, including some dormitories, which the public found fascinating for their spartan nature; Richard Taylor's film and many attractions offered on a day on which, weatherwise, Lancing was at its glorious best.

Also I started a scheme (or had Cuthbert Shaw and was I merely restarting it?) of Chapel Guides, whereby boys could volunteer to show visitors round the Chapel on weekday afternoons, instead of "clubs": a provision which made it very popular with some. I also began (and Trevor Foulkes organised it) a scheme of "community service" as an alternative to corps and Scouting, which took place one afternoon a week. Boys volunteered to wheel old people along the front at Worthing, tend gardens and help the community in various ways. Most of those who did these things were conscientious; but of course the scheme was open to abuse and some managed to give it a bad name and get me into further trouble. I do not know if this scheme survived; but Trevor put his heart and soul into it.

Trevor Foulkes argued with me intensely over everything I believed and did – and wrote! He subjected the drafts of my books to searching scrutiny, questioning every word and every phrase. Maddening! But I expect it was good for me. ("Is"? Perhaps "was" or "might be" or "should be" or "I would like to think that there is at least a possibility that..." "O Trevor!"). I married Trevor to Estelle at Tonbridge Wells one holiday and went to preach for him at the grammar school at which he became Headmaster. We still exchange letters and occasional visits, and continue to argue. He is great on "doing" Christianity without particularly "believing it"; and maybe he is nearer to God than many a steadfast believer.

One thing that Trevor did was to organise Sixth Form trips to the political conferences (at least the Labour one) when they met at Brighton. One year he managed to get President Kenneth Kaunda of Zambia, his wife and his cabinet to come up to Lancing, after a conference in Brighton. So they appeared and were greeted by a select group, including Penelope who handed a bouquet of flowers to the President's wife. We then gave them a tour of the College and Chapel. I asked the man of about my own age, whom I was guiding, who he was in the President's entourage. He answered, as if it were a great joke, 'I'm the Foreign Secretary.' Poor chap. He was assasinated later, as I believe many of them were as part of the tribal warfare that still curses parts of Africa.

The President addressed the school in Great School with a formidable speech. This was the time of the crisis in Northern Rhodesia, and the outome was very important to him. He was asked by a boy, 'What was the best, and what was the worst that Britain did for your country?' He answered that the best was the Civil Service structure, without which the country could not be governed. The worst was the lack of education. This left them with an almost illiterate population and a deplorable vacuum of educated people to give leadership.

Back to the story.

I went to see the Provost about the Chapel situation, but he was useless. He was the Bishop of Lewes, Bishop Morrell. He had taken over from Canon Browne-Wilkinson soon after I arrived; they had all agreed about the "state of the Chapel" and what needed to be done. He agreed with the measures I was intending to take and he encouraged me to go ahead. But when difficulties began to mount, Henry went to see him with Halsey and others in attendance and when I next saw the Provost in his flat in Hove, I found that he was now against everything that he had agreed to. I had a difficult morning with him. He was harsh and disagreeable. Then the telephone bell rang and he answered it. It was

Lord "Someoneorother". Morrell's tone changed to that of silky obeisance as he "Yes My Lorded" and "No My Lorded". When he hung up, I left.

Soon after that I went to see Bishop Roger Wilson, the Bishop of Chichester, at his invitation (Morrell was his Suffragan). Ostensibly I went to "talk about my future", but Bishop Wilson really wanted my account of what was going on at Lancing. He listened with patience and sympathy. It seemed to me (though, of course, he did not say so) that he had no opinion of his Suffragan Bishop's judgement. Anyway, Bishop Wilson gave me his full support.

By now I needed advice from someone I could talk to fully and objectively, so I decided to go to see the Cowley Fathers in Oxford. They might be the most unlikely people to give the advice I wanted to hear, judging from the ultra-Catholic stance I found them taking when I was an undergraduate; but there was good sense in testing the situation from a source that would be sympathetic to those who were opposing me.

I have a rule that I try to keep myself and sometimes urge on other people when I counsel them. "Accuse yourself of the opposite error". My Christian friends, colleagues, opponents, were mostly older than me: perhaps they were right. I was going too fast (but by then I had been at Lancing for six years). Perhaps I was a victim of, rather than just a believer in the Liturgical Movement. Perhaps this was one big error: if so the Cowley Dads would surely not be affected by it. Willie Gladstone once told me that I was too tense. Indeed I was so, and I felt it every morning as I walked up the Sixteen Acre Field to Chapel and prayed in silent preparation for the daily Eucharist. Perhaps I was wrong about the personal act of receiving Communion. Wasn't it enough for the congregation just to be present, and so keep the act of Communion, as it were, pure?

But what nonsense! Of course I was tense. I knew that I should not have worried: just trusted. Henry was so relaxed, as he smilingly kept to his resolution, known to all members of his House, and most of the staff, of not speaking to me for the whole term. This was true. Even when I approached him on the touch-line at a football match, he managed, ever so politely, to turn away without speaking. And there he was in the Chapel on a weekday morning "saying Mass", with me in attendance, about to receive Holy Communion from his hands.

Anyway, off I went to see the Father Superior at the House of the Cowley Fathers in Oxford, Father Bryant, an awesome person of great authority. He had met me before, and knew my father well. He would surely say, "Yes. You are guilty of the opposite error." I would say "Sorry" and set about putting things right, leave Lancing, or whatever seemed called for. I even let Patrick Halsey know that I was going, and as he greatly admired the Cowley Dads I think that he thought that I would return with my tail tucked penitently between my legs.

I told the whole story, from its hopeful beginning to the burdensome present. Father Bryant listened in silence and there was a long pause, and a few sounding-out questions. Then words to this effect: 'Your tenseness is certainly harmful. God is with you. You must trust. Then you will not be so tense, just serene, as were the saints. But your policy has been right. You must not give up on it. This is a local example of new insights which are purging the whole Church, Catholic and Reformed. Witness Vatican Two. It will not stop at "Communion at the Communion Service": it is sweeping away all sorts of unnecessary shibboleths and traditions, such as fasting Communion and "saying Mass" in Latin. Liturgical Revision is on its way – giving back to the laity its proper participation.'

Prophetic words indeed. Soon the General Synod would be with us out of the ashes of Church Assembly. A great deal of liturgical revision would take place; the separated churches would begin to grow together; there would even be new, creative relationships with other religions. Women would be ordained to the priesthood. There would be movement and struggle, and I was going to take my part in it for the rest of my ministry. I am sure that Father Bryant did not see all these things coming – or would have wanted them to; but he knew that there was a "wind of the Spirit" blowing though the Church – and Lancing was beginning to feel the breeze!

So I was to go back and get on with it. He promised to send a Cowley Dad to Lancing for the next Holy Week and Easter spent at school, which would be soon; and he promised to do all he could to help.

I have forgotten the name of the Father who came to us, with high but contrary expectations all round. But did he help? At his first address in the chapel on Monday in Holy Week (everyone present) he attacked the religious set-up of the school and said that some of the so-called Christians were behaving like spoilt children. This did not go down very well! That Holy Week was the most tense of all the weeks I had at Lancing with the divisions sharper and more clearly defined than ever – to the fury of the Head who had devoutly hoped that a Cowley Father, preaching Christianity, would unite the school, not divide it. (In this E.W.G. was rather like the Emperor Constantine in the fourth century who embraced Christianity in the hope that it would cement together the disparate parts of his Empire.) The Provost was furious with the Cowley Fathers and wrote indignantly to the Superior to complain.

One day (I was expecting it to happen) the Head summoned a meeting of senior housemasters (including, of course, Henry Thorold) to discuss the Chapel situation. I was not invited to be present. After this meeting (which Ken Shearwood describes in his book, *Hardly a Scholar*) Mr Gladstone sent for me and told me that I had not got the confidence of the housemasters. He started on the matter of the teaching (divinity groups and all). But we had recently had a full-scale inspection and I had received very high commendation indeed (as good as one could write for oneself!), not only for my work in the classroom but also for the Divinity scheme as a whole. So the Head switched to Chapel. The collections on Sunday evenings were a good sign of morale, and these had been appalling despite my pleas. I had no answer to this; but it transpired after I had left that a master had been regularly stealing the money! He went to prison for it; and his crime certainly had not helped my cause. Then the Head went on about all the things he had originally agreed to. The interview ended inconclusively and unhappily; only he did remind me that he had once said that my long-term future was not at Lancing.

This interview must have happened before the Holy Week crisis. Things went on. I forget the chronological order, but early in the Christmas term of 1967 Willie sent for me again and told me that as I seemed to be unable to come to terms with the Assistant Chaplain, he had decided, with the agreement of the Provost, that we should both leave at Christmas. I went back to the class I was teaching, an A-level set in my study. The boys began to tease me about being sent for by the Head. Had I been beaten? No, but I was in a daze of sorrow and amazement, because although, looking back, the dismissal was inevitable and there was some sort of savage comfort in sharing this fate with Henry Thorold, it seemed a death blow at the time. Much more so, I gathered later, for Henry who was not expecting anything of the sort to happen. Shattered, he left the school at the end of term to take up the post of Chaplain to a prep-school in Oxford, which he had always treated as a "home from home".

I went home and told a very upset Julie all about it, and we set about looking for another appointment. We had started this already. I had applied for the job of Director of Religious Broadcasting for the Midlands and, being short-listed, went to Birmingham for an interview. But I was not appointed and had reason to be glad because the job packed up very soon after the person appointed took office. Another application had gone to Leeds University for the job of Senior Chaplain. I did not fancy my chances because Bernard Pawley (from my Ely days, now Archdeacon of Canterbury) had written for me and had included the true remark that "from southern public school to northern university" was rather a leap!

At the interview I was given the chance to shine when I was asked about *Honest to God*. I had, in fact, been using it with a sceptical Sixth Form group because they found a lot that they could agree with, and a more pious group, because it stretched them. But after the interview I sat in the waiting room dreading being turned down, because I had only a few weeks left at Lancing and no job to go to, and dreading being appointed, because I would have had to tell Julie that we would be living in the upstairs flat of an Edwardian house, with no garden, but a public park across a main road! A man better qualified academically than I was got the job – to my sorrow and relief.

The Provost – most cynically – wanted me to take on an ultra-high church in Brighton and "bring it down to earth"; but Juliet and I (Julie especially) turned this down flat. There was the possibility of a parish in the New Forest, but one of Chute's former curates was now Rural

Dean, and he dissuaded me. Two years before I had been considered for the headmastership of a new Church school in Brisbane: in fact, according to Ivor Church (the Archbishop's adviser), I had been all but appointed, but the telegram from the Archbishop of Brisbane never came. Wisely they had appointed an Australian. I had also been offered the Deanery at Townsville; then the Parish of McKay in Queensland; but Dean Badderly (formerly Dean of Brisbane, preaching at Lancing) had warned me not to accept unless I had the money for the return ticket to the UK. There was also the Teachers' Training College at All Saints, Tottenham. They needed a chaplain and I was short-listed. But the Head of RE took me aside and said, 'You know, old boy, as Chaplain you will have nothing to do with the RE faculty; and we in the faculty have nothing to do with the Chapel. We keep the two apart.' This did not suit me, with my RE books just published. I turned the job down at the interview. And anyway there was not a blade of grass in the place. Julie had been walking round wondering what on earth she would do if she had to live there.

Westminster Abbey came to the rescue. I had volunteered to be an Abbey Chaplain in the holidays. For this I had to be available in the Abbey all day and say two prayers (no more!) from the pulpit every hour. This brought me into contact with Dean Eric Abbott, who asked me to preach one evensong in the Abbey, and was very nice about it afterwards. I now wrote to him and went to see him. He said casually, 'I wonder if Pershore would suit you.' My heart leapt. But the appointment was in the hands of the Resident Canon, Bishop Joost de Blank, and he had a list of candidates on his desk. Nothing could be done, therefore, until he came out of hospital, where he was seriously ill. For weeks nothing happened; but one day Bishop Joost de Blank (famous for his courageous ministry in South Africa) died. Canon Edward Carpenter immediately nominated me for the living of Pershore, and invited me to go to see the churchwardens.

This had been a doubly difficult time for us because, for all those weeks of the Christmas term, Juliet's mother, Kay, had been dying and Julie had been going to the hospital at Clapham every day, I accompanying her whenever I could. She did die, peacefully, with Juliet, me, Tony and Valerie at her side.

'Come along, Christopher,' she said. 'Do your stuff.' I did what I should do as a priest. Then she cried, 'I can hear trumpets,' and soon after that she died. She knew that we were leaving Lancing and we had told her about Pershore although it was not then a certainty. She was cremated at Roehampton Vale; and we drove sadly on our way to Pershore to see the churchwardens.

I had dinner with the two wardens at the Angel Hotel. They could not have been nicer, though they were both wondering if I should be the vicar of such an important parish when I had never been a vicar before. Mr Maple did not like the "youth" of his day, so my experience in two schools did not count for much. But I think that in the end they were pleased to be having me; they were particularly enamoured at the thought of my beautiful wife and family. So we went back to Lancing, a little nervous at the outcome; and there we had to wait whilst protracted negotiations went on. But all ended well.

The Bishop of Worcester invited us to Hartlebury, and seemed pleased at the appointment, though naturally irritated that as the Bishop of the Diocese he had had no say in it. He made me drive over to Worcester to see Archdeacon Peter Eliot, who was delightful, even though he asked me about my "private income". 'None at all,' I said, rather to his dismay. Peter Moore was renowned for being wealthy and Pershore would feel the pinch with a new incumbent who needed such things as working expenses. After that we drove back to Hartlebury and the Bishop and I stayed up late that night watching (in black and white) *Match of the Day*.

So, with a very short time to go before the end of term, I was duly appointed Vicar of Pershore, Pinvin and Wick, and Priest in Charge of St James', Birlingham. I then went through the odd experience of leaving Lancing in a blaze of glory – judging from the speeches and the "obituary" in the school magazine and the generosity of the private and public gifts that I was given. I expect that they were all sighing with relief. I certainly was; but sad relief.

Indeed I can write a happy ending to this unhappy chapter. As if butter had never melted in his mouth, Patrick gave me a fond farewell and began to tell me about his fears regarding the appointment of the next chaplain. I was not particularly interested! Indeed, I once came into the common-room to hear Donald Bancroft berating his colleagues. 'I cannot stand you chapel lot,' he was saying. 'You had a bloody good Chaplain whom you have got rid of. Now you are whingeing about his successor.' I closed my ears and fled.

But Patrick continued to write long, friendly, personal letters. When, in the 1980s, I became Dean of Ripon I heard that he was in a nursing home at Hemel Hempstead, dying, with no priest at hand. So I tore down the Ml and found him very ill indeed, hardly able to speak. I talked to him and gave him Communion and the Blessing. He gave me a seraphic smile which I will always remember: a smile which spoke of his naughtiness, his sense of fun, his profound belief in God, his certainty of forgiveness, of love, of eternal joy in God's presence; all of which completely obliterated any tiny sense of grievance that he may have felt with me or he may have expected me to have against him. Very soon after that he died. His family (sisters) asked me to take his funeral service, which I did; and later I was invited to dedicate the window in the crypt of Lancing Chapel, given in his memory. I hope that one of my addresses on these occasions might be allowed to survive. He was a very special person.

I also discovered by talking to his sisters, that he led a wickedly irresponsible life at home in the holidays, ringing up local clergymen putting on the voice of their Bishop (Runcie, later Archbishop of Canterbury), on some spoof pretext or other. His sisters knew nothing at all about Patrick at Lancing, saying only that he had "some sort of teaching job in Sussex".

Henry Thorold eventually retired to his family seat in Lincolnshire; and through Peter Burman, Secretary of the Council for the Care of Churches, of which I was then the Chairman, I heard that Henry spoke most affectionately about me and hoped that I would stop and see him if ever I were on my way north by car. I wrote and asked him to address our annual conference: he wrote back, delighted, but alas he could no longer undertake public engagements. Soon after that I heard that he was in hospital and I wrote again – a long letter about the best of the "old days". I got no reply, but after his death, his brother John (also a priest) wrote and told me that he had found my letter on Henry's desk; that Henry had been delighted with it – but was too ill to reply.

Juliet and I visited the very friendly Gladstones at their seat, Hawarden Castle in Cheshire, one day on our way to Wales. He and Ros could not have been more hospitable; and I am pleased to say that Sir William Gladstone (at that time the Chief Scout) – (though he had always opposed Scouting at Lancing!) gave a generous gift when I wrote to him about the Ripon Cathedral appeal.

When I went to be Dean of Ripon, the Provost of Lancing wrote and asked me to be the Chairman of the Friends of Lancing Chapel, a body responsible for raising and spending the money needed for the upkeep and completion of that amazing building, one of the finest, I believe, of our age. I said, "Yes: most certainly," and went down whenever I could from Ripon. This was one of the factors (along with the opportunity of living close to my sister Mary) that induced us to retire to Worthing, where we now live "happily ever after", seeing a lot of the College, even preaching there occasionally, and meeting our old friends from Lancing chaplaincy days.

Chapter 18
Vicar of Pershore

During my last term at Lancing – amidst all the furore and anxiety – I received a letter from Aunt Sylvia offering to give me money to be spent (she hoped) on (turn over – wait for it) a skiing holiday with the family. O no, thought I in my feeble-mindedness, not a skiing holiday! Wouldn't carpets for the new Vicarage be more sensible? I mentioned it to my A-Level group, which contained some skiers who used to come back from their holidays bronzed and tough and full of stories of how difficult skiing is and how good they are at it. 'Well, Sir,' said John Trotter, 'I don't really think so. You are not all that athletic. You will find it very difficult.' 'We had a chap in our group,' said another encouraging member of the class. 'He was skiing down a mountain. Unfortunately, he fell over in a heap, and when he sat up he saw the ski going on down the mountain side, with his leg still attached to it.' But Nigel Wheeler stepped in. 'Money for a skiing holiday? Of course you must go, and take your family, and enjoy yourselves. You'll never forgive yourself, and your children will never forgive you, if you miss this opportunity. Don't be closed to the idea. Be open to it.'

"Be opened." "Ephphatha" in Mark 12, 34. Here was to be the substance of my last sermon in Lancing Chapel, with St Mark's story of the man who was "opened" by Jesus to receive (hear) and so to give (speak clearly). I would introduce it with the conversation as above, repeated with embellishments. To be "open" to what is good takes discernment, resolution, discipline; and its reward is ultimate fulfilment. Be open to life, to people, to beauty in all its forms, to God: open to receive and so to give.

So – I was to be open to Aunt S's generous offer. I accepted with delight. She was pleased and enjoyed the holiday vicariously when on our return we drove over to Rye and told her all about it.

Christmas of that year, 1968, was sad with no Kay to spend it with us. I had a service in the Chapel for the few staff who were still around, and I assisted the Vicar of North Lancing with his midnight service. Then we packed and left Lancing in light snow and drove to Pershore. We stayed the first two nights with the Meikle family in Wick and were grateful for their kindness. Then – off we flew to Switzerland, all five of us.

This was one of the best family holidays we ever had. All the conditions were perfect; hotel, weather, food, après-ski (when the children were safe in bed); and the skiing itself. I was not good at skiing because I was too anxious not to have an accident. I did not want to turn up to my Induction on crutches! I never got off the nursery slopes except once when I went up in a ski-lift with Angela who had her eighth birthday in Engelburg. We were an ill-balanced pair and had difficulty getting off the lift at the right moment; so we went too high and when we did get off we had to come down the mountain in slow and careful stages.

On another occasion she and I went on the toboggan-run together. This had been a championship course only a week before, but now it was slow and safe after a heavy fall of snow. We slithered down the course, me terrified as we gathered speed, Angela shrieking with ecstasy, her voice echoing round the mountains. At the end of the holiday, I had a race with Penelope (who had made good progress) and beat her by dint of my greater weight. Peter (aged four) tried hard and fell over again and again, making no fuss at all; but he preferred the toboggan. Julie was best in grace and style, having done some skiing as a schoolgirl. The Anglican chaplain at Engelburg fell ill while we were out there, so I took the Sunday services and was given a free pass up the ski-lifts as a reward. The holiday is immortalised on video tape made on my Super-8 camera. But the film cannot capture the frabjious joy of that carefree holiday. Then we returned to real life: the children to their new school, Abbey Park, just across the green beyond the Abbey; and Julie and I to the Vicarage for our new life together as Vicar and Vicar's wife.

My Induction was a solemn affair, presided over by the Bishop of Worcester (Bishop Charles-Edwards) with Archdeacon Peter Eliot in attendance and the Abbey packed to the door. Patrick Halsey was present with a contingent of Lancing boys who behaved and sang as if butter had never melted in their mouths; so I felt well supported. The Bishop preached using the titles of my four books as his text. This was a nice boost, you would think. But there was suspicion around. Was I just a writer or a youth-centred school chaplain? I had never been a vicar before. Could I be right for such an important and prestigious parish as Pershore? And was I fit to follow such a distinguished vicar (now a Canon of Ely, later to be Dean of St Alban's) as Dr Peter Moore?

As it happened Peter Moore was an ideal person to follow. He had spent much of his own money making the Abbey beautiful in its interior, with the semi-circular apse furnished for the Choir and a fine westward-facing Altar on the chancel steps, illegally fixed so that it could not be moved by subsequent vicars. The Altar had fine frontals, designed by Pat Russell. I asked her to make another one for Lent and Advent, with a super-frontal designed for each of those seasons.

The Abbey had lost its nave in the time of the Dissolution of the Monasteries by the hand of Thomas Cromwell, Henry VIII's minion; but what was left (bought for £800 by the townsfolk) makes a beautiful worshipping space for a congregation of two hundred, just right for Pershore. Peter Moore had made the Abbey beautiful; but his attempt to install John Piper windows had been thwarted by the people of Pershore, who signed petitions against them in all the shops of the town. More the pity, because the glass (apart from a Victorian "picture history" window) is undistinguished. Peter Moore had done many brave things to bring the parish up to highest standards; and had upset some people in doing so. This left me in the position of being able to concentrate on the pastoral side and leave the Abbey itself and the organisation of the PCC intact.

St Andrew's church, fifty yards north and east of the Abbey, was a problem. It had been the parish church for the area of Pershore that had not come under the Benedictine monks of the Abbey, and had therefore not been in the gift of Westminster Abbey. It had been part of the parish of Pershore Abbey now for many years, but there were still those who believed in its independence and resisted its closure. Peter Moore had managed to reduce its services to one a year, at harvest festival, and it was now recognised that this was a problem that the new Vicar would have to face.

I got much conflicting advice. 'Knock it down,' said my curates (quite seriously) 'and sell the bells to America.' 'Get it taken stone by stone to America: I am sure we could find a buyer,' suggested a prominent layman. 'Do nothing,' said the churchwardens. But to me it was clear what should be done. We should ask the ecclesiatical authorities to declare it redundant and have it converted into a parish centre, which was badly needed.

When we were on holiday at Cwm Gloyne Farm in Pembrokeshire, Ralph Sims (a fellow holiday-maker)advised me to employ an architect friend of his, Neil Macfadyen, to design a scheme. Ralph was a civil engineer and had the highest professional opinion of Neil. I followed his advice (after much formal consultation) and the result was a triumph. St Andrew's was converted in a way that preserved its medieval simplicity and beauty, and made it suitable for our present needs. We used the space in the roof for a youth area. The bells were restored to make a teaching tower for beginners – to the approval of campanologists all over the country. A large hall was made out of the nave for social occasions; also a committee room, a stage, a small club room with a porch and door into the Vicarage garden, and a kitchen. I rang Neil the week before the project was due to begin and said that I had second thoughts about the kitchen. It should be larger, capable of cooking full meals. This meant cutting down the size of the committee room; but Neil was patient with me and flexible. He changed the plans, and my second thoughts were proved to be right.

I had some difficult moments with regard to St Andrew's. Colonel Derek Cronin, the Warden and Treasurer (a bad combination), said that we could not afford it. I knew that we could, and felt that we could not afford not to do it, for the negative reason that we had to do something with the building, and the positive reason that Pershore needed a social centre. Derek stood by me loyally once the decision had been made.

Meanwhile, an old lady to whom I used to take Holy Communion every month asked me if she could use the services of the Churches of Pershore Action Committee to be taken into Worcester. 'Yes, of course;

but why?' 'I wish to consult my solicitor and ask him to stop you doing what you are going to do to 'my church', St Andrew's.'

On further enquiry it turned out that there was a window in the church in memory of an ancestor of hers. She thought that we would be destroying it. But I explained that no memorials, tablets or windows would be harmed and that there was no need for her to worry her solicitor in Worcester. She was satisfied and delighted to be told that "her" window would, in fact, be enhanced.

A few days before it was due to be opened, as I was shaving early in the morning, I saw smoke coming out of our garage roof. I rang the fire brigade who were round in five minutes and managed to put out a fire which was spreading through the roof towards St Andrew's next door, almost adjoining. The police blamed a tramp who had been seen the evening before and was suspected of having slept in the loft: but I have to say that Peter and one of his friends had also used that loft – who knows what for? Anyway the situation was saved. St Andrew's was duly opened and was much admired by everyone in Pershore.

Peter Moore left me two curates, Tim Papé and Nicholas Coulton. They both gave me a lot of help as I began to find my feet in the parish, but Tim moved to a school appointment soon after my arrival. Nicholas had been trained in law before seeking ordination, and Peter Moore told me that he was alpha in ability. He was indeed excellent, except that he couldn't sing! When I suggested that it would be better if he were to speak the Responses instead of singing them (such was the amusement he was causing to the choir boys and my daughters), he was most indignant. He had received the "grace of orders" at his ordination. Didn't this include singing? 'Well, I am afraid that in your case, Nick, it hasn't taken.' Years later when he was Provost of Newcastle, we met at the General Synod. 'I can sing now,' he said. 'It's just a matter of confidence.' I was delighted and at the singing of the hymn at the close of the sessions, I noticed that he certainly sang with confidence. But was it in tune?

Nicholas was concerned whether, as a curate, in obedience and under instruction to me, he could fulfil his vocation as Parson ("the person") in the parish. In this he was experiencing one of the dilemmas of the Church of England, that its priests are trained for individual not corporate ministry. I was the same at Basingstoke, though I was less ready to express it. I tried my best to make Nicholas and the other curates feel that we were a team, working together and sharing a "corporate priesthood"; but it never was easy – and never will be.

Nicholas was working for a London BA in Theology. I undertook to help him by getting him to write essays on the texts of the gospels. He resented this and appreciated it, appreciation and gratitude coming out on top. One day Robert Runcie, who had been his Principal at Cuddesdon, rang me to say that he had been appointed Bishop of St Alban's and would like to have Nicholas Coulton as his Chaplain. Would I let him go? 'Yes,' I said, 'for a large transfer fee.'

The curates were an important feature of my life at Pershore. We had a corporate discipline with Matins and Holy Communion every morning at seven thirty preceded by prayer and meditation (aimed at 7 a.m.). We went visiting every afternoon from three o'clock onwards till we all met in the Abbey for evensong at five thirty, full of our afternoon encounters to be prayed about and (if appropriate) discussed. If we were late or missed, we were supposed to explain to the others what had happened. Every Monday morning was spent in "Chapter" at which everything was discussed and plans were laid, pulled apart and put together again.

Robert Runcie had rung me (before he nicked Nick) and asked if I would consider taking David Millar who had a Cambridge "first" in mathematics. His wife, Sue, had been Robert's secretary, but had some problems. David came "to be seen", but more "to see". He had a list of conditions to do with pay, accommodation, days off, parts of each day off, holidays, and time off to go to "cell meetings" with his present friends. I was patient about these, knowing that once he was working in the parish he would find the need to be flexible about "time off" as all priests have to be. He joined us and seemed to settle happily. He preached short, pithy, sermons and got on well with people.

Sue Millar had difficulties. In her good times she had a load of charm and everyone loved her, but in bad times she became depressed. I was proud of the way the parish treated David and Sue – with full

Christian love, understanding and forbearance. I never heard anything nasty said against them; and some people took great trouble to help them, most notably Dr Marshall Wilson and his family.

Philip Barrett also came to us from Cuddesdon. Two days after he arrived many of the Pershore congregation, all the staff, and all the family, including Peter who was then six, plus the new puppy Charlie Girl, went on the Round Bredon Hill Sponsored Walk – all twenty-two miles of it. The object was to raise money for the new swimming bath; our efforts were organised and led by the officers of the RAF (whose Chaplain I was) from the airbase. I was proud of my family, who did the whole course despite Penelope's blisters and all the hardships that such a walk entailed.

But poor Philip! He was not at all used to this sort of thing, physical exercise not being his forte or enthusiasm. However, he hobbled round the course and made a good impression on the parishioners, who appreciated his courage in doing something that was so out of character. What a horrid Vicar I was to press it on him, but he lived to forgive me! He was, above all things, a historian, an academic, keen on medieval churches and plain-song music, and very keen on cathedrals and their history. Years later he wrote a book on cathedrals in the nineteenth century (misleadingly called *Barchester*) which is considered the best authority on that subject. At Pershore he was good with the older members of the congregation, and unexpectedly good with the Youth Club, who respected the fact that he was an unrepentant fuddy-duddy who nevertheless respected them for what they were. His most important contribution at Pershore was the help he gave me to organise the events for the Pershore Abbey Millennium.

Michael Willows came to us from Wells; and Andrew Pullin from Lincoln Theological College. Michael was married with three sons. He was poor, unworldly and saintly, much loved by his own circle in the parish. His hobby was motor-cars, and he was never happier than when he could spend an afternoon off tinkering with an engine.

Andrew had had a tough training at Kelham (renowned for "making or breaking" its priests), where he went when he was sixteen. Like Michael, he was no academic and had difficulty in preparing sermons. I helped him as much as I could.

Andrew was popular in the parish and closer to me than any of them. He had been ordained with special conditions to do with study and supervision, which I gave him; but there was nothing I could teach him as regards spiritual discipline and selfless concern for others.

Sister Christine Dodds of the Church Army came to us at the insistence of the Bishop who said that there were no curates available and that I was the right sort of vicar for her. I found her able and conscientious. She preached well and became resentful of the fact that she was not allowed to carry out priestly duties. It was at this time that, knowing her and knowing the positive as well as the frustrating side of her ministry, I became an advocate for women's ordination, as will become clear in these memoirs. Christine could do all that men could do, better than most of us could do it, so why not let her and others be ordained?

Mike Hatton joined the staff as an ordination candidate "on hold". He had been recommended to do a year in a parish for trial before proceding further with ordination training. He was a way-out young man who told me at once that he had no time for Offices or the daily discipline I insisted on. But he complied and, a rebel himself, he was good with our rebellious youth and made himself acceptable to many in the parish. He came to appreciate our structure of daily worship – even the psalms; and I was able to give him a satisfactory report at the end of the year. I found him in the 1980s in a down-town parish in Leeds where criminality was rife. He had had his vicarage robbed three times and left a note to burglars that there was nothing left worth stealing. I went to preach for him in his parish and was much moved by the degree of love that the parishioners felt for one another and for him. There was vibrant spirituality in that very poor church; and I was proud of Mike.

I had a pleasing sense of freedom when I first went to Pershore. No school routine. No lessons to prepare or books to mark. No one nagging or opposing. No immediate demand to do anything at all! Only the demands of the work itself: parishioners to visit; the growing population of the unchurched on the housing estates; the industrial estate to become acquainted with; house-groups to organise and visit; the Sunday school to be reformed; PCC members to meet; and a growing body of concerns which put together could have overwhelmed me – General Synod, the Deanery (I was soon appointed Rural Dean), ecumenical relations with the other churches, the Millennium.

One Tuesday morning shortly after my Induction I drove to the hospital in Worcester in order to visit (much to his surprise) the Bank Manager who had gone in for a minor operation. As I drove through the countryside I thought, 'Here I am. No one else knows where. I can take as long as I like. No questions will be asked. I could just as well be going to watch a cricket match or playing golf or going for a walk with Julie.' This was freedom indeed, and I have no doubt that clergy can succumb to it and do nothing. But if one has a conscience and is motivated by the longing to bring God to the people of the parish and bring the people to God, and if one tries to be "all things to all people", then the pressures mount up and one has to have a balancing discipline if one is to stay serene and effective. I had to try not to surrender the initiative, to keep the space to think and assess and plan and then do the important things, without neglecting the lesser matters. I also tried not to be seen to be frantic with no time to spare for individuals: much better (and much harder) to give the impression of being laid back.

One parishioner thought that I was lazy and she complained to the churchwarden. She lived next door and was angry with me because her husband was taken ill and died when I was on holiday – so "the curate" (Nicholas!) had to attend her. My routine was that after evensong every day I played with the children, in the garden if possible. She used to hear me with them and thought that this was a poor use of my time. It was in fact important to me; and we always tried to have play time as well as proper family meals, even though I was often busy in the evenings when meetings and house-groups took place, and when people were at home to be visited.

Pershore was a happy place to bring up children. There was a magnificent garden with room for lawn games, a huge hanging cedar, which they called "the dancing tree" and could climb and make their houses in. The garden was bounded by a one-brick-thick wall which bent horizontally in and out to give it strength. The Wilson family lived over the wall and the children were always in and out of one another's houses.

Penelope and Angela started straight away at the Abbey Park School, which was three hundred yards away across the Abbey Park; Peter soon joined them at the infant department. He once came home having been in a fight. 'Was it because I am the Vicar?' 'Well, it would help if you weren't.' But he could give as good as he got according to Mrs Ashworth, the Headteacher.

The girls went on to Prince Henry's Grammar School in Evesham, which later became comprehensive. They both did well, particularly in music under Ronald Edwards, who radiated enthusiasm throughout the school and was particularly fond of our daughters. I used to take Angela to him for private piano lessons (to grade 8) and listen outside the door while they shouted at each other. His wife told us that when he died, tragically soon after his retirement, almost his last words were, 'Angela always had inky fingers." Penelope went up that school on the science side, despite Ronald's pleading with me that she should study A-level music. She did well and got into the medical school at Leicester.

We wanted Peter to be a chorister at Worcester Cathedral, so I took him to the Precentor for a private test to see if he was good enough. He was musical, but not such a good singer at that age as the girls were 'And why should they have not been choristers?' I asked myself, and so did they. When I went to Ripon I determined to open the possibility to girls, and won my way – though very slowly.) Peter was given special coaching in singing by Mrs Vial, a clergy widow and music teacher of the no-nonsense type. She had splendid rapport with Peter and we thought at the time that she was the only person who could get him to do what she wanted. So Peter became a chorister at Worcester Cathedral.

Soon after we arrived at Pershore Juliet decided to train as a teacher. She was already an orthoptist, but practice as an orthoptist would not fit well into family life. Teaching did. So she enrolled at the Worcester College of Education and started to attend as a mature student. Her first specialist subject was History, but then she turned to English and I used to tease her because her "field-work" consisted of going to Stratford to watch Shakespeare! She passed her course with distinction in English and merit in teaching practice. She was then appointed to the delightful village school at Cleeve Prior where she liked the Headteacher and was sometimes left in charge of the school. This was a happy and fulfilled time of her life, in which she had a proper role of her own. We all enjoyed her course. Penelope, Angela and Peter were ready to give her good advice (for instance what TV shows she really should know about); and I once got involved in an exercise of music composition for which she was awarded very good marks!

We made many friends in Pershore, despite a book which I read in my last weeks at Lancing on how to be a vicar. "On no account make friends with your parishioners," it advised. 'Nonsense,' thought I, and threw the book away. Of course there is a professional risk in personal involvement. But was not the Incarnation of the Word of God through the human life of Jesus a risk? Anyway, Juliet and I, partly through our children and their schools, partly through the parish and the goodness of Pershore people, partly through shared interests, made many friends, some of whom we visit when we go for our annual visit to the Friends of Pershore Abbey Festival, of which I am now the President.

Some of my friends were in Rotary, to which Marshall Wilson had me enrolled soon after I arrived. 'You will meet a cross-section of the men of Pershore,' he told me. This was true and a great help to my ministry as well as an enrichment to my life. Eventually I became President. Rotary was concerned with "good works" as well as lunch-time sociability. It did not become my "religion" as it was to some of the members. But was it any worse to them for being so?

One of my responsibilities at Pershore was the RAF station, of which I was the Chaplain. I got to know the officers mostly by going to lunch in their mess every Wednesday, and playing squash afterwards with Dr Warwick Parsons. I married his daughter in the Abbey, and got to know James his son when he was a second lieutenant in the Army, on duty in Belfast. He used to come and share harrowing tales with me and I was amazed that such a young man should be shouldering such heavy – pastoral as well as military – responsibilities.

One of the nicest things that happened when we were at Pershore was that my parents decided to live there. Father was now eighty. We had celebrated his eightieth birthday at Rousham, where he had been looking after the village church. Now we found them a bungalow in Pershore and they moved in with much satisfaction. They had a pleasant garden which Mother tended lovingly. Father and I used to play golf at Fladbury, and he could still play nine holes with his slow, powerful swing and maddening accuracy around the greens. I also used to take him for drives round Bredon Hill during which we would talk and he would share with me his wisdom and his spirituality. He was happy to take services, and he was still a marvellous preacher. He also went visiting in the parish and would send me detailed lists of whom he had seen. They were both very popular in Pershore, and everyone knew Father as "The Canon". We celebrated their Golden Wedding in our house and garden on a glorious day in July with the far-flung family and many old friends present. They were sublimely happy.

Alas Father became ill and the surgeon at Ronkswood told me that he would only live for six months. He was very brave and eventually died in the Pershore Cottage Hospital. I was particularly sad because I had been in London for the General Synod and the train home was delayed for an hour. I was half an hour too late to see him before he died. His funeral was in Pershore Abbey – with the Bishop preaching – on St David's Day 1972.

Soon after that Mother moved to a home at Moulsford, near Wallingford, where she was well looked after and happy enough. We gave her a family party at a nearby hotel on her ninetieth birthday; and she died at the age of ninety-two.

Father's faith was deeply spiritual and intellectual: Mother's was full of feeling and praise and love. They were great Christians and wonderful parents.

Very shortly after Father died, the Bishop, now Robin Woods, made me an Honorary Canon of Worcester Cathedral, an honour which entailed no duties but gave me huge satisfaction, especially as I felt myself to be following in my father's footsteps: for I was now "The Canon".

Chapter 19
Pershore and Beyond

A major event in Pershore was the Abbey Millennium, celebrated in 1972, this being the thousandth anniversary of the establishment of the Benedictine abbey, now the parish church of Pershore. Miss Roden gave me three years' warning. She was the retired Headmistress of the Alice Ottley Girls' School in Worcester. She lived in Pershore and worshipped regularly in the Abbey, and was perhaps the wisest person in the place, always ready to help me when I needed advice, and always with a cigarette in her mouth. So we were able to make our plans – along with the Diocese and (more important) the Town Council – in good time.

Fortunately Philip Barrett joined us at this time and it soon became clear that he was a good organiser, as well as someone with a historical grasp of what this year was to be about. Many events were planned, items designed and put on sale, interest and excitement generated in every way we could devise.

Tim Vivian designed some excellent mugs which had the Norman arches of the Abbey as their motif. These were made by the Benedictine monks of Prinknash Abbey, where David Hollis and I had stayed on our memorable bicycle tour twenty years before. We also asked the Royal Worcester Porcelain to design and make a limited edition of a Millennium plate which we sold for £30. There was also a goblet which Juliet and I could not afford to buy. There were many smaller items and, put together, they helped us to balance the books. I once went into an antique shop in whose window I espied more Millenium (sic) goods. I asked politely about them and got a defensive answer, as if to say, "Why shouldn't we make and sell what we like?" 'Of course,' said I; 'but if you had consulted me I would have told you how to spell "millennium".'

We started with a service in the Abbey, which I introduced in what became a characteristic of Abbey Millennium Liturgy, namely a carefully constructed "Bidding Prayer". Princess Alexandra was present. When she had done her stuff greeting people after the service she insisted on having tea with just Lord Cobham (the Lord Lieutenant), Juliet and me. She asked after us, how we were getting on, and what life was like in the Vicarage at Pershore, as if she were a life-long friend and we were her favourite people.

Lord Cobham, meanwhile, who had been a first-class cricketer, explained to Peter how the English batsmen ought to be treating Lillee and Thompson, who were making havoc with our batting in Australia. (Or was it Griffiths and Hall in the West Indies? I know that England was being humiliated.) I was later invited to preach at Lord Cobham's local church. At lunch, after the service, we had an argument about the "incomparable English of the Book of Common Prayer", and I asked him to justify "Our Father, which art in Heaven".

Then we had a remarkable service at which the Abbey was filled with Benedictine monks, French (from Fleuri) and English, Roman Catholic and Anglican. We fed and wined them in the newly converted St Andrew's. In this service everything had to be carefully balanced, so that, for instance, if a Roman Catholic dignitory "absolved", an Anglican would "bless". The procession was a nightmare to organise. But Philip Barrett knew exactly what was what in the matter of precedence, and the mixed-up monks all appeared to be satisfied.

I had to make a welcoming speech in English and French to the Mayor of Fleuri and his entourage, who also visited Pershore on that occasion. I put this short English speech into my best and much corrected French, then learnt it by heart, pronouncing it as well as I could but not nearly well enough to satisfy Juliet who had spent some months in France in her school days and derided my schoolboy accent. Father John Crighton, who gave me good support throughout the Millennium celebrations and pushed his flock into attending as much as they could, translated the Mayor's speech as it went along. After an hour his translations became shorter and shorter; terse, even dismissive. I do not think that the Mayor noticed.

There was also an enjoyable steam-engine rally. It was held at the RAF base where there was plenty of room for manoeuvres and races. They also made hurdy-gurdy music, and the noise of this plus the engines was terrific. I not only opened this happy occasion: I was told to climb up on to a steam-engine and give an address. So I did – all about the glory of steam-engines, the glory of Pershore and its Abbey, and, no doubt, Hurrah for God.

Not everything was successful. Philip was determined to have a sung Mass according to the Old Sarum Rite; so he got hold of a choir that could sing it in plain-song and printed an elaborate service-sheet complete with historical explanation and the words in Latin and English. This document cost us a great deal of money. As he had not consulted me, I was not pleased. It was the only serious mistake he made, however, and I took responsibility for it.

One could not blame Philip for the failure of the Sealed Knot battle. This was a historical re-enactment of a battle that historians said must have taken place in the Civil War as the Cavaliers (or was it the Roundheads?) made their way from Worcester to Evesham (or the other way round). There surely must have been a battle at the crossing of the River Avon at Pershore! Anyway, historical or not, a battle was devised for the Pershore Millennium and for one weekend Pershore was full of seventeenth-century men-at-arms roaming the streets, drinking in the pubs and coming to the Abbey for the morning service: after which, battle commenced.

Unfortunately it was a dull, misty day, so it was almost impossible to see what was going on and the citizens of twentieth-century Pershore were not so curious that they were prepared to pay money to peer into the mist in the hope of finding out. Also some of the participants had cameras in their hands and between blows took photographs of themselves and their friends, thus spoiling the illusion of a historic and bloody battle. I complained about this afterwards to the Sealed Knot Society; and Philip was much chagrined.

One event was utterly, triumphantly, joyfully successful: *Noye's Fludde*, music by Benjamin Britten, performed in the Abbey for four nights of one glorious week.

There was certain to be a host of production difficulties such as human temperaments, the interruption of Abbey routine, the building of the stage, problems to do with storing the props, the different schools that would have to be involved for singers, animals and instrumentalists; procuring the services of two professional singers – and much else. So I decided that it would be best if I produced and directed the show myself. But who was to conduct the music and be the senior partner in the production? I thought of our own Abbey organist, but could not see myself working with him; nor could I see him being able to cope with the music itself. I wanted to be fair and judge his capability on professional grounds, and for that I needed advice. So I rang up the County Music Adviser whom I had met at Prince Henry's and asked him this direct question. 'Is our organist good enough to conduct *Noye's Fludde*?' 'No,' was the immediate and blunt answer. 'Thank you for your frankness. Is Mr Edwards, the Director of Music at Prince Henry's school, up to it?' 'Absolutely yes,' said Mr. Benoy.

Ronald Edwards was delighted and we were soon meeting together to confer, tell the eighteen local schools of our intention and arrange auditions. He was a joy to work with: strong, ablaze with enthusiasm, and possessing the gift of raising young musicians to heights of achievement that they did not know they possessed.

There was a technical difficulty because the shape of the Abbey and the position of the organ meant that we had to have the ark built stage-right, instead of stage-left as in Britten's instructions. Apart from that I found that the operetta was carefully written to give the right amount of time for every tricky stage operation; for instance building the ark, filling it with animals and sailing it in a rough storm. The auditions were conducted by a third party so that there would be no suspicion of school or family bias. They were successful and produced Angela and enough solo boys and girls to fill the parts. One boy with his voice on the break gave us palpitations as we wondered if it would last out; but he gave us great pleasure too, because there is something special about an about-to-break boy's voice.

Rehearsals began and there were some vivid moments of temperament on behalf of the Conductor and the Director and all the cast individually and severally. We had two good soloists, one from the

Cathedral Choir. The crisis came as word spread about the enjoyability of our production. More and more children from the local schools begged to be allowed to take part. As I kept saying "Yes", reckoning that some would fall out and it was good to have some spare, I ended up with more pairs of animals than could be got into the ark in time. However, we made them enter from all corners of the Abbey where they had been hiding. The sight of the children walking up in their animal pairs from the smallest tots to lanky Sixth Formers to the accompaniment of Britten's noisy, joyful music moved me every time it happened. Furthermore, we had two little "birds" (raven and dove) who were at ballet school and therefore excellent dancers. One of them did cart-wheels down the central aisle of the Abbey as she "flew away" from the ark – and again I wept every night!

(I prepared her later for Confirmation; she told me that the grievous burden of her life was that she had once – most naughtily – eaten a doughnut! What discipline was demanded of her. She became a professional dancer; I have admired professional dancers ever since.)

Bob Ashworth, Head of English at Pershore High School, was at that time running the Pershore Festival. He was a staunch Quaker, and a good friend of mine. He took the part of God and I can hear his voice now reverberating in my memory as on that occasion it reverberated round the Abbey. Penelope was the Right Hand Person throughout the production and gave invaluable help. Angela was excellent in her part as one of the wives. Peter could not be in it because he was at school in the Cathedral Choir; but on a later occasion he was allowed out to sing the part of the boy in *Elijah*, and I was very proud of him then.

Noye's Fludde was the one Millennium event that really took off in popularity. There were long queues each evening, and in the end we were letting people in for nothing, for a "hear but hardly see" show. If it had not been for the absolute necessity of restoring the Abbey to its proper self for Sunday services, we could have kept it going for a fortnight. Directing it was the most enjoyable thing of that sort that I have ever done in my life.

Besides the Millennium celebrations in 1972, there was the Pershore Festival every year. Peter Moore had started it and I was disappointed not to be asked to carry on where he had left off. But the

Festival Committee, not knowing me at all, invited Father Crighton to take the chair, with the result that it went on year by year "as before" when it needed to change and develop. Bob Ashworth then took over and put some new life into it, every year producing a play. One year this was *Under Milk Wood,* and I took the parts of the Organist and the Professor. Another year he produced a play in the Abbey about a young airman encountering Christ and being present at the Crucifixion. I was Christ – to the disapproval of some of the congregation; but most of them were generous about it. The review in the local paper said that the performance had added a dimension to Pershore Abbey, which would never be the same again.

Ecumenism was strong in Pershore with the three churches (Anglican, Roman Catholic and Baptist) being close together physically and friendly in their relationships. Father Crighton was a distinguished liturgical scholar and a much loved parish priest. He had been a close friend of Peter Moore – both of them being unmarried at that time and sharing the same understanding of liturgy, church art and architecture. I could not keep this up as I had a family life to attend to; nor was I so interested in the artistic-liturgical side of Christianity. However, when the scandalous Bull, Humanae Vitae, was promulgated by the Pope forbidding birth-control, Father Crighton, amazed and hurt, came round to see me at the Vicarage. We drank port together far into the night. To him it was not basically a crisis of sexual morality, but of the credibility and authority of the Roman hierarchy. He knew that here was an edict that would be widely disregarded.

I was always ready to invite Father Crighton to Abbey events, "mixed-marriage" wedding services, and occasionally to preach. He was grateful; but there were no invitations to me by way of reciprocation. I expect his hands were tied; and it has been the same one-way traffic all through my ministry, not least, at Ripon.

There was also the Baptist church just round the corner. There were no other denominations in Pershore, so the Baptists catered for Methodists, Congregationalists and all the Free Churches. We were friendly to one another and attended one another's big functions. For instance, I went to the induction of the new Baptist minister and my speech of welcome was the thirteenth the congregation had to endure that day – a fact which allowed me (unlike some of the others) to be very short indeed. I made friends with this particular minister and learnt how difficult it is for them to be so much under the thumb of their lay folk, liable to be sacked if they did not please. This particular minister regretted the fact that he had never had the experience of "speaking with tongues", which to him was the necessary sign of God's approval and his authenticity as a minister. I challenged him on this matter, quoting from St Paul's first letter to the Corinthians. He was grateful, but not satisfied.

In the course of this friendly ecumenism I preached a sermon in which I said that friendliness was not enough. Joint action was necessary. The pleasing result was the setting up of the Churches' Action Committee, which organised much-needed relief for the citizens of Pershore, including an excellent scheme for taking people to hospital, thus saving them from a journey of at least four buses. After I left Pershore, ecumenism was taken further, and a Covenant Scheme was approved whereby the Churches promised not to do separately what they could do together.

The day to day pastoral work in the parish, what St Paul called "the care of all the churches", was the dominating feature of my life in those days, but it is not easy to remember it in detail or describe it. There were four churches, because I was Vicar of Pershore, Pinvin and Wick, and Priest in Charge of Birlingham.

Pinvin was a small outpost on the edge of Pershore. I had an awkward and educating row there with the local farmer. The church was sited in the middle of his land, which had once been Church Commissioner property. In fact, it might still have been so: certainly the farmer had a deeply felt grudge against the Commissioners and therefore the Church of England, and therefore God, and most certainly his "Vicar". The immediate cause was funeral services at which people parked their cars in a way that overflowed the church's meagre parking space; that is, they parked on his land. On one such occasion the curate in charge of the church at Pinvin (David Millar) emerged from a funeral service to find the cars blocked in by farm tractors. They sent word, and waited impatiently for about an hour before being released.

I went to see the farmer in the evening and was determined to listen to what he had to say before deciding what action to take. I consulted my wardens and then decided to seek the advice of the Diocesan Registrar in Worcester. He was simple and direct. 'Legally,' he said, 'you are in the wrong. If you want more space to park your cars you must build a bigger car park, acquiring or restyling the land as necessary.' So we set to and made ourselves a nice little car park behind the church. The parishioners and I (pulled together by the problem we shared) were rather proud of it. By this time I had made friends with the farmer anyway, ironically through a funeral which I took myself. Perhaps God (and his Vicar) were not so bad after all. But don't mention the Church Commissioners! This episode shows how much public policy can affect and embitter individual people – for generations to come.

The people of Wick were hostile to me at first because they assumed that, like Peter Moore, I would want to close their church. The opposite was true; all through my ministry I have backed local church buildings, believing that they should (and this is the condition) be centres of community. I wanted the church at Wick to thrive, and to show my sincerity I gave one of the curates the responsibility of doing all he could to build it up. This was good for him as well as for the village church. For Philip Barrett, Wick was in many ways what he liked most: old fashioned and comfortable. He once produced a choir for an Advent Carol Service held as if this were King's College, Cambridge. I had to field the complaints afterwards that the congregation was "hardly allowed to open its mouth".

Mrs Meikle was uncomfortable with me until she was ill in hospital. I visited her frequently then and she began to unwind and talk and show a new love and understanding. We remained friends with all her family, Malcolm, Mima, Clare (Penelope's age), Tom and Lucy.

Also at Wick were the Elkingtons. Captain Elkington was the other Warden. He did approve of me. He had a devout sister and her friend with whom Juliet and I were sometimes summoned to "afternoon tea". They became allies of mine once they had got used to the new liturgy (Series Two), which I took a lot of trouble to explain.

When the new Member of Parliament, Michael Spicer, came to live in Wick, I did all I could to welcome him and draw him and his family into the life of the parish; but they were too much Westminster-bound. I wrote to Michael Spicer about the mutuality of politics and religion, and the importance to himself of having a spiritual base from which to work. This didn't stop him from hardening his heart against Europe!

My other village was Birlingham. It was not part of the parish, but an addition, with me appointed Priest in Charge: I gave Nicholas Coulton the responsibility of looking after it. It was a beautiful village. Alan Gibbs lived there with his family, and he was one of the most devout men and one of the strongest supporters that I have ever had.

Most of my work, however, was in Pershore itself. Early on we set up house-groups to study the theory and practice of the Eucharist and to consider the old ways and the newly proposed ones in Series Two. This was the beginning of the much-needed and much-resented liturgical revision in the Church of England. "Eucharist" means "thanksgiving". Which form of service (we asked the groups), the old or the new, gives most emphasis to this? "Liturgy" means "the work of the people". Which form gives most scope for "congregational participation"? Which form of the confession is most sensible, dignified, honest? Which form of intercessions best fulfils the need to pray for the world in all its needs? Which lectionary gives the best selection of readings from the Bible? The house-groups came firmly to the conclusion that the new forms should be tried; and in the event there was almost no opposition to them.

After that, we organised eighteen house-groups, all over the parish. The trick was to give each group a definite objective; something to study and the possibility of making recommendations that would be taken seriously. We also fixed a time-limit after which they would be expected to break up. Twice a year we broke up the groups, shuffled the members and tried to find new ones, so that the "groups" did not become "cliques". My belief was that people experience Christian love and personal faith in house-groups more than they do in congregational worship. The new-found love and deepened faith of those who attend these groups adds much to the holiness and joy of common worship, just as it adds a new degree of God-centredness and other-people-awareness to a person's faith.

With some reluctance I also took on a stewardship campaign. I was convinced of the spiritual obligation for full-hearted, generous giving by members of the congregation, not because "the Church needs the money" (though it does) but because people who give themselves to God (the calling of all Christians) are *ipso facto* obliged to give a proportion of their possessions. Some people recognise this, but the majority do not. So I was persuaded to go for a stewardship campaign, with its emphasis on "getting together" and "fellowship meals". Certainly the result was good enough to enable us to fulfil our financial obligations, but it was not a success in the way I had hoped. There was much emphasis on secrecy, but I suspected that the point of this was to hide how little, not how much individuals were promising to give.

We had to revamp the children's work, run by Joan Phillips. I soon found that she was a golden person who gave herself generously to other people: her pupils from the Alice Ottley, where she taught music; the Church; the Choral Society, which she conducted; and many kind ministrations to particular people. She agreed that a Sunday School with no connection to the worship of the Church on Sundays must be wrong, so we divised a scheme of children's weekday clubs which gathered children of different ages, gave them their kind of fun, and prepared them for the Sunday worship. They then came to the Abbey for part of the Eucharist, in time to receive their individual blessing at the moment of communion. A Youth Club already thrived under the leadership of successive curates, but never up to the standard of St Michaels's Guild at Basingstoke – so I averred!

Pershore had excellent churchwardens. Colonel Derek Cronin was bluff, kindly, old-school, wise and conservative. Ian Maple was in charge of the local market and made himself indispensable in the Abbey, doing everything, protecting everything, seeing to everything. He told me that his job was to prevent new vicars from making changes, but there was a twinkle in his eye, and no one could have been kinder. He used to "resign" on principle every now and again, but always retracted. He and Peggy, his wife, suffered a personal tragedy in their family; and this brought us close together in compassion and affection.

Derek retired and was followed by "Lance", as he was universally known. He had been the local policeman and knew everyone in

Pershore from the days when he was ubiquitous on his bicycle. He was the most loyal churchwarden that a vicar could have. He loved to sit with Penelope and Angela at evensong, and if my sermons got too long, he would heave suggestively in his seat.

I was also well served by Major John Irwin, who became the verger. He came to see me to ask advice on what he should do with himself now that he was retired. 'Be my verger and help me run this place,' I said. So he did, handling people and things with dignity and care, and patching matters up when I made mistakes. He had served in the war in Greece (this gave us something in common) and was now married to his second wife. Long after I left Pershore one of his daughters wrote to me about her father, whom she had never known. I wrote a glowing letter in return, but had no acknowledgement.

We had an active Church Council, with every member involved in one of the sub-committees which worked at such things as organising the house-groups, stewardship, worship, children and youth, and social events. I found that the "Eight o'clockers" hardly knew those who attended the ten o'clock Eucharist; and none of them knew the evensongsters; so we tried to arrange events to bring them together. We also acquired a parish bus so that we could take groups around the place as needed. But the Treasurer never liked it!

The curates and I went visiting every afternoon and tried hard to penetrate the new housing estates where people lived in ever growing – generation by generation – ignorance of Christianity. I also went round the factories on the industrial estate; and sometimes we put on a display of their products in the Abbey for an "Industrial Harvest Festival".

We were kept busy with many weddings, baptisms and funerals, which take a lot of preparation. I also had a small group of those who made their confession, some on a life-changing "one-off" occasion, some on a regular "Easter and Christmas" basis. I never pushed. They came; and as always when a priest gives some priestly service, whether it be to Confirmation candidates, the sick or dying, those being married, those he visits or those who find the release and joy of penitence, the priest himself (or herself) is humbled, yet strangely enriched.

I had some rough moments with the bell-ringers and soon spotted the fact that most of them were "ringers only", not worshippers. This made me cross. Why should Pershore Abbey be used for their hobby? So I decided to consult Bertie Webb, Vicar of Evesham, an experienced priest who knew his job backwards and was himself a ringer. His advice was simple. 'If you can't beat them, join them.' So for a short time I did so and succeeded in making friends and seeing things from their point of view. I could not find the time or the concentration to continue ringing, but I had made a point. I then drafted in recruits from my Confirmation classes. Confirmands were instructed in the need "to serve the Church". Bell-ringing seemed to some of them a good way of doing so: but it did not excuse them from staying to worship!

Soon after my arrival at Pershore the Rural Dean died, and to my surprise Bishop Charles-Edwards invited me to take over the deanery. The churchwardens thought that this was right and natural, an honour which should always be held by the Vicar of Pershore. But I had hardly been Vicar for more than "dog-watch" and I wondered if I knew enough to do the job properly. But I soon settled down to what I look back upon as one of the most fulfilling times in my ministry. Pershore was the ideal deanery, consisting of the town with its Abbey, and the villages of the Vale of Evesham scattered around; all thriving and many using Pershore as their natural centre for shopping, market and medicine. So I found myself resembling the early church bishops who had a manageable pastoral district with "elders" (priests) stationed around. I worked hard to give the deanery a unity not just of locality but of purpose. We were to do the work of the Church as effectively as we could – together.

We began by making an inventory of our assets. There were the buildings; Pershore's parish bus, which we were prepared to hire out at a cheap rate (a sop to our Treasurer); the clay-pigeon equipment owned by the parish of White Ladies Aston; other interesting "fête" items; and, above all, the many lay people whose special skills could be used beyond their own parish for the deanery as a whole. Geoffrey Manning, who was the Executive Secretary of Metal Box in Worcester, became the lay Vice-Chairman. Together we devised all sorts of schemes for the work of the Church, thinking and planning in strategic terms of "aims and objectives". (I had just been to the Windsor Long Course which gave me and clergy of similar seniority four weeks of this sort of thing; and I picked up the expression – and some of the practice – there.)

The Bishop used me in the diocese because I was a member of the General Synod, the Diocesan Synod and his Council. He also invited me to join a team of three (two businessmen and me) to examine the committee structure of the diocese and to make recommendations. We found a chaotic mess – lots of committees formed for different but overlapping purposes; all of them inclined to pursue their own agenda without much reference to the Bishop, the diocese or one another. We recommended a new streamlined structure of committees, all of which were to be part of a coherent, line-managed organisation. We went to Hartlebury Castle one evening to present our report and explain it to the Bishop and his staff.

The report was accepted and implemented, and it was just what the diocese needed at that time to make it more effective; but the joke is that I refuted the theory behind this report in later lectures when I argued that "line-management" is not a good model for the Church. The Church is not an organisation built upon hierarchical lines. It is a family of mutually supporting "circles"; from the smallest, which is the individual Christian, a little nucleus of God's love, to the bigger circles of a group, parish, deanery, diocese, see – and the "whole state of Christ's Church". "Lines" are the lateral ones of communication and support, not horizonatal ones of authoritative command. In reverse they are lines of love, learning and co-operation, not simple obedience. However, in this instance our report was helpful, and Robin Woods became a more effective bishop than his predecessor, the much loved Charles-Edwards.

Soon after this I was summoned by the Bishop and asked if I would take on the leadership of the new Education Committee in the diocese. The purpose was to gather into one and direct the various small committees that had existed before. This was to include the voluntary sector (Sunday schools and adult groups) as well as the statutory sector to do with schools. I was to leave Pershore and do the job from the base of being Vicar of Cropthorne.

I went home to think about it and found Juliet very depressed at the prospect. First she did not want to leave Pershore. Second she did not want to go to Cropthorne. Third she did not think that I could do such a widespread job from such a remote place. On all three counts I agreed with her, but did not want to say 'No' to the Bishop.

While I was thinking about it the Bishop summoned me again. This time he invited me to be Director of Education and Archdeacon of Dudley, which was a much more appealing prospect, especially as I would now be on his personal staff. Oh, and would I mind being also the Vicar of Dodderhill in Droitwich, as John Williams, the previous Archdeacon of Dudley had been?

I was advised by some not to take on the parish; but I could see the great convenience of doing so. It would provide me with the Vicarage, now called "The Archdeacon's House"; and I welcomed the prospect of a parish to keep my feet on the ground and (as it turned out) to have the support of a congregation. The matter was settled by Juliet, Penelope and Angela who went to look at the church of St Augustine's, Dodderhill, and decided (quite rightly) that this was the perfect church to get married in: so I was allowed to accept the appointment! The Bishop let us stay at Pershore until the end of the summer, by which time Penelope had finished her A-levels and Angela her O-levels.

We celebrated the end of exams by me taking the girls with a friend each to Wimbledon for the tennis. It was a hot day. We ate strawberries and made our way to a court where Connors and Nastasi were playing in a doubles match. They behaved disgracefully. 'Come on, girls,' I said, 'let's go and watch some better-mannered players.' 'No!' they shouted in unison. 'We want to watch Connors and Nastasi.' So we did – tantrums and all; and it made a lovely day.

American Interlude

One day in 1975 I had received a letter from the British Council of Churches asking if I would be prepared to undertake a preaching tour of the United States of America. This would be administered by the World Council of Churches from New York, who would arrange an itinerary by which I would visit churches of all denominations. I would not be paid for the tour but the Churches themselves would pay me a fee for my sermons which should cover expenses. I would receive hospitality for the weekends, but would be out on my own in midweek.

I found this an alluring prospect, and when I asked the Bishop for his permission he was most encouraging and promised to give me useful contacts. So I put it to the churchwardens and PCC and they too were delighted and helpful. In fact, they said that they would pay for Juliet to accompany me.

So we spent the month of August 1975 in the USA. We started in New York, City and State; Montreal, Niagara and Toronto (for touring not preaching), Lansing in Michigan, St Louis, Washington (for a visit), Philadelphia and Newark. It doesn't look far on the map, but we seemed to travel huge distances, always by Greyhound coach (thus seeing a lot of the local scene) and receiving generous hospitality wherever we went – indeed this often overflowed into the week.

All the preaching was done in Protestant churches – no RCs and no Episcopalian (C. of E.). But I made a point of meeting the Episcopalians wherever we went and we stayed nearly a week with the Vicar and his wife in Holland by Lake Michigan, in which, setting an example to the sun-bathing Americans, Juliet and I most foolishly tried to swim, not realising that the water was freezing. In this parish I celebrated and preached at a midweek Eucharist.

It is impossible to describe the tour in detail, but I will make one or two observations. The tour took place just after the Watergate scandal and morale in the States was low. In every home we stayed in there was trouble with the younger generation – details of which used to emerge when we had stayed a couple of nights and they began to trust us. Once there was a son who was in gaol for drugs and theft; one son had fled the country in order to dodge the draft and military service in Vietnam; one family had a hostile daughter living in their upstairs flat and only communicating angrily by telephone.

One family were thought to be strict teetotallers and their Minister begged us not to let on that he had taken us to watch a St Louis Cardinals baseball match and given us beer to drink. But on the last evening they "opened" the Canoletti picture over the fireplace and produced a whisky bottle from which we drank happily together. They asked us what we would most like to do, and we said "get some exercise". So I played a round of golf, before which I prayed to God to honour the Church of England. He answered my prayer and I excelled myself! On another occasion after the same request we were taken a very long way to bathe "in the ocean". We swam for a few moments with vigour, but had to come in because of the jellyfish!

In St Louis I preached two different sermons to huge congregations, to be met not only by the usual line of people who queued to talk to me about them, but also invitations to all possible meals to say what I had said again to people who had missed them. It seems that I hit on a subject which everyone was worried about because a Methodist professor in the university had been dismissed by his congregation for his non-fundamentalist views. They had never heard of a positive interpretation of the Bible which recognises poetic, mythical, rhetorical, moral truth as well that which is historical.

We found the churches weak on liturgy and sacramental theology but very strong indeed in their sense of membership and obligation to one another. Their readiness to give generously of their time and money would put most C. of E. congregations to shame.

We met some extraordinary people and enjoyed some amazing sights. There was the Minister and his wife who looked after a prestigious church in Montreal. His job was to entertain visitors and to preach the sermons. He went away for six weeks in the summer, he told us, and wrote fifty-two sermons to last him for the next year. As he was coming to England we invited him to preach one of them in Pershore Abbey. The sermon consisted of a conversation (complete with different voices) which might have taken place at the Last Supper. Pershore people were totally bemused by all fifty minutes of it! After treating us with lavish hospitality he booked us into a hotel at Niagara, which we found that we could not afford and we had to make do with only ordering the "starter" (onion soup) at dinner. Niagara is dominated by the sound and the spray of the Falls. We were able to watch and film the smooth river flowing swiftly towards its thunderous fate; and we sailed intrepidly under the cascade of water in a brave little steam-boat (*Maid of the Mist*) and got very wet.

We also saw the huge arch at St Louis which is said to be the gateway between East and West (it was the furthest West we got); the picturesque – but slightly precious – town of Williamsburg, where the inhabitants wear Regency costume to enhance the effect; the many sights of Washington, where we missed our stop on a bus but were warned not to get off at the next stop and walk back, because the district was unsafe for white people; so we went to the end of the journey and back before getting off at our hotel. We spent a day with a delightful and impressive woman priest in the fundamentalist Amish country near Philadelphia. We became separated from our luggage at Newark and our host rang up the head of the Greyhound company himself: the luggage was specially delivered the next day. Our hosts and hostesses were all very kind and generous – more so than we ever expected. They paid me well for my sermons, some of which were broadcast; so if I had not had my pockets picked in Kennedy Airport I would have arrived home with fifty dollars to spare.

And on my first Sunday home I went to a neighbouring village to preach at evensong – a lively sermon, I am sure, laced with juicy stories from America, but with no reponse at all except for the usual, gruff "Goodnight Vicar" at the door of the church. I was back in England.

And back to work. My duties in the Archdeaconry of Dudley began while I was still being Vicar of Pershore, and it was about six months before we went to Dodderhill. We had been in Pershore for eight years. I was ready to move, though Julie and I were both sad to be leaving. The Pershore people were generous; rather pleased, I think, that their Vicar was now a "Venerable Archdeacon".

Chapter 20
Archdeacon; and Vicar of Dodderhill

I was made Archdeacon of Dudley by the Bishop of Worcester in the church of St John's, Kidderminster, Ian Griggs (later to be Suffragan Bishop of Ludlow) being the Vicar. This was towards the end of 1975. But, with the Bishop's agreement, I remained Vicar of Pershore till I moved to Droitwich in the summer of 1976, when Penelope and Angela had finished their exams.

Penelope needed good enough A-level grades in maths, physics, chemistry and biology to be accepted by Leicester University – her first choice because she liked their "hands on" approach to medical training. When the exams were over we all went through the drama of being told that she had undoubtedly failed. However, we went to Newport as usual for the summer holidays and on the last day, before driving home to hear the results, I took her off for a fatherly walk and talk on Newport Sands and asked her what she would like to do in the event of having failed. 'Failed?' she said with great indignation. 'Of course I haven't failed.' End of conversation. Indeed she hadn't and she was duly accepted by Leicester, where she still lives! I drove her there with her bike on the back of the car, passing and being passed by lots of other fathers with sons or daughters inside and bikes on the backs of their cars.

By this time we had moved to Droitwich, where we were to live in what Archdeacon Williams had named "The Archdeacon's House" for the next eight years. It was situated up the hill, about a mile out of Droitwich, a beautiful Edwardian house with a large garden adjoining the practice area of the golf course; so as we gardened or lazed in the

253

sun or played cricket with Peter on Saturday afternoons, we would hear the friendly plop of golf balls with the odd one or two straying into our vegetable patch, most of which I threw back.

Penelope immediately set up business by organising a children's holiday-loose-end course, keeping about a dozen children happy with creative activities as they took part in a show which she wrote and produced, complete with singing and dancing. Producing pantomimes and playlets had always been a holiday occupation for our three, especially on wet days at the farm. All the children took part and we parents were dragooned into proud attendance. So why not do it now for children in our new neighbourhood? It was a very hot summer and almost everything happened out of doors. Penelope and Angela made a commercial success of this enterprise and we all made new friends as a result of it.

A few years later Peter also found profitable scope for his acting. He and his friend set up a two-man theatre company and hired themselves out to local primary schools to perform *Biff and Boff*, slapstick stuff about two men from Mars. Angela earned herself an income by teaching children the flute and piano.

When we moved to Droitwich Angela joined the Sixth Form at King's, Worcester, to study English, French and Music. She was in the second intake of girls at King's, and it became a universally acknowledged fact that Angela Campling's legs were the most shapely in the school. She greatly enjoyed her two years and used to play the flute at the high-class King's concerts.

Peter was still a Cathedral chorister when we first moved, but as we were now in the radius of ten miles from the Cathedral, he was allowed to live at home. From the point of view of his scholastic progress, this was a mistake, because his social life became dominant. He has always been good at making friends – and at this time there were lots of very demanding ones, both male and female. When he left the Choir he became involved in rugger, cricket (first teams for three years running), acting and opera, and the new Head insisted that for his last year he be a boarder, finding some scholarship money to make this possible.

Meanwhile Juliet had been appointed to teach in the Witton Middle School in Droitwich. The Headteacher, Mr Portman, had pioneered middle schools in the country, and Witton was a fine example of what many teachers claim is the most satisfactory kind of school, with an interesting range of age and ability. Juliet took over a class of ten-year olds and found them most stimulating, as I am sure she was to them. Her immediate "boss" was Nell, a dedicated professional teacher who knew all the tricks and had a heart of gold, as well as a strong Roman Catholic faith. The school was within easy reach of home and Julie went backwards and forwards in her precious Beetle. Her teaching career added a whole dimension of interest to our lives.

I now had to buckle down to work on my three jobs. I record without comment the fact that when I left, eight years later, I was replaced by three people!

Job No. 1 was being Vicar of St Augustine's, Dodderhill. St Augustine's might have been the church in which St Augustine of Canterbury met the Celtic bishops of Wales and tried unsuccessfully to persuade them to join the Western Church – a cause in which St Wilfrid of Ripon was successful at the Council of Whitby in the next century. This conjecture arises from the date of the church, which makes it possible, its position (on the way to Wales from Canterbury) and its unusual dedication. But whoever designed the window in the East End cannot have known this as it depicts the two Augustines, Hippo and Canterbury! Like Pershore Abbey, St Augustine's had lost its nave and so consisted of the chancel and crossing – delightful in many ways but inconvenient for worship. It has been very well re-ordered since my time.

St Augustine's is one of the "holiest" churches I have ever encountered. Despite the fact that it had been used by Cromwell's troops in the Civil War and still bears the scars of cannon-balls, the very stones seem to speak of the loving presence of God. Indeed, when Julie brought her class of ten-year-olds to visit the church along with other churches in the town, the children, unused to churches, knelt down of their own accord. It is a beautiful church, crooked physically because, like the rest of Droitwich, it was built over an underground river of salt, so the foundations have slipped: but this adds to its charm.

The congregation was drawn from the families of the former salt miners who lived in the Vines, the street below the church on the west of the town of Droitwich. There lived Harriet (ninety-plus), who was grandma or great aunt to almost everyone, living in a tiny house, quite well off, holding court to all who came to see her, speaking her mind, extremely devout. And there were Loll and Dave, two ex-naval ratings, Loll a stoker and Dave a signalman, who knew everyone, were loved by everyone, and did everything that needed to be done for the church and the church hall.

Loll ran a ladies' football team and when at last, at the age of eighty-plus, he decided to give up, they gave him a party and a huge cake. He then carried on as before because there was no one to take his place. Similarly with the church. He verged and cleaned and cared – but found it increasingly difficult to get up the hill to the church itself. Eventually we had a party for him and said, 'Thank you very much, Loll, for all you have done; now we will find others to take over your jobs.' He gracefully accepted, but turned up next Sunday all the same. He was inseparable from Dave, whom he had known as a child and met again at Shanghai, an incident he recounted often and at length. Dave was as wide as he was high, enormously strong both in body and spirit. He had a rough voice and a strong Worcestershire accent, difficult to understand. Both men were utterly loyal to God, to Dodderhill folk and to St Augustine's church.

There was also a group of women who took care of everything, especially when it came to the annual fête held in the school grounds (a private girls' school next door). There was no organisation for this fête. Indeed, there did not need to be for nothing ever changed and everyone did what they had done last year. If someone had unfortunately died, then daughter or granddaughter carried on the good work.

The school generation was also strong, partly because of a well run Sunday school, and partly because of the annual pantomime (locally not church based) which kept them together, singing and dancing. The two comediennes at this were Winnie and Flo who had us aching with laughter at the same jokes told in the same way every year. For its joyful incompetence the annual pantomime was remarkable and everyone who went to it in the right spirit came away refreshed and entertained and – dare I say? – inspired by the performance. This was the Dodderhill community having its annual fun. The dresses worn by the children (including the smallest) were up to the highest standards. There must have been an army of mums behind the scenes to change the Little Ducklings in Act 1 into Tiny Fairies in Act 2, and the Sweetest Elves in Act 3.

The congregation contained a few "outside" people whose loyalty and service made them indispensable "insiders". Such were the Davidsons, who had brought their daughter to me at Pershore to get married in the Abbey, and had agreed faithfully to the rules of attendance by which they could join the parochial church roll. After the wedding they naturally came less and less to the Abbey; then I found them worshipping in the congregation at Dodderhill, which was nearer their home. They became firm family friends. Charles (and later, Jean) became members of the Dodderhill PCC and managed to add a degree of sense to its proceedings. Then there was Heather Haines, who had been one of Julie's lecturers at the Worcester College of Education. She was wise, devout and very intelligent; a good friend and now a Canon of Worcerster Cathedral. I claim the credit for introducing her into the diocesan education committee: she later became its Chair.

There was also an adult choir, led by Jack and trained by me. The organist was a young man who had learning difficulties but who played the organ quite efficiently and very heartfully by ear: an extraordinary gift. Perhaps it was as much memory as ear because he could also learn a new piece by himself, and then play it later. I taught the Choir and congregation to sing my own music to the new Series Three service. This was later revised by Neil Richardson – a professional composer who had been at Lancing and showed interest in what I told him about my ideas for a congregational setting with passages for a choir. The resulting music (plus some hymns and carols) was duly published by Scalewise, received a good review and was even used in Ripon Cathedral. Dodderhill only had my tuneful but unprofessional version. Our organist understood it and played a certain C Major chord, which the organ is asked to do on its own, with great aplomb. It comes triumphantly after the Affirmations in the Eucharistic prayer, but the organist at Ripon always omitted it! "My" choir was co-operative with regard to my compositional efforts and belted them out, one lady member telling me afterwards that she could not get the tune of the Gloria out of her head. It was a splendid choir: Julie joined it; it always sang with gusto and love.

The power at Dodderhill lay with five men, all stalwart Christians, utterly loyal (like Loll and Dave) to God and St Augustine's.

One was Fred Smith who decorated the church beautifully and served at the Altar with an air of disapproval if the Celebrant omitted any of his favourite bits of ritual. When I suggested that Peter should serve, just after he had been confirmed, Fred tolerated him in a lofty way, but Peter decided that there was not room for them both in the sanctuary. Fred kept the Altar linen and vestments in perfect order through the skill of his needle; and he also lavished much care upon St Peter's Primary School, of which he was the secretary to the Governors – but felt himself to be headteacher, chairman and everything else rolled into one. He was zealous and loyal – but not a man to cross.

Then there was Dennis the postman who had a lovely wife and lots of children, who peopled the Sunday school and the pantomime. Dennis knew everyone in Droitwich by their address, and PCC meetings sometimes came to a halt while he reminded us of who lived where and who was related to whom and whether people were ill or married or not. He was deeply devout and would do anything for the Church.

Then there was the triumvirate of Jack (Churchwarden), Geoff (his son and Treasurer) and Bill Thomas (Churchwarden), who ran the local coffin factory. Bill made Peter a hen-house, for his newly acquired hens, out of wood that had obviously been destined for coffins.

Jack had left school at the age of twelve and became a driver to high-ranking officers in the Army, driving all through Europe from D-Day onwards. After the war he ran a working men's club. He was a man of great ability. He could sing, read and speak eloquently. At meetings of the PCC he used to listen carefully to what was being said, sort the sense from the waffle and irrelevancies, and then sum up with a sensible conclusion and a way forward. He had excellent judgement. He ruled Dodderhill people with a rod made of iron, good sense and love.

Geoff never quite rose above being Jack's son, but he too was an able accountant and a sincere Christian. He worked in the Borough Treasurer's office and was an excellent Treasurer to the church, who did not suffer from "treasurer's syndrome", wanting to keep the money and on no account spend it! Indeed the Dodderhill congregation was one of the most generous in its giving of time and money that I have ever known – even though, or perhaps because, this was a matter of "widows' mites".

Bill was the gentlest of the three and perhaps the most devout in a God-centred, selfless way. He was a person I dearly loved, and still do.

I started in trouble with these men because Bishop Robin Woods had never consulted them about my appointment. So why should they have me foisted on them just because I was the new Archdeacon? This blew up while I was still at Pershore. 'Go along and see them, Chris,' said Robin, 'and sort them out.' So I met them one evening in Bill's house. We started very formally with coffee and a biscuit. I asked them all about the church and its problems and listened attentively and sympathetically. Things began to get more friendly and the whisky was passed round. Soon we put St Augustine's and Dodderhill right; then the Deanery; then the Diocese; then the Church of England; then the world. It was a happy evening.

The parish itself with the visiting (for instance, a day spent distributing harvest produce to addresses given me by Dennis), the preparation of Confirmation candidates (I still keep in touch with Kathrine and her parents), and various pastoral crises which cannot now be described, kept me busy enough without having educational and archidiaconal duties to cope with as well.

However, I had to visit other churches on Sunday mornings, which led to some hectic driving as I dashed off to take a ten or a ten-thirty somewhere in the archdeaconry. One Christmas Eve I was rung up by the Warden of a church near Kidderminster. Their Vicar was ill. Could I take their Christmas morning service at ten-thirty? I could, but I would arrive at the very last minute, or later. In the event I had a minute or two to spare, long enough for the Warden to whisper to me while I was robing that they had a Christmas custom in their church of children bringing their gifts to the Altar at the offertory. 'Excellent,' said I, and prepared to receive the gifts. They were a handsome collection, but as the server and I arranged them round the foot of the altar I became aware of a rebellious attitude from some of the children, who did not seem keen on parting with their presents. The server then whispered to me that I was supposed to receive the gifts, bless them and hand them back. But by then the damage had been done. But no! For in a way that could be interpreted as being full of religious meaning, I kept the gifts at the Altar. Then I gave them back – transformed and ennobled – after the consecration prayer, when the adults came up for Communion and the children for their blessing. The trick then was to get the right presents back to the right children; but they knew well enough whose was what, so all ended happily.

I was once rung in the middle of the night to go to a house where they thought they had a ghost, or at least an evil spirit. It's no good saying that you don't believe in ghosts on these occasions; so I dragged myself out of bed, dressed and went to the house to do whatever seemed appropriate. The family was pleased to see me. They had suffered an extraordinary run of bad luck ever since they had moved into the house a few weeks previously, and they associated this, incident by incident, with a malignant influence affecting each room in turn. I listened to the story – stories – the worst of which was about the treatment the mother had received in hospital where some article of surgery had been left inside her; and she had not managed to get any apology or redress. Wishing to do something practical I promised to go to the hospital with her the next day and try at least to get some explanation and advice, which promise I kept to her obvious satisfaction. Meanwhile, I went round the house and said an appropriate prayer in each room, including the loo. I left them quite happy, ghost forgotten; and apart from the trip to the hospital I never heard from them again. This must be an example of "the Church" (on this occasion through its archdeacon) "doing the work of Christ" without acknowledgement, praise or thanks; yet with deep satisfaction.

It is difficult to write with discretion about the day-to-day grind of a vicar's work as I experienced it at Basingstoke, Pershore, Dodderhill and Ripon: casual visits that seem to lead to nothing but may catch a blaze of anger or searing pain or a deeply troubled conscience; preparing people for marriage, which was nearly always rewarding; baptising babies and welcoming their families, gratifying at the time but often disappointing in the aftermath; and preparing candidates, adults and children, for Confirmation. This was the work I liked best.

Funerals are very personal as one gets involved in a family's grief. It's a painful privilege, but the service itself can be uplifting. Sometimes I have encountered hysterical grief, in one case so severe that I called the doctor in to see a young widow who would not even get out of bed – and blamed me, so I heard later! Hysterics, as opposed to honest tears, can be the result of guilt, when the deceased person has been neglected or there has been an unresolved family quarrel.

Being with people who are dying is another great privilege. If they have been church goers I read psalms to them as well as praying for their forgiveness and blessing; even if they have not been going to church I often read the twenty-third psalm, with its emphasis on eternal blessing in the present moment. Once a very clever woman, well known to me and, along with her husband, an avowed atheist, was terrified of dying and seemed to have the threats of damnation – dating from her childhood but previously scorned – vivid in her consciousness. The twenty-third psalm did wonders for her. 'Don't speculate on the future,' I said. 'Think of God's love for you in the present; and if not 'God's', then just "love", for you are surrounded by it.' Her husband was very grateful in later days.

One of the saddest funerals I ever took was of a boy killed by a milk van when he was four. I went to the house of the parents, whom I knew well in another context. 'No religion,' said the father at the door threateningly. 'Just love,' I said. 'Do let me in.' We sat together far into the night, mother and father smoking continuously. They did not want a funeral in church, but agreed to it in the end for their two families' sake, both families being religious at each end of the churchmanship spectrum. At the service I said that some of us believe in God and say that God is Love. Some just believe in Love, and treat it as God. There is really not very much difference, for certainly love prevails after death, and we are here to celebrate Love even in this moment of great sadness.

I inaugurated two annual events at Dodderhill: one religious, one not so. The religious event was a proper celebration of Ascension Day, a feast little recognised in most parish churches. As Jesus "went up" to the top of the mountain, and then on "up" (which I think of as metaphorical) to Heaven, why shouldn't the congregations of Droitwich churches of all denominations come "up" the hill to us at St Augustine's and celebrate the feast with us? So we invited all the churches to a special evening of Ascension Day Eucharist, followed by bonfire, barbecue and fireworks. When the weather was fine (I sometimes think that God does not understand weather) this made a joyful occasion, and Dodderhill folk were pleased to find themselves as hosts to the town churches.

The other event was a series of cricket matches held on Sunday afternoons, church versus pub, though many of the players – for instance Loll and Dave – were equally at home in both. We played with a tennis ball on the school grounds. Each side batted once and the "elevens" could be reinforced by more players if required. Tea and sandwiches were served, and the stakes were serious. If the church won, all participants, plus followers, would come to evensong; if the pub were to be victorious, then the congregation would go for a drink after evensong. Generally it was near enough a draw to ensure a good attendance afterwards both at evensong (at which I would have the last word!) and the pub. One match was particularly memorable, first for the sixes hit by Angus, the teenage son of the Davidsons. He batted with a windmill action, his bat completing an ark with each strike. Sometimes – rarely – he made contact with the ball, in which case it had to be a "six". We did not keep the LBW rule very strictly, so it was quite difficult to bowl him out through the whirl of body and revolving bat; but his innings did eventually come to an end.

The match finished with a remarkable, somewhat disputed tie. The church needed four runs to tie, five for victory, when the eleventh man came in and was out. Stumps? Certainly not for in marched Angela, the Archdeacon's daughter: and who was going to deny her her innings? The publican fielders closed up and the bowler bowled a soft underarm dolly ball. Angela stepped out and smote it over the fielders' heads, and scampered off for two runs. Another dolly, another confident blow for two more runs. The scores were now equal. But a crafty Pint of Mild (as P.G. Wodehouse would have described him), thinking that enough was enough, stepped back a few paces, and when Angela did her third scornful clout, he was there ready for the catch. So – stumps, evensong and a beer or two afterwards.

We had two family weddings at Dodderhill: Penelope's to Les, and Angela's to Bob. I cannot remember two more happy occasions. I performed the ceremonies; Peter gave his sisters away; and the receptions were at Pershore (St Andrew's) for Penelope and Dodderhill school for Angela. Juliet and the girls were right about the suitability of St Augustine's for these important occasions.

Juliet and I also had our Silver Wedding anniversary at Dodderhill. We had a service of thanksgiving, at which Peter fell devoutly asleep on his knees, and a magnificent party at which the parish gave us a silver sauce-boat jug. We then made off together and had a week to ourselves in the Lake District.

I was right to believe that although the parish would give me a lot of extra work, it would also give me the support that I needed. Indeed the friendship of the Dodderhill people kept us happy and gave me a secure base for my diocesan work. It also gave me a degree of credibility with other vicars who knew that I too had to visit the sick, teach the children, cope with the PCC and raise money for the diocesan quota! All this, however, for eight happy years, was only the backdrop to my two main duties at that time: being Archdeacon of Dudley and Director of Religious Education for the Diocese of Worcester.

Chapter 21
Archdeacon of Dudley

When my appointment as Archdeacon of Dudley was announced I received many letters of congratulation, some of them reminding me in a friendly way that it is a well-known theological fact that an archdeacon cannot be saved. Victor de Waal, however, the Dean of Canterbury, whom I knew at Ely when he was on the staff of the Theological College, wrote to say that in his experience archdeacons are the very grist, backbone, nerve-centre, heart, firing line of the Church of England. Bishops are important and have their glory; but archdeacons do the hard work which makes the bishop's role possible. Vicars bear the brunt; but archdeacons are there to share it with them when the brunt is at its most brutal. Archdeacons are at the coal-face, the cutting edge, the point of contact between the church and the world. They live in the trenches; and they go over the top to attack and be shot at. He may not have used such a mixture of metaphors, but he made the point strongly: that archdeacons matter.

Archdeacons have been described as the ears and eyes of the bishop. I was certainly those things in my area, which included everything north of Worcester up to the borough of Dudley. I used to go to see the Bishop on a Monday morning every two or three weeks. We would sit with a table between us, on which there would be a pile of letters which he would go through and hand over. 'Go and see about this,' he would say. 'Find out what it's about.' 'Go and see this silly ass (of a new vicar). I warned him not to rush things. Tell him not to be so bumptious.' 'There seem to be difficulties in this parish. Go and sort them out.' 'Colonel Bell (diocesan secretary) tells me that this parish refuses to pay its quota. Find out why, and help them to see sense.' 'There is a danger of this curate getting into hot water about – . Pay him a visit.' 'Here is a complaint about a vicarage. Have a word with the parson's wife; and see if you can get some sense out of the Parsonage Board.' And so on. The pile of letters would be pushed across to me, and off I would go wondering how I could fit all these affairs into an already crowded timetable.

Robin was so full of zest that he was a stimulating person to serve – and rewarding, because he was also very humble when he found himself in the wrong, and appreciative of what one did for him. He could also be forgetful. Once he rang me up. 'Chris,' – he was the only person I willingly allowed to shorten my name – 'what are you doing Tuesday evening? Oh? Well, cancel it, would you: I need you to go to St Somewhere's and induct the new priest in charge.' 'O Robin, it really is difficult. I hate cancelling what is already in my diary.' 'Well, you can blame me: I am afraid I have double-dated.' So off I went that Tuesday evening, and when I got to the parish church of St Somewhere's, there was John Williams, my fellow archdeacon, whom Robin had also asked to clear his diary and take over this vital event. We glared at each other and tossed: this gave one of us an unexpected evening at home. Fury – but one could never actually feel that in Robin's penitent presence.

There were many problems: vicars at loggerheads with their parishioners over the new services; a vicar who had taken it into his head to baptise people by total immersion in the local swimming-pool; a vicar's wife in tears because she never saw her husband or they were too poor to keep up such a house and garden; or she went out to work and some parishioners were horrid about it. There was a recently made parson's widow who had no money and nowhere to go. Juliet had strong words about this with the Bishop's wife. Things changed and the C. of E. Pensions Board now does much more for parsons' widows. Once a rich man invited me to dinner and over the coffee and brandy asked me to ask the Bishop (he meant the Parsonage Board) to change his mind about getting rid of the old Rectory. I didn't.

A great deal of my time was spent over matters to do with death. People wanted unsuitable gravestones, feeling that this was a personal matter and had nothing to do with diocesan policy. Once I solved a problem by changing a ghastly poem written in sentimental rhyming couplets into something more seemly. Once we had a new vicar (whom I had found myself and persuaded R.W. to appoint: my worst gift to the diocese) who used to preach thunderous sermons at funerals threatening congregations with hellfire if they attended church as rarely as the deceased had done. In the matter of a death, especially a memorial stone, I always counselled patience. 'Do not argue the point for at least six months,' I said. 'It takes time to get things into perspective.'

The positive side of caring for the churches in the archdeaconry was the joy of working with vicars who were prepared to think strategically about their parishes and plan to do things more effectively. The vicars at whose induction I was present were happy to be visited some months afterwards to discuss some of the problems: parish magazine; work with children and young people; an awkward branch of (say) the Mothers' Union; reluctance even to try the new services; a congregation that would not give; a treasurer who would not spend. There was also so much that was good: excellent relationship with the school; an ecumenical venture; a "care for the bereaved" scheme; new lay people coming into the Church and wanting to make it a better instrument of God's love. Of these I used to say, 'Find out with them at what level (national, diocesan, deanery or parish) they could best serve, and do not expect them to serve at all levels at once.'

I used to enjoy my annual "visitations", seeing the churchwardens and addressing them together about those parts of their parish life that I thought most important, such as education, ecumenical relationships and care within the community which (I dared to think) we had tackled with some success at Pershore. Some of the older incumbents were suspicious of me at first. They did not want interference from a green archdeacon who thought he knew their job better than they did. But I got to be very fond of some of them. Bill, who played golf most days and put my son Peter right on a matter of golfing technique; Leslie whose moment of significance in his life had been as a chaplain with the British forces at Dunkirk and who had written an interesting account of it. He was an eloquent preacher and was disappointed that he had not been noticed by the Church authorities. In defiance he never attended any diocesan or deanery gathering and never used the diocesan services.

I was once asked to give three lectures to potential rural deans at a residentiary conference at Windsor. I made the point that if clergy do not get a response, either from the hierarchy or from their parishioners, they may become sour and resentful. A vicar can survive if he has one or the other, but must not be deprived of both.

I got involved in lots of schemes for the reorganisation of parishes. This was forced on us by the shortage of clergy which the Church was beginning to come to terms with. A scheme for reducing the number of clergy was being forced on all dioceses to make the overall position in the Church fairer. I made a careful assessment of the optimum size of a parish and came to the conclusion that the best situation for a vicar is a parish of nine thousand people with one church. Two churches adds greatly to the strain, and other factors affect it, such as church schools or a hospital. We tried to work a diocesan plan based on a formula I devised, but no situation is ever tidy and it was often difficult to get it right.

Once I went to a PCC to unfold a plan to do with their parish. But a young man opposed me. "Archdeacon," he said, in a very pious voice, 'I have been praying to the Lord about this scheme, and the Lord has told me that it would be wrong and I must oppose it.' 'Oh,' said I. 'That's odd because I have also been praying to the Lord and he has told me that this is the right thing to do.' Tense silence. 'And so,' I added, 'has the Bishop.' Checkmate. And fortunately everyone laughed.

Schemes for uniting parishes could be tricky. There were three possibilities. One was simply to enlarge a particular parish so that it included a wider area and possibly another church or two. This could be difficult because neighbouring congregations do not want to be "swallowed up" by a big new parish, thus losing their identity. Another way was to create a "team" of parishes which would work together. There would be a Team Rector in overall charge, and Team Vicars working at the other churches with him. The third way was less effective but easier to sell: that was to create a "group" of parishes who worked together as far as was possible, sharing one another's resources: a kind of mini-deanery.

There were three essential conditions for any scheme.

One was the proper understanding of "community". No community is complete in itself, but communities can work together in a "community of communities"; each important, but with activities and responsibilities that bind them together into the larger community. There are many church activities such as youth and children's work, mens' societies, adult classes and hospital visiting, which can be shared across parish borders in a community of parishes.

The second essential ingredient is mutual support and affection and willingness to share responsibilities amongst the clergy. Often a grouping would start well with like-minded vicars who were prepared to work together. But then, with change of personnel it would fall apart and a good scheme would fail. This put considerable onus upon those responsible for appointments to find vicars who would "fit"; also an onus on those responsible for the training of clergy to train them as people who can work together and not be egocentric in their concept of ministry.

The third condition for a successful scheme is that it should be a unity of parishes with their people; not just an agreement amongst the clergy.

I once wrote a paper for the Bishop's staff showing that the essence of the life of the Church is "community" and that parsons are there not "to be the Church" supported by the people, but to help the people into realising that *they* are "the Church". With this understanding it is not necessary to have one parson per parish, but it is necessary to have dedicated Christian men and women who are prepared to give a lead from within the community. Sometimes, I believe, such a person can be ordained as the priest in that place, with no expectation that he would be moved away to be a priest in some other place.

I appeared to the Diocesan Secretary to go back on what I had written when he urged – for financial reasons – that when a vicar left his parish he need not be replaced. The idea however of having locally ordained priests from the community, or lay people taking over the running of a parish which would also be served by a shared priest, could not work until those concerned had shown themselves ready for it. In most parishes they were by no means ready.

Bishop's staff meetings happened once a month and took a whole morning, sometimes a whole day. Seven people attended: the three bishops (including the retired Bishop Allenby); the Dean; the two archdeacons; and the Diocesan Secretary. Bishop Robin presided in a loud voice; so we all raised our voices and the decibel count would go up and up. At one of my first meetings Bishop Allenby passed me a note (like a naughty schoolboy). 'You'll have to shout louder if you want to make your point.' So I did – and up went the decibel count another notch. We always sat round a table and had a formal written agenda – which Robin insisted on and I have done at my own meetings ever since: it helps to keep the meeting to the point. The discussions were strategic, tactical, financial, personal. Most of the time was spent on appointments; and difficulties (and difficult people) were prayed about. Sometimes Robin would sum up by saying, 'Right: we'll tell him that it's the will of God that he should go to such and such a parish.' So that is what is meant by "vocation"!

I sometimes held my own Rural Deans' meetings; and these were much more fun, ending in a pub for a beer and a ploughman's. One rural dean was also the Industrial Chaplain for the area (Redditch). He, John Gathercole, who later became Archdeacon of Dudley, made an excellent Rural Dean because, not having a parish, he had a wider grasp of the town's problems. Redditch was an overspill town from Birmingham and was slowly becoming a coherent unit, civically as well as ecclesiastically. I like to think that this was partly due to the team of industrial chaplains and the "Christian ecumenical centre" established in the middle of the shopping spa.

Industrial chaplains went into the factories and got to know the people who worked in them, of all colours of collar. Indeed the Industrial Chaplain at Kidderminster became one of the best-known and most popular people in the town. But it was not an easy job, because chaplains had to make relationships by personal strength and God's grace and not by any formal status. One young man was trained for the job and given some factories to be his stamping ground; but after two or three months I met one of the directors and asked him casually how his new chaplain was doing. He said that he had never heard of him. He then made enquiries and rang me to say that the

Chaplain had not been seen on site. So I went to his home. Sadly he told me that he drove to the car park every morning, stayed in his car all day and then went home in shame. He could not face the ordeal of going in and just "being" a priest, a friend to all, in what seemed a godless, unfriendly place. We took him out of the industrial mission and appointed him to a parish as a curate, where, with his dog-collar round his neck, he was perfectly happy.

One day at a staff meeting Robin Woods told us all that he was going to retire the following year: he would make a public announcement soon so as to give the appointing powers plenty of time to find a successor, also to give all parts of the diocese (deaneries, parishes, boards and committees) plenty of time to say farewell.

I was sad because I loved Robin with his huge stature and powerful voice and his zest for the Kingdom of God. It was always a tearaway excitement working with him on any project. He was a strong leader who pulled people along, making them excel themselves in what they achieved. In churchmanship he was a mixture. He had been brought up as an "evangelical", with a warm love of the Bible which he used to explore during sermons with relish, as if he were making new discoveries. But he had been trained later in a "catholic" understanding of the Church and the sacraments. He was also an advanced thinker in such matters as the possibility (by the forgiveness of God) of a new marriage of someone who had been divorced; the admission of children to Holy Communion; all-round ecumenical relations with other Churches to fulfil Christ's prayer "that they may be one"; and the ordination of women. (His daughter Rachel is now a priest.)

We had a year of farewell parties, many of which his staff were expected to attend, and then a great celebration of his episcopacy and presentation of gifts in the Cathedral. I made the big speech, one of the biggest in my life. Archdeacon Peter Eliot praised me for it, but Colonel Bell said it was too long. 'It had to be long,' I retorted, 'because you had forgotten to bring the presents in from the vestry and I had to go on talking while you went to fetch them!' Touché; and nearly true.

Meanwhile, there was the business of appointing a new bishop. My own part in this was considerable. There was a diocesan "Vacancy in

See Committee" consisting of representatives from all over the diocese. After written evidence had been collected by the Ecclesiastical and Crown Appointment Secretaries this committee met to make its recommendations to the Secretaries concerning the kind of man they would like to have: for instance, first-and-foremost a pastor, a good administator, one with the experience of being a vicar, one who knew how a diocese worked, etc.; just as parishes always ask for their vicar to be the Archangel Gabriel, young, married with a family, a good visitor and an excellent preacher and one who would not want to change anything! Normally the Suffragan Bishop or the Dean would have chaired this meeting; but neither would agree to sit under the other, so they turned to me, the senior archdeacon, to do so – which I did and enjoyed. Refusing the format for the meeting suggested by the Secretaries, I decided to "go round the table" and ask each member to express his or her own feelings. I then made a list of the categories that had been mentioned. We then discussed these and a summary was made under each heading. The Secretaries complained that this procedure made the meeting last longer, but at least the delegates were satisfied.

Three members of the committee then had to be elected to represent the diocese at the meeting of the Crown Appointments Commission; the Dean, Mrs Wendy Roberts (a member of Synod and one of my parishioners at Pershore) and I were elected. So the three of us were summoned to Lambeth Palace to meet with the rest of the synodically elected commission, with the Archbishop of Canterbury in the chair.

The meeting began by all members swearing that they would never divulge what had been discussed; I have no intention of breaking that oath now.

Sufficient to say that, at the end of it all, Philip Goodrich, Suffragan Bishop of Tonbridge, was appointed Bishop of Worcester. He had been one of my favourites from the beginning. He had the experience that was needed, especially as he had been the unofficial (because this was a new invention) Team Rector of a group of parishes in the Norwich diocese that had opted to work together as a unit. Everybody seemed to like him. In marked contrast to the overwhelming, princely leadership of Robin Woods, Bishop Philip was going to be one who would give leadership and professional guidance from his long experience as a parish priest and suffragan bishop.

I got close to Robert Runcie in the course of these meetings. I served for him at the morning Eucharists and we had a long talk in the vestry. I began to realise how deeply hurt he was by Terry Waite's capture and imprisonment and the bad press that he (Robert) had got, despite the fact that he had begged Terry not to venture into Beirut.

Towards the end of my nine years as Archdeacon of Dudley, Director of Religious Education and Vicar of St Augustine's, Dodderhill, I was feeling the strain and my health seemed to be suffering. I got a dose of flu and could not get rid of it; so for months I was dragging myself around, just able to cope with the demands made upon me, but collapsing in a heap when I got home. Sometimes I would find myself driving home from some archidiaconal outpost, along the lanes of Worcestershire, at twelve miles an hour. On holidays I had no energy for walking; and I was causing distress to myself and to Juliet. Bishop Robin was beginning to get the message; and I was told that my health was considered "suspect" by those with the power of appointment and promotion. Julie and I decided that we had had enough and that we would ask the Bishop to find a nice country parish for us to work in for the rest of our days of ministry.

But then, one day, out of the blue, just as I was about to go and play golf with Peter, two identical envelopes arrived with "Ten Downing Street" on them. One contained a letter from the Prime Minister's Appointment Secretary telling me to expect a letter from Mrs Thatcher, which I must answer at once. The other was from Herself, a delightful letter beginning "My Dear Archdeacon", and ending "Yours sincerely, Margaret Thatcher". In the middle was a request that I should allow my name to be forwarded to the Queen for appointment to the Deanery of Ripon.

My knees shook uncontrollably as I putted out on the first green, and I had to tell Peter, even before Julie, who was at her school that morning, what had happened. Julie, of course, was thrilled, but dismayed by the prospect of leaving her beloved school, where she was teaching so happily and successfully. We decided that, despite her secretary's insistence, Mrs T. should be made to wait until we had been to Ripon and seen the Bishop. So I rang the Bishop of Ripon (David Young) and asked to see him. By this time we had studied a map and found Ripon in the far, far north. We would be going into new territory and culture. But first I went to see Philip Goodrich, now the Bishop of Worcester, at Hartlebury. Without looking up from his desk he simply said, 'Have you been invited to Ely or Ripon?' 'Ripon,' I said. 'I am so glad,' said he. 'I thought that it would be a mistake for you to go back to Ely. You'll be much happier in Ripon. And don't worry about its being in the north. Life goes on up there and you'll find a beautiful cathedral and lovely people.'

So, with Juliet, Penelope and Angela in the car, because they were excited and anxious at the prosect of such an upheaval, we drove to Ripon. We found the Cathedral, and Julie and I left the girls to snoop around while we went on to see the Bishop – whom I immediately liked, and have done ever since. We talked and talked and he told me about the diocese, which stretched to the River Tee in the north to, and to include the whole city of Leeds in the south. Geographically Ripon was in the centre of the diocese. 'But,' said the Bishop, 'whereas Leeds is quite near to Ripon, Ripon is very far from Leeds.' He also told me about the Cathedral; and for Juliet's sake, drew a plan of the Deanery, known as Minster House, which he said that he would like to have had himself.

When we got back to Penelope and Angela, they had discovered the outside of the Deanery. 'You cannot possibly accept this appointment,' said Penelope, 'if it means living in this huge house.' She was very sensitive on this issue having just spent a year out of her medical studies at Leicester University writing a study on "homeless men in Leicester and their medical provision". However, I was not to be deterred. The Bishop had told us that we could not look over the house in case word got round about my impending appointment, so we had to be satisfied with his description. Meanwhile, we paid a quick visit to Fountains Abbey, fell in love with it and then returned happily to Droitwich.

So now it was our turn to say "Farewell" to the diocese of Worcester, the archdeaconry of Dudley, the education scene and the parish of St Augustine's, Dodderhill. We had a farewell dinner at Hartlebury with the Bishop and his staff, and some sad, joyful occasions with lovely things said (Julie remembers making four "in reply" speeches) and lovely presents received. Most memorable were the parties at Dodderhill at which we received a very generous gift of crystal glass, enough to last us for ever; and the party at Redditch where we thought we were being invited to a private supper with John and Clare Gathercole, but were kidnapped on the way into their house and driven off to the Ecumenical Centre in the town where all the Churches seemed to be gathered and which we entered literally with a blare of trumpets, played by John's son (now a professional trumpeter) and his band. Presents included: thermal underwear for protection against the icy blasts of the north; Southern Comfort, ditto; and a share in the set of Evesham china which other parts of the diocese also contributed to. The diocese itself (at the end of a Synod) gave us a table-tennis table which we asked for because we thought it would humanise the front hall at Ripon, a capacious clerical cloak lined with the Ripon venetian red material; and a cheque.

And a nice thing happened at Kidderminster.

A few months previously Peter had got himself into trouble with the police by allowing a friend to ride pillion on his awful motor-bike. This had been the worst year of our life as far as our children were concerned. We were always anxious about Peter and his bike, which he had paid for and was entitled to. But we used to be rung up frequently to be told that he had run out of petrol or the bike had broken down. Would I please fetch him from the rugger ground or some motorway service-station? Of course I would, any time of the day or night!

Anyway, for this monstrous crime he and I had to go to the magistrate's court at Kidderminster. The magistrate heard the facts, eyed Peter severely and imposed a fine. Then he turned on me. 'Now, Archdeacon,' he said, 'you must not pay this fine for your son. You must make sure that it comes out of his pocket-money so that he himself pays for the error of his ways.'

Some weeks later the Bishop asked me to go to a parish and induct a new churchwarden, who needed to be "done" with due ceremony. So I stood at the chancel steps of the parish church, and there beneath and before me was the magistrate. I eyed him severely and gave him a telling lecture on the duties of a churchwarden.

Then, at the end of my farewell party with the Kidderminster Deanery, there he was again, in the line to bid me a sad farewell. He added, 'And how is Peter?'

Before departing for Ripon, to get diocese and parish used to doing without us, Juliet and I went to America for five weeks. We had been invited to do an exchange with the Rector at Williamstown, which is equidistant north of New York and west of Boston. It was an exchange of parish duties, houses, cars and golf clubs. We were duly met at Boston and driven to Williamstown, which we found to be a delightful "college town" dominated by the university. It had a lively Episcopalian church and a strongly anglophile population. The parishioners were overwhelmingly kind. The "plant" consisted of: Rectory; church complex, complete with "sanctuary" (for worship) and every kind of provision for office plus secretary; "rest rooms"; babies' changing facilities; and meeting rooms and classrooms. There was a parish bus for outings and holidays, and many flourishing parish groups – enough to make any English vicar envious, especially if you include the salary!

The town itself was pleasant and spacious and contained the famous Clark Institute, which was a picture gallery with a large collection of pictures, particularly Monets and other Impressionists. Julie and I went there almost every day, and generally had our lunch there on the principle, which we discovered during our 1975 tour, that in America the best and cheapest places to eat are the museums and galleries.

The parishioners took us off for exploratory day trips everywhere within reach. We also went to dinner parties where we found that our hosts, some of them history dons, knew more about Ripon and its story than we did. The Sunday morning Eucharist was well sung by congregation and choir, and the good thing about American congregations is that they take seriously what the preacher says! Over coffee and refreshments there would be a long queue to speak to me and ask me to explain further or repeat a point or answer a question or give advice. Once I went to the local "water hole" (a very pleasing freshwater lake) for my daily swim. And there, treading water out in the deep, I was accosted by a parishioner who wanted to discuss yesterday's sermon! That one had been about a Terence Rattigan play that had been on at the theatre the previous week and which I thought had particular relevance to the Gospel of the day. The congregation was amazed because it assumed that I had come with my sermons already composed. But here was one that struck at what everyone was thinking about that week.

One morning at about seven o'clock the telephone rang and a parishioner asked me if I would baptise their son that day. The reason was that he, a youth of seventeen, was about to embark on a drive across the States and would not be expected back this year. He had promised his family that he would "get himself christened" before going. I said, yes – on two conditions. One was that they could drum up a decent-sized congregation to be present at the event. The other was that I could have at least an hour on my own with the boy beforehand to find out if he was seriously wanting this and to give him some much-needed instruction on the Christian faith. He also talked to me about his troubles and fears and the need to break away, if only temporarily, from his over-good and over-protective family. The occasion was a truly uplifting one. Julie, who loved the family, read the lesson.

I was deeply impressed with the Episcopalian Church in Williamstown, indeed, perhaps, in America. At that time the Church was getting a lot of new members, refugees from the Catholic Church with its foolish insistencies and inconsistencies; and the Baptists with their fundamentalist outlook. The church had a strong sense of "community". They all knew each other. If someone missed a Sunday service, someone else would go and find out the reason. They gave generously compared with English congregations, having the simple method by which the Treasurer called on each family to find out and then strongly suggest what that family should be giving. They also had a stern system of mutual criticism between Vicar and "Vestry". They took "the word" very seriously, and when I went to take sick communion to people in hospital or at home, I would find that they had already received and played a tape of the Sunday service, complete with sermon! What they lacked – and what I preached about – was a sense of service to the wider community. They were inclined to be inward-looking and were surprised to find that I thought "those out there" were important.

After five happy weeks we returned home and prepared to move to Ripon.

Chapter 22
Director of Religious Education

It has been my life-long professional passion to teach the Christian faith. When I left school I had a strong personal faith, but very little theological knowledge or understanding. I could not have said anything sensible about the central Christian concepts: the Trinity; Incarnation; Atonement; Revelation. I had read the books of C.S. Lewis (*The Problem of Pain, Mere Christianity, The Screwtape Letters*) which I found helpful at the time but no good as teaching tools when I became Chaplain of Lancing. They argue too much from analogy, too little scientifically. When I went up to Oxford to read Theology I hoped that this would give me the understanding that I lacked.

Did it? It certainly did not give me straight, neat answers or a theoretical blue-print of Christianity. But it did set me going on a lifelong quest. It gave me a historical and literary competence with regard to the books of the Bible and the story of the faith. I learnt that the Bible is a library of books which relate in different ways (historical, mythical, poetical) to the incarnate life of Christ. I gained an understanding of the claims of Christianity by the study of the development of doctrine and the formation of creeds. I was quite "good" at Theology; but my ignorance of Hebrew and German and my weakness in Latin, Greek and French prevented me from getting high honours. But (much more important) I got from Professor Lightfoot a knowledge and love of the four gospels, and from Dr Kelly a desire to search for "the truth", "what is so" (as I think he put it), not expecting wrapped-up certainties, but a demand to go on seeking and learning.

So I wanted Christianity to be seen not only as a "saving faith" for individuals and society, but as a faith that claims to be true. Not that it is the whole truth, of course: how could it possibly be? But it points people to the moral truth of God as this is revealed through the life, teaching, death and continued presence of Jesus Christ.

The life of Jesus was a historical life, the facts of which are there to be discovered, sifted, verified, interpreted in context. It was a significant life, because from it springs the Christian faith; and it is an eternal ever-present life by which people can live today. Christianity is an incomplete revelation, I know; and it stands alongside other revelations, being inclusive not exclusive of other people's insights. It is sensible; it coheres; it "adds up". Through the Cross it confronts the problem of evil, and it assimilates all that is good and true and beautiful in human life and understanding.

Christianity is a life-affirming faith, but it is not so much a system of knowledge, as a way of love; not sentimental love, but a dogma: that the God who is the ultimate intelligent creator is also the ultimate harmoniser who holds all things together in love, because God is the love.

It has been my ambition to communicate this faith, this love, honestly, sensibly and helpfully to people of my generation.

Therefore to be appointed Director of Religious Education for the Diocese of Worcester was an exciting challenge. Here, surely, was the chance to put my Lancing teaching on to a wider and deeper stage, consisting of all the church schools, all the parishes and many cross-parish organisations (such as the Mothers' Union) in the Diocese.

So, thus challenged, I went to inspect my new headquarters in the Bishop's Palace. This was a large building in grounds that adjoined the Cathedral; imposing from the front, hideous inside. It contained a fine staircase that swept upwards to an agreeable clubroom where one could have lunch and sit around for pleasure and for meetings. Downstairs there were corridors and diocesan offices, all very shabby. But my office was spacious and had a superb view of the river and the county cricket ground.

When I first entered, there it was: the cricket pitch. What a good view I would have of county matches, I thought. But, no. This was winter, and when the spring came, so did the leaves on the trees. They blocked the view of the ground and I had to be content with hearing the crack of bat on ball, some flutterings of excitement from the scattered spectators and sometimes a roar when a six was hit or a wicket taken. However, I used sometimes to pop down to the ground and munch my lunch watching part of the evolving pattern of a game of cricket. On some really nice occasions Peter would be playing for the school, which adjoined the county ground, in which case I would have some very important work to do on my knee as I half worked and three-quarters watched!

In my office there were two secretaries who worked for me. One was Helen Buck, who had done the children's work for years. She was knowledgeable and always obliging. The other was Eleanor Robinson, whom I appointed myself and who helped me in every possible way with the archdeaconry, as well as education. She even came to one of my Archdeacon's Visitations and, working in relays with Helen, wrote down and typed my "charge", which I gave from memory. I thought it would be a good idea to have a record of what I had said. "Never again!" was their verdict. I spoke too fast. But no archdeacon/director of education/vicar has ever been better served by his secretaries.

Next door was another office where Caroline Gumley, who had been my predecessor's secretary, worked. She had been in that office for years and knew all there was to be known about the church schools in the diocese. She worked with Canon Norman Atty, who was now the Youth Officer and disappointed not to be the Director. His interest was in state education, church schools and the education authority. I invited him to lunch at the RAF mess at Pershore and we spent an afternoon discussing – me learning about – the education scene. He promised me his loyalty, but made it clear that I had a lot to learn about the administration of church schools.

So it turned out. There were a hundred and twenty-one church schools in the diocese, most of them "controlled" ("controlled" by the State but with a large input from the Church) and some "aided" ("aided" by the State, but the policy as regards admissions and appointments controlled by the Church). They were mostly primary schools; but there were also some excellent middle schools and a few secondary, including Bishop Perowne in Worcester, of which I became

Chairman of Governors. As a board with statutory responsibilities for these schools we worked with the Hereford and Worcester County Authority, sharing our responsibilities with the Diocese of Hereford. The Director of Education for Hereford Diocese was Canon Christopher Herbert, now Bishop of St Alban's. We got on well. I found him a delightful, cultured person with a love for music and art and English literature with which he would enliven his conversation and talks. We were of one mind with regard to church schools and the teaching of RE in all schools.

We felt (as I still do) that Christian "faith schools" can only be justified by the positive Christian input by governors, headteacher, staff and local church. Pupils should be selected mainly by where they live, so that the school serves the community; along with siblings and those in special need (such as a policeman's family at Bishop Perowne!). Only after these considerations should we be looking for so-called "Christian commitment" by parents, which is easy to feign and hard to gauge. I think that faith schools are good for these reasons; but I found that some non-church schools also give a Christian education, by virtue of the faith of the headteacher and staff, and some "church" schools failed in this respect.

The difficulty was to find committed Christians for the staff. What were our C. of E. colleges of education doing? It was also difficult to find churchmen, vicars and congregations who would give the best support to their schools. Some clearly wanted their schools to be sources for recruiting choir, Sunday school and congregation, rather than a source of Christian service to the neighbourhood. Church schools cost the Church – parish and diocese – a great deal of money; so it was important to get this right.

Sometimes I had to wrestle with the clergy on this point, especially if they were in my own archdeaconry. I once had to rebuke a vicar who used to take assemblies in his church-aided primary school once a week and (a) was always late, which is unforgivable in a school; and (b) used to excite the children in a silly way so that the staff had to spend the rest of the morning calming them down. He obviously felt that he was a whale of a fellow, popular with the kids; but he was despised for his unprofessionalism by the headteacher and staff.

Christopher Herbert and I did all we could to encourage Christian staff in all schools and we organised retreat conferences for them. We shared these and found that we could work together well – a rare tribute for clergymen! I had more experience as an RE teacher, but he had more experience of the necessary ties and restrictions for state, even for church schools. This was a time when "indoctrination" was the dirty word and "comparative religion" was the fashion. We tried to temper this so that children should be made open to the insights of other faiths, but also be given a working understanding and experience of their own. We also ran conferences for church school governors, which we made as interesting as possible by giving them juicy problems to consider to do with discipline, objectionable parents, weak headteachers, anxious or bolshy staff, awkward admission problems and intractable (or over-zealous) vicars.

For a few months I enjoyed the schools scene, visiting many schools and making plans for new ones in Redditch, Kidderminster and a joint Roman Catholic/Anglican secondary school in Redditch. There was lots of money to be found; lots of appointments to make; and consultations to be had with the County Education officers about provision of schools for different areas; and meetings to be held with school governors when they had particular problems of staffing or finance.

In my position as Director of Religious Education I used to go to Directors' conferences all over the country at which I met some very able people, such as Alan Chesters, who later became Bishop of Blackburn. These conferences were important for the instructions that came down to us from the C. of E. Board of Education; and some very hot discussions on every aspect of the Church. Directors of Education had strong views and were able to speak their minds on these pleasantly informal occasions. They were aghast – and somewhat envious – to find that I was also an Archdeacon!

The chairmanship of Bishop Perowne School was another important part of my responsibilities. This was a secondary modern C. of E.-aided school in Worcester. It had a noble tradition of giving Christian service to the neighbourhood by educating the children who had failed to get to the grammar school. The "Christianity" of the school lay in its ethos and was fuelled by the teaching staff and the daily acts of worship at which school life was offered to God for his blessing and forgiveness. I loved this school and gave a lot of time to it and its headteacher and staff.

Plans were then announced to reorganise the state schools in Worcester city. Bishop Perowne was to become a comprehensive school, and it was to change its site for the site of another and better (site and building-wise) secondary modern school in the city. But substantial work was to be done on this building to bring it up to the requirements of a much larger comprehensive school. These plans were discussed in detail, and promised by the Authority, but after I left and when all the arrangements had been made, the plans were vetoed at cabinet level – as part of the Tory government's economising measures – which left a vast legacy of trouble for the next decade or so.

As part of the reorganisation, the staff of all the city schools had to give in their resignations, and then be reappointed to the newly constituted schools. This was a huge undertaking which caused a great deal of anger and anxiety. Staff did not want to resign! Nor did they want their schools to change. For two long mornings a week for many weeks I had to sit at a table along with the Headteacher of Bishop Perowne and argue the case for the reappointment (or not) of particular teachers to bring us up to the academic standards formerly required of grammar schools, now required of us. This was a wearisome business and fraught with much argument and bargaining; but in the end most of us were satisfied, and some of the necessary changes in staff were beneficial (we believed) both to the staff themselves and the school.

But it was getting too much for me! I have only described the statutory part of the diocesan education scene. There was also the voluntary sector for which the needs were very pressing. So I came to the sad conclusion that I must hand over to Norman Atty the statutory side of the work, which he was good at. I retained overall authority in the school scene and continued to give personal support to heads, teachers and governors, but I left Norman to do the administrative work to do with the Local Education Authority.

So I was able to turn my attention to where Bishop Robin wanted me, he having no idea at all of the extent and importance of the schools work. This was the the parishes themselves, with their adults, youth and children. This meant approaching the vicars, persuading them to make the "teaching" side of their ministry part of the strategy for the greater effectiveness and growth of the Christian Church. At the time I took over there was virtually no children's work being done at all, very little youth work and little for adults except non-parochial organisations such as the Church of England's Men's Society. To support me there was a Diocesan Board of Education, with a chairman and members elected from the diocese. Like so many diocesan committees the members were people who felt themselves to be "representatives of their deanery and parish" rather than people who were there to work out a strategy for the diocese. But the chairman, Dr Derek Sharples, was excellent. He was a lecturer at the Worcester College of Education and was a man of great intelligence and enthusiasm. He gave me all the backing he could, until, alas, he was replaced. At the meetings the committee would listen to my account of what we were doing and planning – and hoping to spend! They generally gave me their backing.

I also had the "Education Team": but this consisted of people who did not share my vision of promoting Christian learning throughout the diocese. To assist me with the adult work the Bishop appointed Nicholas Brown, a priest who came to us from the church idustrial scene. He could not have been more pleasant to me personally but less interested in my promotional strategy. What I wanted was the equivalent to today's Alpha course, written for the parishes on a broad evangelical catholic basis. Nick thought that this was too ambitious and would have no part in it. So after much heated discussion we agreed instead to produce a series of Buff Papers, named after the colour of the paper we used, in which important topics were laid out for parish discussion groups. Yes, but I had to write them! He and the rest of the team criticised them. I then rewrote them and they were duly issued. We had no word-processor in those days, only slaving secretaries!

The first Buff Paper was on the subject of the proposed "covenanting" with the non-Roman Catholic churches, which had been proposed and debated by the General Synod and sent down to dioceses for their consideration. I was determined that our diocesan debate should be well informed, so in Buff Paper No 1 I set out the story of what had happened, the principles at stake and the decisions that had to be taken. This was a good context in which to lay out some of the fundamentals of Christianity – such as the nature of the Church and its ministry – plus a little church history, in a way that gave the parishes an opportunity to study and learn and then contribute to the general debate.

The next Buff Paper was on the subject of house-groups in parishes, their potential strengths and failures. Here was a vehicle for people to consider the need for both the personal and the corporate aspects of faith. I recently gave a copy of this paper to a parish in Worthing in my retirement; they were most grateful. The third Buff Paper was on the subject of marriage in church after there had been a divorce.

The other members of my team were Norman Atty and Michael Nott. Michael had been the chaplain of the King's School and I had been impressed by the interest he had taken in the younger boys and the enterprise of the worship he devised for them. He was clever, a history scholar at Brasenose College, Oxford, and was keen to join us. I appointed him (with Bishop Robin's permission) to be the Children's Officer, with a church in the city from which to operate. He was euthusiastic and "on my side", but was too busy on Sundays to visit the parishes when they most needed him.

Robin Woods was shocked to find how few parishes were doing any serious children's work. The fashion had turned against "Sunday school", but most parishes had not replaced this with anything that was effective – such as the Wednesday Club plus attendance at the Parish Communion, which we devised at Pershore.

This led to the worst experience I had in the Diocese of Worcester. I became convinced that what the diocese needed was a professional teacher who would be free of parochial responsibilities and therefore be able to visit churches in the diocese on Sundays, as well as weekdays. But the Diocesan Synod had passed a resolution that any new central appointment would have to be approved by the whole Synod – this being part of the notion that it is only at the parish level that significant work is done. So there had to be a debate, and I was ready for it, being convinced of the need. Colonel Bell, the Diocesan Secretary, was against me, being uninterested in children's work; and the debate was held in the north of the Diocese where there was considerable opposition to diocesan officers in Worcester.

This was understandable, but wrong. The fact is that the Church of England was missing out on a generation of people, not just children but young people growing up and needing strong and stimulating spiritual fare. This failure was already having disastrous results both for the Church and for the nation. But to make things more difficult for me in the debate, Bishop Robin felt called to attend a function elsewhere and so left the Synod to the Suffragan Bishop, Tony Dumper, whose wife lived in Dudley and led the opposition to what I was proposing. Worse still, John Dale, the Diocesan Registrar (legal officer), told me just before the debate that I had only five minutes in which to make my speech. This was absurd because he was applying a new rule devised for general debates to this particular situation which was concerned with an executive decision. I did my best in the time given me and then again in the summing up at the end of the debate, trying to convince members that the present situation was intolerable and that doing nothing would perpetuate this for generations to come. But after the closure of the debate Colonel Bell, completely out of order, leapt to his feet and made a speech against me. I protested, but too late; and the weak chairman could do nothing about it. The proposal was narrowly defeated – and I felt very low indeed.

Bishop Robin was furious when he heard what had happened and slated his staff at the next staff meeting. I got some nice letters afterwards saying how sorry some people were that my stand had been to no avail, but I never felt the same about Dudley after that.

After Bishop Robin had retired and Philip Goodrich had been appointed, I had a long talk with him about my work. As regards education I was convinced that I must reduce my work which, on top of everything else, was too much for me to do effectively. I told the Bishop that education should be split into two parts, the statutory to do with schools, and the voluntary to do with everything else. Schools and parishes were different worlds; the former highly professional, with the county authorities to deal with, the latter needing much enthusiasm to get things going satisfactorily. He agreed with me, and in my naivety I thought that arrangements would be made accordingly.

But Norman Atty had different ideas. With his chairman, an ex-headteacher, he persuaded the Bishop that the break should be made along the line of age, with "youth" (schools and parishes) on one side, and adults on the other.

Philip gave in to them, to my great distress. I knew that it was wrong and that this would simply mean that youth and children's work in parishes would be neglected – as in fact happened. But it left Norman in charge of a much bigger area of diocesan work, and me with a much smaller one – adult education. As Norman was forced to resign for personal reasons, this left his side of the work in temporary chaos – something that I hope was repaired when he and I left the diocese. Meanwhile, relieved of a lot of school work, but retaining the chairmanship of Bishop Perowne, I concentrated on what I could do to get the parishes in the diocese enthusiastic about teaching the faith to adults whose instruction was often confined to sermons. I did this partly by making it part of my annual "archdeacon's charge" to parishes. I also found myself presiding over groups of lay people who had formed themselves into study groups across parish boundaries, something I enjoyed immensely as I always preferred teaching itself to the dubious exercise of getting others to teach.

Besides this, I persuaded the local radio to co-operate with a Lent Course. The idea was that I should devise a study course for people to use in groups throughout the region, and at the end of the course people should phone in to the producer with questions arising from the course to be discussed by a panel. But it became clear to me that the chairman in charge of the broadcast had not read the discussion papers, so everything he said was off-track. He told me later, when I confronted him, that he had not had time. I regarded the whole thing as a failure as far as the broadcasting was concerned. But who knows? Perhaps someone gleaned something positive from the Lent Course itself.

Then, after a long talk with the Dean of Worcester, Tom Baker, who had been head of a theological college and was, to my mind, the wisest person in the diocese, I decided to use "modern technology" to get people thinking and learning together. It now sounds elementary compared with what people today do with their computers and the internet, but in those days it seemed a bold innovation. I used audiotapes; with a carefully chosen team I created a set of these to be used in parishes. Consistent with my theories on house-groups, I felt that they needed to be geared to an activity and not be left in some theoretical limbo. So a set of tapes was made on the subject of parish visiting, the notion being that to spread the Christian gospel it was necessary for members of the church to "go out" and practise it and talk to people about it. This was not to be simply a matter of "evangelisation", about which I am wary, but to do with meeting the pastoral needs of the bereaved and the house-bound.

To do this I devised short "plays" which set a scenario with right and wrong ways of meeting it, leaving as much as possible for the users of the tapes to decide. These tapes were aimed and launched upon a surprised diocese, but I left soon afterwards and I never heard how successful (if at all) they were, except that one or two vicars whom I met later said that they had done "rather well". I had planned to try out the first lot and then learn from experience, but events overtook this experiment. For off I went to become Dean of Ripon.

Chapter 23
The General Synod

Soon after I settled at Pershore I received a letter asking me if I knew any clergyman in the Diocese of Worcester who would be willing to stand for the newly constituted General Synod on a "Reunion with the Methodists" ticket, a matter which had already failed in the Synod's predecessor, the Church Assembly. I wrote back to volunteer myself. I was duly proposed and put up for election. My opponent was to be Canon Bartlett, an energetic high churchman with years of experience in the Church Assembly and a reputation in the diocese for sound, conservative views. I thought I had little chance of being elected. However, the Vicar of Evesham, who was entrusted with Canon Bartlett's nomination form, forgot to post it. So – unique in the whole of England – I was elected without opposition.

Canon Bartlett was not pleased. He told me grimly that if I were to fall under a bus, he would get himself elected in my place, and at every meeting of the Diocesan Synod he spoke against me. However, at the next election four years later I won easily on the first count. The next time round I was Archdeacon of Dudley and John Williams (Archdeacon of Worcester) was happy to nominate me without having to trouble the Bishop, who would have had to decide between us if we could not agree between ourselves.

But for the election after that it was going to be difficult. Bishop Robin had had to appoint another archdeacon of Worcester to take John Williams's place and was considering Peter Coleman who was well known in the Synod. 'Don't worry, Chris,' said Robin. 'If I appoint him I will still back you for the Synod if you both wish to stand.' But before completing the appointment Robin forgot his promise and told Coleman that if he accepted the appoinment, he, Robin, would support him, Peter, for the Synod. So when Peter was appointed he came and asked me to give up my place. 'Certainly not,' I said. 'I am here and here I stay and the Bishop will have to decide which promise he keeps and which he breaks when the time for the next election comes round.'

Peter was furious and promised to oust me next time. This was going to be embarrassing because by then Bishop Robin had retired and Bishop Philip Goodrich inherited the dispute. Fortunately, however, shortly before the moment of decision, Peter was made Bishop of Crediton and I was made Dean of Ripon.

Back to those first days of General Synod. My Oxford MA gown was brought out of hiding for the formal opening. We were lined up by Westminster School boys in the cloisters and made to process into the Abbey, diocese by diocese. I found myself worshipping God six inches from a pillar. The Archbishop preached; the Choir sang its bits; we sang the hymns lustily and made our Communion together: thence to the debating chamber in Church House, where the Queen addressed us.

Within a short time I found myself on my feet called to make a speech. It was on the subject of allowing people who had been divorced to marry again in church. I felt strongly about this and had a speech in my head without having any hope that I would be called to make it. After the opening speeches from both sides the matter was up for general debate. Professor Norman Anderson, the chairman, looked up and half left (as he always did), found me in his sights and pointed. I can still remember what I said: that this was a matter of truth and grace and a proper understanding of forgiveness. The speech was received with a deafening hush from those around me, for I was innocently sitting in an Anglo-Catholic enclave, but with enthusiasm from others in the Synod.

In the course of the first group of sessions I had lunch with Colin James (still a humble canon) and Ronald Gordon, two Cuddesdon friends. This was fun, but over the lasagne, glaring at me, they both made it clear that on no account would they ever speak. They were both Anglo-Catholics and did not like my speech. I cannot remember

Ronald ever speaking, but he became Bishop of Portsmouth; Colin later became Bishop of Basingstoke, then Wakefield, then Winchester, and Chairman of the Pastoral Committee – posts that he filled brilliantly. In the Synod he used to read witty, urbane, wise, measured, persuasive speeches.

I was shocked with the state of affairs in Synod, with the Anglo-Catholics and Evangelicals thundering at each other across the chamber. Powerful people such as Oswald Clark, Ivor Bulmer-Thomas, David Silk, who became Archdeacon of Leicester and then a Bishop in Australia,[1] and Margaret Hewitt, on the Catholic side; against them powerful Evangelicals, such as Professor Lampe, who was so kind to me at Ely, and Colin Buchanan, who became Bishop of Woolwich.

The monstrous absurdity of this ecclesiatical friction was demonstrated by the disastrous end of our hopes of reunion with the Methodists, a cause so graciously, valiantly and theologically espoused by Archbishop Michael Ramsey himself. The crux of the debate was the mutual recognition of ministries. We were to recognise their ministry, and they ours. All present priests and Methodist ministers would be "conditionally" (re)ordained at services in which Anglican bishops and Methodist chairmen would act together. Prayers would be said to the Holy Spirit to make up that which is at present defective in the status and effectiveness of the ministry of both churches, our mutual non-recognition being part of that – and all future ordinations would be episcopal. This meant that both Churches would recognise their present limitations, and would go on together, restored and united, as John Wesley himself would have wanted.

But, no. Anglo-Catholics said that there is no deficiency in our present episcopally ordained ministry, and the new arrangement would not guarantee that "conditionally ordained" Methodist ministers would exercise the true ministry of a priest. The Evangelicals, on the other hand, attacked the proposals because, they said, the Methodist ministry is valid as it is and does not need episcopal laying on of hands to make it effective. The two parties thus combined for mutually contradictory

---

[1] Julie and I met David and his wife on a boat going out to the Barrier Reef in 1993. He must have been in Australia inspecting the job.

reasons to thwart the Archbishop and the majority. Unfortunately a two-thirds majority was required, and this was not obtained. So the proposals failed and reunion with the Methodists was put back for – how many years? It is already over thirty. Dreadful. Both churches have been severely weakened by this failure. The Methodists, by the way, had painstakingly accepted the proposals and were much put out by our rejection of them.

Personally I was utterly dismayed. This was partly because I wanted to speak in the debate and make a point that had not been made – namely that the Church is a dynamic not a static community: we should therefore not talk (as they were talking) of "papering over the cracks" but of a process of growth towards one another. But I was not called.

My main anger, however, was because a cause so near to my heart had been defeated. The Archbishop was utterly shaken. He was more "Catholic" minded than the "highchurchmen" who opposed him, and he was deeply hurt by the rejection of his leadership by those who claim to believe most strongly in episcopalian, that is, a bishop's authority. I once heard him saying to himself in his sing-song voice as he left the debating chamber after a defeat, 'Great wickedness. Great wickedness.'

When the Synod was held in London I used to stay in the Naval Club, off Berkeley Square, which I had joined for the fee of one guinea in 1946. I could book a bunk, or, when less penurious, a cabin, and guarantee myself a huge breakfast, which would last me all day. There were about six of us naval synod members who used the club. Sometimes we went to Communion together at the Grosvenor Chapel, just round the corner: it is said that on one occasion the Celebrant intoned, 'Let us pray that the Holy Spirit will see fit to overrule all the decisions of the General Synod.' This caused some mirth when I quoted it in a speech.

The walk across the park became an enjoyable part of my daily routine. I seemed to go by a different route every time and as I strode along I used to compose my speech for the day – generally in vain, for one was rarely called, and anyway I tried to ration myself to one speech per group of sessions.

Not being called, however, could be very frustrating. Most of us suffered from it – and then felt little sympathy for others in the same plight. Once when I was archdeacon I had received diocesan backing for a speech I was to make about joining up parishes and making pastoral provision for an over-churched, under-manned area such as the Teme Valley in Worcestershire. I gave my name in and stood between speeches throughout the debate, but was not called. Infuriated I asked the chairwoman when I met her over coffee, 'Why not?' 'Oh,' she said, she had been advised not to call archdeacons and other diocesan experts. How silly can you get!

But I did speak on a variety of subjects: marriage and divorce, education, Confirmation, children in church, the charismatic movement (I gave examples of the tyranny sometimes exercised by people in the grip of it), liturgical revision, the Church's year and calendar, and some doctrinal matters such as the "filioque clause" in the Creed. This is about the Holy Spirit being the Holy Spirit of Jesus Christ. I was remembering Michael Ramsey's advice when I asked him what to do with people who thought that they were inspired by the Spirit. 'Remind them,' he said, 'that the Holy Spirit is the Spirit of Jesus: therefore they must be humble, not arrogant.' I also spoke on ecumenical matters and, of course, the ordination of women.

I was once invited to propose the acceptance of a report on children's work. This was to the Convocation of Canterbury, that is, the House of Clergy in the See of Canterbury. At that time I was a Diocesan Director of Religious Education, so I agreed to do it; but it was difficult because they could not get a copy of the report to me in good time before the speech had to be made. I had to be content with a long telephone conversation about the principles in the report; and I do not think that I did it justice. However, I emphasised the importance of the subject, and Archbishop Ramsey was nice to me afterwards about the speech.

I was also asked to propose an amendment with regard to the ordination of women, in its very early stages. I forget now what the point was; but Professor David McClean, who was the chairman of the House of Laity, a fellow member of the Open Synod Group and a strong supporter of women's ordination, asked me to do this, thinking that if I did it it would be non-controversial and would help the opposition to come to terms with our point of view. George Austin, Archdeacon of York, a doughty fighter for keeping everything as it was, but quite a friend of mine (I invited him to preach at Ripon when I was Dean) rounded on me and accused me of speaking for the ordination of women itself instead of my sensible amendment (it was to do with a period of waiting): but the chairman rebuked him and said that what I was saying was in order.

My best-received speech was made in York in the days when speakers spoke from the platform facing the assembly – which made speaking much easier, especially for those who did not use notes. I spoke to rebuke the writers of a doctrinal report for failing to emphasise the corporate nature of Christian action and decisionmaking. "Corporate", that is, not by dictat from on high coming down the hierarchical line (as in the Roman Catholic Church) but a genuine sharing and interaction by the whole Church, reflecting the essential "corporateness" of God himself, the God of Trinity. Thunderous applause. Bishop Robin glowed over me later and introduced me personally to the Archbishop, then Donald Coggan, with whom I had a long talk as we walked to Communion together one morning. What a nice, modest, extremely able man.

I was hectored on two occasions. Once I was in the wrong because I came in at the end of an important debate and said something that I had not heard but had already been said. When this was pointed out, I sat down. The other occasion was when we were electing a chairman for the House of Clergy. I was asked to propose Alan Webster, the Dean of St Paul's, a strong upholder of the ordination of women. There was an equally strong Anglo-Catholic up for election, and to my surprise his supporters had packed the meeting and were prepared to shout me down. According to their lights, they did the right thing and duly won. I should have worked harder before the meeting – but it wasn't really my line.

The New Synod Group, at whose invitation I originally joined the Synod, changed its name (after the Methodist fiasco) to the Open Synod Group. Its main activity was to organise a meeting of all its members, plus anyone who would care to come along, on the evening before Synod began, at which the main topics of the week's business would be opened up by some expert on the subject, and the course of the debate foreseen and prepared for. This was particularly helpful to new members who did not know what was going on and did not understand – amidst the confusion of amendments and counter-motions – what the issues were. We always – unlike them – invited members of other "parties" to join us, and they were grateful for the opportunity to review the breadth of opinion before the real debates took place.

Sometimes there would be a debate in Synod on some social, political or commonwealth subject, such as South Africa, arms-dealing, an anti-smoking campaign or employment strikes or Nestlé's powdered milk or abortion or the police or, most famously, because this debate was given national coverage on the media, the Church and the Bomb.

One such debate at York was on the situation in Palestine. It was a bad-tempered debate because we received contrary accounts of the facts, and no one seemed to know accurately what was going on at the present time. This was just after the Gulf War. A message had come through from bishops in the Holy Land saying how important it was for people in England to resume their visits. So Canon Robin Prothero (whom I knew as a Diocesan Director of Education) decided to get up a party to go and explore the situation. This we did, and to my delight I was able to take Juliet with me. We met important leaders from both sides of the divide as well as the British Consul in Jerusalem. The trip was enjoyable and informative and, indeed, deeply moving. I wrote a full account of it and gave many talks on it when I got back to Ripon. This account still exists so I will not repeat or even try to summarise it now. In its tone and conclusions (but not in the brilliance of its presentation) this report was very close to David Hare's monologue *Acting Up*.

After a few years with the Open Synod Group I was elected to the steering committee, and then to be Chairman. As such I chaired two important three-day conferences and some seething pre-Synod debates, for no holds were barred on these occasions. I also spent much energy over two electoral campaigns and wrote election addresses for present and potential Open Synod Group members. My line was clear. We were not the "catholic" nor were we the "evangelical" group; for we were both catholic and evengelical, just as we were "traditional" and "reformed", biblical and rational and sacramental. These were not soft compromises, feeble exercises in fence-sitting. They were expressions of the dynamic, creative tensions within the Church about principles that tended to pull apart but must be held together. I wrote an article about a sailing ship which is steered by the contrary but complementary forces of wind and current acting upon sails, keel and rudder: not wallowing around, but driven forward by "the wind of the Spirit". Our magazine took up this idea with a picture of a sailing ship, which became its logo. They still use it, I am glad to say.

The two most important issues, in my opinion, facing the Church were ecumenical relationships with other churches and the ordination of women priests.

After the Methodist scheme had failed in 1971 there was a pause for a few years and then a new scheme was introduced called the Covenant Scheme, by which the main denominations of Christianity – apart from the Roman Catholics and Orthodox – were to make a covenant together to pursue every possible way towards unification. Inauguration services were to be held all over the country, local churches were to plan to share their resources, including financial, and, if desirable, buildings. Targets were to be set for the combining of congregations and ultimately the unification of ministries. The scheme was expected to be unpopular with Anglo-Catholics (because it could not include Rome) but popular with the "Free Churches" – although they did not take easily to our "establishment" relationship with the State. I was invited to join a group who would study the scheme and go round the country speaking for it, both to Anglican synods and to the appropriate assemblies of other churches.

The theory about the integration of ministries was not difficult. Anglicans believe in "Monarchical Episcopate" – that is, dioceses "ruled" by one bishop. Yet they also insist that the bishop exercises his authority "in synod", with his priests and lay people about him in consultation. Thus, the whole Church is governed by "bishops in Synod" not by lone, lordly individuals. So "monarchical government" in practice means "synodical government". Meanwhile, the Free Churches believe in corporate government by the whole Body. But in practice they then elect chairmen or presidents to personify and express this. Is there much difference between a president who is de facto bishop and a bishop who exercises corporate authority?

So I stumped round the country speaking on these proposals, addressing small groups and one very big one – a Methodist assembly – in Birmingham. My most memorable visit was to the Rural Deanery Synod at Highgrove, Prince Charles's parish, deep in the heart of conservative Gloucestershire. I spoke for forty minutes. Then, at question time, a very grand lady, a veritable Lady Catherine de Burgh, addressed me. 'Archdeacon,' she said (and I trembled). 'Do you mean to tell me that if this scheme were to be accepted we might have a Methodist minister presiding at one of our services?' 'Er, yes, Madam, that certainly could happen.' 'And might this minister be a woman?' 'Well, yes, she could well be a woman.' 'Then I shall certainly vote for it.' Cheers.

But generally when I went to Anglican assemblies I found elderly conservatives complaining that Methodists and Baptists could not be priests as we Anglicans understood priesthood. This comes from seeing priesthood in terms of status rather than function. But Jesus Christ constantly eschewed status and claimed only to be "doing the work of the Father." 'Believe in me,' he once said, 'for the work's sake.' Priests are ordained not for personal status but to work together for the Kingdom of God.

But this scheme, like the Methodist-reunion scheme before it, failed. The majority wanted it to pass. The minority – of just over one third – for their different reasons combined to reject it. A two-thirds majority of the whole Synod and a majority in each House (of bishops, clergy and laity) is very hard to obtain on any matter of profound importance in the Church of England.

It is so important to my philosophy of ministry and way of life, that I am going to write about the ordination of women (in as far as I got involved in the matter) in some detail – though the chronology of my own part is now vague in my memory.

As a cradle "catholic" I learnt from my mother's knee that women cannot be priests; just as men cannot be mothers. When a Methodist layman came to Rotary lunch one day in Pershore, he said to me, 'Of course, we Methodists ordain women.' 'But women cannot be priests,' I retorted. 'Well, think about it,' he said. This was at the time when

Christine Dodd was proving herself to be the best of my curates; and even Pershore parishioners were asking (as Dr Marshall Wilson crudely put it), 'Why do you have to have a man in to do the magic bits?' This question shows how much the matters of priesthood and Eucharist can be distorted.

So – I thought about it. What I thought was this. The statement, "a woman cannot be a priest" might, on the face of it, seem sensible; that is, if "be" implies a generic difference. A dog cannot be a cat. A curry sauce cannot be a musical instrument. But if "be" implies a function, then a statement about "being" can be either true, false, or doubtful. "A baby in arms cannot be a cricketer" (true). "A black man cannot be a cricketer" (false). "An old lady cannot be a cricketer" (doubtful).

What is the "be" in "be a priest"? If "be" is generic and priesthood is a caste (as it is for Hindus) then you cannot be a priest unless you are born into it. But if priesthood is a function within the Church, then it is a matter of performance, not of birth. So anyone who can do the work can be a priest. A Christian priest is a person who is called and authorised to do particular work in the Church such as teaching, serving, counselling, presiding at the Eucharist and pronouncing forgiveness. For this part of Christ's work some people feel themselves to be called by God, and if the Church, through its procedures, agrees they can be trained and ordained.

No one can argue that gender makes any difference to the ability to perform these functions. So it becomes a matter of God's calling. Can God use women, as, we claim, he uses men?

This takes me to America where I met and stayed with a woman priest in Philadelphia during our 1975 tour; and where I worked with a woman priest in Williamstown in 1984. After my experience with these two priests I no longer had any doubts at all. Prejudice was banished. The theory of the ordination of women was vindicated by practice. I also came to recognise, however, that arguments such as I have just used make little difference to those whose opinions have been formed by upbringing or strong emotional, possibly sexual attitudes: though in my simplicity I could never understand why women themselves (oh, and some homosexual men) object so strongly to women priests.

The first hurdle in the Synod was to allow women to become deacons, because at that time they could only be rated "deaconess". For heaven's sake! Some proponents were hardly willing to take this seriously, especially when it was pointed out that, according to Romans 16.1 Phoebe was a deacon, there being no concept in the New Testament of deaconess. Some, however, opposed the new measure bitterly, seeing it as the thin end of the wedge. Anyway, many deaconesses in the Church of England were ordained deacon, including Barbara Chatwin who had retired to Pershore. She was a delightful and dignified lady who – once – in procession, in full regalia, was taken by one of my potential curates to be a retired bishop!

After that the Synod made its cautious way towards women being ordained priests. After a general debate (where only a simple majority was required – but we noted with anxiety that we were nowhere near the two thirds that would be needed) the matter was passed down to dioceses with the instruction that it must also be considered by parishes and deaneries.

It was at the local level that I worked hardest, both in the Worcester and Ripon dioceses. I chaired an active group in the diocese of Ripon, spoke on several occasions, and was also invited by Dame Christian Howard to chair a major conference in York, Dame Christian evidently thinking that I would be a good neutral chairman – but firmly on her side!

I was also asked by the Diocese of Carlisle to be a member of a panel of six (three each side) at a four-day conference at the diocesan Retreat House at Ambleside. We could not help "winning" because the opposition could not agree amongst themselves, having mutually exclusive reasons against the ordination of women. The Evangelical said that he did not mind having a woman at the Altar, as long as she did not enter the pulpit. But the Anglo-Catholic said that he did not mind women preaching as long as they did not stand as priest at the Altar. One lady at this conference became hysterical, demonstrating once more that this can be an emotional rather than a rational issue.

On another occasion, along with George Carey, who wasn't a bishop in those days, I addressed a diocesan conference for the Gloucester Diocese at the Cheltenham Ladies' College (where later, on the strength of that occasion, I was asked to preach). George Carey spread out the biblical evidence in favour of our cause, and I did my bit. It did seem that we won!

On another occasion Canon Ford (a residentiary canon of Ripon) invited me to "meet one or two friends" at his house and talk the matter over with them. I agreed with pleasure – but then found myself facing a room full of antis from all over the diocese, seething with anger, I would even say hatred. I sat on a stool in the middle of the room and was attacked from all sides. I didn't mind. It was easy. The more furious they appeared, the calmer I became. 'It is not fundamentally about women,' I said, 'it is about God: what he can and wishes to do for and through a woman.' To the person who said that he would always refuse to accept the wine of Holy Communion when it was offered by a woman, I answered (quoting Bishop Roger Wilson of Chichester), 'And whom were you refusing?' Calm: but I felt very shaken afterwards. Some of those present were silent, including James Ramsden, once a member of Churchill's cabinet, who wrote to tell me afterwards that he had been a waverer but was now convinced that women should be ordained. He became a staunch ally of mine and a good friend.

My last speech on this subject was at the Convocation of York before the main debate in Synod. The motion had to be passed by both Convocations, so it was an important occasion, and the length of speeches was unlimited. I was called first of the floor speakers and decided to be brave and spend the first part of my speech trying to refute what had just been said, taking the arguments head on. Then, as briefly as possible, I made my own points. I think that the speech lost its punch, but it was certainly made in the true spirit of debate. Everyone else, I noticed, read prepared speeches.

I was not called to speak in the final debate in General Synod, but almost everything that I wanted to say was said and the points on both sides were weighty and well argued. The Proposer, Bishop Michael Adie, made his case with sweet, unanswerable reason. This debate was unbearably tense and was watched by many (including Juliet) on the television. It was well known that about three members of the Synod would have to change from No to Aye if we were to get the required two-thirds majority. When we all tramped out through the voting doors

(Clergy/Laity, Aye/No) I could not bear to go back straight away; so I went into the Hoar Memorial Hall where coffee could be had and where, if one listened, one could hear what was being said in the Debating Chamber over the PA. I distinctly heard George Carey say, 'then we've done it.' I rushed back to my seat to hear the result announced. The ayes had it by the majority required. No applause was allowed. Some wept – with joy or dismay.

In the melée afterwards I grabbed hold of Sister Carol of the Order of the Holy Name. She was weeping – with joy, she said, but with sadness too for her Sisters in the Convent, some of whom were so vehemently against it. She herself had made a persuasive speech. 'Come on,' I said. 'Come and hear Beethoven's Fourth Piano Concerto at the Festival Hall.' We did, sitting together in the front row. She continued to weep, perhaps, now, because of the beauty of the music.

(The evening before I had heard Mahler's *Resurrection Symphony* at the RFH. It had cast me into the depths of despair; and then lifted me to heights of joy. Very appropriate. And an omen?)

Three last points, a pleasing aftermath, and a bonus.

1. Some people grudgingly complained that we only scraped a Yes by the narrowest margin possible. But a two-thirds majority in the General Synod for any decision affecting the life of the whole Church is a huge margin.

2. The best argument "against" was the ecumenical one, that by agreeing to the ordination of women we were driving a further wedge between ourselves and the Roman Catholics. And there are those who think that the Church of England had no right to go it alone on such a major issue. Against this, however, one can quote important examples of the C. of E. "going it alone", being fiercely resisted by Rome and then being proved right. The priority of Mark's gospel is one. Anglican married priests are another. When will Rome follow?

3. But the main rift with Rome, from the Anglican point of view, is its refusal to recognise our ordained ministry. Thus, to Roman Catholics I am not a priest. A Roman Catholic/Anglican commission was set up to examine the matter and came out with a report to the effect that Rome should recognise Anglican orders. We in the Synod

had debated this report and accepted it about two years previously. The Vatican went silent on the matter; then, shortly before our debate on the ordination of women, announced that it rejected the report and would still not recognise Anglican orders. Why then should the Church of England refuse to admit women to priestly orders, when Rome does not recognise these orders anyway? I believe that there were some who would have been ready to "wait for Rome" if it had not been for this singularly ill-timed snub by the Vatican. Two or three votes would have been enough.

(I know, of course, many Roman Catholics who privately recognise our orders and even allow our priests to celebrate Holy Communion at their altars – this being especially true in France. Even in England there is much mutual friendship and recognition.)

The pleasing aftermath. The Movement for the Ordination of Women wished to have a final conference and a service to celebrate the ministry of women. Some cathedrals were asked to host this service and refused. Ripon was asked and we gladly accepted. What a service. The Cathedral was packed. The singing was such that I began to fear for the roof. I (as Dean) concelebrated with a woman priest from the Diocese of Winchester who had been ordained the day before. The (woman) Bishop of Dunedin in New Zealand preached – a down to earth, "now-get-on-with-it" sermon. A solitary protester marched up and down outside the Cathedral with a rude banner about "priestesses", but he was ignored. Meanwhile, representatives from all the dioceses in England processed into the Cathedral with their banners. The last to enter was received with a huge roar of approval from the congregation. 'What was that about?' I enquired afterwards. 'Oh that was a group of Roman Catholics carrying a banner saying, 'Women Priests for the Roman Catholic Church'.'

The bonus. When I retired in 1995 members of the Movement for the Ordination of Women in the Diocese gave me a copy of a picture by Picasso of hands joined round a bunch of flowers. It had been their logo. It now hangs in my sun-room.

One of my proudest moments in the Synod was when my son Peter came to see me when the Synod was being held at York. Peter (aged twenty-one) was just back from Nicaragua, where he had spent more than a year picking coffee, working on a hospital building site and gathering information and ideas which would find their place in his play *Hey Nicaragua*. It happened that Alan Webster had recently been there on behalf of the Archbishop of Canterbury on a fact-finding mission. When I told him that Peter too had just got back and was bursting with love for the people, indignation for what their rulers with American support were doing to the country, admiration for the local churches, but not for the hierarchy that governed them, he asked if he could meet him. So Peter came over from Ripon and compared notes with Alan. Alan immediately sent a message to the Archbishop of Canterbury asking him to come and meet Peter and hear what he had to say. So there we sat round a large table: the Archbishop and his advisers, the Dean of St Paul's and some of his friends, a very proud me (who didn't say a word once the introductions had been made) and at the end of the table, holding court and answering everything asked of him, large, bronzed, confident, modest, articulate and altogether impressive, Peter. The Archbishop never met me on any occasion after this without enquiring after him.

The Council for the Care of Churches

When I was Dean of Ripon I took part in a debate about church buildings, to support my friend Eric Evans, formerly Archdeacon of Cheltenham, at this time Dean of St Paul's and Chairman of the Council for the Care of Churches, who was getting stick from the floor of the Synod. I spoke to say that church buildings are not just a useful commodity, "plant" in the jargon: they are symbols of God's presence in a locality. Two days later the secretary of the Council, Peter Burman, congratulated me on my speech and said mysteriously that soon "I would be hearing from on high". I didn't know what he meant: but a few weeks later I received a letter from the Archbishop of Canterbury, inviting me to become Chairman of the Council for the Care of Churches (henceforth, CCC).

This is the Church's top body with regard to church buildings. It gives advice to chancellors, dioceses and parishes; writes pamphlets;

interprets the law; and guides C. of E. policy with regard to structure, architecture, conservation, alterations and additions, organs, fabrics, glass, bells, pictures, redundancy and re-ordering. The committee consists of experts in all these matters: architects, art historians, an archdeacon or two and members nominated by the Synod. It also has expert sub-committees who deal with such things as organs and bells. It has a professional secretariat of seven who worked in the church of St Botolph's in the City, where there were offices, a hall, a committee room and a library with a full time librarian. I was to be their Chairman. 'Why?' I wondered, not being in any sense a buildings expert. I met Robert Runcie in a lift in Church House and asked him. 'You have experience of buildings from the user's point of view,' he said, 'what with Pershore Abbey and Ripon Cathedral: and we want someone who will see the problems from a parish as well as an art/historical angle.' Antiquarian considerations had been too strongly emphasised in recent years, he thought.

I received a somewhat grudging "go ahead" from my cathedral colleagues; then a generous "Yes" from David Young, my Bishop; but he said that I would have to give up something in the Diocese and released me from being the Chairman of the Board of Education. So I said "Yes" to the Archbishop and went to London to inspect my new domain.

The secretary, Peter Burman, was away on an extended tour abroad (at which my eyebrows were rightly raised); so I was briefed by the Vice-Chairman Mary Hobbs, wife of the Archdeacon of Chichester. I invited her to lunch at the Naval Club so that we could talk together on neutral territory, and she gave me a low-down on the personal difficulties with which the Council seemed to abound, the professional problems it wrestled with and the conservation ideals that it was there to pursue. She hoped that I would be "on their side", which meant taking a stern line against innovations to churches and being on my guard against some of the schemes that vicars seemed to think necessary. I then talked to the Assistant Secretary who warned me darkly to beware of "the electronic organs lobby".

I soon knew what he meant. After my appointment had been announced, the Chairman of an electronic organ company came to see me at Ripon to tell me his woes and to add that he and the Chairman of another firm were going to sue the Church of England for libel! Really? Yes, because of a pamphlet being published by my Council in which untrue things were said about electronic organs, to do with the cost of maintenance, sound-quality, etc. He urged me to use my influence to withdraw the pamphlet, abolish the Organs Sub-committee and to make sure that churches throughout the country would be better informed and allowed to install electronic organs where appropriate. I gave a non-committal answer and set about investigating the matter.

First, I asked to see the pamphlet and was horrified by its negative tone, doubtful claims and accusations. I then talked to some organ experts I knew, including Harry Brammer who had been assistant organist at Worcester, when Peter was a chorister, and was now Chairman of the Royal School of Church Music – the top dog in this line. He agreed to meet me – hush hush – at his club, the Athenaeum. There, from the depths of leathery armchairs, I told him the situation and he whispered his advice, so that the sleeping gentlemen around would not overhear us and spread word of his treachery. The pamphlet, he said, was certainly over the top. Most organists preferred pipe organs, but there was a lot to be said for electronic organs in certain situations. A sensible and balanced attitude was necessary on an advisory committee.

I then sent the pamphlet to the Synod's Legal Officer, Brian Hanson, whom I knew from the Open Synod Group, and asked his advice. Brian said that the pamphlet was probably libellous unless we could prove its assertions.

I then talked to Ronald Gordon, over lunch in the House of Lords. Ronald was at that time the Archbishop's episcopal Chief of Staff. I wanted to warn without bothering the Archbishop that the Church of England might be on the verge of a public row, feeling that he ought to know about it before it burst. Ronald himself was a fine organist and was delighted with the whole story. 'Typical!' he said, chuckling over the House of Lords soup. 'Go ahead.' I do not know whether or not he bothered the Archbishop with all this silly business.

I then spoke to the Chairman of the Organs Committee, Dr Lionel Dakers, who had been organist of St Paul's. He said that he agreed with me really, but found that one of his members had strong opinions and had persuaded the rest of the committee. I told him that as Chairman of the CCC I would not allow the pamphlet to be published in our name. It was to be withdrawn. Meanwhile, I would re-write the pamphlet myself in a way that I thought the committee would find satisfactory, but would be balanced and judicious. This was an error of judgement. Members of the organs committee were furious with me for tampering with their pamphlet. So I persuaded the main committee to agree to the pamphlet's withdrawal and did not bother them with my version.

All this took place over several months, including the time of the CCC conference, held in Lancashire. We went to the Blackpool Tower on the last evening and I danced with the Vice-Chairman, Mary Hobbs. In the course of this conference I was taken into a darkened room with one of my committee colleagues and asked to listen to a tape which had been made secretly during a conversation at which £1,000 had changed hands for a promise by a Diocesan Organs Adviser always to recommend a particular firm of organs. Hot stuff. But there was nothing that I could do about it unless someone were prepared to sue: which they weren't. However, it put me on my guard – and made me regard this particular organist with a somewhat knowing eye.

When I got back from the conference I was asked to speak on the *Today* programme about electronic organs. 'I hear you are an expert on organs,' said Brian Redhead aggressively. 'Certainly not,' said I. 'Well then?' 'I simply represent the view that when a church is faced with the problem of repairing or replacing its organ there are factors besides musical purism – such as expense and space – to be considered.'

I then set about drafting new members onto the sub-committee, hoping to change its attitude. Meanwhile I won back some grudging favour from the present members by attending their day conference and "singing" the Eucharist with my best Minor Canon technique!

The CCC was a difficult committee to handle because I was not expert in church architecture or the history of art. But I was well advised and tried to draw the right line between pastoral and liturgical needs, on the one hand, and a proper sense of conservation, on the other – and still be decisive. The turning point was when Peter Burman resigned and we appointed Dr Thomas Cocke to be his successor.

Thomas was already a member of the main committee and I liked him very much. He was an art historian of distinction with a Cambridge doctorate, and he was also a committed Christian, unlike Peter Burman, who had become a Buddhist. I was glad he applied for the job, but there was a strong field against him. This appointment was so important that I insisted on interviewing all the candidates myself in the presence of the Synod's Personnel Officer the evening before the interview with the committee. I found that of all the candidates only Thomas understood ordinary, week by week, parish life, with building and financial problems looming so large. I felt sure that he was the right person for the job. The committee agreed and Thomas was appointed. He came and stayed with us at Ripon to discuss the situation and became a personal friend to Juliet and me. I also stayed in his home at Cambridge, got to know Carry, his delightful wife, and two teenage children – and actually went to church with him and listened to a very donnish sermon from a retired professor priest.

I did my best to get to know the staff at St Botolph's and I used to go regularly to London to see them and talk through their work with them. I was, of course, the learner in this situation; but this was good for me. I once travelled to London from York by train in the company of John Habgood, Archbishop of York. He was a man I much admired. He asked me why I was going to London and was pleased when I told him. He got on fine with Angela, our daughter. It was after he had conducted the Three Hours in Ripon Cathedral. Julie and I left him in the drawing-room with Angela, who had read Theology at Oxford, but was herself shy. When we got back they were chatting merrily to one another with no inhibitions.

Electronic organs dominated the beginning of my time with CCC, yet they were only a small part of the whole. As chairman of one of the boards and councils of the Church I was entitled to a seat on the Archbishop's Council, which I used to attend in some trepidation when there was something that concerned me on the agenda. It was a powerful body, elected by the Synod but with some *ex-officio* members.

The "parties" sat in solid lines round the huge table, with the Archbishop trying to keep the peace and ensure some forward movement. I remember him once saying that he hoped that the Council would give unanimous support to some proposal. But no. One of the parties was determined to put its objection on record even although it knew itself to be in the minority. I did not vote, and only spoke when asked. Once Robert Runcie turned to me for a report and opinion. 'But make it snappy, Christopher,' he said, eyes tired and sad.

I also had to answer questions in the General Synod at Question Time at the beginning of each group of sessions. This occasion was 75 per cent boring as chair-people like me trotted up to the rostrum to give the answers prepared by their secretariat to questions that were printed on the order-paper; and it was generally little more than an opportunity for authority-, particularly archbishop-, baiting. After the prepared answers members could ask awkward supplementary questions, so one had to be alert and able to think on one's feet. This could become exciting, heated, even hilarious. I was always well briefed and on the rare occasions that they came at me was able to field the supplementaries successfully. Once I was taken by surprise when Professor David McClean asked if my Council had considered the continental way of handling a particular problem. We hadn't: but I remembered that one of our staff was about to go to Belgium for an international conference which could be relevant. So I was able to say, 'Yes, a representative is going ...' This was accepted without demur. Indeed, I think I scored a point.

On another occasion Prebendary Michael Saward, a Canon of St Paul's Cathedral and a friend and sparring partner of mine from the Windsor Long Course, asked a difficult question about bats. We had had a whole session on bats at our last conference and I had had to insist on giving the lady who came to talk to us on the subject some protection as what she said was unpopular. Bats are a protected species; but they can do great harm to churches. So our protecting, conservation instincts were at war with themselves. I had a nice, noncommittal answer ready for Prebendary Saward, in which I admitted that I was "batting on a sticky wicket". M.S., not impressed, asked a supplementary, and someone then jumped to his feet (out of order, I think) and said that the best way of discouraging bats was to use a lot of incense. Someone else (I wish it had been me) suggested that Prebendary Saward should note this as it would do a lot to brighten up the services in St Paul's. There was general laughter and everyone was pleased – though the problem was far from solved.

When there were problems to solve or situations to report we generally sent one of the officers and perhaps a member of the committee to investigate. But when we were asked to make a report and give advice about the churches in Liverpool, I decided that Thomas and I would go together and spend a night there. One interesting feature of this visit was those churches that had been built to serve both Roman Catholics and Anglicans. Perhaps such an arrangement could only work in Liverpool where the two bishops were famous for their friendliness and determination to do everything they could together. The churches concerned were certainly working well together – but there were difficulties. 'We are both in trouble with our superiors,' said one of the Roman Catholic priests. For going too far by getting too close? It was interesting to hear that the crux of the matter was sometimes the Reserved Sacrament in the Aumbry. The Anglican vicar explained that the hosts that had been consecrated by the Roman Catholics had to be kept distinct from those which had been consecrated by the Anglicans, with each priest having his own key. But as time wore on, we gathered, the distinction became confused and priests of both denominations would go to the sick with whichever consecrated host came to hand.

My last act for the CCC was to write and present a report to Synod on the value of churches and the responsibility for their maintenance. It was not quite the triumphant occasion I had hoped for. Thomas wanted to write both the report and the speech; but I insisted on writing my own speech and delivering it in my usual way. Perhaps this was a mistake. It made the speech slower and therefore longer; and it could not be as polished as a written and read speech would have been. Thomas was very het-up because he had heard of a plot from members of the Standing Committee to attack church buildings and our report. I was not worried. One expected opposition; and we had the perfect answer. The Church had churches whether people liked it or not, and had a statutory – as well as a moral – duty to keep them in good order. But my speech was about more than that: it was about the religious, quasi-sacramental value of churches, and the belief that their aesthetic and cultural value was a bonus of which we should be proud. Many people came to God, I said, through their church. We must not let the buildings become idols ('Goods made into gods,' as Bishop David Jenkins had put it); but we must value them for their religious purpose and also fulfil our responsibility to the country and future generations by preserving and enhancing them with all the skill and expertise at our disposal. I added a strong plea that churches be kept open.

I guessed that the cost of our committee work would be questioned so I kept my ammunition on this subject dry and ready for my reply to the debate. Apart from the few officers, I said, all the members of the committee (including the specialist sub-committees) were men and women of the highest professional calibre and distinction; and they gave their services free. If they were to be paid for the invaluable work that they do the cost would be very much higher. So the Church of England was in fact getting most of the services of the CCC as a free gift. This was a telling point and when it came to the vote there was hardly anyone against us. Most people were nice about the debate afterwards and the Archbishop of York congratulated me most warmly.

It would be easy to write about the General Synod negatively: the party warfare, boring debates, motions, amendments and voting by Houses; the strutting and posturing of self-important people; snidery, pomposity and intrigue; concern with the vote rather than the truth, parliamentary procedures rather than the glory of God. But the truth is that over the years the Synod managed to lead the Church of England forward in many ways to do with its worship, its service to the nation and its administration. Also a great deal of mutual respect and affection developed between people who were hotly opposed to one another's point of view. There were, of course, the bores who regarded the Synod and its procedures as their whole world. But there were also those who did not like the Synod particularly, but filled the debating chamber (emptying the coffee hall) whenever they were called to speak. Bishop David Jenkins was one of these.

There was a chapel in Church House and a church at the University of York with daily prayers and the celebration of Holy Communion and a continual run of people as they came in and out to pray. On one notable occasion at the Sunday morning Eucharist at York (held this time in the theatre) someone who had been slanging his opponents the evening before crossed the floor at the moment of the Peace to share the Peace of Christ with one of them. The whole congregation then broke up to share the Peace with one another. Was there ever such a Peace? People who were enemies last night embraced one another. Michael Ramsey, who was presiding, stood at the Altar looking bewildered and a tiny bit impatient while the "Peace" went on and on. Eventually he was allowed to resume the service and we all made our Communion. From this moment onwards (I decided) there was a genuine feeling of affection between us whatever our ecclesiastical persuasion. Indeed Bishop Howe, who was at that time the General Secretary of the Anglican Communion, told us in a speech that he "collected" national Synods as he was always having to address them; and he judged them not by the amount of agreement that they showed but by the degree of affection between the members. In the twenty-two years I knew it I think that our Synod ranks high in that respect. We did worship. We did pray together. At York our days began with Bible study in small groups. Friendships were formed; and there was no doubt at all that we were a "Christian" assembly. In fact we found that Christian unity is not a unity of agreement but the unity of the Spirit, a gift of God through the Spirit of Christ.

I enjoyed my time as Chairman of the Open Synod Group and (later) as Chairman of the Council for the Care of Churches, as I did with the Synod in general: but as I drew near to the dreaded year of retirement, I decided that I would give myself at least a year without either of them, so that I could concentrate my ministry on my chief love, which was Ripon, the Cathedral and its people. Timing in the matter of chairmanship is important to the smooth running of the Church and the Synod, so I wrote to the General Secretary and told him that I was prepared to resign from the CCC when he thought it would be most convenient for me to do so from the Church's point of view; that would be some months before or some months after the next election of Synod. He was grateful for being consulted and a date was duly fixed.

While I was away in Australia an IRA bomb badly damaged St Botolph's church, the CCC headquarters. I returned to find the staff bravely working in tin helmets in rooms that were still deep in dust and rubble. The new Archbishop of Canterbury (George Carey) came to see us and I have a photograph of the occasion.

Soon after that I left CCC with a party and ceremony and a generous present of CD tokens. At the last session of the General Synod I was one of those mentioned by the Archbishop and specially thanked; so I left it with some pride and affection.

I cannot resist a wry smile as I read my *Church Times* today, 12 July 2002, about the Synod's meeting in York last weekend. On its agenda there were: Anglican/Methodist reunion; the marriage in church of those who have been divorced; Crown involvement in the appointment of bishops; the admission of women to the episcopate; conflict in the Holy Land; Christian witness in a plural society; the constitution of the Synod. Everything changes; but everything stays much the same.

Chapter 24
The Family and Holidays

We received a little money from Juliet's mother when she died in 1967; enough, we hoped, to buy a cottage one day and meanwhile to acquire an old, large and lovely family wagon: a Volkswagon caravanette in which we could sleep and, with the help of a tent attached to the door, camp. It had a double-bed that spread across behind the driver's seat, a cooker, a roof that opened, and some cupboard space for necessary equipment. Julie and I could sleep in the double-bed; the girls in the front, and Peter under our bed, with his head sticking out by the door.

We tried it out on our way via "the lake" to Wales for one of our holidays at Cwm Gloyne, our beloved farm at Velindre, near Newport, Pembroke. "The lake" was a favourite stopping point on A481 which we passed when we took the prettiest, friendliest, slowest way to Newport via Leominster. We decided not just to stop for a picnic, but to sleep the night there in the wagon, roof wide open. Of course it rained, but a little wetting did not trouble us, and the venture was a decided success.

We made some good family friends on the farm. The Gills were always there when we arrived, Brian, Rosalys and Nicholas and his cousin, Julia. They were quiet at first, but the children soon broke down the reserves. There were also the Williamsons. Bernard had been Father's churchwarden at Roehampton and had used Craig y Mor for his family holidays. When that was sold, Bernard and Diana discovered this remote farm and persuaded us to share it with them. The other friends were the Sims: Ralph, a civil engineer, Jill his artistic wife, Adrian, who nearly became a concert pianist and gave two recitals for me, at Hartlebury Castle and Ripon, before some muscular debility stopped him playing professionally; and his brother Justin and sister Jeanette. They were an emotional, noisy family: we came to love them all and Ralph used to invite Julie and me to prestigious events in London in later years. Sometimes Mary and Michael and their families were there too. We had needly games of inter-family cricket and boistirous romps in the sand dunes.

The farmhouse was large with everything centred around the enormous, higgledy-piggledy kitchen, where the food lay about, and our cheques in payment were pinned to the beams and sometimes not cashed for months. One endearing feature of the farm was that Mrs Thomas did not know about inflation and for years and years she always charged us the same: seven pounds a week for adults and half that for children.

Mrs Thomas presided over everything that happened, including the huge breakfasts and suppers which we had every day. She was helped by Rose, a cockney lady of great kindness and wit. Mrs Thomas's husband had had a stroke and sat happily in the kitchen doing nothing: her two boys, Hugh and Anthony, seemed to manage the farm between them.

The farm was up a long and bumpy lane, about which a family song was composed and sung with vigour every time we went up and down it. There was a variety of beaches to go to: Newport Sands, the nearest and most convenient, four miles away; Mwnt, a delightful and remote little cove the other side of Cardigan; Cwm-y-Eglys, the other side of Newport, from where we could walk up and round Dinas Head; and the "mountain" (Carningli), which we used to climb about twice a holiday. And there was much more: hills, mountains, rivers, woollen mills, golf courses; St David's, with the Cathedral for Sunday worship and Ramsey Island for sailing round and seal-watching, some fifteen miles away. For a really wet day, there was Carmarthen with a cinema, where the families went to watch *Chitty Chitty Bang Bang*, whilst Ralph and I played appalling golf in the rain, with Jill's cousin, an American, who was not used to such courses (or, indeed, to such a farm).

Daily breakfasts developed their own routine. Over massive portions of bacon and eggs we would all discuss the day's programme, pondering the merits of each particular beach in relation to such considerations as the weather, the distance away and the availability of ice-cream. When the talking had ceased with everything said and nothing decided, Bernard would raise his head from *The Times* and announce that he was going to Newport Sands – or wherever. So that was that. He had an old and stately Rolls which took up the whole lane and allowed no other car to pass in either direction. This would be carefully parked on the beach and Bernard would then attach a box-kite, which flew straight up and marked the spot for members of the family to make for if they got lost. Bernard would then settle down for the day with his study of Egyptian Mythology or the Theorems of Euclid – or, indeed, New Testament Greek, which he and Angela, when she was going up to Oxford, studied together.

Parking on the beach was at once the advantage and disadvantage of Newport Sands, and it occasionally led to crisis moments when someone's car would be stuck in the sand with the tide pounding in. Everyone on the beach rushed to the rescue, and at worst a tractor was hired from the golf club, at considerable cost.

Newport Sands had many attractions, including a scambly walk along the cliff and over the rocks to the headland; another walk "up to the top" and back; super bathing; and the golf course when we tired of sand and preferred the gorse. Once when Angela was small she disappeared altogether. Panic. Our children generally wore red so that they could be seen from afar. But on this occasion Angela couldn't be seen. However, all was well and she turned up having gone for a walk along the cliffs with John Willamson. What was all the fuss about?

Farm life itself had lots to offer and sometimes when the children were a bit older they preferred a "day on the farm" to going to the beach. I remember the horror I felt when I found, after a strangely quiet morning, that they were making houses for themselves, linked by passages, in the hay barn. What would have happened if the hay had slipped? In the evening we used to go off with the tractor to bring in the harvest: another perilous procedure on the swaying, tipsy, high-piled cart with the children all over it. No sensible present-day parent would stomach the risks we took so happily and innocently in those carefree days. But no harm was suffered. Juliet and Penelope and I once had an encounter with the farm bull, Penelope later declaring that we left her to its mercy. One wet day Angela and I decided to walk to Ceibwr, a rocky beach about four miles away, however wet we got – which was very wet indeed. She was preparing for Oxford entrance and I went over philosophical and ethical questions with her to arm her for the General Paper, just as I had done with pupils at Lancing. Often in the evenings we played noisy games of mah jong, which became our craze. The Finn family were also with us at that time and enjoyed these games. Mike used to play me golf and ask me searching questions about God just as I was about to drive or putt.

One year we arrived at the farm tired and excited. We had played a noisy game of "milk-churns" to while away the miles, and here we were. Out came Mrs Thomas to greet us, but with the words, 'Ooh, I am in a pickle: I thought you were coming tomorrow, and there's no room.' The upshot was that she arranged for us to stay the night elsewhere and return to the farm the next day.

Our children had to manage with very little money in their pockets; but what they had was supplemented by going round the beach regattas winning prizes. Peter could swim and scull faster than anyone around; Penelope and Angela did well in swimming and canoe races; and Penelope made a speciality of building sand-castles in the shape of a Norman church, complete with square tower and Norman arches. She always won – for originality!

One year Brian Gill arrived with a new sailing boat, a Mirror. He was enormously proud of this boat as it sat on the lawn outside the farm and he polished every bit of it and practised hauling the sails up and down. But when he first took it to the beach and launched it in the creek, he took a dislike to the wind which made the sails flap and the boat lean over in a most threatening way. However, he soon learnt to cope with it, and Penelope and Nicky's cousin Hilary used to sail intrepidly out to sea leaving us on the beach wondering if they knew how to turn round and come back. They always managed it.

Another adventure was when we were with the Leahys in their caravan at St Justin's Bay, round the cliff head from White Sands, the beach of St David's. It was (so we thought) a particularly calm day, so we decided, Michael Leahy, Angela and I, to row our new little boat (appropriately, called *Lucky Dip*) round the headland to White Sands, while John and Joan Leahy and Juliet walked round by the cliff path.

But once out to sea the Atlantic rollers were much too heavy for our bouncy *Lucky Dip*. In no way could we row in without being overturned. So life-belts on, we prepared to swim. We then rowed as hard as we could for the shore. A huge wave came chasing up from aft. We "pooped". 'Help,' shouted Michael. 'Abandon ship,' shouted I; and we all swam calmly ashore, helped on by the waves and the surf and the incoming tide. All the gear was rescued, including *Lucky Dip* herself. By this time the shore party, who had witnessed the episode from the cliffs, came rushing to the rescue. If I had to do it again I would keep the boat beyond the breakers and wait for the others to be on the beach before venturing shorewards. But I would not do it again.

Other friends in Newport were the Kenyon family. Christopher was at Lancing and I had prepared him for Confirmation. He introduced us to his parents and they were most hospitable. Their house was in a commanding position on the cliffs, just a field between themselves and the sea. They had a boat for rowing in the regattas, and John (a retired Army major and prep-school headmaster) and Christopher used to play golf with me, and helped Peter to start.

We once had a particularly wet month at Cwm Gloyne, but just as we were leaving, the sun came out as if for ever. So we decided to stay thereabouts and set up camp in the wagon at Mwnt. There we had a happy week during which I did a lot of painting. Yes, pictures. Exceedingly bad: but I loved doing it and it gave me a feel for texture, contour and different lights which I had never noticed before. Our art-teacher friend Tim Vivian took one look at my efforts and said, 'Ah! Primitives.' At the end of this week we had to go back for Angela's friend Penny Larner's party, to the disgust of the rest of us!

We went to the farm every summer until moving to Droitwich, when we bought Berian, a delightful cottage on the south side of Newport. We did not have holidays there with the whole family, for by this time the children were going their own ways; but they themselves and their friends and many of our friends and colleagues used the cottage. Sometimes – so they said – the family used it for a university "reading party"; and Peter took his travelling theatre company there to rehearse his plays prior to the Edinburgh Fringe and touring. Mr and Mrs Owen, who lived opposite, looked after Berian when we were away and got it ready for us when we went down there. Mr Owen was also caretaker of the village hall next door: he allowed Peter to use it for reheasals. Julie and I had restful, recuperating holidays at Berian, sometimes by ourselves, sometimes with friends.

We had other holidays besides those at Newport. We used the wagon for day expeditions to the Wye Valley with the Leahys; and to Ashes Valley at Little Streatham, my old schooldays haunt where Michael and I had the week by ourselves in 1941. We duly explored the source of the stream, climbed the hills to pick blueberries and clambered down to the stream to play Pooh-sticks. It has all been immortalised on film.

Peter once cycled to Berian from Pershore with a friend. They separated on their way home because Peter wanted to go back over the hills. But darkness descended when he was out in the wilds of Wales. Peter, who had no lights, sensibly rang the police who came and escorted him to the police station at Llandovery. The police rang me and told me that they "had him"; but I needn't worry. He spent a comfortable night in a cell and rode on home the next morning, with kind-hearted me meeting him at Brecon and driving him home.

One Easter holiday we went to Paris and camped in the Bois de Boulogne – all five of us. The wagon, unfortunately, went badly wrong in its engine, so we had a very slow journey from Calais to Paris. There the engine stalled when a traffic-light went green, and every car in Paris hooted at us. But we found the Bois safely and used the offending wagon simply as a tent for the week.

It was a week of joyful exploration. We have a film showing the bright spring weather, the Eiffel Tower, the trip down the Seine round Notre Dame, a pond near the Louvre where Peter and I played boats while the others looked at the pictures; monmartre, with Peter counting his change on the steps of the church after a horrid clergyman had made him pay for his candle; having our portraits done; and the clean and efficient camp itself.

The children had their own trips abroad. I drove Penelope home from Wales to go with a school party to France; she also went with exchange friends to France, Germany and Spain. One friend, Elizabet, stayed with us at Cwm Gloyne and discussed Jane Austen all the way from Heathrow. She also left her passport at the farm when I was driving her back. I rang the farm and Brian Gill chased us with it, and we just caught the plane. Angela went to Germany with a German friend; Peter had an unequal exchange with a French boy who was too young for him, and was a very difficult guest indeed when he came for his return visit.

Penelope, Angela and Peter can write their own memoirs about their school days. To us they seemed happy and fulfilling, though there were some difficulties. We became dissatisfied with the Abbey Park Junior School, but the music was good. When Peter took his entrance to King's Worcester for the Cathedral Choir the Head said that his maths was not nearly good enough – so we had to send him for two terms to a local private school to catch up. I remember Peter's dreadful French teacher at that school, but also the excellent cricket at which Peter was already beginning to shine.

I still have a copy of a letter I wrote to Penelope's Head at Prince Henry's, and I certainly worked hard on her behalf. I was furious with one of Angela's teachers when she said that, of course, Angela was not Penelope. But they both did well academically, Angela going to the King's, Worcester, Sixth Form when we moved to Droitwich, and then on to Oxford; and Penelope doing well enough in science (though the arts were her obvious forte) to get to the medical school at Leicester University. Both excelled in music, and Penelope gave a brilliant acting performance in *Roots*.

Peter excelled at rugger and cricket at King's, being in the First teams for three years running. He also acted with distinction and sang the leading bass part in *The Bartered Bride*. These activities came to the fore when his voice had broken and he had ceased to be a chorister. I had to stick up for him too when the Head took agin' him. I complained that all the masters seemed to want him all the time for rugger or cricket or music or acting or opera, not to mention academic studies; and they should get their act together!

One feature of Peter's full life was the cricket eleven that beat all the Worcestershire schools one year and the following year reached the finals of the Lord's Taverner Cup, competing against schools from all over the country. We parents and followers went to the Oval for the final to support them; but alas our boys got the worst of the conditions and were beaten. Peter was "out" LBW from a ball which bruised him high up the thigh; and he bowled steadily for over after over, but with no luck. It was an exciting two years because all the boys in the eleven were heroes at at least one of the matches and we parents became very friendly in mutual admiration.

On one occasion Anne Vint, my secretary, had an embarrassing party for her daughter at which the young guests wrecked her house. I wrote in the parish newsletter an article to the effect that parents should not abandon their houses when their teenage children had parties. This was given headlines in the paper, and I was not popular with my children and their friends. For one of Penelope's parties Julie and I duly stayed around in the kitchen – and were delighted with the way everyone behaved and cleared up afterwards.

The three children had varied and demanding social lives which meant driving them all over the district. Peter's, indeed, was deemed to be a threat to his scholarly progress: the Head insisted that he became a boarder for his last year and generously found the money to make this possible. He had a good last year and did much better in his A-levels than had been predicted.

Cathedral music became a feature of our lives, especially for the three years in which Angela and I sang with the Worcester Festival Choral Society for the Three Choirs' Festival, doing the rounds of Hereford, Gloucester and Worcester. As Peter was also singing in the Cathedral Choir, this became a way of life, the summers dominated by rehearsals and the festivals. We sang some memorable works, including the usual repertoire of Bach, Handel and Elgar; but also *Caractacus* by Elgar, in which the words were so stupid that they almost cancelled the beauty of the music; *The Music Makers*, which we sang again in the Albert Hall; the new *Mass of Christ the King* by Malcolm Williamson, which we rehearsed adding a page or two of score as they were handed to us each week, the ink still wet. We sang this again at Westminster Cathedral. We also sang Poulenc's Christ-affirming *Gloria* and David Fanshawe's *African Sanctus* complete with tapes from the African jungle and a slinky Lord's Prayer. Crowning all we sang Mahler's Eighth Symphony, as I described in *The Food of Love*.

Juliet and I took parties to Oberammergau every ten years to see the Passion Play: eighty boys from the Kings' School, Ely in 1960; the parish of Pershore in 1970; the Archdeaconry of Dudley in 1980; and the congregation of Ripon Cathedral in 1990. The play itself was always moving and rewarding to watch, with its slow, measured progress, punctuated by the Old Testament tableaux; Christ himself, perhaps too passive, "being done to", rather than, as in the Fourth Gospel, in command of events. There was too much emphasis on Judas and his motivation; wonderful crowd scenes; adequate music (Mozartian but not memorable); a desperately sad climax, with Jesus (as somehow you do not expect) moving on the cross; an unsatisfactory, "happy ending" Resurrection; and an overall effect of deep devotion and love and suffering and sadness: a tragedy rather than a victory.

We stayed with the "characters" in their homes and were treated by them with great friendliness. The organisation was perfect; and the wood carvings – especially in 1960 before they were priced out of our pockets – were very special. Memorable moments: the lunch-hour out of the village in the peace of the country with Penelope and Angela, so beautiful with their long and lovely hair and their Tyrolean costumes, hushed in awe; the Eucharist in the Lutheran church after the performance with the Pershore group; Christ approaching the temple on the donkey at the beginning of the play; the striking clarity of the tableaux; the long time it took to pass round the bread and the wine at the Last Supper – and the awful moment when Jesus gives the "sop" to Judas; and the agony in the Garden, with the much repeated, woeful cry to "Mein Fater".

When I was Dean of Ripon I was invited by the Principal of St Francis' College, Brisbane, to give the first "Ivor Church Lecture" in honour of Ivor who had retired from being the Principal. This was the college in which I had been born, and Ivor was one of my best friends at St Edmund Hall. I was delighted to accept, and with the permission of the Bishop and the chapter, I flew to Brisbane with Juliet in 1993.

We decided to make a holiday of it. So we went via Perth, where we had an adventurous week in the bush with our Ripon friends the Danishewskis, and Sydney where we were met by Andrew Bett (my godson) and his sister, Jenny. We stayed in the Deanery at Brisbane for a week and I took a full part in the cathedral services, preaching twice. Then we went to the college where we were handsomely treated and I duly gave my lecture on Creative Tensions within Christianity. Besides that I taught a class of potential deacons (mature men and women of very high calibre) on the subject of worship. I celebrated Communion and preached at their College Eucharist. At the end of the week Juliet and I were "dined out" by means of a trip down the river calling at different places for the stages of the meal.

After that we stayed for a week with an old Lancing friend, John Crowther, who lived in Toowoomba but had a cattle station, now run by his own son, far away in the outback near Roma: that is, thirty miles from Roma – with nothing in between. It was three miles away from the house to the gate of his estate; and five miles to the nearest inhabitant. We helped to go round up the cattle as we watched it begin herded along not by a man on a horse but by a man on a motor bike! After that we went to Townsville and the Barrier Reef; then home via a week in Penang where John joined us with his car and drove us all over the island. Penang was much developed and much noisier but just as hot as it was when I went last from HMS *Nelson* in 1945.

These were a memorable six weeks.

If there is one thing that vicars are good at, it is having holidays. This is partly because it is hard to relax at home with people constantly coming and the telephone always ringing and the difficulty of getting a genuine day off each week: so holidays are indeed important. There were many more than I have described and many more memorable incidents. The car journeys themselves were always good for "family time" – games, songs, rounds, talk, argument and chatter. We relished these holidays, as we relished our family life; and it's good to see now how our children and grandchildren enjoy their family lives – and their hoildays.

Chapter 25
Ripon Cathedral

Our move to Ripon coincided with the appalling affair of the miners' strike. The policemen who battled with the miners in October 1984 were stationed at the Claro Barracks in Ripon, so early every morning a fleet of coaches filled with policemen drove down the A1 to the battle grounds; and every evening they returned. Pictures of the fights were shown in lurid detail on television screens; but stories were circulating in Ripon that things were much worse than they appeared on the news. The city was amazed and horrified. In the Cathedral we prayed for justice and peace, but it was difficult to see how these would come about. "Mercy and truth are met together", says the psalm about the Ideal Age to come: but it hasn't come yet.

Ripon is a delightful city, claiming the word "city" because it has a Cathedral. It is a market town with a square, and a hornblower who blows his horn there every evening "to set the watch". The square contains a tall obelisk, the Town Hall and its balcony on one side and a thrum of busy shops all round. Down a twisty lane lies the Cathedral; grand in a homely way, with a magnificent West Front and two towers, dominating, guarding, blessing the city. If you approach the city from the south or east you see the Cathedral standing above it, a physical symbol of God "dwelling amongst his people".

Sociologically there were two features, apart from the Cathedral itself, that made Ripon special. One was the fact that the Royal Engineers were based there. Soldiers were always to be seen on leave in the town, sometimes the cause of fisty quarrels with Ripon lads over the local girls; and whenever anything needed doing in the city or the

Cathedral, the Engineers were ready to help, build or repair. Alas, this ubiquitous usefulness performed under the name of "exercise" was stopped by the Ministry of Defence under new regulations shortly after I arrived, but the Royal Engineers continued to perform public functions which made them popular in the city. The Regiment also had the "Freedom of the City", entitling them to march through it with bayonets drawn, standards flying and trumpets blaring, on certain occasions in the year.

Secondly, there was the College of Education, the Ripon campus of the College of Ripon and York St John, whose other campus was in York, twenty-four miles away. We were to see a lot of the staff and the students; they played an important part in the life of the city. The Cathedral Precentor was also the Chaplain of the college, making a link that was useful and pleasing to both establishments.

The Minster House, which had been bought and renovated for my predecessor Dean Edwin Le Grice sixteen years before, was to us the best house in the Church of England! I know of no other deanery or bishop's "palace" that I would prefer to live in: we felt greatly blessed and privileged to have it. It is a much adapted Queen Anne house; the rumour (unsubstantiated) was that it had originally belonged to the Cathedral but had been sold by some unscrupulous dean to his cousin, an admiral, for a pocketful of change. Its condition was poor when it was acquired for Dean Le Grice, and he had been unable to live in it for a long time. But now it was magnificent; standing nobly under the lea of the Cathedral with a garden around, and down the steps an area of grass and stately trees which the Bishop dubbed "the deer park". This was brilliant for Cathedral occasions (fêtes, Scouts, receptions, adult and childrens' parties) and perfect for family games of hide-and-seek with grandchildren, and hockey, which we played with walking sticks and much vigour, our family against the Glanville-Smiths on Boxing Day. There was also room for windy badminton with the choristers, and golf practice for Peter and me.

Inside the house there is a large hall with a magnificent fireplace, a huge and valuable picture of the Cathedral in former days by "De Paris" (a painter unknown to the expert who came and examined our pictures: could it mean "from Paris?"); and plenty of space for our grandfather clock, the sofa that saved my life (see Chapter 4); and our new table-tennis table given us by the Diocese of Worcester. This made the front hall a friendly place, but we wheeled it away on state ocasions.

Opposite the front door there was an arch and beyond that another hall containing an enormous oil painting of one of my predecessors, who always seemed to be frowning at me in disapproval; and then a staircase sweeping round and up to the floor above. The choir could perform from this staircase, using the stage halfway up; and be photographed for those who like sentimental pictures of choir boys. The two halls together made a superb space for receptions and parties. We felt it was right to let it be used for such purposes as people's wedding and golden wedding occasions, charity coffee-mornings and Victorian – or Edwardian or Queen Anne – parties. There were concerts and recitals and many fundraising events that we hosted.

We reckoned to give nine parties every Christmas. The choristers' party was particularly good fun. After an enormous tea – wishfully designed to quieten their high spirits – the boys played (by tradition and demand) Murder in the Dark. This was not successful. The younger boys enjoyed a good scream but there was little chance for the older boys to exercise their skill at detection. In the following years Juliet found a conjuror who had just the right mixture of mystery, see-through magic and scatalogical humour to keep them cheerful and entertained. (On one such occasion granddaughter Rosy was a big hit.)

Another memorable party was when the choir from Eton College was giving a recital in the Cathedral. Michael Abrahams, whose son was at Eton, was organising this occasion and he asked me if we could have the choir and its supporters in for a short "thank you" reception after the concert. 'Certainly,' said I: but two days before the event Michael rang me to say that I was giving them a meal, wasn't I? 'A meal? How many for?' 'Sixty'. Panic. So we rang up one of my adult Confirmation candidates, Poppy Millington, who did outside catering. 'Easy,' she said – and produced a marvellous repast, including quantities of sticky toffee pudding.

On the right of the hall was my spacious study; beyond that a beautiful drawing-room just right for the Bechstein and grand occasions, beyond that our family snug room in which we kept the television and which we tried to keep for our own; but not always successfully.

On the left of the hall was the dining-room with its Tudor panelling and its royal portraits. These had been found in my predecessor's time somewhere in the hidden reaches of the Cathedral. Possibly they had been put there by their owner in times when it was politically incorrect – indeed dangerous – to have royal portraits in your family gallery. I decided that they must be properly restored, whatever the cost; and with the aid of grants from the Pilgim's Trust we had them done, one or two at a time. They were eventually "opened" in the presence of our appeal patron, Prince Michael, along with an expensive lunch in the Old Deanery Restaurant in aid of the appeal. It was a very happy occasion and Prince Michael took a lot of trouble to chat to people, not least the stonemasons and members of the choir. Towards the end of lunch he leant over to me and said, 'Mr Dean, would you very kindly write me a speech to thank you all for this occasion?' so I scribbled out some words on the back of a menu, and he haltingly read them! On that occasion our dentitst was present. He was not one who worshipped in the Cathedral, but he was a good friend and prepared to pay for a royal occasion. I introduced him to Prince Michael as we did the rounds together. 'And what do you do for the Cathedral?' asked the Prince. 'He has promised to give a large donation,' said I. Enormous relief on the face of our dentist; and a nice cheque arrived the next day.

These were some of the great occasions when we used the Minster House creatively. But there were many lesser occasions too; and we tried to keep an open house where people felt they could drop in on us and come together and meet each other. But it was also our home, a beautiful house for living in, and a splendid place for family gatherings: Bethan's and Patrick's christening; brother John's sixty-seventh birthday; and lovely Christmases with all the family, children and grandchildren. I can remember dancing round the hall to the *Pastoral Symphony*; and carol singing in the drawing-room, the floor still littered with discarded wrapping paper and piles of presents, and the room vibrating with the rhythm of *Jingle Bells*, even Bethan in her cot bouncing up and down in joy.

Sometimes Peter would come with his acting troupe. They would be doing one of his plays, such as *Hey Nicaragua*, in the College, Harrogate or York. They would park their vividly decorated van in our drive. It was adorned with acting-props tied to the roof, and had the startling name of the company (AK 47) painted in aggressive lettering all over it. They would come home on a high after an evening's performance, clatter noisily to bed, and then reappear at about eleven-thirty the next morning, looking cheerful and scruffy just as the Bishop or the Mayor or the Honorary Canons were arriving for some important meeting. But Julie and I loved "the troupe". They were so generous to one another and grateful to us: splendid actors; and Peter led them with gruff humour and affection. *Hey Nicaragua* is a brilliant play, which hits hard at the cruelty of American policy towards Nicaragua. The Reagans are shown in *Spitting Image* masks having to watch the dreadful results of this policy. But while it is telling and exciting, it is also entertaining with its songs and moments of stylised buffoonery; but oh so sad. The rave review in the *Observer* at the Edinburgh Festival was well deserved.

My Induction and Institution service was a grand affair, the Cathedral packed with people and all the clergy of the diocese there in procession. In my sermon I described my ambition that the Cathedral should be a "Jacob's Ladder" bringing God to people and people to God. I began with a reference to all the beautiful church buildings that I had had the luck to serve in: St Michael's, Basingstoke; Ely Cathedral; Lancing Chapel; Pershore Abbey; the quaintly crooked St Augustine's, Dodderhill; and now – Ripon Cathedral. After the service there were receptions in three places at once: the Town Hall; the Old Deanery Restaurant; and the Cathedral Primary School. Julie and I (chauffered by Patrick Bickersteth, who had organised the whole affair) visited them all and met as many people as possible.

Amongst those we met was the the Chairman of the Royal Naval Association. When he learnt that I had been in the Navy he invited me to be President of the local RNA. I accepted and this led to a happy association with the local ex-mariners, most of whom had served in submarines. The Chairman himself had been a coder! We used to meet on Monday nights in the Red Lion, and, after a minute's silence, reminisce over sandwiches and rum.

They were extraordinarily kind to me, so much so that on Armistice Sundays I used to join them in the ranks. I would take the service in the

Cathedral, preach a rousing sermon, then nip into the vestry, take off my robes, and join the parade as it assembled outside the Cathedral. Once in line, the rum bottle would pass round the ranks; then, to the rousing sound of the RE band, we would march up Kirkgate and pass the saluting base. If you want to feel close to people, march with them! We would then make our way up to the Memorial Gardens, and I would contrive to step out of the ranks and conduct the ceremony; and so back to drinks in the Red Lion afterwards. When I left Ripon the RNA gave me handsome presents, including a small "rum fanny" – which sits on my piano now as I write. It is still full of rum!

Back to my Induction. When it was all over my family and immediate friends gathered for dinner at the Warehouse in Kirkgate. All the family were there (except Mary) and many old friends such as Rosemary and Andrew Betts, Rosalys Gill, Bernard and Diana Willamson. I cannot remember a more happy occasion. The proprietor gave me a "Ripon Hornblower" to remember it by. I have got it by me now – and still do.

On the day of my Induction I received a letter from Her Majesty the Queen suggesting that she perform the ceremony of the Royal Maundy at Ripon the following April, 1985. I was to answer at once, but not tell a soul for three weeks. So I told Patrick Bickersteth, whom Edwin Le Grice had appointed as the Honorary Chapter Clerk. He agreed with me that we must say "Yes, delighted" to Her Majesty and that we must also tell the other two members of the Chapter, Ronnie McFadden and David Ford, interpreting "Dean" to mean "Dean and Chapter". We then decided that the Bishop must be consulted, because arrangements would have to be made for people to be chosen from all over the diocese to be invited to receive the "royal pence".

The numbers invited are the same (for both men and women) as the number of years the sovereign has reigned – in this case, thirty-one: so sixty-two people had to be found. They were to be chosen for their record of public service and the fact that they were "not wealthy". We wanted to have a spread of people from all over the diocese, so at a meeting with the Bishop, we decided to invite rural deans to submit names to go to Buckingham Palace for royal approval. Invitations would then be issued from the Palace itself. The result was an amazing list of wonderful people of all sorts and colours and professions and worldwide service, voluntary and professional. The Queen, when she came, had obviously studied the list and mastered it, for she was able to speak personal words here and there to the recipients as she went round them, and she commented to us on the humbling nature of the exercise. Many good and selfless people came together on that occasion. We did everything we could to make it enjoyable for them; and the Queen and the Duke were exemplary in the concern and admiration they showed to the recipients.

The Maundy Thursday event threw me into the deep water of responsibility and organisation; and all this was in the first weeks of my incumbency. It was an opportunity to meet people in the Cathedral, city and diocese and I was determined to do everything as well as I could. We had meeting after meeting. Besides the matter of communicating with the diocese and starting the process of selection, there was transport, catering, parking and lavatories (the Cathedral did not contain this facility!) to arrange. Then there was the service itself, the music and ritual and readings. The Duke read the lesson, and I was told that in one cathedral they had forgotten to put the Bible in place, so I took the responsibility of doing that myself. When it came to the rehearsal the day before, I decided to take charge of this, though there were others expecting to do so. So I went into the pulpit, called for silence and began to explain and order and boss and make them do it again; till we got it right. Bishop David Saye (Bishop of Rochester) was the Royal High Almoner for this occasion: with his experience he helped me considerably.

I had already had meetings with the police and representatives from the Palace who came to see that all was in order for Her Majesty's reception in the Minster House itself. We were told what she liked and didn't like and the provision she would need for her comfort both before and afterwards. We gave up our en suite bedroom; Julie would not let me sleep in it the night before in case I left my pyjamas lying around. The Duke had our spare room (the old Victorian nursery) and was delighted to find a picture of HMS *Hotspur*, in which he had trained in his naval days, on the wall. Security men came along with sniffer dogs to make sure there were no hidden assassins around; We were instructed on matters of etiquette and were told that "if the Duke asks you a question and you don't know the answer, don't guess, because he does!"

Whom to invite to the reception was a question that needed careful handling.

The greater the circle of those selected, the greater the number of people who would feel themselves left out. So we decided (Juliet and I, for it was our responsibility alone) to invite all the employees of the Cathedral; that is, those who were paid for their services, including the cleaners, stonemasons and secretaries. This meant not inviting the many volunteers. This gave us an easily handled number, eighty in all, a social mix, and a definite line of demarkation. "Volunteer" could have included almost everyone.

When the day came everything went to perfection. The service, I believe, was as good as it could be and included (rather daringly because the Queen and the Duke did not know it) the anthem *The Apple Tree* deliciously sung by the choristers, as well as the rousing and royally approved *Zadoc the Priest*. We arranged the seats all round the Cathedral looking inwards, so that the Queen could go round the recipients and see them face to face. After the service was over I escorted Her Majesty out on to the West Front, where photographs were taken, and then across the road to the cheering crowds who had come to see and applaud. The Queen was in high spirits and seemed to enjoy chatting to people and receiving flowers and gifts which she promptly handed to me, ignoring the multiple click of cameras that went on in a barrage around us.

And so into Minster House, where Juliet was ready and waiting to receive us, with invited guests already in position. We arranged them not in a line (such as we had on the similar occasion at Worcester) but in groups standing round in circles. I took the Queen round the groups one way and introduced the individuals to her; and Julie took the Duke the other way; so the Queen and the Duke both met everyone. Then there were drinks and refreshments.

We had a butler lent to us for the occasion! Fred Asker had been a stable-boy, head of a stable, a general's batman and was now working for Major Ingham. When he retired, he offered himself to Julie and me to help in any way he could. He gave tone to our dinner parties by waiting at table, looked after the Cathedral silver and would demand my trousers at unsuitable moments so that he could give them a press. He was a deeply devout Christian: I took him Communion on his death-bed a few years later. The Royal Maundy reception was the highlight of his life, and he hung a picture of himself handing a tray of sherry to the Queen, in his sitting-room.

The Duke knocked over a plate of goodies; and went down on his knees amongst much laughter to pick them up. He gazed at the royal portraits (not yet restored) and said he bet they were fakes; and was hotly rebuked by me when he doubted the validity of the Royal Charter which we had specially placed for their Majesties' perusal in the dining-room. But he did not mind being told that he was wrong; and he submitted to a lecture on the history of the Cathedral by Dr Foster, the Senior Verger.

After the reception in Minster House we escorted the royal party to the Town Hall where the Mayor and Councillors were waiting, for lunch. They then departed; leaving Ripon, its people, its Cathedral and its Dean on a high wave of loyal enthusiasm.

A year later Queen Elizabeth, the Queen Mother, came to the city for the celebration of a thousand years of its charter, which dated back to King Alfred (so they say). This began with a service in the Cathedral at which I escorted Her Majesty to her place, and then preached. I recalled the occasion when as a "boy on a bike" I met the King and herself inspecting a bomb-site in the East End of London (see Chapter 4). The Queen Mother said afterwards that she was delighted with this recollection. Where exactly did it happen? 'Somewhere near the Elephant and Castle,' I thought, but could not be sure. After the service we had another reception in our house, having been carefully instructed about what Her Majesty liked to drink (gin and vermouth): then she went to the Town Hall for lunch at which she made a speech; then with us to Fountains Abbey to watch *Robin Hood Revels* – in the rain. She chatted to the players, then hopped into a helicopter and flew to Windsor for a dinner party that evening!

The city's Millennium (in 1986) gave rise to much activity in the city itself and the beginning of the custom of a New Year's Eve celebration in the Cathedral and market square. After a short service in the Cathedral we had a torchlight procession to the square. Then, on the stroke of midnight, I blessed the city from the Town Hall balcony, the Mayor made a speech and people danced in the square. Every year the numbers attending this jolly occasion grew, and by the time of my eleventh year the Cathedral was packed and the market square became a sea of faces as I did my "Pope Act", as my family called it. It could not be a very solemn blessing although I myself took it seriously. There was barracking and cheers and a pleasing shout of "Good Old Dean".

Another custom which started at this time was the Boxing Day walk from the Cathedral to Fountains Abbey; following in the footsteps of the Cistercian monks who had fled from York and taken refuge in the monastery at Ripon. They had then ventured forth on the day after Christmas and began to establish themselves at what we now call Fountains, taming the valley there and building a monastery and abbey church. I believe that this, with its extensive grounds, is the most beautiful historical site in England. After a short service in the Cathedral conducted by the Bishop, we set out, Cathedral congregation, citizens of Ripon plus their dogs, and family parties from far and wide, bent on walking off their Christmas dinners. We made our way through the streets of the city, across the fields to Fountains Abbey, the grounds of which had been opened for the occasion. There we sang carols in the ruined nave of the abbey itself, and drank rum punch prepared by the Fountains' stewards. Then home, sometimes wet through, to a late Boxing-Day lunch.

My first year there were four hundred people on this walk. After eleven years it was two thousand. Sometimes we would have a special guest to accompany us: on one occasion, Monsignor Gordon Wheeler, who had once been Chaplain of Lancing and was now the Roman Catholic Bishop of Leeds. He was very nice to Juliet and me and asked us to lunch. He wanted to know all the Lancing gossip and was ready with some juicy stories from his own days.

Once I had been installed as Dean I had to set about the work of running the Cathedral. The daily routine, of course, had its own momentum and would keep going without my interference. But in matters of direction and policy there were several things that I wanted to get right. Appointing Patrick Bickersteth as the Chapter Clerk, properly paid and given definite responsibilities, was the first important move I made. This put the supervision of the Cathedral lay staff into his hands, including their wages, pensions and employment rights. It also gave a greater formality to our Chapter meetings, as he took the minutes and produced agendas for each meeting. This was a change from previous meetings to which members brought their own bits of agenda to be discussed, whether the others were prepared for them or not. It also meant that decisions were minuted, acted upon and recalled at the next meeting. I also had excellent secretarial help from Avril Widdowson, whom I inherited from Dean Edwin, and later, when Avril went to the Chapter office, from Carol Oldroyd whom, with Julie's help, I appointed myself, and who (with Mike her husband) became a personal friend. In the office she helped me with all my duties (CCC as well as Cathedral) faithfully and efficiently for ten years.

But I could not "run" the Cathedral by myself. I was the "first among equals" with the other two members of the Chapter, Canons Ronnie McFadden and David Ford; so while they were two and I was one, they could always out-vote me, making my statutory "casting vote" useless. It was not that I wanted to defy them: I always worked for consensus; but the feeling that I had no real power of my own was frustrating. So I asked the Bishop to fill the vacancy by appointing a third canon. Patrick Bickersteth agreed and told the Bishop so himself. But any new canon would also have to have a diocesan post; and it was known that the Bishop wanted to appoint a Director of Ministry. Some said that the new Director should live in Leeds, where most of the parishes were situated. 'But in that case,' I argued, 'the" cannot be done.'

The Bishop agreed and decided to appoint a Director of Ministry and Residentiary Canon of the Cathedral. He could have made the appointment without reference to me; but he decided to ask me in on the selection process, for which I was grateful. There was a strong list of applicants and the Bishop and I agreed that the strongest of them all was Peter Marshall, a canon of Chelmsford. My colleagues were angry when they found that they had not also been consulted; but I was pleased with the appointment. I needed a strong man in my Chapter who would help me with some of the reforms that I thought were necessary. So Peter (now Dean of Worcester) was appointed, and the balance in the Chapter was changed for the good. Not that Peter and I always agreed. Far from it and he was to prove an awkward colleague in some respects; but we agreed on the fundamentals and could stand up to one another when necessary.

I continued to search for consensus, and always achieved it except in two instances. The important one of these I will describe later. The other might seem trivial. Not so. It was the matter of the colour of the carpet to be placed under the new nave altar which we were so proud of. The architect said it should be red. I agreed: so did David Ford. But Ronnie had been talking to a parishioner who was by profession an internal decorator. She said that it should be gold. He and Peter agreed. Deadlock. I could not give way, especially as red was the architect's choice.

But Ronnie and Peter were determined on gold. So my first recourse was to claim the casting vote, and so win – if not the argument, certainly the decision! But I thought that that would cause a breach in our unity which would be difficult to repair. So I said that we would vote formally at the end of the meeting, having done our other business, hoping that one of the others would relent. But no. We voted: two two. By then I had decided what to do. I gave my casting vote to the Chapter Clerk who attended all our meetings and on this issue had not spoken. This was Robert Lambie (Patrick Bickersteth having retired) and he voted – against me! So the carpet was – and still is – gold. I have never regretted the decision, but continue to think that it would be better still if red. Judge for yourself if you go to Ripon Cathedral.

The liturgy was the one thing that Ronnie and David did not want to change. 'We worked at it with Dean Edwin,' they said, "and we have got it perfect." But by its nature the worship of God can never be perfect; and I felt that it was wrong for Ripon Cathedral to ignore the liturgical changes that were taking place in the country – changes which reflected new insights and a determination to bring the "people" into the act of worship; also to be sensitive to the revised liturgies of other denominations.

Dean Le Grice had achieved the most important object of making the Sunday Sung Eucharist the main service of the week; complete with the Cathedral Choir singing the best music, but also having it a "congregational" service with the laity playing their proper part. This was a hard balance to find, and there were complaints from both sides. "Not enough choir singing", from the Lay Clerks. "Not enough congregational singing", from some of the congregataion. I felt that as long as both sides were complaining, we had probably got it about right. Anyway, gradually, gradually we made some changes that were necessary; and we managed to stay together on these, with Peter Marshall helping. I felt humbly proud of the service that we developed, and it was certainly popular.

Once a quarter we put on a full Choral Eucharist with an orchestra and a musical setting, such as Haydn's *Nelson Mass*. This was popular and drew a large number of new people into the Cathedral. I insisted that the balance of "word" and "sacrament" should be maintained and that a proper sermon should be preached on these occasions.

We maintained a high standard of preaching. Ronnie was a very good preacher indeed who could read his script without appearing to do so; and he always took infinite trouble to get it right. Peter was good – though sometimes intellectually above people's heads. Michael Glanville-Smith could also be very good; and I did my best. The preaching "chart" was always prepared by me; and this caused some annoyance in the Chapter. Fortunately the Cathedral Statutes played into my hands on this matter. They laid down that the Dean should preach on three Sunday mornings a month; and that he should invite the Bishop to preach at Christmas and Easter. If we had kept to this I would have done nearly all the preaching myself; so I told my colleagues that if they did not like my arrangements we could go back to the Statutes!

The most serious problem that I found on my arrival at Ripon was the state of the Cathedral building. With my archdeacon's eye I looked up at the parapets and saw that the stonework was crumbling. Surely it was not safe. Norman McDermid, my old friend who had rowed in the boat I coxed at St Edmund Hall (I had displayed a picture in the Chapter

House to prove it) was Archdeacon of Richmond; and he advised me to do something about it. The architect had been in office for forty years and was now unable to climb up to the roof; so he relied on the reports of Jack Yarker, the resident stonemason, who assured him that all was well. When I found Jack's phrases being repeated in the architect's report, I was suspicious; and asked my colleagues if I could have an independent report made of the fabric of the Cathedral. They too were sensitive to the problem; so they agreed and I invited Neil McFadyen, of Pershore St Andrew's fame, to make a report.

Neil's report was devastating. The stonework, he said, was in a serious state of disrepair and in a year or two would be dangerous. The reason for this was that for sixteen years no serious work had been done as all the stonemasons except Jack had been dismissed because of the shortage of funds. Now we would have to put things right. I had a grim meeting with Ronnie and David and we agreed that the architect must be asked to resign (after many years of loyal and splendid service to the Cathedral), a new architect appointed and an appeal started in order to raise the extra money that would be needed, as the expected cost would be far beyond the means of the capitular funds available.

Of course, I wanted to appoint Neil; but my colleagues were not going to let me do so too easily. All the formal procedures had to be carried out: consultation, advertising, short-listing and appointment. Our short-list consisted of extremely able architects, including the architects of other cathedrals. We had to consider vision, competence and administrative support. Neil, with a strong recommendation from the Master of Worcester College, Oxford, had all the required qualities; but he was clearly "my" candidate.

So there we were, the three of us (before the time of Peter Marshall), in my drawing-room trying to agree about whom to appoint out of the three left for consideration. I decided to say as little as possible and to let them take the initiative keeping my "but"s in reserve. Then the telephone rang in my study. I went to answer it leaving Ronnie and David to themselves. When I returned they were all smiles. 'We've decided to let you have your architect,' they said. 'Let's appoint Neil McFadyen.' So we did and it was one of the best appointments I have made in my life. He was superb: careful; creative; flexible; always seeking to please us and reflect our views, but strong enough to be firm when he felt the need to be so. He won the hearts of the local stonemasons – including Jack Yarker and the local Ripon experts, who regretted the retirement of the former architect ('Who does this new Dean think he is, sacking our architect?'). Years later a senior man in English Heritage said that in his opinion we had got the best cathedral architect in the field.

I decided that I must take responsiblity for the appeal myself. One and a half million pounds were going to be needed over the next few years, and it was essential that I should be fully involved in the process of raising the money. This was not my line! I hated asking for money and had the conviction that I should be the person offering, not the person asking, if I were to be a true promoter of the Gospel. But there was no alternative.

We started by approaching fundraising firms – and in doing this we were very fortunate. We came across Brigadier David Ryatt, who had worked for one of these firms and was now going to go freelance. Furthermore, he had recently managed an appeal for Fountains Abbey, so he knew the immediate neighbourhood and its fundraising potential; he wanted to employ his former secretary (Roz Waddington) to help him. She was a bright and delightful person who could win anybody's heart who had a heart to win, but was also swift and efficient in everything she did. The two of them made a formidable pair. He had a big personality and could mix it with anyone he met, and she made sure that everything was well organised and efficient. They were quite expensive – and we had to set them up in a properly equipped office; but the expense was justified.

I also invited Neil Balfour to be our Chairman: he in turn invited Prince Michael to be our President. Neil lived with his wife Serena and his large family, some of whom were at the Choir School, in Studley Royal House in Fountains Abbey. They became good friends to me and Juliet and to Ripon Cathedral. Neil was full of ideas and was prepared to twist people's arms to get them to work hard on our behalf. Very soon we had a committee of influential people and big prestigious events were being organised in Ripon, Harrogate, Richmond and Leeds. We were told firmly that we were not to organise coffee-mornings because people who attended them were inclined to think that they had thereby done enough. We needed hundreds, not pounds; and thousands were better still!

One such event was a glamorous fashion show, with top international designers, organised by Serena Balfour at Harewood House – too expensive for me even to attend, but Julie was taken as a guest of the Balfours. After the dinner and show, things such as a cruise round the world or a trip across Europe on the Orient Express or a life-long supply of nylons were auctioned for vast sums of very welcome money.

Another event was horse-trials, run by Michael Abrahams (a very generous friend and supporter) in the grounds of his estate. Each jump was sponsored by an industrial firm and the event ended with a sumptuous lunch at the end of which a spontaneous auction took place. 'If you had any sense,' said one of Michael's gruff friends, 'you would auction a picture of the Cathedral. Have you got one?' 'Well, actually, yes; and I have not hung it yet, so I will see what it can fetch.' The result was five thousand pounds! 'Are there any more of my possessions you would like me to sell off while I am about it?' asked Michael. 'My sheep or my cattle or my wife?' That event raised £35,000 and set us on our way.

I got some nasty letters later from the anti-fox-hunting lobby, but the event had nothing to do with fox-hunting: it was a way for the local rural community (plus some firms in Leeds) to show their generosity to the Cathedral at Ripon, which was sometimes known as "the Cathedral of the Dales".

On top of the many public activities I conducted my own personal campaign. I wrote an individual letter in my own hand to all the shops and companies in Ripon, but got a poor response. I think the feeling was that every Dean in turn makes some sort of "appeal": the Cathedral was always wanting money, and always would. Why should they bother? I once went to the home of a wealthy man in a village nearby with a house that looked over the fields to the Cathedral. 'Why should I give money for the Cathedral when I do not believe in God and do not believe in the things the Cathedral does or stands for?' 'Look out of your window, Sir,' said I. 'If that building were to fall down, wouldn't it spoil the view?' He graciously saw the point. Indeed he appreciated my visit. We talked of many things, religion and God included; I felt that in the end this (like other similar visits) was essentially a pastoral situation. The truth is that people's beliefs often follow their actions. When they show generosity, they begin to discover for themselves the generosity of God. As for the shops and businesses of Ripon I always followed my letter with a visit, sometimes drawing their fire, or just their irritation, but at least making contact, which is so important in the mission of the Church.

The first £100,000 or so came quite easily; but the middle part of the appeal was a hard slog. It was difficult to keep the momentum up, and by now we were working our way through the register of charities getting small donations from lots of remote charitable sources. The final sprint came when we were able to say that our target was within reach. By this time we had lost our original director and his team and I was doing the work myself with the help of a bright new secretary, Caroline Rigg.

The Cathedral building took a great deal of my time and attention when I was Dean of Ripon. Too much so? I thought the matter through and came to the conclusion that this was my responsibility: if I did nothing and concentrated my attention away from the Cathedral, the state of disrepair would get worse and the building would become dangerous and a shabby reflection on God and the spiritual dimension to life for which it stood. Neil McFadyen made us work our way round and over the top of the Cathedral, piece by piece. This included lots of dull but necessary matters such as installing safety harness for the masons up aloft, the building of fireproof partitions across the inside of the roof, and, of course, not dull but contentious, the cleaning of the stonework.

Even the Chapter was divided on the desirability of this, some feeling, with most of the citizens of Ripon, that people liked the comfortable, shabby blackness of their Cathedral. I did not agree; nor did the architect; and the fact that this dirty stone was also unsafe clinched the argument. To inspect it for myself I went up with Neil in a "cherry-picker" to look at it in detail. Besides that scary feat, we invested in an expensive process called photogrammatory by which every stone could be assessed and a decision made about whether or not to replace it. Also the world's leading expert in the matter of cleaning stone was invited to come from Belfast to inspect and give us advice, which was to clean the stone by force of water and sand, not by any harmful, chemical application.

Our plans were made public and I received some stiff letters of opposition. Who were we, the Dean and Chapter, ephemeral non-entities who would be gone tomorrow, to change the colour of Ripon's beloved Cathedral? I always replied as politely as I could and sometimes visited the person concerned. I was sad to find this combination of love for the Cathedral building and distrust for those who managed it; but as soon as the work was done and the Cathedral was restored to its pristine honey-gold glow, everyone was delighted and said that we should have done it years ago.

Two incidents occurred as a result of the scaffolding which enwrapped the building. One was the fact that it challenged the youth of Ripon into adventurous climbing feats aloft. What proper young man could resist the challenge? We were told that we could smear the scaffolding with a vile stuff that would get on the climbers' clothes and mark them for life; but I refused to allow this. So we contented ourselves with a pregnable fence and notices of dire warning to trespassers – enough, I hoped, to cover us in the case of accident.

Once I went out and confronted the miscreants, declining to chase them aloft, but waiting to catch them at the moment of their descent. On another occasion the young men had been drinking, and I found myself surrounded by three or four who abused and threatened me. I reasoned with them and promised to go and talk things through with one of them the next day. I did so, but he had given me a false address.

My family (son-in-law Les in particular) were furious with me when I got home after this encounter (it was on Boxing Day); and told me that I should never let myself be confronted with drunks who are always unreasonable and sometimes dangerous. Probably they were right.

The other occasion was on the eve of the Gulf War. One morning it was evident that the friendly Cathedral clock was not striking as it usually did, every quarter of an hour. All one could hear was a pained silence. So I asked Jack Yarker to have it put right. 'But, Mr Dean,' he reported when he had investigated the matter, 'the clapper has disappeared.' 'How can a clapper "disappear"?' I asked. 'Find it.' But no: it had "gorne". This strange fact became known to all who frequented the Cathedral, and after evensong one of the lay clerks came to see me. He was a policeman who was sometimes called in to the Cathedral Choir to sing tenor. Whenever I saw him being a policeman I could not bring myself to believe that he was also one of our tenors; and whenever I saw him becassocked and surpliced in the choir, I could not believe that he was really a policeman. But he was: both. Anyway he told me that one of his colleagues on duty in the market-place the night before had encountered two soldiers carting a heavily wrapped object across the square. Asked what it was they gave a humorous but evasive answer. Could it, he now wondered, have been our clapper? Definitely yes, I thought; so I rang the Commanding Officer of the Royal Engineers and told him the story of the lost clapper and the policeman/lay clerk's suspicions.

He immediately paraded all his men and asked who had done it; adding that they would stay on parade until he was told the truth. Two miscreants stepped forward – and lo! the clapper was found and returned. The CO wrote most apologetically to me and told me that the men concerned had now gone to the Gulf; but that they had been reprimanded and docked a day's pay. A week later I received letters of apology from the men, who told me that they had had a few drinks, and it being the night before their embarkation, had climbed the scaffolding into the tower as a "dare"; bringing back the clapper to prove that the deed had been done. I wrote an amused letter back wishing them luck in whatever part they were to play in that nasty war.

There was a lot to do to the inside of the Cathedral. Of paramount importance was the matter of heating. My first winter we had a service on Ash Wednesday at which all who were brave enough to attend nearly froze to death, because the heating used to be on at full blast for the weekends and then turned off for the week. Sunday's "full blast" was clearly not enough to make up for the days of cold; so we invested in a new system which provided a steady heat all the time and was more economical in terms of expense and the preservation of the fabric.

The second, more visible change was the erection of the new westward-facing altar and choir stalls at the east end of the nave. The Chapter agreed on this matter and a new altar with choir stalls around it was designed and constructed. The result was very satisfactory and met with only a flutter of opposition from the congregation. I am proud of it as the best central altar I know in any cathedral: it is flexible and easily changed for concerts; in its normal position it is at the focal point of the nave and yet matches the eastward orientation of the Cathedral.

We made a beautiful window out of some broken pieces of medieval glass, in memory of Dean Le Grice; and (my first achievement) we emptied the ancient crypt of the clutter of museum pieces, leaving it as empty as the "empty tomb of Christ" which is what St Wilfrid designed it to resemble. As for the treasures, we built a new treasury (helped by a handsome grant from the Goldsmith Company) in what had been a junk store in the north choir aisle; and we invited the parishes of the diocese to put their treasures into it for display. We had burglar-proof cases made for this purpose and the treasury became an important feature of the Cathedral. But where were we to put all that we needed to store, such as the extra chairs used on special occasions? Not having had a monastic foundation, we had no cloisters and literally no space for anything extra within the bounds of the building. Another problem was the staircase to the library. This had been designed by Gilbert Scott and must have been one of his worst constructions. It went straight up into the library at a dangerous angle with no break at all. Many elderly people refused to go into the library for books or the events that we held there, because of these daunting steps.

The first suggested solution to the storage problem (that of building an underground chamber) was rejected, because the archaeological authorities demanded an expensive exploratory dig first, and said that in the event of any archaeological remains being found, everything would have to be put back and permission for our store would be refused.

The architect solved the problems of storage and the staircase together by designing a new curved staircase which went up to a gallery and then on up to the library: under the gallery, was a space for storing. I was thrilled with this plan. But how to pay for it? It was too expenssive for our capitular funds; and it did not come under the terms of the appeal. I could only have it, I was told, if I could find the money for it.

So I invited Paul and Valaria Sykes to lunch. They were now living in Studley Royal. Paul was a Yorkshireman; blunt, direct, highly intelligent, outspoken in his opinions, forthright in calling spades spades and fools fools, with a strong love for his adopted city of Ripon and its surroundings. I had already written to greet him into the neighbourhood, having been introduced by Neil Balfour. I had officiated at the funeral of his father and the baptism of his grandson and was preparing Valaria for Confirmation. After lunch we took Paul on a tour of the Cathedral and showed him the new work, making him climb over the roof to see what was being done, round the clearstories, out to see "my head", which had been carved as a gargoyle over the library roof; and all the plans, of which he approved, and all the details, which he admired. We then showed him the plans for the staircase, gallery and store, and a beautifully drawn picture which would win much support for the scheme. There was a memorial to one of Paul's predecessors at Studley Royal which was to be restored and would be a central piece in the new gallery.

'But what do you want me to do about it?' he asked. 'Pay for it,' said I, getting used to his blunt way of talking. 'Oh,' said he, 'well, give me a month to think about it.' One month later he rang and asked me to visit him at Studley Royal. There he had his cheque book at the ready. 'How much did you say it was?' I reminded him; he wrote the cheque there and then. After the usual fuss of official procedures the work was put in hand and completed – in English oak.

The library was a problem. It was a beautiful room above the south choir aisle, messed up with a mixture of books, chairs, tables and junk. Neil had it cleaned, repaired and rearranged and we were able to make it into a genuine, well-stocked theological library with a volunteer librarian, the meticulous Joy Dean, and an excellent space for receptions, lectures, classes and meetings.

We also possessed some valuable and ancient books. Plans were already being made for these to be taken to the university library at Leeds where they could be properly stored and looked after. Critics of this plan accused my colleagues of bouncing me into accepting it before I knew what I was doing. Not so. As archdeacon I had had to insist on parishes making proper and expensive arrangements for storing their records and ancient documents, or else sending them to the county archives centre. When I asked the Verger to show me round that part of the Cathedral and asked him to open the safe in the library where these documents were stored, I was shocked at their condition and insisted that we sent them to Leeds where they would be properly looked after. In fact, they were named the Ripon Cathedral Collection and they remained on view for anyone interested in inspecting them; and the university was well pleased.

After five years the appeal ended with a service of thanksgiving attended by the Bishop, the Lord Lieutenant and Prince Michael. This took place on a day of heavy snow which blocked all the roads around, including the A1. The service was due to start but the Important People had not arrived. The Bishop, Juliet and I sat in our drawing-room getting messages from their car phones to the effect that they were "making slow progress" or they were "stuck again". Neil Balfour and the Lord Lieutenant at last arrived and we decided to start the service without Prince Michael. Halfway through, however, he arrived at the West Door. I halted the proceedings and asked everyone to turn around. We greeted him with a fanfare of trumpets and a cascade of triumphant chords on the organ. Everyone was pleased; especially as the Cathedral, as a result of the appeal, was looking its proud and gracious best.

A building cannot be "perfect", any more than an act of worship can be. But I did my best to leave the Cathedral in good repair and as beautiful and useful as I and my colleagues could make it. We were concerned with a process. Dean Edwin had contributed much in his sixteen years. I had tried to continue the good work, I pray, to the glory of God.

Chapter 26
Dean of Ripon

Soon after I came to Ripon the Bishop asked me to be the chairman of the Diocesan Board of Education. The Director of Education at that time was Ken Stott. He had risen through the ranks of church schools in the diocese and had ended up as the headteacher of St Aidan's, the C. of E. comprehensive school in Harrogate, a splendid school with a Sixth Form that we shared with the Roman Catholics. He knew the scene well and wherever we went on our tour of church schools the headteacher seemed to be someone he knew inside out from the past. And like those doyens of archdeacons, John Williams at Worcester, and now, I discovered, Norman McDermid at Ripon, he always knew the story from years ago. Ask them about some problem, and the answer would be, "Well now, back in 1946, just after the war, when so-and-so was Vicar and such-and-such his Curate (or headteacher, or school Ggvernor) there was a difficulty about ... Years later ... Then in about 1980 ... So you see the problem now is ... "

Not only did I meet the people, headteachers and vicars, on my tour of church schools, I also saw the diocese itself: the sweep and folds of the Dales, the stretches of moor, picturesque villages with their greens and pubs (Ken knew the best ones for eating in) and their churches; also the urban wastes of Leeds, the slums, Armley's dreadful jail, the posh leafy districts – and some excellent schools.

After Ken retired, I persuaded the Bishop to appoint Ian McKenzie as Director. He had been an administrator with the Leeds Board of Education, and so had inside knowledge of the system. This was as well because a difficult situation was blowing up in Leeds.

The Church of England was proud of its middle schools. But the Leeds Authority decided to change these schools so that they could establish a three-tier system with sixth form colleges. Unfortunately for us, the Church of England was particularly strong in its middle schools and our contribution to the system was much valued; but the Church did not have the clout to influence decisions as regards the overall organisation.

When the plans were announced there was fierce opposition from parishes that had church middle schools, and I was sent sacks of letters from those who objected plus those who were dragooned into writing: there was a suspicious conformity of phrases which reminded me of the Synoptic Gospels. The opposition, however, was obviously strong so I decided to organise public meetings at which officers from the Authority could explain their policy and people could air their grievances. We had three such meetings with me in the chair. People crowded the halls to be present – and shout at me! 'If you can't stand the heat, get out of the kitchen,' shouted one angry vicar. Juliet, who was present, was shocked. I found that I did not mind at all. Opposition from my churchwardens or PCC or my colleagues could trouble me; but this sort of fiery fury did not touch me at all because it was not personal. Perhaps that is how politicians manage. Anyway, I remained calm and gave measured answers; to the effect that the Church of England could not control the policy and make things happen in favour of ourselves and our schools. It was as simple as that.

But when it came down to particular schools, possibly closing some, changing others, bartering for these, negotiating the best way forward for those, I decided that the Bishop of the diocese himself must be brought in – not for the details but for the principles; so I arranged a meeting of the Board with the Bishop in attendance. I wrote a paper and put it before the Board. When the decisions were made, we published them and then arranged to have a debate in the Diocesan Synod. I had flu coming on as I addressed the Synod; but in the excitement and with the adrenalin coursing around, I gave them an exposition and a defence of our policy. In my reply to the debate I congratulated the vicar who had given me most trouble, and told the Synod that he had a brilliant school and was quite right to want to resist the change that was being proposed; but it was necessary now for us to look beyond our particular schools to see how we could serve the system as a whole, for our responsibility as an established church was to the nation, not just our own parishes. Was I right? 'Only the local is rea,l' said G.K. Chesterton. But right or not, we had no choice. The Synod accepted our policy, albeit sadly. I then retired to bed!

Soon after this I had a letter from the Archbishop of Canterbury inviting me to be chairman of the Council for the Care of Churches. I went to see Bishop David, who said, 'Of course you must: but you'll have to give up the Board of Education.'

So much for my efforts to cover the diocese. Apart from preaching engagements, which came thick and fast, I rarely escaped from the local scene. Invitations to preach always contained the hazard of losing one's way. Once I was nearly at a church in Leeds for a nine-thirty Eucharist when I came head on with a marathon run and was diverted by the police. Although I could see the church's steeple, I could not find my way to it until I persuaded a boy on his paper-round to guide me on his bicycle (an adventure I turned into a sermon on some later occasion)!

The Vicar of Leeds was Canon John Richardson. He gave me a tour of Leeds and introduced me to the Mayor, who told me of his ambition to make Leeds into a centre of culture, now that the woollen mills were things of the past. "Culture" included football and cricket as well as theatre, art and opera.

Indeed, cricket, I discovered, was a serious subject in Yorkshire. Little jokes and pleasantries about Boycott or the lowly position of the county cricket team were met in stony silence. Julie and I were introduced to Geoffrey Boycott and Freddie Truman at Paul Sykes's house. Truman also came to give away the prizes at a raffle we organised at the annual race-meeting put on for the benefit of the Cathedral Appeal. I took him and his wife to dinner. He did not bet; but seemed to know all about it and taught me some of the terms (such as BF – beaten favourite). When someone approached and began to berate the performance of the English test team, Freddie went for him and asked him if he thought he could do better than they were doing:

would he care to face the West Indian fast bowlers? And did he imagine that the players were not all doing their best?

Canon Richardson persuaded me to speak at the annual meeting of a society devoted to giving the deprived children of Leeds a holiday. I did my best; they rewarded me by inviting Julie and me to join them on their next visit to the children's holiday-home by the seaside. We accepted and joined them and some city dignitories for a journey to the coast on a day of unremitting rain. Julie and I were dressed casually, as for a day by the sea. This was a mistake for the committee members were dressed up in suits and (the ladies) hats. We also took a picnic lunch to eat in the coach. This was also a mistake for at our stops in both directions we were expected to join the members in a slap-up meal. The children at the home were a delight. A little boy of eight was put in charge of Julie and me to show us round the home. With solemn importance he showed us where he kept his toothbrush – in a slot marked with his name. (This proved a point made by the inspectors who once came to the Choir School. Children like to have their own bits of space.)

One of the most enjoyable features of life at Ripon for me, its Dean, was the Cathedral music, the Choir and the Choir School. Music of great complexity and profound beauty was offered to God every day in the Cathedral, and three times on Sundays, in the course of our regular worship. I could hardly believe my luck – and thank God enough – for the fact that it was my duty to join in this worship and to have considerable responsibility for it. The justification for "cathedral music", which I defend vigorously in *The Food of Love*, is that the best we can devise should be offered to God. Those who are present but do not join in the performance of the music, join in the worship by positive listening and offering what they hear in prayer to God. The Choir sees to the musical excellence. The rest of us make it an act of worship. This I tried to do myself, and I had the additional responsibility of reading the New Testament lesson and sometimes leading the prayers. Occasionally, in the absence of the Precentor, I sang the priest's part myself, having done so in my Minor Canon days at Ely.

For the first nine years everything to do with the choir was blissful. Ron Perrin, the Director of Music and Master of the Choristers, had his faults as a conductor, but he did not lack inspiration. Once at a Three Cathedral Choirs concert in Durham Cathedral, he conducted a piece by Monteverdi with blazing inspiration that lifted the choirs and the huge audience far above the expected level of enthusiasm. On another occasion he conducted the same combination of choirs in Ripon Cathedral, when they performed a motet written by Thomas Tallis *(Spem in Alium numquam habui)* for forty voices. Ron held them together, each a colourful thread in a rich tapestry of sound, a triumph for his inspiration and control. He was also an excellent composer; composing a vibrant piano quintet and a particularly effective *Magnificat* which combines the spontaneous joy and the moral demands of that poignant New Testament canticle.

My favourite occasion was *The Ceremony of Carols* by Benjamin Britten, performed by the choristers and a harpist every year on the Sunday before Christmas, after evensong. It started in darkness: then the choristers could be heard in the distance as they processed into the Cathedral singing their haunting plain-song melody. They took their place in candlelight in a half-circle round the conductor, with the harp in the middle, and began the utterly beautiful set of carols: emphatic and triumphant, hushed and sad, searing solos from the best boys of the year, a wild and furious three-part canon. *The Ceremony of Carols* made one feel the pain and joy, the beautiful, harsh reality of the birth of Jesus. I always wept. At the end the boys with their candles processed out and away to the same plain-song tune, fading in the distance.

After the *Ceremony* the lay Clerks and other musicians came for their Christmas drinks and supper and a musical jolly, as we got them round the piano to play (several on the piano at a time) and sing. They wore aggressive bow-ties on this occasion: so I used to put one on myself, just to show them!

I managed to persuade the Choir, in my early days in office, to record my Eucharist which I had written for the Rite A service, and which we had performed regularly at Dodderhill. Neil Richardson (OL and professional composer) had "realised" it, improving the harmony and writing the organ accompaniment. I had also written some carols and canticles. The men were never nice about my compositions, perhaps for the reason (as Peter Marshall explained to me: he was equally sour) that by writing music I was stepping out of my proper role as Dean! Or perhaps because the music was not as good as I thought it was. But the fact is that the boys liked it and told me so when they need not have done; the congregation took to it when we needed a setting for congregation and choir; and Ronald Perrin twice performed my carols at the Christmas carol service. He told me that he was not trying to please me, but they fitted his scheme of keys – a mystery I have never understood. One of my carols, written for three flutes, piano and choir, was performed by the grammar school at their Christmas concert; another was performed by the College of Education and was used in parishes around Ripon, being taken to them by the music students as part of their practical experience. Another was written for the primary school – and they recorded it, with a jazzy accompaniment written by Robert Lambie. But my moment of glory came when the BBC did a series of programmes on music for the Eucharist. For the last one they asked for newly composed music to be submitted; they chose Ronald Perrin's *Gloria* (for choir) and my *Creed* (congregation and choir). I have their recording on tape.

My favourite carol was written for the secondary modern school's carol concert, but they did not perform it and I have never heard it. It consisted of a testy dialogue between the angels and the shepherds, who did not at all want to leave their sheep, although the angels promised to look after them. Angela tells me that the modal tune (sung fast) is difficult for children to get hold of. I was also asked to write a canticle for three unaccompanied voices for the College of Education to be sung at their end of year Eucharist. As I was giving Communion while they performed it, I was not able to listen; and as they forgot to record it, I have never heard it sung. Kerry Beaumont did not perform it with the choristers, so perhaps it "doesn't work"! It's very sad, but I like it so much that I am going to have another go at it when – if ever – I finish writing these memoirs. When I left Ripon the Choir gave me a tape of all my music that they performed, including a Te Deum for two (treble) voices, with a difficult organ part added by Philip Wilby, who taught composition at Leeds University.

"My music", however, even to me, was only a very small part of the musical scene at Ripon. There were regular concerts and visiting artists such as Janet Baker, Jennifer Bates (playing Messaien: she sent me a tape every Christmas!), Heather Harper, Rosalind Runcie, James Bowman and Richard Baker, who gave an amusing and informative lecture for the appeal, and wrote the foreword to *The Food of Love*. We also had the Vienna Boys' Choir – who made me cross because of the huge audience who came to drool over them, when our boys sang just as well, but in a different style. The VBC were older and sang fruitily and throatily; and looked bored stiff.

We also had a choir of Russian girls, tightly disciplined and not permitted by their draconian lady director to enjoy the music or the occasion; a deep-throated choir of men from the Ukraine; the BBC Northern Orchestra; Opera North; the Orchestra Camerata; and brass bands, which are very popular in the north of England. We once had a brass band competition in the Cathedral, at which "my" band competed. This was the Ripon City Band. I was its President and used to go and drink beer with them after their rehearsals: more of them later.

Our own choir gave many concerts. There was the annual Three Choirs of Ripon, Durham and York, performing at Ripon once in three years; and the other Three Choirs: Ripon, Wakefield and Leeds Parish Church, which also did its triannual round. We had several television occasions with one Midnight Mass, *Songs of Praise* and ITV's *Allelujah*, starring Harry Secombe, who had us all to a jolly lunch in the Old Deanery Restaurant.

They have changed *Songs of Praise*. When we did it at Lancing in the 1960s I wrote and compèred it, and its aim was to draw people into the worship of God. Now they centre it on local interests and individual experiences. This gives it a "human" interest, but it is less focused and possibly less uplifting. The producer decided (at my suggestion: this was in Advent) to do one such programme by candlelight. But every time they stopped to reorganise their resources or do something again, the candles went on burning. This spoilt the sequence, and there was nothing they could do about it except change all the burnt candles for new ones that were of the same height as before. The producer told me afterwards that he would never again do a show by candlelight. I thought, 'Serves you right for keeping me waiting so long, just to say the Blessing at the end!'

*   *   *

353

I used to visit Ronald Perrin regularly to talk over policy and plans: but this was unrewarding. He could not have been nicer; but he rarely went through with what we had decided. The lay clerks became very critical of Ronald Perrin, his methods and his state of mind: they kept warning me that "things could not go on like this". There was a row over a visit the Choir paid to Scotland at which Ron was said to have behaved badly; and one day the men refused to sing at Sunday evensong. So the boys sang alone; and that was the climax of a sequence of events that led to Ronald Perrin resigning and being appointed Organiste Titulaire.

Peter Marshall and I had a difficult interview with him and his lady solicitor, who began by saying that they regarded my letter to Mr Perrin as "constructive dismissal" and that they intended to sue the Dean and Chapter for large damages. When she heard the whole story, however, she asked if she and her client could go away and consult. After half an hour they returned and agreed to our terms.

When all was decided I rang up Kerry Beaumont, who was then organist of St David's, and invited him to become our Musical Director and Master of the Choristers. He had been a chorister and a lay clerk himself, so he was well known and liked by the lay clerks and much respected for his formidable musicianship. So one day after evensong, I went down into the choir vestry, told the boys to skedaddle, and told the men about Ron Perrin's resignation and new appontment, and the fact that we had invited Kerry Beaumont to be the new Director of Music – all in one sentence! – to their amazement and the scotching of rumours and speculation about who should follow Ron. Ron himself went on playing the organ in the Cathedral whenever he wanted to and seemed strangely content with the new situation.

So Kerry came amongst us with Lesley his wife and two children, Jesse, who won the top musical scholarship to Eton, and Victoria who became a star in the Girls' Choir when it was eventually formed. Kerry was a great success: a superb organist, brilliant improviser who had won an international competition at St Alban's Cathedral, a quiet but excellent conductor, and very good with the boys. I attended one of his rehearsals and was amazed at how quickly he could teach them complicated music, treating them as young professionals, all in it together for the love of the music and, indeed, the worship of God, for he was a devout Christian. The result was an immediate raising of morale and an improvement in the standard of singing; without, perhaps, the moments of dazzling inspiration that Ronald Perrin could sometimes achieve.

The eighteen choristers had scholarships in the Cathedral Choir School. I was the Chairman of the Governors and bore a great deal of responsibility – and derived much satisfaction – from the school. When I talked to the accountant at the beginning of my time at Ripon, he told me gloomily that the school would have to close in two years if it did not pick up in numbers. It had a young headmaster whom Dean Edwin had recently appointed, but this was his first post. He found the children easy to manage, but the staff and the parents difficult. We started off with a crisis. Some parents came to me to report the misdemeanours of one of the staff. I arranged an enquiry, and with the almost total support of the governors, dismissed this particular person, who had been warned before and was obviously a worry. "Almost" because the two Canons, as members of the Board of Governors, refused to back me. In fact they both resigned! This shattered but did not deter me. It was foolish to grumble against "parent power" in a private school, which depends upon the goodwill of the parents who pay the fees; and it was irrelevant to say that this man's dismissal would weaken the choir. His offence, thrice repeated, was too bad to tolerate; his dismissal (which I delivered immediately after the meeting, in front of his weeping wife) cleared the air and improved the atmosphere in the school. A year or two later he was divorced and his wife married again into the close Cathedral circle, to everyone's delight. That was crisis number one.

Crisis number two was much worse. For reasons that were good, but not generally known, the headmaster's wife said that she would not be returning to school and after much hair-tearing I told the headmaster that he must resign and leave. I had consulted the headmaster of Sedburgh, a Choir School governor, who agreed to meet me on a certain bridge halfway between Sedburgh and Ripon. I told him the story and his advice was that the headmaster would have to go; but in order to avert a crisis with a head-less school beginning a new school year, he recommended one of his retiring housemasters, Ian MacDougal, to be appointed acting headmaster until we could make a permanent appointment. I explained what I could of the situation to the staff and they, though much shaken, rallied round. We met the parents together as they brought their children for the first day of term and I handed them a written statement, promising that all would be well. The temporary head then turned up with his wife and two huge dogs, who were extremely popular. I am sure that it was the dogs who persuaded everybody that all would be well. As indeed it was because, although he had no experience of prep-schools, he made everyone feel that things were safe in his hands.

We then had to set about appointing a new headmaster. Unfortunately the first short-list failed to produce anyone with the experience and creativity to save the school, so I rang Richard Moore, who had applied and had then withdrawn his application. He was already a headmaster. He wanted a change, but was hesitant about coming so far north. We saw at once that here was the right man for the post. He had a delightful wife, Sheila, and Julie and I sat far into the night persuading them that life does go on in the north and that Ripon with its Cathedral and the Yorkshire moors on the doorstep was a superb place to be. So they agreed to come, and in my time the Choir School never looked back. In addition to his personal qualities and his knowledge of schools Richard and Sheila came to love the Cathedral, its music and its worship; and they became close friends to us both.

When I had been Chaplain at Ely, the Dean himself insisted on preparing the choristers for Confirmation. They worshipped alongside him every day, he explained; so he wanted to share with them his love and understanding of Christianity. I now decided to do the same for the same reasons. I knew how choristers, singing the services every day, could be hardened against Christianity. I felt that they needed to be taught about it and Confirmed, as soon as they were ready. It was difficult to fit my busy life into their tight timetable; but the headmaster lent me his sitting room (I refused the offer of his study!) and was prepared to let the boys off the odd French lesson; so we managed it.

The Confirmations took place on Easter Sunday mornings, at crack of dawn, as part of the Easter ceremonies and Eucharist. We included a Baptism whenever possible, this being in line with the custom of the early Church in catacomb days. This gave them an experience never to be forgotten, but it was hard work for all of us, especially me, who had to fit in their individual preparation with all the other joyful activities of Easter. The parents and godparents too were rather dismayed at having the service so early in the morning and for my last two years we abandoned the scheme. But we kept to the joyful Choir Easter Breakfast that had been such an important part of the proceedings.

Did we work the choristers too hard? Addressing a gathering of choir school Heads at Ripon, Ted Maidment, once a valued colleague at Lancing, now Headmaster of Shrewsbury, said that in his experience ex-choristers nearly always did well at school, often outshining their contemporaries. The discipline of singing in a top-class choir, which demanded individual excellence and a strong sense of interdependence, plus the ability to "perform" on the occasion, plus the experience of the music itself and the use of the English language in the daily recitation of the psalms, plus the fact that by the end of their time they could read music as easily as you and I can read the newspaper: all this together was brilliant training and made for excellent education.

I once put it to a boy after the leaving ceremony after their "Last Evensong". This was an occasion I invented. I used to make a speech and mention the leaving boys' individual contributions and excellence, sometimes poking fun at their particular quirks. There was Roly, very proud in his Old Choristers' tie, but quite ready to be leaving. 'Roly,' I said, 'tell me honestly, did we put too much on you – for instance at Christmas and Easter?' Pause for thought. What would he come out with? Would he tell the truth? Then a "words-can't-express-it" shrug of the shoulders. 'Magical,' he said.

We had a family of three Roman Catholic boys in the Choir, spread over six years. The oldest, Ralph, began to take the sacrament at the Sunday Eucharists. 'Ought you to, Ralph?' I asked him. '" don't see why not,' said Ralph, 'I do at home.' 'Yes, but that is when, you are in you own church. I think you had better clear this with your parents and your priest.' The message came back. 'Yes, certainly. If he is in an Anglican Choir in an Anglican cathedral he should receive Communion along with the rest.' Hurrah for such ecumenical understanding. 'But, Ralph," I said. "The others have been through the Confirmation classes. Would you like to join them next time round?' 'Oo yes, please,' said Ralph, a glutton for punishment. But he sensibly added the condition, having discussed it with his parents, that I should be honest and tell him the differences between the Anglican and the Roman beliefs and customs as they occurred. Which I did. He was a good member of the class, with a better grasp of Christianity than his contemporaries. He also had a strong influence on them, telling them straight that they ought to go to confession! 'It won't do you any harm,' he chortled. 'Indeed, you could do with it.' However, as we drew near to the occasion of the Confirmation itself, I began to wonder what would we do with Ralph. I consulted the Bishop: he agreed to *affirm* Ralph when he *confirmed* the others. This fitted in very well, especially as on the same occasion I was preparing a lady from the Lutheran Church, who was eager to be instructed in Anglican ways, but did not want it to be thought that she was not already a confirmed Christian. Ralph's brothers followed suit when they came of age; except the third boy, Tudor, who insisted on being "properly" confirmed. I told them all that from now on they were recognised members of both Roman Catholic and Anglican churches; and that whenever they were in one, they were to think and speak kindly about the other. They were to be human bridges.

Although we had a "pastoral canon", Ronnie McFadden, until he retired, then Michael Glanville-Smith, this did not exclude me from parish and pastoral affairs. As the "incumbent" I used to visit whenever I could. Several people, including priests, came to me for counselling and confession. I always felt that I got more back from those I saw in a pastoral situation than I gave out to them. If ever I were in the dumps, Julie would say, 'For heaven's sake, go out visiting.' I did and always came home refreshed.

Nothing would stop me from teaching. During my first Lent I gave a course on "Christianity" as I had given to the combined Churches at Droitwich. The reception, however, was different. At Droitwich there were loud alleluias to my open, intellectual, forward-looking, critical, David Jenkins-like approach (but he was not then a bishop); the only serious opposition came from a strong fundamentalist who believed in the devil and hell-fire, and accused me of "not taking evil seriously" because I made the classical claim that ultimately evil is a negative. True, it accumulates to become something horribly positive; but fundamentally it is the denial of God's will. It is the darkness where there should be light, hatred where there should be love, chaos where there should be order.

At Ripon, however, attitudes were more old fashioned. One elderly and bemused member of the congregation said to me afterwards that David Jenkins (he was by now the Bishop of Durham) was surely doing great damage by shaking the traditional faith of Christian people. I said that Bishop Jenkins was giving Christianity back to thousands of intelligent people who had been deterred from faith by obscurantism and a silly insistence on "believing five impossible things before breakfast". Anyway, my talks and the discussions that followed were taped, spread around, much discussed and generally appreciated.

I also took study groups in my drawing-room made up of people who were prepared to study St John's gospel or one of St Paul's letters or one of the Creeds. I enjoyed these classes, and so I believe did they. (Julie will testify because she attended most of them.) I also took adult Confirmation classes, often consisting of couples whom I had previously prepared for marriage. These were successful in enlarging the congregation and making, for me and Julie, some lasting friendships.

Once a young girl from the grammar school (Christine) turned up at my St John's Gospel group, lowering the average age by about fifty! 'Who are you?' I asked her afterwards. 'I'm Christine,' she said, 'and I am going to do A-level Divinity at school. But I do not think that the Chaplain knows much about the subject.' 'Would you like me to help?' 'Definitely, yes.' So I gave her essays to write and books to read and particular subjects to prepare: to my delight, and the amazement of the school, she got an A. She became one of our first girl servers in the Cathedral. Later she went to Oxford to read a branch of anthropology, and is now, after many false starts, studying medicine. She still writes to Julie and me now and again.

Some of my classes of married couples were disappointing in terms of "cathedral-going"; but the members were responsive at the time and I believe enriched at a deep level of their lives by what they learnt of themselves and one another and what they learnt about the habit of prayer, which is relating life to God. I have been better at teaching "prayer" than I have been at teaching "going to church". One couple worked as chef and assistant chef in a hotel. They told me that in no way was it possible to attend worship regularly and together. Another was very honest. They loved the classes, they said. Why hadn't someone told them all this before? But the "culture" (my word, not theirs) of the Cathedral "just isn't us". It made me realise that the alienation of many people from Christianity is not intellectual or religious, but cultural. There were some from the groups who became seriously committed members of the congregation; but their background was different, so they took easily to the dignity of Cathedral worship and its glorious music.

When George Carey, the Archbishop of Canterbury, came to Ripon to spend a weekend in the diocese he preached in the Cathedral and came to lunch with us afterwards – very late because he spent ages talking to individuals after the service. One of the things he said in his address was that when we have Lent courses we should not hold them in the church: we should take them out into the "market-place", that is, some convenient, secular meeting place. So, always ready to follow my archbishop's ideas, I asked Bishop David Jenkins to come to give a Lent course, and arranged for this to take place in the Town Hall. David had now retired, and we gave his lectures a great deal of publicity. On the first occasion he came to supper with us before the lecture and then we walked to the Town Hall together, only to find it seething with people who were queueing but could not get in. So I said, 'All right, we'll go back to the Cathedral,' and sent a messenger ahead to prepare the Verger for the invasion. When everyone had settled down in the nave, David gave the first of his superb lectures and then answered questions with patience and insight. On his third visit he came early so that he could go with me into the country and meet a bed-ridden doctor who had told me that David Jenkins was the only kind of Christian apologist he could listen to; and oh how he would like to meet him. So I arranged it. David actually said very little to him: this was no occasion for argument or discussion: but he gave him a Blessing.

That particular doctor (he died soon afterwards) was deeply moved and grateful. The defence of Bishop Jenkins against the so-called committed Christians who claim to abhor him, is that he is one of the most holy and loving people you could meet. "By their fruits you shall know them."

In the course of answering a question after that evening's talk, David became extremely emotional and stopped the proceedings suddenly, leaving us all to wonder what was up. The next week he apologised. 'That question,' he said, 'opened up a train of thought and new insights which I had never had before. I was so moved that I could not go on. This is the point …'

Of course, there was a lot of personal work to be done with and alongside those I worked with. We had regular and formal Chapter meetings and twice a year we used to spend a day together in the sitting-room of the Sportman's Arms, some miles from Ripon, with a good lunch and much talk. On these occasions we would hammer out major matters of policy and direction and try to come to one mind. We did not take minutes, and the practice was to bring any decisions that we made to a later Chapter meeting to be formally ratified. This gave us a chance for second thoughts.

Canon Ronnie McFadden was someone I learnt to love and appreciate for his spirituality and professionalism. In a way he was the "ideal priest", an assiduous listener and a wise confessor, trained to be such in the hard school of Johannesburg. David Ford had an easy friendliness, which made him good company. Michael Glanville-Smith was an old friend from Worcester days whom I had persuaded to come to be our pastoral canon when Ronnie retired through ill health. Sometimes I felt that I had landed Michael in it! But Juliet and I loved him and his family. Michael always had a joke on his lips, and sometimes these went awry. Someone once said to me, 'I don't like this new canon of yours, Dean.' 'Oh, Peter, why not?' 'Well, you see,' he said, deadly earnest in his leathery Yorkshire voice, 'I haven't got a sense of humour.'

Peter Marshall was the "training officer" of the clergy for the whole diocese; and this, he decided, included me. I sometimes had to resist this! But he was most helpful when it came to planning my "sabbatical", during which I not only wrote the first draft of *The Food of Love* (at Rosses Point in Ireland) but also managed some genuine holiday and a Retreat – with a fresh study of St Luke's Gospel. It included a trip to the Holy Land. Peter was cleverer than all of us and was a rock of strength when it came to really difficult matters. I relied on him a lot, but he needed to be in charge, and I did my best to get him a senior appointment.

There were two vergers at Ripon, and for our first view of the Cathedral Juliet and I were taken round by them. Dr Bill Foster, the Senior Verger took me; George Thorpe took Juliet. Dr Foster was a scientist by training. He had a first-class degree in chemistry, and had then come out of the greedy world of industry to what he thought would be the sheltered harbour of the Church of England. I am afraid that he may have been disillusioned and his job as Senior Verger of Ripon Cathedral turned out to be no sinecure. But he was very good at it, being meticulous in his administration and acquiring an encyclopaedic knowledge of the Cathedral, its history and its architecture.

If Dr Foster guided you round the Cathedral, he would tell you the facts: the dates and the way the different parts of the building were constructed into one another as disasters and new construction followed one another century after century; a fascinating story, with still much to be discovered. George, on the other hand, liked to tell the story: of kings, archbishops, deans, canons, heroes and rascals. Were some of his stories a little tall, somewhat embellished in the course of constant repitition? No doubt: but they gave people the essence of the Cathedral and its life down the ages; and, indeed, because of George's warmth and good humour (his laughter at his own jokes would reverberate round the echoey vaults of the Cathedral) people would feel something of the holiness and wonder that was all around them. I once preached a sermon about the Bible, using the complementariness of Bill and George as an illustration: to show that the Bible needs to be studied scientifically, with careful analysis of its sources and texts, but also in love, so that the Spirit of Christ, which is at its centre, can be found and worshipped.

Bill found it difficult to accept some of the changes we proposed making to the structure and fabric, although he spoke with relish about changes that had been made in the past. Nevertheless, his combination of Christian devotion and high intelligence was good for us all. George sometimes made blunders, but he too was a cheerful, hard-working member of the Cathedral staff.

In the course of time both vergers retired and were replaced by Gill Steer, who I claim to be the first woman Senior Verger in any cathedral in England. She was a trained theologian and came about halfway in disposition between Bill and George. She was meticulous, knowledgeable and totally professional, unlikely to make mistakes. To assist her we appointed Alastair Betts, the son of a local vicar, as Assistant Verger. At first Gill thought that he was too young. How would he cope with all the people and the obstreperous youths who occasionally came marauding in? Answer: very well indeed. He could speak their language and was physically strong enough to deter them when necessary. He was also sensitive to people's particular needs. This old lady always needed to be escorted up the aisle and helped up the steps: this man liked to have a chair placed just so: Canon "So-and-so" liked ... the Dean was fussy about ... Both Gill and he were excellent during services, always ready to save a situation, such as the time when I was so horrified at what a Muslim speaker was saying at the lectern that I was thinking of stopping and contradicting him. But Alastair came up to me, bowed low, and said in a whisper, 'Don't worry, Mr Dean. The microphone is off and no one can hear what it is he is saying.'

This story should be told in full. The occasion was an important anniversary service of thanksgiving that the Masons wanted to have in the Cathedral. Two other cathedrals in the north had turned them down; but I agreed to have it. The service would be "Anglican evensong", I said, according to the Book of Common Prayer; and I would preach. But could there be additions? Of course, prayers and thanksgivings for the present and the past. Could a Hindu and a Muslim Mason (both from Leeds) be allowed to read something from their scriptures? I examined the passages proposed and, finding nothing that would offend a Christian in them, said, 'Yes,' The Hindu, when it came to the point, did his bit exactly as promised. But not so the Muslim. 'I am going to sing to you from the Koran,' said the Mullah. '"Sing", because these words are too sacred to recite in the spoken voice.' So sing he did: and soon the choir boys were having to call on all their discipline (prompted by my fiercest scowls) not to giggle. Then he said, 'And now I will translate these words.' Whereupon he began on a passage about Jesus that was not acceptable in a Christian cathedral. But, as already recounted, the combination of his accent and the lack of microphone ensured (and I asked people afterwards) that his words were not understood by anyone.

I preached a sermon about Solomon and the process of "building", a process which (witness the temple: witness our cathedral) never stops; so the Masonic purpose now should be to "build" what is best for society. This sermon was printed in the Masonic magazine. At the reception afterwards, everyone seemed pleased.

The organiser (a churchwarden in his own parish church) was delighted but embarrassed by the unscripted contribution from Islam. There were some nasty letters written to me afterwards about allowing the service to take place. But why shouldn't we have "evensong" and, in God's world, is there anyone that we should not pray for? Letters of complaint were also sent to the Bishop who asked me for a complete account of what had happened. I told him and even sent him my sermon. But he never made any comment, which was rather discouraging: I never knew whether he supported me or not.

Golf was important to me at Ripon, even though I only played a few times a year. The friends I played with included Bill Emerson, who was the kindest and politest person I have ever known. 'Oh, good shot, Mr Dean,' he would exclaim as my ball soared into the air and swerved away to the right. 'Rubbish, Bill: look where it's gone.' 'Well, perhaps it should have been a little bit more to the left.' Another doughty opponent was George Thorpe, who came into his own on the golf course, though he had a reputation for being an over-handicapped "bandit". Out on the course he would tell everyone about the Cathedral; and in the Cathedral, leading me out of the vestry into a procession, he would turn and whisper, 'Yesterday I got a three at the fourth, Mr Dean.' We had an annual match of "The Cathedral" against the club. I would procure the service of some good players from diocesan clergy and a stonemason who played from scratch and used to partner me! The day would end with an excellent dinner and speeches. I also gave a speech at the annual Yorskshsire Golf Captains' Dinner (they were all dressed in red). I regaled them with stories from P.G. Wodehouse, telling them as if they were true and quoting him as a learned and moral authority on golf.

I did all I could to serve the city of Ripon. Julie and I went to dinner with our first Mayor, John McGrath and his wife; we remained on good terms with subsequent mayors and the members of the council. One such member asked me to marry him to his partner, with whom he had been living for years, and then prepare them both for Confirmation. 'Why?' I couldn't help asking. 'Because I want to be Mayor,' he answered, unashamed. Most motives are mixed: who wants to be judged by their basest ones? Jim had been beyond death's door in a motor accident, and he had a sublime faith in the all-forgiving love of God whom he had met and would meet again in the after-life. My job was not to condemn his motive but to enrich the lives of him and his family (I also prepared his daughter for Confirmation and married her to her farmer husband) with the sense of forgiveness and purpose that the Gospel brings.

I got myself involved in the politics of the cottage hospital, making a strong speech at an open meeting; and the two secondary schools. Edwin Le Grice had already been sacked from the governing body of the grammar school because of his left-wing attitudes; and I was never invited to join, even though the staff asked that I should be. However, I became a governor and vice-chairman of the secondary modern school; I wrote and spoke in favour of the two schools being run together as one comprehensive school. As things were the two schools stood on opposite sides of the same road (pupils being supposed to keep to their own side), each with special resources that could have been shared to their mutual benefit, but kept apart by a system which divided Ripon disastrously. But there were many grammar school old boys who resisted all change to this divisive arrangement.

In some years I was the Mayor's Chaplain and this gave me the opportunity to make myself acquainted with the local Council and Councillors, some of whom became our friends. Certainly one of the proudest moments of my professional life was when the Mayor and Council invited the Dean and Chapter to accept the "Freedom of the City of Ripon", an honour we were to share with the Regiment who were the only other "freemen". We gladly accepted, and organised a massive occasion in the Cathedral at which a concert was performed by our Choir and other local musical groups; the hornblower blew his horn; the Mayor (Connie Birkinshaw) made a flattering speech; I replied with a gracious "Thank you"; gifts were given both ways; and on behalf of the Chapter I was presented with a plaque to mark the occasion. In my speech I asked what privileges could we actually exercise? The Army could march through the streets with bayonets drawn, banners flying and trumpets blaring. We did not want to do that. But could I park my car where I liked? Alas no, I was told; but we would be allowed (by ancient tradition) to set up a stall in the market-place on Saturday mornings.

One exciting event, one generous gift, one nasty personal experience and one (to other people) amusing one, before I describe my last months at Ripon.

I had made a good relationship with the RAF squadron at Dishforth. Sadly, the squadron was to be disbanded and they asked if they could have a farewell service and a ceremonial placing of their colours in the Cathedral before this happened. Yes, of course: but they wanted a particularly inconvenient Sunday, the Sunday on which the Archbishop of Canterbury was coming to celebrate and preach. I said, 'All right: but it will have to be a nine o'clock service in order to make way for the Archbishop's Eucharist at eleven.' This meant tight timing and a strain on everyone. However, it happened and the Cathedral was full that morning for two very different services – each with the Choir and full ceremonial.

A week later I had a telephone call from the RAF station. Would I like (a) to go with Juliet to their farewell dinner? Yes, delighted; and we went. The occasion was graced by a very senior officer who lambasted the government for its ill-thought-out defence strategy. After the dinner Julie and I slipped away leaving the officers to dance on the tables and be as riotous as they liked.

The other offer (b) was: would I like to go for a flight in a Tornado? Would I not! The day was fixed. I spent the morning having an exhaustive medical examination; then, after a briefing session, I was strapped into the navigator's seat behind the pilot (with all the charts in front of me) and up we shot. Julie was present at the briefing session and was then taken to a simulating machine where she was shown the controls and given a flying experience. Meanwhile, I was up in the stratosphere. We had another Tornado in company, so I could take pictures of it with my video camera. At one point the weightless camera stood up without my holding it. We flew northwards to Scotland and then came down to ground level to roar along Loch Ness. After that we turned sharply upwards and accelerated incredibly, leaping upwards and leaving my stomach behind. I was actually feeling very rough at this time, but the pilot, who was on the intercom, knew that I was all right. He could hear me panting, but I refused to be sick. Up and up we went, over the North Sea then back to Ripon.

When we were about to land, the sky cleared, so we took off again in order to circle round the city and have a look at it with the tiny Cathedral there in the middle, and faces, I am sure, looking up; the scene dominated by the race-course and its lake, bigger than the rest of Ripon put together. On landing I felt shocked and they said (having foreseen this), 'I expect you would like Juliet to drive you home,' which she did. We went up into the hills to sit peacefully and recover from this exhilarating experience.

The generous gift was a holiday every year in Majorca. Malcolm Beer was an occasional and honorary lay clerk. He and Joan owned an apartment near Palma, and they invited Juliet and me to use it for a fortnight every year after Christmas. This we most gratefully did, spending the first few days basking in the sun on the balcony overlooking the sea, letting the sun, sea and champagne-air assuage our tiredness. Then we would explore the island by bus or hired car, and return to Ripon much refreshed.

The nasty incident happened when my accountant rang me to say that the Inland Revenue had challenged my return and accused me of not declaring my full income: this for a couple of years back. Hadn't I? I simply could not remember all the facts, so I buried myself in my old diary and all that I had of the accounts for that year, and could only find one trivial matter that might be held against me. The accountant clucked, but was told that this was not what they were after. I should look for a "considerable sum", to do with fees. I decided to consult Robert Lambie, now the Cathedral Chapter Clerk, who came up with a suggestion. That year a sum of money had been paid to the Cathedral for a broadcast. The cheque had been made out to the Dean and Chapter. Could this be what they were thinking of? He was right. Some stupid accountant had shortened "Dean and Chapter" to "Dean", so it looked as if all the money had been paid to me personally. End of story: but no apology was received from the Inland Revenue; and all I got was a bill from my accountant for the letters and time he had spent on the matter! But my fears of arrest, arraignment and public obloquy were over: I felt more relief than anger.

The other embarrassing moment was when the Mayor asked me if I would abseil with him down the tower of the Cathedral in support of his charity. 'Of course,' I said. 'Anything to help.' The architect ruled out the Cathedral tower, so the fire-brigade's tower was to be used instead. The day came with this appointment irrevocable in my diary. I hadn't really thought about it; but Julie said, 'At least you ought to wear proper shoes.' So I put on my trainers, made for the fire-brigade's tower and found a large and expectant crowd awaiting their entertainment, like Romans at the Colosseum. It was not all that entertaining. The Bishop, who had also been asked, was a practised mountaineer. He came down swiftly like a wild cat. The Mayor had been rehearsing for the occasion and made his way down in a gingerly but dignified way. Then it came to me. I found myself climbing the tower and wondering what on earth had induced me to agree to this hazardous way of raising money. But there was no going back. 'Now, Sir,' said a fireman as he strapped the reins to my body, 'just do as you are told and you will find it easy and perfectly safe.' 'Really?' 'Yes: so climb over the parapet and start your descent.' I peered over. There, far below, were people gaping up at me. Panic! But it would have taken more courage to turn back, so over the parapet I climbed and tried to listen to the instructions which were being barked from above. 'Stretch your legs and lean outwards,' said the stentorian voice. This was the last thing I wanted to do. I wanted to bend my legs and cuddle inwards. 'Stretch your legs, Sir.' The voice was louder, more imperious. So I stretched them, and began to feel at ease. I could feel the harness securely in my back, and by taking oridinary steps, I was making good progress – downwards. All was going well and I was feeling quite pleased with myself until I came to a hazard: an open window, put there on purpose to make things more difficult. The Bishop, I remembered, had just hopped across it, gravity and harness pulling him in a gracious ark round the obstacle. But my "hop" was ineffective and I found myself swinging into the window then out again, then side to side like the pendulum of a clock. The crowd was oohing and ahing, and it was clear to Juliet, who was filming the proceedings, that they were more entertained by me than all the others put together. When at last I arrived on terra firma they gave me warm applause. I hope that it induced them to give more to the charity. The Mayor seemed well pleased.

My last few months at Ripon were spoilt by two matters. First, I had to have half my colon removed at the Harrogate General Hospital, spending ten uncomfortable days there. I was very well treated by all concerned, and I was sent more "Get Well" cards than they had ever known! Bishop Ralph, the retired Suffragan Bishop of Knaresborough, who lived in one of the Cathedral chapter houses and was a true friend to us all, came and gave me a Blessing just as I was about to be wheeled away and done. This was the right moment, and he was just the right person, for a Blessing. Two days after the operation Bishop David came to tell me that Canon David Ford had resigned, but as David himself came an hour later as chirpy as ever and gave no hint of resigning, I thought that I must have dreamt it. The story of this will emerge later.

After my operation I had a week at home doing nothing; then a week in a hotel at Scarborough going for slightly longer walks every day. The annual meeting of the National Society of Town Planners had asked me to give the initial address at Scarborough that week. Julie agreed to my doing this on condition that I wrote the lecture before my operation and then read it out. This I did and got paid a handsome sum for expenses, which made the hotel bill possible! I forget what I talked about, but it aroused some lively discussion.

Just before I left Ripon, Canon David Ford resigned over the matter of the ordination of women. We had talked it through together very thoroughly (he and I: then all the Chapter) and although he kept saying that it felt like "bereavement" (a term that was being widely used by those who were opposed) we told him that no harm, only good, would ensue. The practical question was, "What should the Cathedral do about it?" We agreed that if a woman were to be appointed or invited to officiate in the Cathedral, due notice would be given so that anyone who felt that this was wrong could stay away. David agreed and we published a statement saying that the majority of us welcomed the Synod's decision, but that we recognised the difficulties, especially to one of our number, and that we would therefore ensure that people would always be able to choose whether or not to attend a Eucharist at which a woman priest was to preside.

A few weeks later the Bishop said he would like to appoint the Reverend Penny Driver to be Minor Canon of the Cathedral, to look after the cathedral parish of Sharow and retain her position on his staff. We were ready to agree to this – but David wasn't. Despite the published statement, David said that by accepting her we were "driving him out". So there was an impasse, which ended in David's resignation. It was even sadder because we knew that David was also motivated by marital problems. His resignation was accepted and a farewell service and reception were arranged in the Cathedral. David invited parishioners from his former parishes and many of the townsfolk with whom he had made a strong relationship and who believed that we were "casting him out". David arranged the service himself – full of thanksgiving and joy. In my speech I said I was not sure whether we were rejoicing for his past ministry or mourning his departure. I then told the story of what had happened – in such a way as to commend his courage in deciding to leave rather than compromise his principles. People told me that they were astonished at what I had said, for they had been given a very different picture. But what I said was true and well documented. So, sadly, because he was so likeable, he left. Very soon afterwards he was divorced. He is now a priest in the Orthodox Church. We did everything we could for Anne his wife, who had been very loyal to him and was broken-hearted in her disillusionment. She remained as a secretary in the Cathedral office, but then left Ripon to resume her life in Cambridge.

Julie and I had nineteen farewell parties and many generous presents. The last one was in the hall of the Choir School. Never was such a party. Everyone was there including all the family. During the reception Kerry Beaumont and a friend played Beethoven's *Spring Sonata*. Then we sat down, Julie and me, on the stage. The choir performed an amazing psalm, rather cheeky in its illusions, words and music by Malcolm Beer. Then we had "This Is (Has Been and Will Be) Your Life", including the Navy in the past and washing-up in the future. (A bowl and sponge were presented to rub it in.) Then, at half past ten, when I thought it was all over, in marched the City Band, uniform on, instruments ready. They had been waiting an hour! They performed as in the Last Night of the Proms, a chorister's mother singing *Rule*

Britannia and *Land of Hope and Glory* the audience waving flags and throwing streamers – and me conducting even if the speed of my beat did not seem to affect the speed of the music! We have it all on video, dubbed with one of the BBC Symphony Orchestra at a real Last Night in the Albert Hall; so the BBC are seen to be making the Ripon Sound, and the City Band sounds just like the BBC – all to the beat of my baton and resounding joy from all present – including my excited grandchildren.

Margaret Evans took us to *A Midsummer Night's Dream* in Harlow Gardens in Harrogate on the evening before we left Ripon; after a night in her flat we drove the very long way to Worthing, where we still are today, enjoying our retirement.

Coders Campling and Paris and the
Parthenon: November, 1944

Christopher Campling

Sub-Lieutenant
C. R. Campling

A Japenese admiral coming
aboard the *Nelson* to begin the
process of the surrender at
Penang: August, 1945

Married to Juliet Marian Hughes:
July, 1953

Penelope Campling presenting
a bouquet of flowers to Mrs
Kaunda (the wife of the
President of Ghana) at Lancing
College: Summer, 1964

The family (Penelope,
Angela and Peter, with
Juliet and Christopher
entering Pershore Abbey:
January, 1968

The Dean of Ripon coming out of the Cathedral after his Induction: October, 1984

Presenting a goblet to Her Majesty the Queen after the Royal Maunday: Maunday Thursday, 1985

Juliet and Christopher on a working holiday in Ireland, 1997